Mistassini
Normandin
Vauvert
Péribonca
St-Amédée
Petite Péribonka
Péribor
Grande-Décharge
St-Prime
Lake St John
Roberval
St-Gédéon
Ste-Hedwidge
Val-Jalbert
Ouiatchouan R.
Chambord (St-Louis)
St-André
Belle R.
St-Jérôme (Métabetchouan)
Alma
Hébertville
Jonquière
Kénogami
Ste-Anne
St-Fulgence
Bagotville (St-Alphonse)
Chicoutimi
L. Kenogami
Laterrière
Grande-Baie
Baie Ha ha
Saguenay R.
Tadoussac
Baie-Ste-Catherine
Rimouski

Métabetchouan R.

CHARLEVOIX

La Malbaie
St-Pascal
TÉMISCOUATA

Baie-St-Paul
KAMOURASKA
Ste-Anne-de-la-Pocatière

St. Lawrence River

L'ISLET

CANADA
UNITED STATES OF AMERICA

La Tuque
R. St-Maurice
Batiscan R.
h-de-Mékinac
Gosford
St-Vallier
Harouxville
St-Tite
St-Timothée
Ste-Thècle
QUEBEC
Lévis
Grandes-Piles
Grand Mère
Ste-Flore
Shawinigan
St-Séverin
Lac-à-la-Tortue
St-Narcisse
Boniface
t-Élie
ne-des-Grès
ulin
Radnor
Batiscan
St-Maurice
Trois-Rivières
Cap-de-la-Madeleine
Nicolet
St-Joseph
St-Léonard-de-Nicolet
anoraie

EASTERN TOWNSHIPS

Wotton
Weedon
cinthe
East Angus
Mégantic
EAL
Sherbrooke
Magog

SCALE OF MILES
0   50   100   150

THE CLERGY AND ECONOMIC GROWTH IN QUEBEC
(1896 – 1914)

William F. R Y A N

The Clergy
and
Economic Growth
in Quebec
(1896–1914)

LES PRESSES DE L'UNIVERSITÉ LAVAL

QUEBEC, 1966

© LES PRESSES DE L'UNIVERSITÉ LAVAL

FOREWORD

We live in an age when the Christian Churches are reassessing their attitude towards progress and especially towards economic development. In December 1965, at Vatican II, the Roman Catholic bishops of the world in their Pastoral Constitution on The Church in The Modern World *(#34) clearly committed Catholics to building a better world. They confidently stated that "men are not deterred by the Christian message from building up the world, or impelled to neglect the welfare of their fellows. They are rather more stringently bound to do these very things." And the World Council of Churches in the same positive spirit is convoking a world conference in the summer of 1966 on the theme "Christian Response and The Technical and Social Revolutions of Our Time."*

These developments within the Church contrast sharply with the growing tendency, especially among social scientists, to correlate "economic backwardness" with "traditional" religious values in both developed and underdeveloped countries. For example, it is not surprising, to find the sociologist John Porter, in The Vertical Mosaic, *generalizing concerning the clergy in Quebec:*

> Quebec's hierarchy assumed a reactionary attitude to the industrialization of the province... Quebec's industrialization was a tide to be stemmed because it was seen as a threat to French national survival. The solution to the question of national survival became confused with the solution to the problems of industrialization. The solution was expressed in a clerical-national creed: Those who had not left the village should remain there, and those who had left should return.[1]

1407847

The present study is economic not theological. Its purpose is to search out the facts of the situation in Quebec. No attempt is made here to portray the Church as a champion of economic development or to judge whether or not such a role should be an integral part of her mission. I merely try to accumulate and analyze sufficient empirical evidence to arrive at some tentative conclusions on what the Church in fact did—and perhaps what she is likely to do elsewhere—under conditions of an initial economic spurt. Such knowledge will be of interest to all who are concerned with closing the gap between the developed and the underdeveloped, between rich and poor countries throughout the world.

William F. Ryan, S.J.

---

[1] John Porter, *The Vertical Mosaic* (Toronto: University of Toronto Press, 1965), p. 333.

ACKNOWLEDGEMENTS

In the preparation of this book, I am much indebted to Professor Alexander Gerschenkron of Harvard University for his direction and encouragement and to the members of his graduate seminar in economic history for their valuable criticism. I am likewise indebted to Jean Hamelin of the Institut d'Histoire of the Université Laval for his sustained interest in my work. Among the dozens of those who kindly furnished me with valuable documentation and helped me to interpret it, I can mention here only Msgr. Victor Tremblay of the Société Historique du Saguenay, Msgr. Albert Tessier, Archivist of the diocese of Trois-Rivières, and Antoine Dubuc of Chicoutimi. For reading and criticizing my text I am indebted among many others to John Buell, Arthur Cotter, Jacques Cousineau, Patrick Malone, and Jacques Monet. To the administration of Loyola College and my colleagues there as well as to Rev. Jack Shea and the staff of the Social Action Department of the Canadian Catholic Conference I must also express my sincere appreciation for their continued encouragement and support. I am especially grateful to my Jesuit Superiors and brethren for without their financial support and enthusiastic interest and encouragement this study would have been quite impossible. I am likewise grateful to my publishers, les Presses de l'université Laval, for their collaboration.

Finally, I am pleased to make known that this work has been published with the help of a grant from the Social Science Research Council, using funds provided by the Canada Council.

W.F. R.

TABLE OF CONTENTS

LIST OF TABLES

ABBREVIATIONS

ASC: Archives of the Séminaire de Chicoutimi

ASHS: Archives of the Société historique du Saguenay

ASTR: Archives of the Séminaire de Trois-Rivières

DA: Dubuc Archives

EAC: Episcopal Archives of Chicoutimi

EATR: Episcopal Archives of Trois-Rivières

MLPC: *Mandements, Lettres pastorales, Circulaires.*
      The directives, pastoral letters, and circulars of the bishops of the various dioceses in the province of Quebec to their clergy and the faithful.

INTRODUCTION

It has become almost commonplace to say that Catholicism has impeded economic development in the French-Canadian province of Quebec. For example, Professor S.D. Clark, of the University of Toronto, readily accepts this allegation and suggests that the Catholic Church in Quebec, as an "essentially status institution" teaching a philosophy of "otherworldliness," imposing heavy taxes on her people, and holding them in a position of excessive dependence, confirms his general thesis that in Canada "the promotion of the religious interest in itself has involved a weakening of the economic interest, because of the fundamental antagonism of the one for the other."[1] And Professor Conrad Langlois, of Sir George Williams University, in a recent article reviewing the literature on this subject, suggests that "the official doctrine of the Roman Catholic Church itself may have had an influence on the lag of industrial development of French Canada, but the influence of the nationalist clergy may have been greater. From these combined two [sic] influences, the French Canadian people have acquired a philosophy of life, which has been responsible to a certain extent for the lag in economic development."[2]

It is our interest here to discover how these allegations stand up in the face of detailed research into Quebec's economic development. Such research, although directly concerned only with the particular situation existing in French Canada, nevertheless has an indirect bearing on the more general question of whether there is any stable relationship between a man's religious beliefs and his economic activity. This question is especially relevant at a time when dozens of so-called "underdeveloped" countries are desperately trying to marshal all their material and spiritual forces to emerge from "economic backwardness." Because the popular tendency has been more and more to correlate "economic backwardness" with "traditional" religious values, this study can perhaps throw some light on this more general discussion. It may do so at least as far as this concerns the influence of one major religion, Catholicism, which is often

---

[1] S.D. CLARK, "The Religious Factor in Canadian Economic Development," *Journal of Economic History*, Supplement, VII (1947), 94, 95. Reprinted in his book *The Developing Canadian Community* under the title "The Religious Influence in Canadian Society."

[2] Conrad LANGLOIS, "Cultural Reasons Given for the French Canadian Lag in Economic Progress," *Culture*, XXI (June 1960), 163.

pictured in "underdeveloped" countries as having a negative influence on economic progress both through its teachings and through its peculiar authoritative structure.

This book is a case study of the influence exercised by the Catholic Church on the economic spurt that took place in the province of Quebec in the period 1896–1914. For methodological purposes it side-steps the ambiguous concept of "Catholicism" in favour of the concrete institution that is its empirical source, namely, the Roman Catholic Church, which is here arbitrarily defined as the élite or power-structure in that Church. For this study, the Catholic Church is summarized in those who have the authority to teach, interpret doctrine, enforce policy, and organize action towards specific goals in the name of the whole Church, that is, the bishops, the priests, and authorized Catholic teachers, as well as the organizations, institutions, movements, and publications immediately inspired or directed by them. In other words, instead of trying to study Catholic economic attitudes, as most authors have in the past, I have preferred to adopt the approach of studying the process of formation of Catholic attitudes in concrete circumstances, for this process appears to be more easily observed and controlled. The primary emphasis is, therefore, on the élite, who legitimately teach and interpret value orientations, and only secondarily on the community of the faithful, whose awareness and acceptance or rejection of this guidance is much more difficult to observe and measure.

French Canada is particularly well suited for this kind of study because here the people are relatively homogeneous in both racial origin and religious belief, 80 per cent being French Canadian and 86 per cent Roman Catholic. The difference is made up almost wholly by the 5 per cent Irish in the population.[3] In Quebec, unlike more primitive societies, the distinction between the Church and secular powers is well established, and constant interaction between the Church and the State is accepted as both normal and legitimate. Because the Church's influence is here considered to be especially strong, one may hope to detect more easily how she marshals her energies in the face of rapid economic development. The interesting observations of those who have already studied this area suggested that this research would prove fruitful. For example, Raoul Blanchard,

---

[3] Province of Quebec, *Statistical Year Book*, II (1915), 148–51. It is clear that these percentages remained almost constant over the decade 1901-1911. Hereafter this annual publication will be referred to as the *Statistical Year Book*.

the noted French geographer, has said that no major changes, even on the political level, have been adopted in Quebec without at least the tacit approval of the higher clergy.[4]   And more recently, a sociologist at the Université de Montréal, Hubert Guindon, has proposed the highly controversial thesis that the Catholic clergy have not only influenced but actually manipulated to their own advantage the bull-dozing impact of industrialization, and thus have managed to consolidate and even to gain greater control over the whole of French-Canadian society.[5]

Does the province of Quebec in the period 1896–1914 provide a suitable geographic unit and a meaningful economic period for such a study?   Quebec is not a separate nation, but merely a province in the Canadian Confederation.   But traditionally both French Canadians and students of French Canada have thought Quebec sufficiently different from the rest of Canada in race, religion, culture, and language to merit particular and separate study.   Moreover, the possibility of Quebec's becoming one day a separate state has always been the preoccupation of not a few French-Canadian intellectuals, and even some economists.   Ever jealous of her provincial autonomy, Quebec continues to study her particular economic problems and to initiate such studies as that published in 1961 by the Ministère de l'Industrie et du Commerce of Quebec, *Croissance et structure économiques de la province de Québec*, prepared by Professor André Raynauld and his associates.   This approach does not minimize the very close economic interdependence that exists between Canadian provinces, and especially between Quebec and Ontario. Nor does it reject the thesis of A. Faucher and M. Lamontagne who have held that "Quebec's industrialization had nothing specific to do with, and was not fundamentally influenced by its cultural environment; that, rather, it was a mere regional manifestation of the overall economic evolution of the North-American Continent."[6]   Certainly the present study does not assume that the Church's influence was a major determinant in Quebec's economic growth, but the question still seems meaningful: in what direction did the Church throw her weight during this period of economic growth?   Whether that influence was sufficiently strong to differentiate Quebec's economic growth

---

[4] Raoul BLANCHARD, *Le Canada français*, p. 296.   Blanchard is apparently referring to the situation in Quebec since 1867, for both the Constitution of 1791 and the Union of 1840 were, in fact, opposed by the clergy.

[5] Hubert GUINDON, "The Social Evolution of Quebec Reconsidered," *Canadian Journal of Economics and Political Science*, XXVI (November 1960), 546.

[6] A. FAUCHER and M. LAMONTAGNE, "History of Industrial Development," in Jean-Charles FALARDEAU, ed., *Essays on Contemporary Quebec*, p. 34.

"specifically" or to affect it "fundamentally" is quite another matter, but on this too the present research may be able to shed additional light. Raynauld discovered that, although total production in agriculture, mining, and manufacturing has grown at almost identical rates in the provinces of Ontario and Quebec since 1870, both per capita income and wages have always remained substantially lower in Quebec. This observation would seem to indicate further that there are good economic reasons—quite apart from the racial, cultural, and religious ones—for making a separate if not independent study of the province of Quebec.[7]

The period 1896–1914 commends itself for several reasons. First and foremost, it was a time of great economic significance for Quebec. Without entering into a detailed description of this period—a task for a later chapter—we can say that both Canada and Quebec experienced rapid economic development during these years. Rostow, basing himself on Firestone's detailed statistical studies, concludes that it was the "take-off" period for Canada.[8]

> La province de Québec, comme le reste du Canada et grâce à lui d'ailleurs, a connu une période de "take off" entre 1896 et 1913. Si on compare, par exemple, la production manufacturière du Québec entre 1900 et 1910, on observe un accroissement *en volume* de 76.5 pour cent, tandis que la population n'a crû que de 21 pour cent au cours de la même période. La production per capita a augmenté de 4.2 pour cent par année, soit plus que le double de la croissance moyenne de longue période au Canada. Pour le Canada dans son ensemble, on observe également qu'en dollars courants, la proportion de l'investissement, par rapport au revenu national brut, passe d'une moyenne de 12.6 pour cent par an de 1870 à 1900, à 18.2 pour cent en 1910. [O.J. FIRESTONE, *Canada's Economic Development, 1867–1953*, p. 100. The corresponding net investment figures given by Firestone (p. 112) are 4.7 per cent and 9.5 per cent respectively.] En outre, contrairement aux impressions premières que l'on a, la Province, dès avant la première guerre mondiale, disposait déjà d'une industrie manufacturière très importante et très diversifiée tournée déjà principalement vers le marché des autres provinces canadiennes; les industries du fer et de l'acier auxquelles on attache toujours un intérêt primordial dans les plans de développement et qu'on a toujours cru inexistantes dans le Québec, comptaient en 1910 pour 20 pour cent de la valeur ajoutée de toutes les industries manufacturières en dollars constants 1890–1900. Et si nous comparons l'Ontario au Québec à cet égard sur une base de valeurs ajoutées en dollars courants de 1910, nous trouvons une industrie du fer et de l'acier qui contribue à 14 pour cent de l'ensemble dans le Québec et à 18

[7] A. RAYNAULD, *Croissance et structure économiques*, p. 63.
[8] W.W. ROSTOW, *The Stages of Economic Growth*, pp. 38, 42-43.

pour cent de l'ensemble dans l'Ontario. Comme ces chiffres sont une indication suffisante que la province de Québec a participé à la croissance du reste du Canada, on peut ajouter que le revenu par tête du Canada en dollars de 1935–1939 était égal à $434 en 1910, soit un chiffre qui correspond à peu près à la moyenne du revenu per capita de 1953 pour 55 pays du monde.[9]

Clearly, this is a period of significance in Quebec's economic development; and this statement is true whether we accept or reject all the assumptions underlying Rostow's theory of the stages of economic growth. The choice of the spurt years has the advantage of presenting us with a period which is at once economically significant and at least potentially well suited to shed some light on similar spurt periods in other countries where currently every effort is being made to launch rapid economic development. Furthermore, such a period reveals rapid structural and institutional changes which a powerful, homogeneous Church, such as the Catholic Church in French Canada, cannot be expected to ignore, and so we can rightfully expect to observe interaction between this "economic development" and the "Church," and an attempt on the latter's part to exert an influence on this process of change in which she may be willy-nilly involved.

The year 1914 was chosen as the upper limit of the period under study because by that time the "artificial" forces of war had taken over and lent new vigour to Quebec's faltering economic spurt and the controversial issue of conscription had caused French Canadian nationalism to overshadow other influences such as that of religion in Quebec's affairs. French Canada thus ceases to be of interest to the purpose of this study, which is to investigate what potential energies and resistances the Catholic Church and religion generally bring to bear on the earlier stages of economic development. Already by 1910, and certainly by 1914, Quebec, together with the rest of Canada, was no longer an "underdeveloped" country in the current sense of that word. Quebec's economy thereafter continued to grow, to boom and bust, and Quebecers to quarrel among themselves about how the spoils and roles in this growth should be apportioned between the races; but even if the Church had an important role to play in this later phase of economic growth it will not directly interest us here.

From the economic point of view, the lower limit of the period is quite easily selected and defended. June 23, 1896,

---

[9] RAYNAULD, *Croissance et structure économiques*, pp. 28-29.

marked the beginning of the Liberal era of Sir Wilfrid Laurier, a period of economic progress unprecedented in Canadian history during which Canada pushed her western frontier to the British Columbia coast. The year 1896 also marked the bottom of the business cycle, and it was in that year that wholesale prices, which had been slowly dropping since the 1870's, finally started to climb once more. However, though 1896 has been taken as the initial year and the bulk of the research relates to the period 1896–1914, the year 1896 has not been taken too rigidly as an end date, since one of the chief interests of this study has been to see whether the Church did in fact modify in any marked way her value orientations as the pace of economic development quickened at the turn of the century. To appreciate such a change, we must, at least in a general way, follow her teaching and activities from the time of Confederation in 1867.

It may perhaps be repeated that there is no question here of attempting to prove that the Church's influence is the determining variable in this process of economic growth: we shall rather simply study the role—positive, negative, or neutral—played by the Church in this dynamic process, which obviously in most cases was initiated by other agents. That the Church herself was greatly influenced by the process of economic development is most likely, but that study may be left to the religious sociologists. We are interested rather in observing the élite or power-structure of the Church in action. The relevant questions to be asked are these: (1) Who took the action? (2) Why? and (3) With what results? With the first question we must beware of mistaking the activities of an exceptional person as typical of the Church in general. The answers to the second question give us a clue as to whether the justification of the Church's action is given in terms of ultimate values, or in terms of concrete local situations. And, finally, the answers to the third question enable us to evaluate the effectiveness of the influence exercised in achieving the results sought.

The selection of sources has had to be made with care. The relationship between the Church and economic development is seldom treated explicitly or in detail in economic or historical studies. The political bias of much of history tends—even in a very laissez-faire society, such as existed in Quebec at the turn of the century—to attribute all achievements in national welfare during a period to the government that happens to be in office at the time. Religious publications, perhaps because they are usually written by clergymen, tend to be excessively reticent and almost apologetic concerning the priest's involvement in economic affairs. If they happen to devote more than a few passing sentences to the fact that a certain *curé* played an important economic role in his parish, they invariably hasten to add that he was primarily a man of God, for fear people might take offence or be scandalized. Often it is quite impossible to determine exactly what is the empirical content behind the expression which we find repeated in parish histories: "the curé did much to promote the material betterment of the parish." For these reasons I attempted to organize source materials on a very wide base. Only by gleaning marginal remarks and observations from many different sources has it been possible to accumulate a respectable amount of evidence. It was also useful and at times even necessary to have recourse to informal interviews with older people who lived through this period in French Canada and whose memories could help to fill in some of the more glaring gaps in documentation.

Another difficulty in documentation is that much of it, even serious official communications, is in a rhetorical style often little given to exactness of figure or fact, and quite impatient of the many shadings between black and white. Particularly where the sources are speeches and articles for special occasions, the reader must beware of taking words for facts, and programmes for concrete realizations. We would do well to bear in mind the criticism which Édouard Montpetit, Quebec's first professionally trained economist, levelled against this rhetorical flair long fostered among his fellow Canadians. He writes in his memoirs:

> Notre enseignement a vécu longtemps au delà de la réalité, dans le domaine de l'esprit. Il a été surtout littéraire et philosophique, d'une philosophie livresque, sans contact avec la vie. Cet enseignement, que l'on corrige aujourd'hui avec raison, accentuait nos défauts, développait en nous le goût d'une logique irréelle, l'appétit des mots et des dissertations, la manie de l'éloquence satisfaite d'elle-même et considérée à l'égal d'un acte, en sorte que, quand elle avait parlé, elle nous laissait repus de verbiage, en face d'un adversaire armé de volonté et d'action.[10]

Yet with all their shortcomings, the documents are still quite adequate for the stated purpose of writing neither an economic nor a religious history of this period in French Canada but rather of trying to uncover the "typical" facts and situations which reveal how the Church acts in and reacts to the process of rapid economic development.

---

[10] Édouard MONTPETIT, *Les Forces essentielles*, vol. I of *la Conquête économique*, pp. 22-23.

The procedure is the following. Chapter I has a brief description of the general situation in Canada and particularly in the province of Quebec at this time, and a somewhat more detailed description of the economic development that took place during the period to enable us better to situate, understand, and evaluate the influence of the Church therein. Industry, as we shall see, was quite early concentrated in the city of Montreal, and there was no marked tendency towards decentralization before World War I. Ideally, therefore, Montreal should be the object of detailed study in this project. But here the phenomena of industrialization and Church influence and their interaction are too complex and subtle to be the object of a pioneer study using quite unsophisticated tools of analysis. Since Montreal presented a serious methodological problem, a study in some detail was made of two other regions which were experiencing industrial revolutions at this time, even if, in strictly quantitative terms, they were of much less importance than that taking place in Montreal. They are the St. Maurice River valley and the Chicoutimi-Lake St. John region, where large-scale development of hydraulic and electric power was just being initiated. Precisely because industrialization was just getting underway in these regions it is much easier to detect the Church's attitudes and actions than in an older industrial city such as Montreal. Then, too, we can expect that the changes that took place in these regions during this period have more in common with the phenomenon of current development in underdeveloped areas.

The marked contrast between these two regions also helps us to understand better the total process of economic development: the St. Maurice valley is almost exclusively an industrial region, but in the Chicoutimi-Lake St. John region industry grew up side by side with land settlement and agriculture. Both regions have for our study the added advantage of containing a cathedral town from which pastoral letters and directives are regularly issued by the local bishops to the clergy and faithful.

The more detailed section of the study begins with a description of the economic development that took place in each of these two regions and the role played by the Church. Chapter II considers the case of the St. Maurice River valley, and enters into some detail to catch the flavour of the changes that were taking place in Quebec at the time. Chapter III discusses the Chicoutimi-Lake St. John region, following the same pattern, but in less detail in the interests of brevity.

The core of this study is a series of chapters which attempt to evaluate how typical are the findings in these two regions in the light of the more general changes taking place in the rest of the province, including Montreal. This discussion is grouped under the major headings of settlement, communications, and agriculture (chapter IV), industry (chapter V), and education (chapter VI). The conclusion (chapter VII) attempts: (1) briefly to summarize the key attitudes and initiatives adopted by the Church during the development spurt and to note how they changed or were modified during this period; (2) to evaluate very roughly their significance for the actual economic development that occurred; (3) to relate this present study to the general discussion on the relationship between religion and economic development; and finally (4) to suggest certain lines of future research.

A few observations should be added on the limitations of this study. It is quite clear that the research behind it has nothing to contribute to the discussion inaugurated by Max Weber, and continued by such economists as H.M. Robertson and Kurt Samuelsson, concerning the question whether religion exercised an important influence on the genesis of the spirit of capitalism which later sparked the industrial revolution. This is a matter of disputed historical fact and has nothing to do with French Canada in the twentieth century. However, the present empirical study does have some bearing on the current discussion engaged in by such economists as Hagen, Rostow, Kindleberger, Meir, Baldwin, Buchanan, Ellis, Boulding, and others, about whether there is an inconsistency between religious attitudes and growth attitudes, between "the religious ethos" and the "development ethos" as they are sometimes called.[11] Such discussion, however useful, risks falling into an empty exercise in logic unless it is backed by careful empirical research. For example, it is interesting to know that there is no necessary conflict between "the Catholic ethic" and "the development ethos,"[12] but it would be much more helpful to know under what particular set of circumstances the Catholic Church could be expected to cultivate the radically different attitudes of enthusiasm, of discouragement, and of indifference towards the process of economic development. This study, by examining

---

[11] For a clear, well-documented discussion on this whole question of the consistency between these two sets of attitudes and a brief critical review of the literature involved, see Mario ZANARTU, S.J., "Roman Catholic Ethic and Economic Development" (unpublished Ph.D. thesis, Faculty of Political Science, Columbia University, 1962).
[12] Cf. *ibid.*

in concrete detail an economic spurt in a particular region, should be able to enlighten this discussion, at least in what concerns the Catholic religion; for though this study is limited to a particular region it can undoubtedly suggest tentative hypotheses concerning the relationship between Catholic religious belief and economic activity, which might later be tested for generality in other areas where the Catholic religion is also predominant. Thus, little by little, a body of tentative consistent hypotheses based on relevant empirical studies could be assembled to guide both the economist and the churchman in an area where their fields and interests overlap.

The present author would not claim by his approach to be able to detect all the religious influence, or even all the Catholic influence, that has a bearing on the development process. For example, *a priori*, the possibility cannot be ruled out that the greatest single impact of religious influence is really to be found in the great initiatives elicited in the province at this time by English and American Protestant entrepreneurs and financiers. Nor can one hope to detect all the religious influence exercised on a people's economic activity by the mere fact they were born or raised as Catholics. I have chosen rather to study Catholic influence, as it were, in-the-making, because here it is more subject to direct observation, and, besides, over time Catholic attitudes are essentially reducible to what Catholics are taught to believe and practise by legitimate Catholic authority.

This book does not claim to determine the role the Church has played in French Canada's economic history, which dates back over three centuries, but merely studies her role in a period of vital importance in French Canada's economic development, the initial big spurt that took place after Confederation. However, to the extent that it considers how the Church modified her value orientations in the face of rapid economic change, it can contribute thereby to a better understanding of the Church's role in the entire history of French Canada's economic development. But the immediate purpose always remains to study the inverse relationship, that is, how the Church influenced or modified economic development and not how she herself was modified by this development.

Nor does this study take up directly the very interesting question of why the French Canadians themselves seem to have played such a minor role in initiating industrialization in French Canada, except insofar as this question overlaps a particular subject matter during the given period. In fact, the Church was always chiefly preoccupied with the role which French

Canadians played in the development process, but that did not prevent her from encouraging or discouraging various initiatives undertaken by English Canadians and Americans, both Catholic and Protestant. We have to face this question of the role of French Canadians in the development process, at least indirectly, when we discuss the Church's role in education over which she had considerable control at that time.

Another worrisome limitation of this study—and one which the author freely admits—is that it does not include separate detailed research into the Church's property holdings, her sources and methods of collecting revenues, and especially the nature and size of her investments during this period. Only such a detailed study could serve to confront directly and weigh the merits of Clark's general contention that "the heavy drain upon material resources of the country in maintaining institutions of religious ownership has weakened the economic energies of the population... In French Canada heavy ecclesiastical taxation in one form or another has meant that the capital required for the establishment of industry has come either from outside capitalist groups, from the state, or from the Church herself."[13]

The reason for not undertaking such research is at once simple and decisive: fully reliable sources were not easily accessible. One must not yield to the easy temptation of substituting popular speculation for facts in this controversial area. However, as the reader can see for himself, this lacuna in data has not proved to be a major obstacle. By watching how the Church acted in many different concrete situations and by using fragmentary information to the full, we can, I submit, discover the role of the Church in the process of economic development, at least in its essentials. And, for the moment, one can only impatiently wait to discover whether in fact the findings of future research in this mysterious field of Church finance prove unexpectedly to be in some way inconsistent with the tentative conclusions here concerning the role of the Church in French Canada's economic development.

In carrying out a study such as this, one must confront the famous "agriculturalist thesis," so dear to the hearts of some French-Canadian historians and social scientists,[14] who contend that the chief economic preoccupation of the vast majority of

---

[13] CLARK, "The Religious Factor in Canadian Economic Development," p. 94.

[14] See, for example, Michel BRUNET, "Trois dominantes de la pensée canadienne-française: l'agriculturalisme, l'anti-étatisme, et le messianisme. Essai d'histoire intellectuelle," *Écrits du Canada français*, III (1957), 33–117.

French-Canadian intellectuals, and, *a fortiori*, of Catholic clergymen, was to direct all French Canadians towards agriculture.
The study has turned up much empirical evidence bearing on the
thesis in our particular period, but no attempt is made to cor-
roborate or refute it for other periods of French-Canadian economic history.   Likewise, there is no serious discussion of how
French-Canada might have developed economically had she
not been largely protected from the secularizing effects of the
French Revolution and such other major changes as tended to
create a more clear cut separation between Church and State
and to reduce the Church's influence considerably by confront-
ing her with a strong anti-clerical State.

Finally, no attempt is made to portray the Church as a
great champion of economic development or to judge whether or
not that should be an integral part of her mission in these particular circumstances.   Nor is there discussion of whether economic initiatives should be the exclusive domain of the layman.
The attempt has been merely to try to accumulate and analyze
sufficient empirical evidence to arrive at some tentative conclusions on what the Church in fact did—and perhaps what
she is likely to do elsewhere—under conditions of an initial
economic spurt.

CHAPTER I

GENERAL SETTING AND ECONOMIC DEVELOPMENT

TOPOGRAPHY, CLIMATE, AND POPULATION

Quebec was one of the four original participants in Confederation in 1867 and emerged as the largest province in the newly constituted Dominion of Canada.[1] In 1867 the new province had an area of about 188,000 square miles, but with additions carved out from the Northwest Territories in 1898 and 1912 its area was increased to about 703,635 square miles, or roughly 19 per cent of the area of Canada. The result was that, in spite of a rapid growth in population over the period, from 1,192,000 to 2,006,000, the density of the population was only slightly increased, from about 3.38 inhabitants per square mile in 1871 to about 5.69 in 1911.[2] In fact the population remained largely concentrated in the southern fifth of the province, in the area bordering the St. Lawrence River. At the turn of the century, the areas newly opened for land settlement—the "colonization regions," as they are always called in the literature—were Abitibi, Temiscaming, the regions north of Montreal and the Ottawa River, and, finally, the Lake St. John, Temiscouata, and Matapedia regions. But it is clear that the rugged topography and the severe climate have prevented Quebecers from settling permanently too far north of the St. Lawrence valley. For although average temperatures in the coldest month range from 14° to 7° F in areas nearer the St. Lawrence, and from 3° to -1° in more northern regions, extremes of cold as low as -40° and even -50° are not at all unknown. Frostless days range from an average of fewer than 80 in the northern settlements to a high of about 140 per year in the St. Lawrence Lowlands.[3]

The topography of the province can be generally described as composed of three structural units—the St. Lawrence River

---

[1] Two excellent sources for a more detailed study of the geographical, cultural and political situations are Mason WADE, *The French Canadians, 1760–1945* (Toronto: Macmillan, 1956), 1136 pp.; and Raoul BLANCHARD, *Le Canada français* (Montréal: Librairie A. Fayard, 1961), 314 pp. The latter is a summary study of his earlier five-volume series, *les Études canadiennes* (Montréal: Librairie Beauchemin, 1935–1954).

[2] *Statistical Year Book*, II (1915), 138.

[3] BLANCHARD, *Le Canada français*, pp. 35, 38.

Valley or Lowlands, the Laurentian Highlands, which form part of the Canadian Shield, to the north, and the Appalachian ranges to the south.   The shield, which covers an area of some 2 million square miles in Canada, forms an immense "V" with arms outstretched on either side of Hudson Bay and occupies about fourteen-fifteenths of the total area of Quebec.   It is only in recent times that industry and tourism have succeeded in piercing its long forbidding rocky heights and thundering waterfalls. Beyond the south shore of the St. Lawrence lie the Appalachian ranges which often peak to over 3,500 feet.   This rugged hilly region contains many fertile valleys and plateaus which, however, become more rare as one moves to the northeast towards the Gaspé peninsula.   Between the Laurentian Highlands on the north and the Appalachians on the south lies the plain described as the St. Lawrence Lowlands.   It widens upstream, in a southwesterly direction from Quebec City.   The vast majority of the province's population is concentrated in this relatively small plain.

In 1910, French Canadians formed about 80 per cent of Quebec's population.   This proportion represented an increase of about 2 per cent since Confederation.   Roughly 16 per cent of the remaining 20 per cent were of English, Scottish, and Irish origin.   Quebec's birth rate was amazingly high, averaging about 36.8 per 1,000 over the period 1894–1913, and reaching a maximum of 41.2 in 1909.   The death rate was likewise high, averaging about 19.8 annually, although it did fall from 21.3 in the period 1894–1897 to 17.7 in the period 1910–1913.[4]   As late as 1913, over 47 per cent of the deaths were occurring among children under five years of age.   Had there been no demographic movements in and out of the province, population would have grown at an annual compound rate of about 1.7 per cent over the period, but, as we shall see later when we discuss the settlement movement, during the period 1891–1911 Quebec suffered a net migration of about 150,000.[5]   As a result, in spite of a small steady flow of immigrants, population increased only at an annual average rate of 1.7 per cent instead of at a compound rate of the same magnitude.   And what is more significant, in the prosperous decade 1900–1910 population grew at an average rate of 2.16 per cent, or twice as fast as the average rate of 1.08 per cent during the preceding decade 1890–1900, because during that decade of recession there had been a net migration of 121,000

      [4] *Statistical Year Book*, II (1915), 152, 183, 190-191.
      [5] RAYNAULD, *Croissance et structure économiques*, p. 251; see also Nathan KEYFITZ, "The Growth of the Canadian Population," *Population Studies*, IV (June 1950), 47-63.

as compared with 29,000 in the subsequent decade. During these two decades, owing to heavy European immigration into western Canada, Quebec's proportion of the total Canadian population fell from 30.6 per cent in 1890 to 27.8 per cent in 1910, but began to rise again once the waves of mass immigration came to an end.

POLITICAL ORGANIZATION

The British North America Act granted to the provincial legislatures power over what were considered provincial interests: education, local public works, property and civil rights, civil law, provincial company charters, licences, municipal institutions, the management and sale of public land, and so forth. As their source of revenue, the provinces had the right to direct taxation.

The federal government's powers included control of the armed forces, the regulation of trade and commerce, banking, credit, currency, criminal law, postal services, fisheries, patents and copyrights, the census, and the raising of money by any mode of taxation. Likewise, interprovincial public works and services such as navigation, shipping, railways, canals, and telegraph came under its control. Immigration and agriculture were the joint concern of both legislatures.

Immediately after Confederation, federal subsidies to railway and navigation facilities were of the utmost importance in equipping the country with the necessary infra-structure for later economic development. In addition, the central government granted the provinces a subsidy on a per capita basis to help them meet their financial needs. But by 1915 this direct subsidy to the Quebec government had dropped to $2 million or about 13 per cent of the provincial government's total receipts of $15,151,986 in that year.[6]

The two political parties in Quebec were the traditional Liberals and Conservatives, often referred to as the "rouges" and the "bleus." The June election of 1896 brought the Liberals to power in Ottawa under the capable leadership of the French-Canadian Wilfrid Laurier, and his popularity and influence enabled the provincial Liberals in the following year to sweep Quebec, where they remained in power under the successive leaderships of F.-G. Marchand (1896–1900), S.-N. Parent (1900–1905), Sir Lomer Gouin (1905–1920), and Alexandre Taschereau

---

[6] *Statistical Year Book*, II (1915), 367.

(1920–1936). Their economic policies will be considered later when the various attempts of the Church to influence them are discussed.

THE CATHOLIC CHURCH IN QUEBEC

It has been accepted as a truism that the Catholic Church has been and remains a very important institution in French-Canadian society. For example, the French author André Siegfried, after a prolonged visit in Canada at the turn of the century, set down his impressions of the position of the Catholic Church in Canada as follows:

> Of the 5,371,000 inhabitants of Canada, 2,229,000 are Catholics, and of these 1,429,000 belong to the single province of Quebec. The Church of Rome has its stronghold, therefore, upon French Soil, and if we except the Irish element which is somewhat numerous, it may be said that, speaking generally, the French of Canada are Catholic and the British Protestant. This fact contains the key to the entire political situation of the Dominion. There need be little fear of our exaggerating the part played by religion; both with Protestants and Catholics it is immense. In the case of the French Canadians the ascendency of the Church is so great that it may be regarded as the principal factor in their evolution.[7]

Years before, in the report to the Crown on the situation in Canada after the rebellions of Upper and Lower Canada in the 1830's, Lord Durham had also remarked on the dominant position of the Catholic clergy in French Canada:

> The Catholic priesthood of this province have, to a remarkable degree, conciliated the goodwill of persons of all creeds; I know of no parochial clergy in the world whose practice of all Christian virtues, and zealous discharge of their clerical duties, is more universally admitted and has been of more beneficial consequences. Possessed of incomes sufficient and even large according to the notions entertained in the country, and enjoying the advantage of education, they have lived on terms of equality and kindness with the humblest and the least instructed inhabitants of the rural districts. Intimately acquainted with the wants and characters of their neighbors, they have been the promoters and dispensers of charity, and the effectual guardians of morals of the people, and in the general absence of any institution of civil government, the Catholic Church has presented almost the only semblance of stability and organization, and furnished the only effectual support of civilization and order.

He commented, too, upon the importance of the parochial institutions in new settlements, for

---

[7] André SIEGFRIED, *The Race Question in Canada*, p. 11.

> ... the religious observances of the French Canadians are so inter-
> mingled with all their business, and all their amusements, that the
> priests and the church are with them, more than with any other
> people, the centres of their little communities.[8]

Siegfried went still further and observed that the Church
had even learned to live in "complete independence" of the
State:

> ... the Church really achieves that perfect condition of complete
> independence of which its high functionaries love to talk. It lives
> outside the jurisdiction of the civil power; *above* it, the ecclesiastics
> sometime maintain and always feel. No one ventures to assert
> in Canada, as in France, the supremacy of the State.
> The very conception of a civil State does not seem indeed to have
> ever taken root in Canadian France.[9]

Some 86 per cent of the people of Quebec were Roman
Catholic at the time of Confederation; the proportion increased
only .5 per cent during the period 1871–1911.[10] In 1911, An-
glicans accounted for 5.13 per cent, Presbyterians for 3.2 per
cent, Methodists for 2.12 per cent, and Jews for 1.51 per cent
of the population. There are no exact statistics on the racial
origins of Catholics, but, traditionally, to be French Canadian
and to be Catholic have been considered synonymous. French
Canadians, therefore, accounted for about 93 per cent of the
Catholics, and the remainder were mostly of Irish origin.

Because our chief interest is in the élite or power-structure
of the Catholic Church, which was predominantly French Canadian, the English-speaking Catholics, though not deliberately
excluded, will receive only incidental attention. And, in general,
we abstract here from the influences exercised by religions and
churches other than the Catholic Church.

Prior to World War I, the civil province of Quebec comprised
three ecclesiastical provinces under the pastoral care of three
archbishops: the ecclesiastical province of Quebec consisting
of the dioceses of Quebec, Trois-Rivières, Rimouski, Chicoutimi,
Nicolet, and the Apostolic Prefecture of the Gulf of St. Lawrence;
the province of Montreal consisting of the dioceses of Montreal,
Saint-Hyacinthe, Sherbrooke, Valleyfield, and Joliette; and the
province of Ottawa—partly in the civil province of Quebec—
consisting of the dioceses of Ottawa, Pembroke, Mont-Laurier,
and the Apostolic Vicariate of Temiscaming. The rapid growth
and spread of the Church are evident from the fact that several of

---

[8] C.P. Lucas, *Lord Durham's Report*, vol. II, 138-39.
[9] Siegfried, *The Race Question...*, p. 15.
[10] These and the following percentages are taken from *Statistical Year Book*, II (1915), 148-50.

these dioceses were founded after Confederation.   For example, Sherbrooke was constituted a diocese in 1874, Chicoutimi in 1878, Nicolet in 1885, Valleyfield in 1892, and Joliette in 1904; the Apostolic Prefecture of the Gulf of St. Lawrence was established in 1903, and the Apostolic Vicariate of Temiscaming in 1908.   Mgr Taschereau, archbishop of Quebec, became Canada's first cardinal in 1886, and the same honour was later bestowed upon Mgr Bégin, who succeeded him in the diocese of Quebec at Mgr Taschereau's death in 1898.

Dioceses are divided into parishes, each under the pastoral care of a parish priest or curé.   In the province of Quebec it was common practice for the civil authorities to constitute municipalities so that they would coincide as far as possible with the territory of established parishes.   In the material affairs of the parish, the curé is assisted by the *fabrique*, the council of churchwardens elected by the freeholders of the parish.   In fact, a parish cannot be established unless a formal petition is made by the representatives of the local people to the bishop.   Once named to a parish, a curé usually remains there for life.   This permanency gives great stability to the parishes and causes pastors to identify themselves more completely with their people.   As Mgr Victor Tremblay writes:

> Le curé canadien, établi à demeurer parmi ses paroissiens, subissant leurs conditions de vie, dénué par leur misère et riche par leur prospérité, honoré par leur respect, soutenu par leur confiance, malheureux de leurs divisions ou de leurs désordres, réconforté par leur vertu, en contact continuel avec eux par ses devoirs multiples et par leurs multiples besoins spirituels et temporels...; le curé canadien a vite fait d'épouser tous les intérêts de ses fidèles.[11]

For the French Canadian—even the anti-clerical—the curé frequently emerges as the hero of the popular histories of his race.[12]   This is due, at least in part, to the peculiar situation that existed among the French Canadians when the English so rudely severed the umbilical cord that tied them intimately to "mother" France.   At that time, the return of about one-third— some 2,000 or more— of their lay leaders to France only served to deepen the atmosphere of discouragement and defeat that continued to hang over this infant colony with its meagre population of 65,000.   Both business and education would be long in recovering from this major set-back; for entire decades French

---

[11] Mgr Victor TREMBLAY, "La Paroisse et la race canadienne-française," *Rapports de la Société canadienne d'histoire de l'Église catholique* (1947-1948), p. 77.
[12] For example, see Robert CHOQUETTE, *le Curé de village*. This is a series of radio programmes presented in 1935, giving a colourful idea of the active role of the curé in a village in French Canada.

Canadians would continue to live what Michel Brunet calls "une vie diminuée."

> Plusieurs négociants, déjà appauvris par la guerre et ruinés complètement par la concurrence de leurs rivaux britanniques, se retirèrent du commerce.   Les hommes d'affaires canadiens devinrent des producteurs marginaux, des intermédiaires, de modestes boutiquiers.   La société canadienne n'avait plus sa classe d'entrepreneurs.
>
> L'instruction publique, qui avait progressé normalement pendant la période coloniale française, rétrograda après la Conquête... Le système scolaire attendra près d'un siècle pour se réorganiser.[13]

This vacuum of leadership was filled by the Church.   She won acceptance and prestige with the British conqueror by preaching loyalty to his legitimate authority, but at the same time she adopted an unwavering policy of steadfastly defending the integrity of the French-Canadian race.[14] Siegfried's impressions are typical of most observers who had an opportunity to study the situation at the turn of the century—and even much later.

> Without the support of the priests, our compatriots in Canada would undoubtedly ere now have been dispersed or absorbed.   The village church formed a rallying-point for them when their country abandoned them and withdrew from them even the social authorities round which they might have organized their resistance.   It is the country curé who, by dint of daily instruction, has kept alive in them those modes of thought and manners and customs which characterize the French Canadian race.   It is the Church that by taking under her care the collective interests of the people has enabled them to withstand successfully all attempts of the English at persecution or seduction.   The bonds between the clergy and the laity in French Canada are as strong today as they were a hundred years ago.   Now as then the maintenance of Catholicism would seem to be the most essential condition of the continuance of our race and tongue in the Dominion.[15]

The Church's secret for remaining a strong popular institution was that at every turn in history she has espoused the one cause which French Canadians of every blend have closest at heart— "the development of their race as a distinct unit, and the preservation of their integrity.[16]

In her solicitude to keep French Canadians both Catholic and French, the Church's policy has usually been one of cultural isolation.   Even when a substantial group of French Canadians have settled elsewhere, such as in New England and the Canadian

---

[13] BRUNET, "Trois dominantes...," *op. cit.*, p. 37.
[14] SIEGFRIED, *The Race Question*..., p. 47.
[15] *Ibid.*, p. 50.
[16] SIEGFRIED, *Canada: An International Power*, p. 227.

west, the Church showed remarkable resourcefulness and ingenuity in helping her people to reproduce their particular way of
life almost integrally in these new circumstances.   The French-
Canadian clergy seem to have been convinced that everywhere
in North America their flock had to be protected from the dangers
that continually threatened on every side—from English "Protestants," from American "materialists," from French "anti-
clericals and Free Masons," even from Irish Catholics, and,
strangest of all, from the local governments.   Growing state
power has been a bogy for the Church ever since the conquest.
The days of economic planning under Talon were completely
in the past.   Immediately after the conquest, the state represented the "Protestant English enemy" who was trying to
assimilate the small French colony through the creation of an
English public school system.   Later, the government was, in
the eyes of the clergy, a group of Englishmen and those French
Canadians who had bought the rulers' favour. And their diffi-
dence grew as the radical ideas of the French Revolution began
to leave their mark on certain French-Canadian politicians.
After 1840, under the Union Parliament, the French Canadians
became a minority, but even when Quebec finally got its own
truly French Catholic parliament, the Church had long since
through its integrated parish and school system learned to
dispense almost entirely with the aid of state bureaucracy.
Moreover, at the turn of the century, the Church's experience
of persecution at the hands of anti-clerical governments in
France and other European countries and the resultant stream
of "refugee" priests, brothers, and sisters who sought asylum
in Quebec, had once again roused all the old misgivings about
the true motivation behind constant efforts to push the state's
power into new areas.

Although Brunet sometimes oversimplifies and exaggerates,
as there will be occasion to see later in concrete cases, his sweep-
ing summary statement of the situation after Confederation
does catch the atmosphere of the times, especially in what the
Church regarded jealously as her own domain—that of general
education.

> Les dirigeants ecclésiastiques gardent leur ancienne méfiance à
> l'égard du pouvoir civil.   Ils n'ont pas oublié les longues luttes que
> l'Église québécoise a dû livrer, depuis la Conquête, pour obtenir et
> conserver sa liberté d'action.   Le programme de plusieurs chefs
> politiques 'rouges' et les outrecuidances de quelques francs-maçons
> et esprits forts qui se donnent l'illusion d'être la majorité ne sont pas
> de nature à les rassurer.   Le clergé, en général, a encore une confiance
> très limitée dans les chefs laïcs canadiens-français.   Il cherche à

s'allier aux plus traditionnalistes d'entre eux. Il croit toujours un retour à la période 1820-1840. La situation pénible des catholiques dans plusieurs pays d'Europe continentale où l'Église est victime d'une persécution ouverte et systématique, inspire aux chefs religieux du Canada français une prudence extrême. Ils surveillent étroitement tous les gestes et toutes les initiatives du gouvernement québécois. Celui-ci devient comme paralysé et n'ose pas adopter les réformes qui s'imposent dans deux domaines qui relèvent de sa juridiction: éducation et législation sociale. En 1875, un gouvernement conservateur se sent même obligé de supprimer le ministère de l'Instruction publique. L'enseignement et la prédication des religieux français chassés de leur patrie par un législateur sectaire contribueront à préciser davantage la pensée anti-étatiste des principaux interprètes de la société canadienne-française. Quiconque propose une réforme, une initiative, une mesure, un projet nécessitant l'intervention de l'État provincial se voit soupçonné de conspiration maçonnique. Une équipe de journalistes et d'écrivains se spécialise dans le dépistage des conspirateurs, quelquefois réels, souvent imaginaires.

Un phénomène vraiment paradoxal s'ensuivit. Dans un État démocratique où l'immense majorité de la population était catholique pratiquante et où un gouvernement n'aurait pas pu gouverner sans son appui, les autorités ecclésiastiques adoptèrent à l'égard du pouvoir politique l'attitude que l'Église a dû prendre dans les pays où les fidèles catholiques formaient une minorité obligée de se protéger contre l'incompréhension et la persécution d'une majorité hostile ou indifférente. Un peuple catholique avait déclaré la guerre à son gouvernement catholique.[17]

It is only against such a background that much of the later discussion in this book, especially of education, will become intelligible. Here, this very summary introduction to the situation of the Church in French Canada may conclude by recounting the quaint device—a parable and its explanation— used recently by Gérard Pelletier in introducing a similar study written for a popular magazine. However nebulous, this parable with its over-simplified explanation does provide a key to many of the mysteries of Quebec. Pelletier's parable is taken from a passage in which Archbishop Roy of Quebec recounts the typical history of a French-Canadian parish. His description runs as follows:

Jusqu'au jour où les paroisses jugèrent plus pratique d'ouvrir un compte de banque, il y avait dans certaines paroisses un coffre muni de deux serrures. L'une des clefs était confiée au curé, l'autre au premier marguillier et, sans ces deux clefs, on ne pouvait ouvrir le coffre. Le curé ne pouvait donc pas toucher à l'argent de la Fabrique sans la présence du premier marguillier. A la fin de décembre, pour rendre compte de l'administration de l'année écoulée,

---

[17] BRUNET, "Trois dominantes...," pp. 101-102. See also on the same theme Pierre Elliot TRUDEAU, "Some Obstacles to Democracy in Quebec," in Mason WADE, ed., *Canadian Dualism*, pp. 241-59.

on ouvrait solennellement le coffre de la Fabrique devant tous les marguilliers assemblés.

Pelletier sees in this simple story a symbol of the whole history of the relations between the Church and lay society in French Canada:

> Pour décrire les relations entre l'Église et la société canadienne-française, il suffirait de distinguer les époques et les régions où le marguillier détient l'une des deux clefs et celles où le curé, les fourrant toutes deux dans sa poche, exerce une autorité abusive. Bien entendu, les clefs prendraient alors valeur de symboles: l'une représenterait le pouvoir spirituel, l'autre le pouvoir temporel. Le curé figurerait la puissance cléricale et le marguillier résumerait en sa personne toute la diversité du laïcat.
>
> Ce coffre à deux serrures, ce serait non seulement la richesse matérielle, les ressources économiques mais la source même de toute puissance: autorité politique, pouvoir sur l'enseignement, sur l'édition et la presse, sur tous les leviers de commande qui déterminent la marche et l'évolution d'une société.
>
> Il faudrait rappeler le temps où les marguilliers ne voulaient pas s'embarrasser de leur clef, trop heureux de laisser au curé seul le soin des deux serrures; puis celui où le curé vit d'un mauvais œil, interpréta comme une intolérable méfiance qu'on voulût être présent pour l'ouverture annuelle du coffre; enfin l'époque présente qui complique tout avec ses comptes en banque, invention funeste et si complexe qu'elle brouille complètement les rapports traditionnels...[18]

ECONOMIC DEVELOPMENT IN CANADA, 1896–1914

A brief sketch of the economic development that took place in Canada after Confederation is given here in order to situate more clearly Quebec's own economic development which was intimately related to it.[19]

The role of government in economic development gradually changed. The federal government had early adopted what was called the "National Policy" of subsidizing transportation and communications facilities to unite the country and stop the steady drain on population through emigration to the United States. This policy also included the establishment of tariffs

---

[18] Gérard PELLETIER, "La Société canadienne-française et l'Église," *Le Magazine Maclean* (September 1961), p. 11.

[19] For this sketch I rely largely on O.J. FIRESTONE's basic study, *Canada's Economic Development, 1867–1953*, especially on Part I, "Summary of the Analysis," 3–27. Firestone's rough estimates are adequate for the general lines of Canadian economic development, although his estimates of national income per capita for 1910 and of GNP for 1880 may be too high, and his population estimates for the period 1870-1920 may be too low (see, for example, Kenneth BUCKLEY, "Review of *Canada's Economic Development, 1867–1953* by O.J. Firestone," *American Economic Review*, XLIX (June 1959), 431-33). I base my own detailed estimates of total output and value added in manufacturing in Quebec directly on the available census data.

to protect Canadian industry. The first Canadian transcontinental railway, the Canadian Pacific, was built between the years 1874 and 1885. Both federal and provincial governments followed a policy of making generous land grants to the railroads. In the period 1900–1915 two further transcontinental railways, the Grand Trunk and the Canadian Northern, were completed, thus increasing Canadian railway mileage from 7,657 to 34,882 and giving the nation both the highest railway mileage per capita in the world, and, among modern countries, the lowest railway mileage per square mile of territory. By 1916 the federal government had granted 31,864,074 and the Quebec government 13,324,950 acres of land to the various railway companies to stimulate their expansion.[20] As the provincial governments in the east began to benefit from new property revenues at the turn of the century, direct federal subsidies to them fell off rapidly.

The rate of economic growth in Canada has been uneven. Soon after Confederation the "great depression" threw its sombre shadow over the economy, and it was not until 1896 that prosperity returned with all its brightness. Thereafter it continued strongly until 1913 with slight waverings in the years 1903-1904 and 1907-1908. World War I brought new vigour to the Canadian economy in 1914, and it surged ahead once more.

The period 1896–1914 was one of rapid industrialization and urbanization in the east and of rapid land settlement and railroad building in the west. Between 1890 and 1910, Gross National Product in constant dollars (1935–1939) increased by 122.7 per cent or at a compound rate of 4.09 per cent.[21] At the same time, "the number of persons in manufacturing doubled, real output rose 130 per cent, and the value of fixed capital employed increased 2-¾ times in real terms... Real output per person working increased about 11 per cent, representing an annual rise of one-half of one per cent."[22] Analysts usually attribute the great prosperity of the years 1900–1914 to the facts that in this period between $4.5 and $5 billion were invested in capital goods, and that the net inflow of foreign capital exceeded well over $2 billion.[23] Also, between 1890 and 1910 gross investment measured in constant dollars increased from

[20] Canada, *The Canada Year Book*, 1916, p. 430.
[21] FIRESTONE, *Canada's Economic Development*, p. 68.
[22] *Ibid.*, p. 210.
[23] Canada, *Report of the Royal Commission on Dominion-Provincial Relations*, book I (Ottawa: King's Printer, 1939), 75-76, cited by FIRESTONE, *ibid.*, p. 103, in note. See also Penelope HARTLAND, "Canadian Balance of Payments Since 1869," in *Trends in the American Economy in the Nineteenth Century*, vol. XXIV of *Studies in Income and Wealth* (Princeton: Princeton University, 1960), p. 723.

13.9 to 18.2 per cent of Gross National Product; net capital formation increased from 6.3 to 9.5 per cent; and per capita income in constant dollars (1935–1939) rose from $240 to $434.[24] Already, during World War I, Canadians were earning as much and more from manufacturing as they were from agriculture, although it was only with World War II that industrial employment finally overtook and passed agricultural employment.[25] Nevertheless, it is quite clear that by 1914 Canada had little in common with what today are referred to as "underdeveloped countries."

In recent years, there has been an attempt to reinterpret an important phase of Canadian economic history and to consider the "great depression" years, 1870–1896, as rather "dynamic" depression years. The earlier interpretation of this period has been based largely on the evidence of net migration, the failure of per capita exports to rise, and the steady decline of prices in this period. But, as Gordon Bertram has rightly pointed out, this interpretation overlooks the fact that in eastern Canada there was a constant growth in manufactures—Ontario's manufacturing showing an average annual compound rate of growth of 4.58 per cent in constant dollars, and Quebec's manufacturing one of 4.11 per cent. Moreover, per capita Gross National Product in constant dollars was increasing at a rate of .02 per cent above the long-run annual rate of 1.65 per cent already noted.[26] Bertram sees the major difference between the decades 1870–1890 and the later more prosperous decades 1890–1910 as due primarily to exogenous factors, and especially to easier access during the later period to huge sums of foreign capital.[27] These considerations go far towards dispelling the common illusion of a very sharp break in the continuity of growth in the year 1896, the year in which the trend of wholesale prices which had been falling steadily since 1872 finally hit bottom and turned upward.[28]

Once the "depression" decades are shown to be decades of steady if not explosive growth in manufacturing in eastern Canada, it becomes exceedingly difficult, as Bertram has shown, to find evidence to verify the succeeding spurt in the period

---

[24] FIRESTONE, *Canada's Economic Development*, pp. 100, 66.

[25] *Ibid.*, p. 24.

[26] Gordon W. BERTRAM, "Historical Statistics on Growth and Structure of Manufacturing in Canada, 1870-1957," paper read before the Canadian Political Science Association, McMaster University, Hamilton, Canada, June 11, 1962, p. 47.

[27] *Ibid.*, p. 49.

[28] See H. MITCHELL, "Statistics of Prices," in *Statistical Contribution to Canadian Economic History*, vol. II, 56.

1896–1914 as a "take-off" in the special sense in which that term is used by Rostow.[29]   But even if this latter spurt lacks the characteristic of sharp discontinuity and so does not deserve to be called a "take-off," it still remains a period of great importance for Canadian economic development and was the period in which Canadian manufactures experienced their highest rate of sustained growth prior to World War I.

ECONOMIC DEVELOPMENT IN QUEBEC, 1896–1914

General Perspective

The purpose of this section is merely to describe adequately the economic development that took place in the province and thus to establish that it was a period of sufficient importance to warrant this study and its attempt to discover the role of the Church's influence in economic development. Presented here is an over-all view of the more important changes that took place so that when he comes to the later chapters, which discuss the influences of the Church in particular sectors of the economy, the reader will already have a sufficiently clear picture of the relative importance of these sectors for the total growth process.

It has long been fashionable to refer to Quebec as the "backward" or "underdeveloped" province of Canada. For example, quite recently Walter Rostow compared Quebec to the American South: "Canada has had its regional problem of a sort of traditional society in Quebec. The take-off of the American South is a phenomenon of the last two decades; while the take-off in Quebec may only now be getting whole-heartedly under way."[30]   And the French-Canadian historian, Michel Brunet, in alluding to Quebec's high rate of unemployment and relatively low wage scale at the present time, disdainfully observes that "the economic equipment of Quebec remains that of an underdeveloped area."[31]   The reasons alleged for such "backwardness" are usually the "specific cultural factors" or "the traditional society."[32]

---

[29] See Gordon W. BERTRAM, "Economic Growth in Canadian Industry, 1870–1915: The Staple Model and Take-off Hypothesis," *Canadian Journal of Economics and Political Science*, XXIX (May 1963), 159-284. Here Bertram systematically shows that none of Rostow's key indicators is clearly verified in the period 1896-1914, which Rostow himself proposed as Canada's "take-off."

[30] W.W. ROSTOW, *Stages of Economic Growth*, p. 18.

[31] BRUNET, "Trois dominantes...," p. 58.

[32] See A. FAUCHER and M. LAMONTAGNE, "History of Industrial Development," p. 23, and ROSTOW, *Stages of Economic Growth*, p. 18.

Recently, both the theory of "backwardness" and its alleged explanation have been sharply challenged. The French-Canadian economists, A. Faucher and M. Lamontagne, concluded their essay study of Quebec's industrial development by categorically denying that French-Canadian culture had left any specific trait on Quebec's industrialization for the obvious reason that the latter was not a regional phenomenon:

> Quebec's industrial development has never behaved in an autonomous and isolated way. On the contrary, it has always felt very deeply the impact of the North-American evolution. Its development has been mainly a response to change affecting the whole continent. Thus conceived as part of a larger unit, Quebec cannot be said to be backward or forward economically. In an economy of coal and steel, when locational factors were not favourable, it developed less rapidly than other regions in a more advantageous position. On the other hand, when these factors became favourable, progress was immediately felt.[33]

These authors seem to imply that Quebec experienced no serious industrialization until about 1911, for the "simple fact that Quebec, in the steel economy of that period, had no coal and iron and was located too far from the Appalachian coal fields."[34]

More recently still, in the first serious quantitative study of Quebec's modern economic history, Professor Raynauld of the Université de Montréal and his associates marshal statistical evidence to show that by 1913 Quebec, along with the rest of Canada, had already achieved its "take-off," and that since 1870 the rate of growth in Quebec's economic production has been almost the same as that of Ontario, which is recognized by all as Canada's bell-wether in economic performance.[35]

Such divergence of opinion reveals only too well the lack of research on Quebec's economic history as well as the ambiguity of such concepts as "backwardness" and "industrialization." For present purposes, it will suffice to outline the major gains in economic development achieved before World War I. We are directly interested in all those projects which the province

---

[33] Faucher and Lamontagne, "History of Industrial Development," pp. 34-35.
[34] *Ibid.*, p. 30.
[35] A. Raynauld, *Croissance et structure économiques*, pp. 28-29, 63. He bases this conclusion on his findings that over the long-run period 1870–1935 agriculture production grew at an average annual rate of 3.2 per cent in Quebec and 2.9 per cent in Ontario, and during the period 1935-1955 the rates of growth in agricultural production were 8.58 and 8.45 respectively; mineral production grew at an annual average rate of 8.2 per cent in Quebec and 6.4 per cent in Ontario in the period 1900-1955; and manufacturing production over the whole period 1870-1955 grew at an annual average rate of 5.53 in Quebec and 5.48 in Ontario (pp. 43-48). His rates of growth are measured in current value terms. This method is quite adequate for his purpose of comparing the rates in the two provinces, but it does, of course, considerably exaggerate the rates of real growth involved.

initiated to increase its productive capacity and ultimately its per capita consumption potential. Even this brief sketch should contribute something towards an understanding of why there is a difference of opinion on the economic record of Quebec.

At first glance, the economic picture in Quebec after Confederation does not appear bright. Quebec City, which had had a prosperous shipbuilding industry and long been a major commercial centre, was now in full decline, and the future of the province's famed logging industry was already clouded as the prized pines became scarcer and scarcer. The deepening of the St. Lawrence together with the construction of canals opened up the interior Great Lakes system to cheap navigation, and the new flood of western wheat threw Quebec's cereal-based agriculture into crises. What industrial prosperity remained in the province began to be concentrated in its southwest corner around the fast-growing ocean port and railroad centre of Montreal, whose population tripled between 1861 and 1891, rising from 90,000 to over 265,000, and again doubling to 530,000 by 1913. The Vieilles Forges near Trois-Rivières, the seat of Quebec's ironworks for almost three centuries, succumbed to the cheaper American product and was finally abandoned in 1883 owing to rising costs involved in using poorer ore and more expensive wood. Worst of all, in the eyes of the French Canadians, lack of new employment opportunities in the province was forcing thousands to emigrate to the United States. Blanchard estimates that about 700,000 French Canadians left their native soil definitively between 1851 and 1931.[36] And Keyfitz estimates that net migration from the province, independently of racial origin, was about 280,000 in the period 1881-1911, but that it rapidly decreased towards the end of this period as prosperity returned.[37] The picture was only the more dismal for the French Canadian because the federal government was encouraging and subsidizing mass European immigration. In the prosperous decade 1901–1911, Canada was host to 1,515,822 immigrants, and during the following decade she received 1,200,000 more.[38]

---

[36] BLANCHARD, *Le Canada français*, p. 95.

[37] See KEYFITZ, "Growth of Canadian Population," p. 54. His estimate of net emigration from the province of Quebec is as follows: 1881–1891, 132,000; 1891–1901, 121,000; 1901–1911, 29,000; 1911–1921, 99,000.

[38] In reality, Canada was for many immigrants merely a doorstep to the United States. For example, it has been estimated that in the period 1901-1911 only about 55 per cent of the new immigrants remained in Canada; however, it is one thing to lose a stranger and quite another to lose a natural born Canadian. See Georges LANGLOIS, *Histoire de la population canadienne-française*, p. 142.

The chief reason for this gradual movement of economic prosperity from eastern towards central Canada—as towards the central United States—was, as Faucher and Lamontagne explain, "the substitution of steel for wood as the basic economic product of industry and the construction of railroads was the decisive element in this change." They conclude, perhaps too sanguinely, that, "thereafter, only those regions where coal could be found would experience rapid progress."[39] In fact, Quebec has no coal, and her vast iron ore deposits were still firmly locked in the Laurentian Shield. So Quebec looked elsewhere, and following the example of New England—where many of her workers had gained factory experience—concentrated on cheap labour industries such as textiles, shoes, flourmilling, sawmills, tanning, gloves, bakeries, cigars, and cigarettes. Quebec was forced to join the "sweating-system" industry belt of the continent while Ontario had the good fortune to be located near the steel- and tool-producing belt, as Faucher and Lamontagne describe it.[40]

But there are several qualifications to this too sombre picture, which tends to the view shared by many currently underdeveloped countries that there is no genuine economic development or industrialization unless it is centred around a basic steel industry. Happily for Quebec, two new industries were already on the horizon before 1896: the hydro-electric, or "white-coal" industry, and the pulp and paper industry— the latter destined for almost half a century to be Canada's, and especially Quebec's, most important industry in terms of total production. The Laurentian Shield which had hitherto provided only giant pines had now begun to unfold her other treasures. John Dales describes how Quebec is ideally situated for the development of hydraulic power:

---

[39] FAUCHER and LAMONTAGNE, "History of Industrial Development," p. 25.

[40] *Ibid.*, p. 26. Here they write: "In Canada as well as in the United States, economic activity moved towards the centre of the country. In this region of industrialism, southern Ontario was strategically located with respect to waterborne and railway traffic. It was adjacent to the Appalachian coal fields and could command the cheapest routes to the western hinterland. To these advantages was added a decisive factor, the tariff walls which according to geographers played 'a vital role in causing manufacturing to be more important on the Canadian side than otherwise would be the case.' [C.L. WHITE and E.J. FOSCUE, *Regional Geography of Anglo-America* (Englewood-Cliffs: Prentice Hall, 1950), chap. XIII.] Thus the Great Lakes sub-region of Ontario emerged as the Canadian wedge into the United States and forged ahead in stride with the Cleveland sub-region of the manufacturing belt. The importance of tariffs in this development cannot be too much emphasized. In the words of Bruce Hutchison, the wedge 'is physically almost an island surrounded by lake and river. Economically it is still more insular behind a Chinese wall of tariffs.' " [*The Unknown Country* (Toronto: Longmans, 1948), chap. VII.]

The PreCambrian, or Laurentian Shield and the river system which it has fashioned provide the favourable mould within which the hydro-electric power industry of Quebec has developed. The southern boundary of the shield is Quebec's "fall line." Moving westward, the line follows the St. Lawrence River to Quebec City where it arcs gently to the north. Rejoining the St. Lawrence, it sends a spur of granite across the river to form the rapids just west of Mont-real. At no point are the Laurentian hills more than 100 miles from the north shore of the river, and thus the drainage from the immense area of northern Quebec thunders down from the ancient uplands directly into the fertile and populous St. Lawrence valley. Virtually the entire settled portion of the province is within 100 miles from at least one of the large power sites on the north shore of the river.[41]

Dales' thesis is that if Quebec had had to depend on imported coal to generate her power she would have had a very slim chance of achieving large-scale development. He claims that

... without hydroelectricity, central Canada would have only some 40 per cent of the materials required for an industrial structure, and would have had virtually no chance of industrialization. Water-power has been a *sine qua non* of industrial growth in central Canada, and the same could be said of the region's agricultural resources. Central Canada's large mining and forest resources, on the other hand, would have been unavailing for the region's industrial develop-ment if they had not been coupled with good hydroelectric and agricultural resources.[42]

Hydraulic power organized on a large scale, cheap electric power, almost limitless spruce forests, cheap, abundant, energetic labour, and the rapid transformation of agriculture from a cereal to a dairy-farming base—these were among the chief economic factors at work at the turn of the century, and they not only succeeded in keeping Quebec's economy from falling into stagnation but even enabled it to retain a major role in Canada's economic development, second only to the more favoured prov-ince of Ontario. Quebec's was not to be a steel-centred devel-opment, but, as is clear from Raynauld's study, she was not to be outdistanced by Ontario in annual rates of growth of production in either agriculture, mining, or manufacturing. Raynauld's conclusions are confirmed by Gordon Bertram's more recent study.[43] The latter's statistics on manufacturing indicate that, despite the extremely rapid economic transformation of Western Canada between 1896 and 1914, Quebec managed almost to hold her own in the percentage of Canada's total manufactures

[41] John H. DALES, *Hydroelectricity and Industrial Development, Quebec, 1898–1940*, p. 26.

[42] *Ibid.*, p. 175.

[43] Gordon W. BERTRAM, "Historical Statistics in Growth," p. 22.

which she provided (see Table I). If we omit the war year, 1915, in which Ontario's iron and steel industry had an obvious advantage, and consider only the period 1890–1910—coinciding roughly with the period which Rostow refers to as the "take-off" period in Canada—Quebec's share of total Canadian manufactures fell by 1.7 per cent as compared with a slightly smaller drop of 1.2 per cent for the province of Ontario.[44]

TABLE I

Percentage Distribution of Canada's Total Manufactures, Quebec and Ontario*

YEAR	QUEBEC	ONTARIO
1870	34.5	52.1
1880	33.7	51.2
1890	31.0	51.5
1900	31.9	50.6
1910	29.3	50.3
1915	27.3	52.2
1926	30.7	51.1

* Based on Gordon W. BERTRAM, "Historical Statistics in Growth."

The economic development that took place in the province of Quebec at this time will now be considered in more detailed quantitative terms. The discussion will centre on the areas of manufacturing and agriculture, which particularly concern this study, and will be based on two reliable measures of the rate of economic development—the values in constant dollars of total output and of value added in manufacturing for the period 1896–1914. Discussion of certain other important economic indicators will have to be more casual, for there are still

---

[44] Quite obviously Bertram's findings are not in perfect agreement with those of Raynauld (cited in note 35 above) because the latter found that Quebec had a slight edge over her neighbour. But these differences are not large enough to be of major significance.

no sufficiently reliable estimates of Gross National Product, of per capita income, or even of capital formation in industry to attempt to verify whether Quebec really did undergo a Rostovian "take-off" in this period. Raynauld appears to have proven, not necessarily that Quebec had her "take-off" in this period, but only that if Canada experienced its "take-off" in

TABLE II 1407847

Distribution of the Labour Force in Absolute Numbers and as Percentages of the Total Labour Force, Quebec and Ontario, 1911*

	QUEBEC		ONTARIO	
	Absolute numbers (thousands)	Percentage of labour force	Absolute numbers (thousands)	Percentage of labour force
Total labour force............	653†		991‡	
Agriculture.................	205	31.3	307	31.0
Manufacturing.............	142	21.7	231	23.3§
Commerce..................	71	10.9	112	11.3
Construction...............	68	10.4	83	8.3
Personal and domestic services..	54	8.3	79	7.9
Transportation..............	43	6.5	76	7.6
Other services..............	31	4.8	45	4.5
Government.................	18	2.7	28	2.7
Forestry...................	11	1.8	11	1.1
Mining....................	6	.9	17	1.6
Fishing and Hunting.........	4	.7	4	.4

* Sources: *Census of Canada*, 1911, VI, Table 2; *Statistical Year Book*, II (1915), 157.
† Represents 32.7 per cent of Quebec's population of 2,006,000.
‡ Represents 39.1 per cent of Ontario's population of 2,527,000.
§ It should be observed that Ontario's edge over Quebec in employment in manufacturing all but disappears if construction is included under manufacturing, as it often was at that time.

this period Quebec also experienced hers, because, as he shows, her economic development formed an integral part of Canada's during this period. In any case, Raynauld's brief explanation of how Quebec fulfills the conditions of the "take-off" would not stand up to the searching criticism which Bertram has made of Rostow's suggestion that Canada had its "take-off" in the period 1896–1914. There will be no attempt here, therefore, to prove that Quebec underwent her "take-off" in the period 1896–1914, but only that during this period she experienced important economic change and growth, her biggest sustained spurt since Confederation.

Occupations

One of the more interesting points of the occupational picture in Quebec is the fact that already in 1910 only 31.3 per cent of the labour force were employed in agriculture, while 21.7 per cent were engaged in manufacturing, and an added 43.6 per cent were engaged in such occupations as commerce, construction, transportation, government, and services—all occupations that were associated more with urban than with rural life (see Table II).

Indeed, this was a period of rapid urbanization. The rural population in Quebec decreased by almost 30 per cent in the period 1870–1910 (see Table III). By 1915 the province was no longer predominantly rural, but had an urban population of 49.6 per cent. And, if we adopt the new definitions introduced into the census in 1951, which consider as "urban" any city, town, or village with 1,000 or more inhabitants, whether it is incorporated or not, we find that in 1915 Quebec was already 53.5 per cent "urban."[45] During these decades, the cities, especially Montreal, were expanding and improving their facilities; in addition all over the province, towns and villages were being founded and incorporated, and public works projects

---

[45] Under the old definitions only incorporated towns and cities were counted as "urban." But in 1915 there were 13 centres listed as towns with under 1,000 occupants, and 49 listed as villages which had over 1,000 occupants. So the acceptance of incorporation as a town was a very arbitrary norm. In 1915 Montreal contained 70 per cent of the strictly city population, that is 650,000 out of total of 957,129; of the 14 other cities, only Quebec City had a population exceeding 100,000. An indication of the rapidity of urbanization is seen in the fact that in the brief period 1911-1915 city population increased by 27.2 per cent; town population increased by 32 per cent, from 142,776 to 192,759, as 15 new towns were incorporated; and village population increased by 38 per cent, from 116,338 to 160,143, as 43 new villages were incorporated (*Statistical Year Book*, III [1916], 65–71). It might be added that, even under the old definitions, in 1910 Quebec was more "urban" than Canada as a whole, for 48.4 per cent of its population was "urban" as compared with the Canadian average of 45.4 (FIRESTONE, *Canada's Economic Development*, p. 60).

TABLE III

Percentages of Rural and Urban Population in Quebec*

YEAR	URBAN	RURAL
1870	19.5	80.5
1880	22.8	77.2
1890	29.2	70.8
1900	38.8	60.2
1910	48.4	51.6
1915	49.6	50.4

* SOURCE: *Statistical Year Book*, III (1916), 65.

such as local town halls, court houses, market places, churches, school buildings, waterworks, and electric lighting, were being undertaken. Improved communications were first on the agenda of all town councils; attempts to get on at least a branch line of the railway, to improve roads, and to instal the telegraph and telephone, all had top priority. Usually these towns and villages were centred around a few small factories, power installations, flour and sawmills, and the new creameries which were blossoming everywhere. Some towns were the natural commercial and market centres of farming settlements. Many sprang up out of the wilderness at the site of a waterfall which had attracted a new pulp and papermill or a hydro-electric installation. Still other towns and villages grew because they were host to new light industries which came in search of the cheap labour these people were only too eager to provide.

Mining

Mining was still relatively unimportant in Quebec. If we exclude cement production, which increased from 17,000 to 2,881,000 barrels annually in the period 1901–1913, the only mineral of importance was asbestos, the annual production of which increased over the same period from 33,466 to 136,609 tons. These two products accounted for $6.2 million or 47.3 per cent of Quebec's total mineral production in 1913—the remainder being made up of small quantities of gold, silver, iron, and copper ores, and various quarry products.[46]

Manufacturing

In manufacturing we shall concentrate on the decade 1900–1910 for whose terminal years there are the detailed census data on manufacturing. We are here dealing with rough data collected by the census before the Dominion Bureau of Statistics was organized to refine definitions, assure complete coverage, and prevent overlapping. The lack of refined data has caused some students in the past, for example, Faucher and Lamontagne in 1952, to shy away from quantitative studies of Quebec's economic history.[47] Because they are not really essential to this discussion, I have relegated to a statistical appendix (Appendix

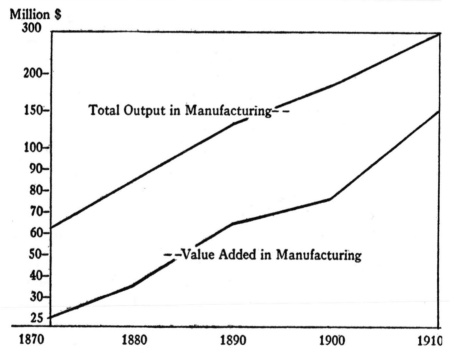

Growth of Total Output and of Value Added in Quebec's Manufacturing, 1870–1910, in Constant 1900 Dollars (see Appendix I).

[46] *Statistical Year Book*, II (1915), 493–503.
[47] FAUCHER and LAMONTAGNE, "History of Industrial Development," p. 23, where they write: "Due to the scarcity and, in many instances, the complete absence of statistical data, our approach has to be non-quantitative".

I) my own attempts to face squarely several of the weaknesses found in the census data. The chief aim therein has been to measure with a certain degree of refinement the extent of the spurt which took place in manufacturing during the decade 1900–1910. The quantitative estimates mentioned hereafter, unless otherwise indicated, refer to this appendix. In later chapters we shall touch on other aspects of the spurt that are more directly relevant to the central theme of this study.

In Quebec, any more than in Canada as a whole, the spurt of 1896–1914 did not represent in manufacturing a sudden sharp upturn from a situation of deep depression, as has been often suggested. The so-called "depression decades," in particular those of 1870–1880 and 1880–1890, achieved an increase in constant dollar terms (1900 = 100) of 47 and 51 per cent respectively in gross value of manufacturing production, and of 40.6 and 69.6 per cent in total value added in manufacturing (see Figure on page 38). The decade 1890–1900, though less buoyant, still managed to show an increase of 26 per cent in gross value of manufacturing production and of 24.5 per cent in total value added.

In 1890 the bulk, about 60 per cent, of manufactures was still to be found in the industry groups of food and beverages (23 per cent), leather products (13.5 per cent), clothing (10.1 per cent), and wood products (13.3 per cent), and much of industry was still carried on in small shops and factories. But already other industry groups were beginning to show strength. Iron and steel products accounted for 11.1 per cent of total manufactures, transportation equipment for 7.2 per cent, textiles for 5.6 per cent, paper products for 2.8 per cent, tobacco products for 2.6 per cent, and chemical products for 3 per cent.

After 1890, and especially after 1896, large-scale production made rapid gains. In 1890, 81.5 per cent of total manufactures were produced in establishments with five or more employees, whereas in 1910 the proportion in such establishments was less than 2 per cent.

The decade 1900–1910 was one of very rapid growth and structural change in Quebec manufactures. The total gross value of production in constant dollars (1900 = 100) increased by 74.9 per cent, or at an annual compound rate of 5.79 per cent, in spite of two short-lived, minor recessions in 1903 and 1908. Total value added in manufacturing increased by 81.6 per cent in the same decade, or at an annual compound rate of 6.14 per cent.

TABLE IV

Percentage of Total Quebec Manufactures Contributed by the Various Industry Groups (in Terms of Constant Dollars, 1900=100) in the Years 1900 and 1910*

	Gross Value of Production			Value Added in Manufacturing		
	1900	1910	Percentage change	1900	1910	Percentage change
I. Food and beverages............	20.7	14.2	–6.5	12.2	9.0	–3.2
II. Tobacco and tobacco products..	4.9	6.4	1.5	7.5	6.0	–1.5
III. Rubber products.	0.002	0.003	0.001	0.002	0.003	0.001
IV. Leather products.	14.8	9.1	–5.7	12.0	8.5	–3.5
V. Textile products.	7.3	7.3	0.0	7.2	6.8	–0.4
VI. Clothing (textiles and furs).......	10.7	10.1	–0.6	11.8	10.2	–1.6
VII. Wood products..	11.1	10.8	–0.3	13.2	11.2	–2.0
VIII. Paper products..	3.8	7.2	3.4	4.8	8.3	3.5
IX. Printing, publishing, etc.	2.2	2.5	0.3	3.6	3.7	0.1
X. Iron and steel products........	8.8	10.9	2.1	10.3	12.4	2.1
XI. Transportation equipment......	5.2	7.9	2.7	4.9	6.9	2.0
XII. Non-ferrous metals	1.07	4.2	3.15	1.3	5.6	4.3
XIII. Electrical apparatus, etc.........	1.14	2.8	1.7	1.9	3.3	1.5
XIV. Non-metallic products........	1.06	2.3	1.2	1.5	3.9	1.4
XV. Products of petroleum and coal...	0.17	0.3	0.13	0.06	0.09	0.03
XVI. Chemical products	3.3	2.9	0.41	3.2	2.7	–0.5
XVII. Miscellaneous manufacturing industries	0.92	1.1	0.18	1.2	1.4	0.2

* Source: See Appendix on Manufacturing Statistics. The percentages for 1910 are slightly biased downward by the omission of the industries which could not be redistributed into the new Standard Industrial Classification. And the value added figures of the same year are slightly biased upward by the omission of fuel and electricity costs among the material costs calculated at the individual industry group level.

In this decade the traditional consumption-goods industry groups of food and beverages, leather products, textiles, and clothing, while still looming large in the total volume of manufacturing production, all lost ground in their percentages of total value added, as did the wood products industry group, which had long been the pivot of Quebec industry (see Table IV). Although the latter group did benefit from the booming construction industry and thus make a rather sharp recovery from the previous decade in terms of total gross value of production, it still failed to regain its former dominant position. Other faster growing industry groups, such as paper products, non-ferrous metals, iron and steel products, transportation equipment, electric apparatus and supplies, and non-metallic products increased their percentages of total value added. The impetus that the active construction industry gave to cement production in turn instilled new life into the non-metallic products industry group. The new aluminum industry was the chief source of drive in the non-ferrous metals industry group, and its rapid growth would soon lead this group into a predominant position in Quebec industry. The individual industries of boilers and steam engines, iron and steel bridges, and foundry and machine-shop products were responsible for the new boom in the industry group of iron and steel products. Because the large railway shops recently established in Montreal were building and repairing much of the new rolling stock required by Canada's rapidly expanding railway system, they accounted for practically all the growth noted in the industry group of transportation equipment. The sharp increase in the production of local electrical apparatus and supplies, in spite of the fact that most heavy electrical equipment was still being imported, is merely a weak index of how quickly Quebec's industry was turning to this new source of power as well as of how rapidly the province was being electrified and provided with the telegraph and the telephone. With the threatening exhaustion of readily available forest resources in the United States and the development of large-scale hydraulic projects to provide cheap water and electric power in Canada, the American newsprint industry began to move northward, and Quebec mills would soon come to win a predominant position in the paper industry of America.

The cheap labour industries also continued to grow rapidly. It was during this decade that the Canadian cigarette industry settled permanently in Quebec; but its gains were largely offset by losses in other earlier tobacco products such as pipe tobacco and snuff. Likewise, growth in factory-made textiles and clothing was made largely at the expense of custom-made clothing and domestic production. The leather industry also faltered, partly owing to the withdrawal from the industry of many artisans' small shops. With the development of refrigeration, the new slaughtering and meat-packing industry boomed, but its gains were largely offset in the industry group of food and beverages by slowing rates of growth in dairy products.

But perhaps the two most interesting growth leaders were the industry groups of paper products and of electrical apparatus and supplies. Newsprint and electricity were in many ways the key to Quebec's industrialization in the first half of the twentieth century. Both industries are based on the extensive development of hydraulic power. Over the decade 1900–1910 installed hydraulic power increased by 310 per cent, from 82,876 to 334,763 hp., and by an additional 140 per cent to 803,786 hp. by 1915.[48] This was the dawn of the age of electricity in Quebec. The value of total output in the electrical light and power industry increased by 358.7 per cent (in constant dollars) in the decade 1900–1910, and by an additional 388 per cent by 1915. And, as we saw, the industry group of electrical apparatus and supplies kept pace as industries as well as cities, towns, and villages began to switch to this new source of light and power.

The pulp and paper industry was the first to profit by the new large-scale hydraulic power developments. This industry grew rapidly during this decade in anticipation of capturing the American market. Newsprint was perhaps the first Canadian manufactured product to penetrate successfully the protective tariff wall that President McKinley had built around the United States. This penetration soon became an open invasion, because the Canadian newsprint industry, largely centred in the province of Quebec, rapidly took over the growing American newsprint market, supplying 4 per cent of its needs in 1909, 25 per cent in 1916, and 62 per cent by 1932.[49]

Two other new industries were closely associated with the emergence of large hydraulic and electrical power developments —the aluminum and carbide industries. The former, which, along with the reduction of other non-ferrous metals, would soon form Quebec's third largest industry group, increased its production in its first small plant at Shawinigan from 1,983,252 to 18,368,542 pounds in the period 1901–1914, an increase of 827 per cent. As late as 1886 aluminum was still counted among the

[48] *Canada Year Book*, 1931, p. 282.
[49] Herbert MARSHALL *et al.*, *Canadian-American Industry*, p. 36.

precious metals and sold for $12 a pound, but by 1910, owing to the discovery of how to use electricity in its reduction, it was selling for 22.7 cents a pound and was already being used extensively in Quebec's new high tension cables to carry electricity across the province. The carbide industry also started humbly with an initial output of 2,000 tons at Shawinigan in 1904, but it had increased its output fivefold by 1913 and was destined to form the base of the future chemical industry at Shawinigan. There will be occasion later to note the importance of both these industries in the economic development of the St. Maurice valley.

Agriculture

A basic transformation had already begun to appear in Quebec's agriculture in the 1880's, a concerted effort to replace systematically the former cereal-based agriculture by dairy farming, stock raising, and the crops associated with these two activities, since the province's soils were too poor to compete with the vast new wheat fields of the West. In the conclusions of his doctoral thesis on "Agricultural Development and Industrialization of Quebec," Charles Lemelin summarizes a few of the more important quantitative indications of the progress achieved in the period 1881–1911.

> The first cheese factory was organized only in 1865 and the first butter factory in 1873. In 1881 the number of dairy factories was 162, and in 1911 it was 2,142.
>
> In the three decades 1881–1911, the number of farms had increased by only 15.7 per cent as compared to 43 per cent in the previous thirty years. Yet the number of milk cows had gone up by 30, and the number of hogs by 140 per cent. Horses were more intensely used on the farms and they were also sold for use in urban centers and for export. Their number increased by 35 per cent. The area in farm land increased more than the number of farms: by 24 per cent as compared to 15.7 per cent. Similarly, the area in field crops increased by close to one third. The production of wheat decreased by more than one half, while the yield increased from 9.05 bushels per acre in 1880 to 14.82 bushels per acre in 1910. The output of oats and barley increased by 69 and 36 per cent, with yields of 24 and 22 bushels per acre respectively. Hay and clover production increased almost three times between 1880 and 1910, the yield being slightly over one ton per acre in 1880 and 1.5 tons in 1910. In 1910, there was 41,750,000 pounds of butter and over 58 million pounds of cheese coming out of dairy factories.[50]

[50] Charles LEMELIN, "Agricultural Development and Industrialization of Quebec" (unpublished Ph.D. dissertation, Department of Economics, Harvard University, 1951), p. 211.

In the period 1890–1910, the production of dairy products in constant dollars (1900 = 100) increased by 152.2 per cent and of field crops by 60.7 per cent.[51]   The spurt in agriculture seems to have started earlier than the spurt in manufacturing and the bulk of the growth was concentrated in the decade 1890–1900 when the new dairy farming made its greatest gains and the number of creameries increased from 729 to 1,992.   The movement towards specialization in dairy farming continued during the following decade, though this is less evident if we rely solely on the change that took place in the total value of dairy products, which increased by only 4.7 per cent.   Nevertheless, during this decade, a new and more balanced orientation was given to the dairy industry.   The manufacture of cheese was cut back by 27.9 per cent from 80,630,199 to 58,171,091 pounds, and more emphasis was put on winning a reputation for the quality of Quebec cheese on the Canadian and international markets.   The making of domestic butter and cheese was more and more discouraged and the quantity of milk delivered to the creameries increased by 118.2 per cent from 865.8 to 1.889 million pounds.   The creameries used the bulk of this additional supply of milk to produce creamery butter, whose production increased in the decade by 70.3 per cent from 24.6 to 41.9 million pounds.   This progress and healthier balance were achieved in the dairy industry despite the fact that the average number of cows per farm, after dramatically rising from 3.5 to 5.1 in the previous decade, now fell back temporarily to 4.7.   But their value per head rose 44 per cent, and better feeding and care contributed to the increased volume of milk delivered daily to the creameries. That cattle were being better fed is evident from the fact that the acreage devoted to the hay crop rose 22.8 per cent in this decade.[52]

The census data for 1910 also indicate that field crops increased by only 15.5 per cent in the decade 1900–1910.   However, the year 1910 seems to have been poor in agriculture and not fully representative of the progress achieved.   For if we choose the following year, 1911, as a terminal year, we find that the total value of agricultural products over the period 1900–1911 showed a healthy annual average increase of 9 per cent in current dollar terms, and of about 3.5 per cent in terms of constant dollars.[53]   In this decade, when new industrial towns were

---

[51] *Statistical Year Book*, II (1915), 442.
[52] *Census of Canada*, 1911, IV, 408.
[53] See Appendix on Agricultural Statistics.

blossoming almost overnight, farm land still increased by 8.09 per cent; the number of acres under field crops by 4.1 per cent; and the tobacco crop by 32 per cent. As agriculture became more diversified and the city markets more easily accessible, the average number of hogs per farm rose from 2.7 to 5, and that of hens from 21.8 to 32.3.[54] The number of farmers increased by 8,955, or by 5.9 per cent. And, in 1910, 92.3 per cent of the farmers owned their own farms, and 76.1 per cent of them had holdings exceeding 50 acres.[55]

All in all the period 1890–1910 was a sort of golden age in Quebec agriculture compared with the lean years of the earlier decades. The shift to dairy farming was the decisive factor in this evolution, but it coincided happily with and was strongly encouraged by the opening of new industrial and city markets. There might appear to be here a solid incentive for farmers to adopt new methods to improve both the quantity and the quality of their products. But in Quebec's agriculture, as in Quebec's industry, labour was everywhere both abundant and cheap, and hence there was little real incentive to make dramatic increases in investments in farm machinery. It is true that such investments did increase by 113 per cent in current dollars, or by about 94.4 per cent in constant dollars in the decade 1900–1910,[56] but, for the most part, the increases in mechanization that did occur were largely concentrated in such essential equipment as cream separators rather than additional field equipment. What major capital investments there were, went mostly into equipping the new creameries and into improving the breed of the milking herds. Thus Lemelin correctly concludes, the transformation in Quebec agriculture was largely a response to growing markets and not the result of the adoption of new methods arising out of labour scarcity, or the availability of cheap new farm equipment.

> One can safely conclude that Quebec agriculture had undergone a basic transformation between the two periods 1850–1880 and 1880–1910. The fertile and favorably located regions of the south-western areas no doubt weighted heavily in shaping the general trend evidenced by the statistics. The capital investment underlying these

---

[54] *Census of Canada*, 1911, IV, pp. xiv, XXXVI, 405, 411.

[55] *Statistical Year Book*, II (1915), 422.

[56] However these estimates are only approximate, for, as indicated in Appendix I, we have no precise information on how such capital stock was evaluated in the census data of either 1900 or 1910. That in spite of such encouraging increases, the degree of mechanization in Quebec agriculture remained relatively meagre is evidenced by the fact that in 1910, the average farmer had farm implements valued at $345 (current dollars), which represented only about 35.7 per cent of the value of his farm products for that year (*Ibid.*).

changes was minimum especially as far as mechanization is concerned... The change in type of farming enterprises and the production was not the effect of decrease in price of capital goods originating in the industrial sector. Neither was it a change brought about by the scarcity of manpower resulting from industrialization because at all time the labor supply was plentiful... These changes in Quebec agriculture were rather due to a shift upward in the demand for agricultural products resulting from the long-run trend in urbanization, particularly conspicuous after 1900.[57]

Standard of Living

One further comment seems in place before taking up the central theme of the relationship between the Church and economic development. Thus far we have discussed Quebec's economic development only from the side of production, yet growth in per capita income is the standard usually employed by economists to measure genuine development. As already noted, in the period 1910–1914, Canada had an estimated per capita Gross National Product of $453 (1935–1939 dollars).[58] Per capita income had increased at an average rate of 2.15 per cent annually between the periods 1890–1894 and 1910–1914, and at 2.3 per cent in the shorter period between 1895–1899 and 1905–1909, in spite of massive immigration and the high rate of natural increase in these periods of 2.31 and 2.77 per cent respectively.[59] Quebec's population growth did not exceed the national average; in fact, for the decade 1901–1911 it grew at an average rate of 2.16 annually. We have no precise estimate of per capita income in Quebec at this time, but we have good reason to believe that growth in per capita income in Quebec kept pace with the national average while nevertheless remaining below it and considerably below that of Ontario in absolute terms. As already indicated, since 1926 (when we have more reliable data), Quebec's per capita personal income has remained consistently about 27.5 per cent below that of Ontario, and about 11.6 lower than the Canadian average; and since 1870 wages in manufacturing in Quebec—which are a fairly good index of the trend in personal income—have always remained about 10–15 per cent

---

[57] C. LEMELIN, "Agricultural Development and Industrialization of Quebec," p. 215.
[58] O.J. FIRESTONE, *Canada's Economic Development*, p. 280. As already noted, it has been suggested that these rough estimates of per capita GNP and income may be too high.
[59] *Ibid.*, pp. 242-43.

lower in Quebec than in Ontario.[60] And, as Gordon Bertram has shown, even if Quebec holds its own when compared with Canada as a whole, yet it is still far outdistanced by Ontario when the population factor is introduced and the provinces are compared under the heading "Per capita manufacturing output expressed as a per cent of Canada per capita manufacturing output." For the years 1900 and 1910, we find Quebec with percentages of 103.1 and 105.0 respectively, while under the same heading Ontario, owing to its much lower rate of population growth, had the higher percentages of 123.4 and 143.1 for these two years.[61] In fact, during the decade 1900–1910, Quebec's population increased by 5.8 per cent more than that of Ontario, and, owing to the age structure of its population, Quebec showed a much lower rate of participation in the labour force. In 1910, owing to heavy immigration into Canada as a whole, 394 per thousand of the population were active in the labour force, but in Quebec only 326 per thousand were counted in it, and these included some 8,000 boys and girls between 10–14 years of age.[62] While Quebec was still losing many of its best labourers to the United States, the rest of the Canadian provinces were gaining immigrants of working age from Europe. Besides, in the province of Quebec, subsistence and sub-subsistence farming was common, especially in areas of new settlement where families depended on the logging industry to supplement their farm income. Low productivity, cheap labour industries, non-mechanized agriculture, and subsistence settlement projects combined with a high rate of natural increase and low labour-force participation to foster lower per capita incomes in Quebec than in Ontario and in Canada as a whole, though this gap

---

[60] A. RAYNAULD, *Croissance et structure économiques*, pp. 63, 210. Charles Lemelin is of the opinion that, because of the surplus labour market, wages in Quebec industry faithfully reflected the standard of living prevailing in Quebec's agricultural areas until quite recently (C. LEMELIN, "Agricultural Development...," p. 196).

The earliest national wealth estimates made by the Bureau of Statistics confirm this gap. They show that Quebec was estimated to have 25 per cent of the national wealth but 26.87 per cent of the population; however, Quebec was also estimated to have almost double the per capita wealth of the Maritime provinces. These annual estimates were later discontinued as not being sufficiently refined, but they had already confirmed a gap of about the same dimension as revealed by the more accurate personal income estimates made after 1926. (See *The Canada Year Book*, 1926, p. 802.)

[61] Gordon BERTRAM, "Historical Statistics on Growth and Structure of Manufacturing in Canada, 1870-1957," p. 25.

[62] These estimates are based on the data provided by the *Statistical Year Book*, III (1916), 96. The national average estimate is based on FIRESTONE (*Canada's Economic Development*, p. 58). A. RAYNAULD assigns this low rate of labour force participation as the principal cause of lower per capita incomes in Quebec in later decades (*Croissance et structure économiques*, p. 61).

showed no long-run tendency to widen substantially.[63]   Hard
work and long hours were not an adequate substitute; and there
was little labour-scarcity incentive to promote productivity
gains by mechanization or better mechanization of either industry or agriculture.

Faucher and Lamontagne rightly insist on the importance of
Quebec's population problem.   For them, "the only phenomenon which was specific to Quebec was its population problem."
They find in that fact the explanation of the drive towards
agriculture and land settlement pursued by the government
and the Church for almost a century in "a region which is not
naturally destined for agriculture."[64]

It is my conclusion that the fact that per capita incomes
have been consistently lower in the province of Quebec than in
the neighbouring province of Ontario has helped to foster the
idea that Quebec was much more backward economically.   Is it
not possible that at least in the earlier decades of the century the
French Canadian, steeped in the tradition of domestic economy,
continued to live much more independently of the market than
the majority of his fellow Canadians and that the estimates of his
personal income were therefore to be biased downwards?   As
was noted, the new goods that were pouring out of the factories at
this time were, in bulk, processed foods and beverages, factory-
made cloth and clothing, boots and shoes, cigarettes, iron goods,
wooden furniture and utensils, etc.—in all of which the *habitant* was often quite self-sufficient, and not necessarily poorer.
Nevertheless, there remained a foundation in fact, and, in the
absence of serious research into its causes, uninformed opinion,
fed by national and religious prejudices, helped to create the
myth that Quebec still remained the one "underdeveloped"
province in the otherwise highly developed nation of Canada.[65]
Moreover, French Canadians have by and large been "the hewers
of wood and carriers of water" in the growth process; they
have provided the "cheap labour" element in many of the industries which have been plagued with cycles of unemployment.

---

[63] For example, in 1960, Quebec had 24.4 per cent of total personal income in Canada
and 28.6 per cent of the total population (*The Economic Almanac*, 1962, p. 534).

[64] A. FAUCHER and M. LAMONTAGNE, "History of Industrial Development," p. 30.

[65] Another reason why visitors often had the impression that Quebec is a very underdeveloped province is that industry has been excessively concentrated in the Montreal area
and a few other centres such as Shawinigan and Sherbrooke.   The result has been that
subsistence farmers in the more distant regions have not had a strong market incentive
for improvement and possible enrichment.   Because of this, whole areas have developed
subsistence farmers depending for additional income on winter work in the logging industry.
Hence, pockets of underdevelopment, backwardness, and poverty.   But this is a peculiar
regional problem which the present study does not investigate.

They have not to any significant degree been either the owners or the entrepreneurs of the new industry. In this situation they quite naturally develop the feeling of being "backward" or "underdeveloped," of being second class citizens in comparison with their English and American employers. They long for the economic liberation of their race. It is only in this context that one can understand how their spokesmen have talked at times of their economic situation as one of "slavery," and how Canon Groulx, for example, could refer to the high wages paid to French Canadian workers in industry as "the golden chains which still remain chains."[66]

In brief, the present writer concludes with Raynauld that there was a period of rapid economic development and industrialization in Quebec prior to 1914, and that this province, in spite of serious demographic problems, which kept its per capita income somewhat below the national average—a problem to which we return later in more detail—still fully shared in the important economic spurt experienced by Canada during this period. In the absence of more refined economic indicators of per capita GNP and income and of capital formation, no attempt is made here to verify or reject his contention that this was for Quebec her Rostovian "take-off." Even so, it is clear that whatever serious problems of distribution and reorientation of industry still remained to be solved by Quebecers after World War I, the province had sufficiently developed by that time for her problems to have little in common with those of present-day underdeveloped countries.

---

[66] See *le Devoir* (Montréal), October 24, 1962, where Canon Groulx recalls how this was one of his favourite themes in the twenties.

CHAPTER II

THE ST. MAURICE RIVER VALLEY: DEVELOPMENTS UPSTREAM

EARLY DEVELOPMENT

The St. Maurice Valley has been chosen as one of the areas for more detailed study prior to World War I, and especially in the period 1896–1914, because here we can see the launching of a new dynamic industrial area based on an abundant hydro-electric potential and limitless evergreen forests. It is an area which was destined within a few decades to become the world's biggest supplier of newsprint and for a time the forerunner in Quebec's aluminum and chemical industries. Here we can watch how the Church reacted when directly confronted with the abrupt changes of industrialization at a time and in an area where she still had great influence over the general population even if less over the employers, who were ordinarily neither Catholic nor French Canadian, nor even Canadian.

In the next chapter this same phenomenon of industrialization will be studied in the Chicoutimi-Lake St. John region. Here, however, agriculture and land settlement progress simultaneously with industrialization, and we can see whether the Church takes a different attitude under these different circumstances. To facilitate the comparison the limits of these two areas will be set to coincide roughly with the ecclesiastical dioceses of Trois-Rivières and Chicoutimi. We shall not be able to consider the changes taking place in the dozens of little villages in the area, but rather only in the more important town or city centres. The diocese of Trois-Rivières at this time comprised the counties of Saint-Maurice, Champlain and Maskinongé. Later it included also the new town of La Tuque and this too will be considered here.

With the industrial development of the St. Maurice Valley in the early twentieth century, the site of Quebec's first large-scale attempts to harness her abundant "white coal" to replace the "black coal" she lacked, we are at the heart of a new industrial era. John Dales writes of the large-scale effect of the linkage of hydroelectricity and industrialization in Quebec:

When the large power site rather than the small water fall became the center of interest in Canadian electrical circles, the whole character of the industry changed abruptly. From an enterprise of local significance, the central station became a developmental project which provided the social capital for the power requirements of a whole region, and, in contrast to the relatively modest requirements of money and skill involved in local stations, the promotion and construction of a major hydroelectric plant became an essay in finance and engineering. Although on a somewhat smaller scale, the hydroelectric industry resembled the railway in many respects. The power station succeeded the railway as the main developmental agency in the country, as a major field for investment, and as an outlet for engineering energies.[1]

The St. Maurice River drains an area of about 16,350 square miles in a southeasterly direction through the Laurentian Highlands into the St. Lawrence River at the city of Trois-Rivières, which is roughly half-way between the cities of Montreal and Quebec.[2] It is about 325 miles in length. Over time its turbulent waters have cut deep channels into the rock formation of the Laurentian Shield. In the 235-mile stretch below the Gouin Dam, which now seals off its upper sources, it falls about 1,300 feet. This river is ideal for hydroelectric development for in the final 180 miles of its course it drops 1,150 feet in ten distinct major falls, apart from other numerous rapids and cascades.[3] By a system of reservoirs and controls the primary capacity of the St. Maurice has been more than tripled. Beyond the short distance near its mouth, where it flows through the St. Lawrence plain, it drains a very heavily wooded region, rugged in its physical features, severe in its climate, and little suited to agriculture.

At the turn of the nineteenth century, when Britain was suffering a critical shortage of timber due to the continental blockade, she sent out timber-hungry pioneers who began the ravage of Quebec's flawless pines. But it was only after 1830 that the wood-merchants turned their eyes on the timber of this valley, hitherto all but forbidden to settlers by greedy fur traders and forbidding to woodsmen because of the untamed torrents of the river. The first concessions were granted in 1831, and soon the Nesbitts, the Collinses, the Youngs, the Morrises, and the MacKenzies began to feast on the valley's

---

[1] John H. DALES, *Hydroelectricity and Industrial Development*, p. 184. In note 2, page 264, Dales shows how many ex-railway men were associated with the promotion of hydroelectric enterprises.

[2] For a detailed study of the geography of the region, see Raoul BLANCHARD, *la Mauricie*.

[3] See H.M. FINLAYSON, "Hydrology of the St. Maurice River," *Engineering Features of the Shawinigan System*, pp. 9-11.

rich forests.   The king of the valley was a Scot, George Baptist, who set up a large sawmill at Les Grès in 1846.   The pattern of development in the valley was already set.   An anonymous local author describes it graphically as management by others with the French-Canadians as the sturdy workers of the forest and river.

> Tandis qu'Anglais, Écossais et Étatsuniens se partagent *nos forêts*, les Canadiens français, fidèles aux traditions qu'ils conservent jalousement et qu'ils nous ont transmises intactes, procréaient "à la tanne" pour la revanche des berceaux et donnaient au pays une illustre lignée de robustes portageurs, de rudes bûcherons, de courageux draveurs, d'infatigables porteurs d'eau.[4]

Among all those who acted as entrepreneurs along the St. Maurice forest one can pick out the name of only one French Canadian, that of a native of Trois-Rivières, Georges Gouin. All unknowingly, Georges Gouin, the single French Canadian among the lesser wood-barons, seems to play the role of the typical French Canadian entrepreneur, ever seeking that governmental preference so graciously bestowed upon Englishmen and Americans.[5]   The French Canadian's role in the timber industry was to be limited to being "Bob's man" or "Alex's man," that is, to work for such timber kings as Bob Grant or Alex Baptist.

The latter's settlement at Les Grès together with the Vieilles Forges were long the only two industrial centres in the valley and both were "closed" villages.   At Les Grès there was not even a school—probably because the successful Scot saw no particular advantage in educating his French Canadian workers.[6]

The year 1852 is an important date in the early history of the valley, for it was then that real money—that is, other than the "pitoun" or company money—appeared in quantity for the first time.   In that year, at the wood merchants' request, the federal government undertook to build sluices and booms at Shawinigan and elsewhere along the river to prevent the logs from being dashed to bits as they dropped over the falls.   The workers were paid in dollar bills.   In that year also the forests of the upper St. Maurice valley were opened for exploitation. And now as exploration and surveying went forward, despite the pessimistic reports of three earlier official government commissions, submitted between 1829 and 1847, which had found the St. Maurice valley unsuitable for agriculture, some agricultural enthusiasts still saw in the opening of the valley a ready

---

[4] SYLVAIN [pseud.], *Horizons mauriciens*, p. 101.
[5] *Ibid.*, p. 103.
[6] Thomas BOUCHER, *Mauricie d'autrefois*, p. 21.

alternative to the recurrent waves of emigration to the United States.[7]   In 1856, for example, a new Crown Lands Commission reported happily on the finding of the experts:

> Ces explorations et ces arpentages ne tardèrent pas à révéler le fait que la vallée du Saint-Maurice renferme non seulement une provision inépuisable de bois d'un grand prix, mais aussi une terre excellente pour des défrichements et sur lesquelles on n'avait jamais compté. C'était, pour ainsi parler, comme si le peuple du Canada venait d'acquérir un territoire, non pas dans une partie éloignée de la province, mais à son centre même, adjacent aux établissements les plus populeux, situé à moitié chemin entre les deux ports de mer de Québec et de Montréal, offrant une suite de bonnes terres jusqu'à quelques milles du Saint-Laurent, ouvrant un nouveau champ vaste et facilement accessible pour l'extension des défrichements.[8]

New roads began to be built with government aid, mostly for the convenience of the woodsmen, but settlers encouraged by their curés followed along to make land and to supplement their scanty income by selling wood to the companies or by working in the lumber camps during the winters.   We find a parish at Saint-Tite in 1863, at Saint-Boniface in 1849, at Sainte-Flore in 1856, at Saint-Élie-de-Caxton in 1870.   And other parishes were sizeable enough to require resident curés in later years: Saint-Séverin-de-Proulxville   (1886),   Lac-à-la-Tortue (1882),   Saint-Timothée-d'Hérouxville   (1897),   Saint-Joseph-de-Mékinac (1897), Sainte-Thècle (1897).   Deeper in the valley, on the west side of the river, Saint-Michel-des-Saints became a parish in 1883, and Saint-Zénon in 1889.[9]

But agriculture never really succeeded as an independent industry.   It remained almost totally dependent on the logging industry.   And when the latter industry fell on hard times in the 1870's many of these settlers, with their ready markets and supplementary income cut off, in their turn took the well-worn road to the factories of New England.[10]   The simultaneous closing down of the Vieilles Forges and Baptist's sawmill at Les Grès in 1883 proved catastrophic for the region.   Thomas Boucher, a native of Saint-Boniface, whose family emigrated to Manchester, Massachusetts, in 1888, recounts the experience of his own parish as typical of the valley.

---

[7] Cf. SYLVAIN, *Horizons mauriciens*, pp. 66-67.

[8] La Commission des Terres de la Couronne, *Rapport de la commission* (Ottawa: 1856), p. 25; cited by Auguste DESILETS, *la Grand'Mère*, p. 13.

[9] See for more détail T. BOUCHER, *Mauricie d'autrefois*, pp. 159-205, and BLANCHARD, *la Mauricie*, pp. 57, 60-61.

[10] As late as 1950, the geographer Raoul Blanchard still held that neither the soil nor the climate were serious obstacles to much better agriculture than actually exists in this region.   See *la Mauricie*, pp. 73-4.

En ce temps-là, la région du Saint-Maurice passait par une très grande dépression économique; c'était l'époque de l'émigration à l'outrance aux États-Unis. Les jeunes gens robustes s'en allaient dans les forêts de pins ou dans les mines de fer du Michigan tandis que des familles complètes s'en allaient travailler dans les filatures de la Nouvelle-Angleterre. Pour sa part, M. Bellemare perdit, dans l'espace d'une dizaine d'années, au delà de cinquante familles et il en était ainsi dans les paroisses limitrophes.[11]

But the seeds of the new industrial era for which the early lumbering prepared were not long in bearing fruit. Two events of great significance took place in 1878 and 1890. In 1878 a branch line of the newly completed Quebec-Montreal railway was extended 34 miles into the valley to Les Piles, and, in 1890, John Foreman set the first pulp mill in action at Grand'Mère. It was driven by the mighty waters of the St. Maurice, never before harnessed for industrial purposes. Blanchard points to the significance of this use of water power:

Arrêtons-nous à cette date de 1890: elle est aussi capitale dans l'histoire de la Mauricie que celle de 1852. Cette dernière signifiait l'ouverture de la région à l'exploitation de la forêt; la première annonce que cette exploitation va comporter de vastes développements industriels, vivifiés par l'emploi de la force hydraulique. Les deux colonnes sur lesquelles bâtir l'édifice mauricien sont désormais en place.[12]

New towns were born in this new industrial era—Grand'-Mère, Shawinigan Falls and La Tuque—and the old city of Trois-Rivières was revitalized by these developments. But before turning to study them we may consider briefly the role of the Church in the development of the area that preceded the establishment of stable industrial towns.

Sources of knowledge are scanty, but they do give some general idea of the role of the curés in the valley. It had long been the custom of the curés to frequent the logging camps during the winters to bring to the men the consolations of their religion. On these occasions, we are told, it was almost unknown for a single man to refuse to confess and receive communion.[13] Likewise, it seems, the curés were the chief promoters of the limited settlement that took place in the valley in the latter half of the century, and it was also they who tried to keep the settlers from emigrating from the valley to American industry. Certainly the two parishes of Saint-Michel-des-Saints and Saint-Zénon owed their beginnings almost exclusively to the indefati-

---

[11] *Mauricie d'autrefois*, p. 149.
[12] *La Mauricie*, p. 86.
[13] Pierre DUPIN, *Anciens chantiers du Saint-Maurice*, pp. 109-18.

gable endeavours of Abbés Brassard and Provost.[14]   Abbé Brassard spent six years and all his personal fortune of $16,000 to
found the parish of Saint-Michel, which he settled with people
brought from the older parishes of Joliette and Brandon.

Boucher tells us of the Abbé Bellemare, curé of his own
parish, Saint-Boniface, near the site of Shawinigan Falls, that
he was "toujours soucieux du bien-être matériel de ses paroissiens."   It was he who organized a co-operative for the manufacture of cheese in the parish in an attempt to arrest the steady
drain of his parishioners to New England and Michigan.   This
was considered a hazardous undertaking since it was probably
the first of its kind in the region.   But, according to Boucher,
the curé's efforts were so successful that the factory earned
$10,000 for its stockholders in its first season.   Never had
so much money come to the parishioners of Saint-Boniface in
the course of a single year![15]   Another priest, curé Jean-Baptiste
Grenier of Saint-Tite, set about building better schools and invited in the Brothers of St. Gabriel to teach in them as soon as
the railroad brought prosperity to his parish.   He was likewise
the champion of every local initiative, whether it was to organize
agitation for a station on the railroad, to install a local waterworks, or to have his village incorporated.[16]   At Sainte-Thècle,
the missionary Maxime Masson literally built the church, presbytery, and school with his own hands.[17]   And we find another
missionary, Adélard Milot of Grande-Anse, taking advantage
of the improvements made in the river-bed to buy the *Saint
Louis*, a 45-foot powerboat, to ensure a regular service between
the Grande-Anse and La Tuque; not until later did the government pay a subsidy to continue this regular service.[18]

Though the evidence is scanty, these curés do not seem
to be exceptional.   A similar story is repeated in parish after
parish.   It seems to be the local priest who organizes not only
the church but the entire enterprise of settlement—including
bringing in settlers, seeking government help, organizing public
works such as the schools, roads, etc., as well as improving
agriculture and introducing the dairy industry.[19]

---

[14] BLANCHARD, *op. cit.*, pp. 60-61.
[15] *Mauricie d'autrefois*, p. 150.
[16] *Ibid.*, p. 163.
[17] *Ibid.*, p. 179.
[18] SYLVAIN, *Horizons mauriciens*, p. 92.
[19] Cf. BOUCHER, *Mauricie d'autrefois*, pp. 159-209; and also the same author in "La Grand'Mère" (unpublished manuscript, Archives of the Séminaire de Trois-Rivières, 1952), pp. 25-26.   Hereafter these archives will be referred to by the letters ASTR.

What was the economic significance of these subsistence farming settlements? They were simply an adjunct of the logging industry and the forges. They supplied, in a certain measure, ready-to-hand manpower, farm products, and horses for the timber industry—though some of the wood-merchants also had their own farms, since they could not rely on outside supplies because of the very poor transportation facilities. These settlers also supplied manpower and charcoal for the Vieilles Forges at Saint-Maurice and later at Radnor. And finally, they managed to develop sufficient economic activity to keep themselves from being compelled to abandon their native province for the United States—which the vast majority of them considered a type of forced exile.

It is ironic that it seems to have been the alleged "prophet" of the agriculturalists,[20] Mgr L. Laflèche of Trois-Rivières, who cooled the ardor of Curé Labelle, the apostle of the settlement movement, to promote farm settlement in the St. Maurice Valley. Whatever his predilection for agriculture, this bishop reveals a keen insight into the economic realities of the situation. In a letter to Curé Labelle, in 1879, he encourages him in his great work of colonization—but elsewhere in the province! Nature, he believes, has reserved his valley for industry.

> La direction que vous donnez à votre activité dans l'œuvre de la colonisation est certainement l'une des plus patriotiques et le Bon Dieu la comblera de ses plus abondantes bénédictions. Les vallées de l'Ottawa et du lac Saint-Jean offrent un vaste champ au surplus de notre population et c'est là qu'il faut le diriger. La vallée du Saint-Maurice présente peu de chance à l'agriculture. Son sol aride et rocheux ne contient que bien peu de terres fertiles et il sera difficile d'y former des paroisses prospères. En compensation il est riche en minéraux et en bois de commune, et les pouvoirs d'eau pour mettre en œuvre ces matières premières sont nombreux et puissants. L'agriculture et l'industrie doivent donc dans les plans de la Providence se donner la main pour faire de notre pays une contrée prospère et heureuse. Comme l'industrie doit suivre l'agriculture, vous marchez donc dans les vues de la Providence en lui donnant toute l'impulsion possible par la colonisation de nos terres les plus fertiles.[21]

We now turn to a study of the industrial developments in the valley at Grand'Mère, Shawinigan Falls, La Tuque, and finally at Trois-Rivières.

---

[20] See, for example, BRUNET, "Trois dominantes...," pp. 54-55.
[21] Letter from Mgr L. LAFLÈCHE to Curé Labelle, November 18, 1879; cf. Mason WADE, *The French Canadians*, p. 433.

COMMUNICATIONS

In 1878, as we saw, the railway linking Trois-Rivières to Les Piles finally put settlers and woodsmen in contact with the outside world and provided the former with a market in which to buy and sell. Hitherto the makeshift roads had been subject to all the vicissitudes of the weather, and river traffic had to contend with the falls and the rapids. Any future large-scale development was conditional upon the construction of railroads.

If the first railroad to Les Piles helped the wood-merchants bring in their supplies, it was still quite inadequate for the new industries that would blossom in the next few decades, for it did not follow the river closely enough. Transportation facilities remained primitive. The first woodpulp produced at Grand'Mère had to be loaded on a barge to cross the river and was then carted by horse to the station still a few miles away. After 1894, the pulp was hoisted across the river by cablecar to the opposite bank where the new railway junction had been established. By 1898, the Great Northern had connected Grand'Mère with Saint-Boniface, Joliette, and Hawkesbury, and a little later with Lake St. John and Quebec. But it was only in 1903 that the new industrial centres obtained direct connections with Montreal. Until that date, Shawinigan was on a branch line constructed by the industrialists which connected with the Great Northern at Aldred Junction. And because of the alleged fear, on the part of the Great Northern, of rivalry with the Canadian Pacific, it was 1906 before Shawinigan had direct connections with the latter line, which connected Trois-Rivières directly with Montreal and Quebec. The development of La Tuque also was handicapped initially by lack of railway connections, but it soon ended up on two railways, the branch line of the Quebec-Lake St. John Railway promoted by the Brown Corporation, which planned to open a pulp and paper mill there, as well as the Transcontinental which arrived at La Tuque in 1908 even before the projected pulp industry. It was the Transcontinental that finally made the valley easily accessible. It followed the river for about 120 miles and supplied all the forest outposts, thus making possible the installations of huge reservoirs and dams near the source of the river to control the water level. In particular, it facilitated the construction of the Gouin Dam, begun in 1912, which has a storage capacity of some 280 billion cubic feet of water and remains the key to control of the St. Maurice.[22]

---

[22] See H.M. FINLAYSON, "Hydrology of the St. Maurice River," p. 10.

And so by 1911 the new industrial sites had good railway connections and the valley was left with only one deficiency in its railway system.   It lacked a direct connection between La Tuque and the other towns downstream.   And thus it remains.[23]

GRAND'MÈRE

The story of Grand'Mère is the story of the most prosperous pulp and paper mill in Canada prior to World War I.[24]   A Scot, John Foreman, who was the Montreal agent for various British manufactures, was the first to conceive the idea of harnessing the hydraulic power of the St. Maurice to fabricate woodpulp, and though he was soon eliminated by the more powerful financial barons of American capital, he remains the authentic "father of industry" in the valley.   When he first launched his project, in 1882, there were only five such mills in Canada with a total capital of $92,000 and with only 68 employees.[25]   He chose the site of Grand'Mère because of its falls fifty-two feet in height. In May of that year the local village council of Sainte-Flore, in whose parish the site was located, unanimously voted him a tax-exemption for twenty-five years.   Foreman, with the help of some Montreal businessmen, formed the Canada Pulp Company with a capital of $50,000 (of which only $29,000 was subscribed) and in October work was begun on the power canal by local workers from Sainte-Flore.   Lack of money, lawsuits, and bankruptcy all came within a year, even before the canal was completed.   But Foreman bought up the liquidated assets and a few years later succeeded in getting richer partners, this time American industrialists with experience in the pulp and paper business.   They were A. Pragenstecher of New York and Warren Curtis of Corinth, who in 1887 joined with a few English Canadian businessmen to form the Laurentide Pulp Company Limited with Pragenstecher as president and Foreman as secretary.   The capital initially subscribed was $100,000, but it soon proved totally inadequate.   However, Pragenstecher's credit was good and by 1890, with the help of a German-American, Baron Von Kessler, the 5,000 hp. mill, installed at a cost of $750,000, was producing 45 tons of pulp daily.   Its operation

---

[23] For a detailed discussion of these railways, see BLANCHARD, *la Mauricie*, pp. 82-83.

[24] The name "Grand'Mère" comes from a large boulder that formerly stood in the middle of the falls.   It had the appearance of an old Indian woman.   The Laurentide Company dynamited it out and set it up in the town, much to the satisfaction of the French Canadians.

[25] A. DESILETS, *la Grand'Mère*, p. 35.

was far from ideal; the mill was two miles from the railroad which passed on the opposite bank of the river, and costs all round were too high.

After the Great Northern put Grand'Mère on its line, the mill was expanded to a 50-ton daily capacity in 1895, and to a 60-ton capacity in 1896. But the manufacture of pulp exclusively still proved unprofitable. What was needed was a giant paper mill. And here again American capital came to the rescue. General R.A. Alger bought $150,000 worth of stock for cash in 1896 and became director of the company, associating himself with William Van Horne and R.B. Angus of the wealthy Canadian Pacific Railway after he had failed to interest English money in his project.[26] They soon bought out the Pragenstecher-Curtis group, and Foreman was quietly squeezed out as the business giants moved in. We hear little of him at Grand'-Mère after 1895.

Soon between 400 and 500 men set to work to build a dam which would raise the height of the falls from 52 to 85 feet, and in the following year some 1,300 men were at work building the new pulp and paper mill, which could now benefit by the full driving force of the river. By 1900, it was producing daily 120 tons of pulp, 40 tons of manilla, and 30 tons of cardboard. And when shortly thereafter the mill installed three "foudriniers," it had a daily capacity of between 150 and 200 tons of newsprint, which in the paper industry was "unprecedented in Canada."[27] By 1906, the *Pulp and Paper Magazine* estimated, Laurentide was producing 44,500 net tons of roll newsprint per year, whereas the entire Canadian consumption was only approximately 27,200 tons.[28] And it continued to hold its lead in progress and profitability thereafter.

In the period 1899–1904, the company was able to pay out 37 per cent dividends on its ordinary shares in spite of its expansion programme and big losses suffered in two major fires in 1900.[29] Net profits failed to rise in a single year, the so-called "depression year" of 1908, when they fell by $30,000 to $251,458, on a gross business of $429,779. The president announced that "in view of the world-wide depression, the results

---

[26] DESILETS, *op. cit.*, p. 55, gives Alger's shares as worth $500,000. I prefer to stay with the more conservative figure of $150,000 which is given in G. CARRUTHERS, *Paper in the Making*, p. 601. This chapter relies on him also for other technical details in the history of the paper industry.

[27] CARRUTHERS, *op. cit.*, p. 601.

[28] *Pulp and Paper Magazine of Canada*, March, 1906, p. 66.

[29] See *Annual Reports of the Laurentide Company Limited*, "Corporation Records Collection," Baker Library, Harvard Business School. In 1901, it became the Laurentide Paper Company and, in 1909, the Laurentide Company Limited.

of the year's business are considered satisfactory." In 1909, the Laurentide was shipping regularly a car of newsprint to the United States daily, and between 500 and 1,000 tons monthly to Great Britain, South Africa, and Australia.[30] In 1912, optimism was so high after the reorganization of the company, and after the Quebec government prohibited further exportation of pulp wood cut on Crown lands to the United States, that, from January to November, Laurentide shares rose from 155 to 240 on the Montreal stock exchange. As the editor of the *Pulp and Paper Magazine* remarked, "This wonderful prosperity has been a veritable gold mine for the shareholders, and it is little wonder that so much attention has been attracted to the Canadian pulp and paper industry as a field for investment."[31]

In 1913, Laurentide was producing 320 tons of newsprint daily, much of the higher production being achieved by speeding up the paper-machines which had never before been run at more than 600 feet per minute.[32] And in that year, the *Pulp and Paper Magazine* again did reverence to the name "Laurentide": "today, the word stands for efficiency and expansion in the pulp and paper industry as the Laurentide Co. Ltd. is undoubtedly the best known pulp and paper manufacturing company in Canada."[33] In the same year the company had between 800 and 1,000 men at work on the construction of a new power unit to develop 100,000 electric horsepower, 12,000 to be used for the mill and the rest to be sold for industrial use in the valley. In 1916, they allied their power interests with the Shawinigan Water and Power Company, which was then rapidly gaining control of power interests in the province.[34]

It is quite clear that the major factors of this successful industrial development were Foreman's initiative, the improvement of the railway facilities, the plentiful supply of American capital when it was desperately needed to expand and to shift quickly to integrate paper with pulp production, and the alert management represented in these decisions. But all these changes did not take place *in vacuo*, as Heilbroner likes to remind us.[35] This industry was only part, even if the more important part, of the newly organized boom-town of Grand'Mère, which had been transformed from a bare river site on the outskirts of

[30] *Pulp and Paper Magazine*, August, 1909, p. 238c.
[31] *Ibid.*, November, 1912, p. 367.
[32] *Ibid., Anniversary Issue*, May, 1953, p. 147.
[33] *Ibid.*, September, 1913, p. 605.
[34] *Ibid.*, November, 1913, p. 751, and *Annual Report*, 1916.
[35] R.L. HEILBRONER, "The Literature of Development," *Harper's*, May, 1961, pp. 96-97.

the parish of Sainte-Flore in the 1890's into a town of more than 6,500 by 1914.[36]   Initially, in 1882, and again in 1887, most of the workers came from the villages around, especially from Sainte-Flore and Lac-à-la-Tortue.   As Boucher, a native of the region, says, in wonderment, "Jamais de mémoire d'homme on n'avait vu tant d'argent dans la région et dans la paroisse." Whereas formerly monthly salaries paid by the wood-merchants had varied between 8 and 10 dollars, and men working on the sluices had received 15 dollars, now any worker could have **90** cents a day plus 10 cents for former experience, and steam drillers were paid 2 dollars.[37]   There was also a sudden revolution in working conditions.

> En considérant le travail et les conditions de travail préexistantes pour nos ouvriers des forêts et nos draveurs, il y avait une grande amélioration à Grand'Mère.   On sait que, tout récemment encore, la perte d'un outil valant un dollar était considérée plus importante chez nos exploiteurs de la forêt que la perte d'un homme: il se noyait annuellement plusieurs hommes sur le St-Maurice et, presque chaque fois, les contremaîtres demandaient: "Y a-t-il noyé son Canthook ?" C'était l'oraison funèbre d'un pauvre 'Canayen'![38]

The company staked out an area for a village for its personnel in 1887, but the majority of the local workers still lived at home.   In 1894, there were still only about 50 families living at Grand'Mère; but as the mill expanded it grew rapidly.   When disease threatened, the company along with some representatives of the French Canadians took the initiative to have the town incorporated.   But the company itself and many French Canadians stayed outside the municipality, for both had "une sainte horreur des taxes."[39]   In 1898 the town got its post office and improvised church and school.   Except at times of additional construction at the mill, the vast majority of the workers in the company were French Canadians, who organized their own part of the town, while the company organized a typical "English town" for its personnel and for English-speaking specialized workers.[40]   In its early years, Grand'Mère suffered greatly from the instability, inexperience, and inefficiency of its successive mayors and councillors, as well as from exaggerated partisan politics and what seemed a traditional

---

[36] *Statistical Year Book*, II (1915), 141.   The population had increased from 2,511 (1901) to 4,783 (1911), to 6,500 (1914).   Of these 6,500, all but about 260 were Catholics. See *Canada ecclésiastique*, 1914, p. 96.

[37] *La Grand'Mère*, p. 37.

[38] *Ibid.*, p. 61.

[39] *Ibid.*, p. 68.

[40] Beckles WILLSON, *Quebec: The Laurentian Province*, p. 163.   When he visited Grand'Mère in 1912, he compared the English section of the town to "a village in Surrey."

fascination for endless and costly lawsuits. The case of the
waterworks is typical of what happened in many public endeavours in these early years. Boucher recalls the amusing
details of that sad story of the town council's vacillation:

> L'on accorde une franchise pour la construction d'un aqueduc à une
> compagnie; on la retire pour la donner à une autre, puis on la retire
> de cette dernière pour la remettre à la première. Et quand surgit
> le projet d'acheter le fameux aqueduc, même tâtonnement; on décide
> de l'acheter pour $30,000, la population n'en veut pas. L'année
> suivante on décide de nouveau d'acquérir tout l'actif comprenant
> l'aqueduc et les égouts de la Cie Hydraulique de Grand'Mère, mais
> cette fois-ci pour la somme de $65,000: la population approuve. Ce
> n'était pas tout. Après 5 ou 6 mois, on s'aperçoit qu'en acquérant
> le dit actif, on n'avait pas acquis son outillage. Il fallut l'acheter.[41]

Inexperience and indecision were only worsened by this
constant resort to lawsuits as the solution to all problems. During the term of Mayor Nault it seems that almost every contract
let out ended up in a lawsuit; finally the Mayor himself became
the object of a lawsuit and it cost the town $10,000 to exonerate
him.[42]

All the while the company modernized its own section of
town, made some generous gestures to the workers, especially by
organizing a model farm and dairy to provide milk for their
children, and continued to try to escape pressures to pay taxes.[43]
The local commerce was soon entirely in the hands of French
Canadians, but all the bigger industrial initiatives continued to
be the exclusive domain of English Canadians and foreigners.
The only exceptions were small sawmills, the organization of
river traffic, small local hydroelectric stations, and the old iron
forges. But even these, when successful, usually fell into English hands.

What was the role of the Church in all these developments?
Bishop Laflèche first visited the site three months after the new
company had begun work in 1887. Abbé N. Caron, his companion, gives a detailed description of the new constructions
which he visited with his bishop.[44] And as soon as the pulp
mill was completed, the elderly bishop came up from Trois-
Rivières at the invitation of the manager to bless it. After the

[41] *Mauricie d'autrefois*, p. 122.
[42] *Ibid.*, p. 144.
[44] In 1910, the young American manager succeeded in getting the tax-exemption
extended until 1931. And, thereafter, he launched a campaign in favour of introducing
a town-manager—obviously in the hope that the city would be set on a better financial
and physical basis before the company finally began to bear fully its share of community
responsibilities. Until then the bone of contention of local politics remained the tax issue.
[44] Abbé N. Caron, *Deux voyages sur le Saint-Maurice*, p. 322.

blessing, "il fit aux travailleurs réunis dans la cour de la Compagnie une vibrante allocution, les exhortant à sanctifier leur travail et exprimant des vœux de progrès à l'adresse de l'entreprise."[45]

The parish church continued to be at Sainte-Flore, but the local priest came each fortnight to celebrate Mass at Grand'Mère. And owing to the new prosperity the curé of Sainte-Flore was able to complete his new church in 1897. However, after sounding out the local manager, J.R. Reilly, Bishop Laflèche now decided it was time to organize a Catholic parish and school in the new village.[46] He wrote to Curé P. Boulay, in January, 1898, urging him to try to acquire the necessary property as a gift of the company:

> Tâchez d'obtenir gratuitement ces terrains de la Compagnie de la Pulpe, attendu que ces constructions sont aussi avantageuses à la Compagnie qui a certainement intérêt à avoir une population religieuse, morale, et honnête, et aussi des édifices qui feront honneur à la future ville.[47]

The Bishop enclosed a letter to be delivered to Sir William Van Horne, president of the company, in which he outlines his plans to build in order to meet "les besoins religieux et l'éducation de la population catholique de cet établissement qui prend des développements considérables et que je serai heureux de voir grandir de plus en plus et prospérer." He tells Van Horne that the most urgent need is for a school which can also be used for religious services; later, he will collect money to build a church that will do honour to the establishment.[48] Shortly before his death, in 1898, the Bishop came to visit the spot donated to the parish by the company, planted a cross thereon, and named Father Louis-R. Laflèche as curé to organize local education and religious services.[49]

Curé Laflèche was immediately elected president of the new School Commission, and he was re-elected each year until he resigned in 1916. Adhering strictly to democratic procedures, he seems, nevertheless, to have ruled the Commission with a strong hand. The meetings were regularly held in the pres-

---

[45] *Cinquante ans—Paroisse Saint-Paul de Grand'Mère, 1899-1949*, ASTR.
[46] Copy of letter from Mgr L. LAFLÈCHE to J.P. Reilly, October 21, 1897; Episcopal Archives of Trois-Rivières, hereafter abbreviated as EATR.
[47] EATR, copy of letter from Mgr L. LAFLÈCHE to Abbé Pierre Boulay, January 31, 1898.
[48] EATR, copy of letter from Mgr L. LAFLÈCHE to Sir William Van Horne, January 31, 1898.
[49] BOUCHER, *op. cit.*, p. 77.

bytery. A perusal of the minutes of the meetings confirms Boucher's observation that there was better organization here than for the town itself:

> A la Commission scolaire on n'a jamais vu ces tâtonnements ni ce manque d'esprit de suite dans l'administration. C'étaient pourtant les mêmes hommes qui pour la plupart sont passés au Conseil pendant cette période. Mais ici un homme de grande valeur par son éducation et sa grande culture, M. le Curé Laflèche, a toujours présidé aux délibérations de cette Corporation depuis son organisation en 1900.
> De plus, les séances de ce corps se tenaient au presbytère où il était difficile de manquer de décorum.[50]

All measures were generally passed unanimously when the President had given his considered opinion, Boucher says. In fact, I turned up only a single case where a measure was not passed unanimously. This did not mean that Curé Laflèche had everything his own way—especially in money-matters. For example, when he wanted the Commission to make a grant to help enlarge the Convent School in 1905, neither he nor the bishop prevailed, and peace was only re-established when the Commission bought the Convent School outright in 1907.

In the beginning, Laflèche handled both the borrowing of money and the supervising of work for the school. But soon laymen took over these tasks. It was on his initiative that the Commission got in the Ursuline Sisters to teach the girls' school and the Brothers to teach the boys' school. And he insisted that they be taught English efficiently.[51] He led the Commission in its pursuit of lax tax-payers, the company as well as local citizens, threatening the former with legal action in 1902 unless it paid its assessed school tax of $3,951.32. However, more amicable relations prevailed under the new manager George Chahoon, and they granted the company tax exemption for two lots in 1903. By 1904, the Commission's schools had achieved the inspector's grade of "excellent," meriting 28 out of 30 possible points.[52] Under Laflèche, the Commission also tried to bring action against lax school-tax payers by requesting the Premier to make the right to vote in municipal elections conditional on the payment of one's school taxes, and later, in 1910, the Commission pursued delinquent tax payers in court. In 1907, the Commission requested permission from the pro-

---

[50] *Ibid.*, p. 122.
[51] *Livre des minutes de la Commission scolaire de la municipalité du village de Grand'-Mère, P.Q., du 9 août 1900 au 14 février 1916* (Grand'Mère School Commission), p. 241.
[52] *Ibid.*, pp. 80, 83.

vincial School Commission to hold evening classes for adults free
of charge.[53]

The relationship between Curé Laflèche and the young
American manager, George Chahoon, was quite intimate.   As
his daughter, Mrs. M.E. Browne of Grand'Mère, describes it,
"Dad never did anything without talking it over with Curé
Laflèche."[54]   It was to the Curé and the local mayor, J.-A. Robert, that Chahoon turned for help in 1908, when he was embarrassed by a sympathy strike started among the American
and English Canadian papermakers and departmental heads,
who were members of the American Federation of Labour.
The union was trying to prevent Chahoon from supplying
newsprint to the International Paper Company during the strike
of its employees in the United States.   Laflèche's suggestion was
simple and straightforward: Chahoon should fire the English
speakers—most of them were Americans—and replace them by
local French Canadians, who aspired to those good jobs hitherto
closed to them.   As Chahoon described the pre-strike situation
later, "the mills were entirely manned by hobo papermakers
and foremen, because the management didn't consider that the
local untrained men were capable of assuming responsibility."[55]
Chahoon accepted the Curé's suggestion and his labour problems
were solved for decades to come.   The local AFL unit was
dissolved and an open shop declared.[56]   Recalling this strike
settlement in 1912, the newspaper *le Bien public* claimed that
on that occasion Chahoon had reflected to his associates: "Nous
manipulons des millions, nous qui commandons; à côté de nous
un pauvre homme qui n'a pas de millions et qui est cependant
bien plus puissant que nous sur les hommes, et cet homme c'est
Father Laflèche."[57]

Many old-timers suggest that thereafter it was the Curé
who was the "unofficial" arbitrator between the company and
the men.   Whatever the case, labour conditions did improve
and Laurentide was one of the first Canadian companies to
adopt the three-shift system of work.[58]   Many years later, after
Curé Laflèche's death, Chahoon described his relationship with
him as follows:

[53] *Ibid.*, p. 144.
[54] Interview with Mrs. M.E. Browne, June 1962.
[55] George CHAHOON, "A Speech on Labor Relations," given probably in 1943 (in the private collection of Mrs. M.E. Browne, Grand'Mère).
[56] See W.E. GREENING, *Paper Makers in Canada*, p. 38.   Greening blames the clergy for inciting sentiment against the American unions on this and similar occasions.
[57] *Le Bien public*, November 22, 1912.
[58] BOUCHER, *op.cit.*, p. 117.

Shortly after our arrival, we went up to pay our respects to Father Laflèche, and found in him a very kind and helpful friend, so much so that one day when leaving him I apologized for taking so much of his time. He smiled, and putting his hand on my shoulder, said, "Mr. Chahoon, you and I are partners—I look after the spiritual welfare of my people while you are responsible for their bodily well-being." The partnership was never dissolved.[59]

In a letter written by the Curé to Chahoon, in 1905, we find the same warm affection expressed for the young manager, who had been very kind to him. He ends the letter in his inelegant English,

Consequently, being at the head of a great but poor congregation, and seeing how you are allways [sic] good for me and my people, in exchange for your kindness, I regard as duty to pray God to bless you and your very honourable family, and to render the business of your company more and more prosperous.[60]

Besides attending to his spiritual duties, the Curé seems to have been in this boom town primarily an educator and a peacemaker in the many quarrels among its citizens, and between the workers and the town officials, on the one side, and the company on the other. Boucher sums up his life in the phrase "il fut un précieux conciliateur."[61] And from the company's point of view it was obvious that he was a very important figure in the community. In the first volume of *Le Digester* [sic], the company's newspaper, he merits major articles in both languages and the largest individual photograph. He is especially praised for "his balanced spiritual leadership," and the editors sum up their praise as follows,

... no one has been for so many years identified with everything that spelt the progress and welfare of the town, has taken a keener interest in its development and contributed so widely to the maintenance of that spirit of harmony and bonne entente which is prevailing at Grand'Mère.[62]

The only issue that seems to have divided Chahoon and Laflèche was "Sunday work." The Curé always fought it, Chahoon was always promising to stop it soon. But here as elsewhere there was never any open conflict.[63]

---

[59] G. CHAHOON, *op.cit.*

[60] Letter of Rev. L.-R. LAFLÈCHE to Mr. G. Chahoon, February 25, 1905. (Private collection of Mrs. M.E. Browne, Grand'Mère.)

[61] *La Grand' Mère*, p. 142.

[62] *The Digester*, Vol. I, No. 32, May 28, 1919. By that time he had introduced three schools and was busy working on the project of a new hospital.

[63] This is confirmed by Oscar Gélinas, who has worked with Laurentide since 1912. He remembers how the Curé would often urge the men at the early Mass not to work on Sunday, only at a later Mass to say that he himself would see their boss and make arrangements.

From the various older people of the town whom I interviewed, I could obtain no evidence whatsoever of anything having been said against industry by the Church, or of village people having been discouraged from quitting their farms to work in the mill at Grand'Mère. They all simply said they were extremely poor at the time, and the curé knew they could do better in the town and so never tried to stop them from leaving the farm.

We might also examine, here, the content of Curé Laflèche's sermons to his flock as well as the content of the teaching given in the schools, but it will be more useful to do this later through the bishops' pastoral letters and directives to their clergy and the instructions of the directors of the provincial School Commissions.

SHAWINIGAN FALLS

If Grand'Mère was the pioneer industrial town in the valley, its neighbour, a few miles downstream, Shawinigan Falls, or Shawinigan, as it is usually called, was destined to have more brilliant and sudden success. The story of Shawinigan is the success story of a bold enterprising company, the Shawinigan Water and Power Company.[64]

The Shawinigan Company was not the first to develop electricity from waterpower in the region. In the 1890's a local entrepreneur, Édouard Lacroix, backed by a Sherbrooke banker, William Farwell, and others, had organized what was to become the North Shore Power Company at Saint-Narcisse on the Batiscan River. By 1897, this company was supplying Trois-Rivières with electricity by means of an 18-mile transmission line—reputed, at the time, to be the longest in the British empire.[65] Once the initiative was given and interest in electricity aroused, a second local group headed by A. Carignan and H. Mailhot formed in 1895 the Shawinigan Electric Light and Power Company Limited to attempt to harness the mighty Shawinigan falls.[66] But they had to become owners and their purchase of the falls was delayed by a three-way quarrel about who really owned the falls and the surrounding land: the federal

---

[64] Cf. J.H. DALES, *Hydroelectricity and Industrial Development*, p. 97, where he gives a good summary review of this company's history.

[65] Gérard FILTEAU, *L'Épopée de Shawinigan*, p. 87.

[66] The name "Shawinigan" is most likely derived from the Algonquin word for 'crest' though this is disputed. See FILTEAU, p. 37.

government, the provincial government, or John Foreman, who claimed he had purchased this land earlier.   The delay was fatal for the new company, for though the sale at auction was announced for June 15, 1897, at a price of $10,000, a provincial election intervened on May 11 and gave to a new Liberal Minister, S.-N. Parent, control of such sales.   He proceeded to cancel the sale at auction and to put what seemed exorbitant conditions on the sale of the falls: $50,000 for the site and $2 million to be invested within 18 months, and another $2 million in the next year thereafter; and the purchaser had to be producing electric power within 20 months and paying at least $200,000 in wages.   Failure to fulfil the conditions would mean annulment of the sale and confiscation of the deposit.[67]   Quite obviously Parent was trying to bypass the local French Canadian entrepreneurs in favour of English and American capitalists—a practice which seems not to have been at all rare in Quebec politics.[68]

In short order the falls were bought ostensibly by David Russel on September 9, 1897, but really by John Joyce of Andover, Massachusetts, who had large holdings in the Boston brewery business.   The latter interested J.E. Aldred of Lawrence in the project, and thereafter it was Aldred who became the driving force behind the new Shawinigan Water and Power Company which was formed in the following year. Failing to find sufficient ready capital in Boston, Joyce and Aldred were forced to turn to Canadian financiers, and they found solid backing in two figures who dominated the Canadian scene at the time, Senator L.-J. Forget, a French Canadian financial wizard, and H.S. Holt, an Irish engineer.   Together these two industrial promoters had their finger in nearly every successful industrial and financial venture of the period.[69]   Construction got underway in 1899, the project being undertaken by Wallace Johnson of Holyoke, Massachusetts, who had worked on Niagara a few years before.   The new company remained desperately short of capital until 1903, when it proved it could deliver electricity to Montreal about 90 miles distant.   In the meantime, it earned revenue by selling water power to the aluminum and pulp and paper companies, which it had invited to share its

[67] FILTEAU, *op.cit.*, p. 90.
[68] See for example, François-Albert ANGERS, "Naissance de la pensée économique au Canada français," *Revue d'histoire de l'Amérique française*, XV (Septembre 1961), 211, where he makes a good case for the thesis that it was precisely this failure of the Quebec government to second the efforts of French Canadian entrepreneurs that finally caused their ruin.
[69] FILTEAU, *op.cit.*, p. 92.

industrial site, and happily the construction company was willing to work for stock in the new company. The simultaneous emergence of three industries brought 1,500 workers to this deserted spot in 1899, and Shawinigan was born with a boom.

Now a word on the development of each of the major companies.

The Shawinigan Water and Power Company

The record of this company is impressive. It started to produce 24,000 electrical hp in 1903; by 1914, it had raised this production to 150,000 hp. Between 1904 and 1914, it increased its annual sales from 26 to 432 million kilowats.[70] At the latter date, it already had 600 miles of long-distance transmission lines. Its common stock rose from $6.5 million in 1907 to $12.4 million in 1914, and its annual paid dividends increased from 4 per cent to 6 per cent in the same period. By 1917, Aldred could report to the stockholders that the company was now so strong that by lowering its rates it could prevent any prospective competitor from entering the field.[71] Before World War I, the Shawinigan, as it was called, was already supplying much of industry in Montreal, in the St. Maurice Valley, and on both sides of the St. Lawrence with electric power besides distributing it to 40 local communities. By means of its longterm contracts it insulated itself against fluctuations in industry. Through its initiative and that of the other power and timber companies, the provincial government set up the Quebec Streams Commission in 1910. The huge reservoirs constructed by this commission over the next few years solved the serious problem of the irregular waterflow of the river.[72] To dispose of its surplus off-peak power, the Shawinigan invited Thomas "Carbide" Willson to produce carbide on the site by implementing his patent which was designed to use electrical reduction. The Canada Carbide Company Limited was founded in 1901, and by 1909 it was completely absorbed by the Shawinigan Company.

Calcium carbide as a cheap source of acetylene gas was still in commercial competition with electric lighting, and its industrial uses for the welding and cutting of metals were just beginning to be realized. The output of the new company increased from 2,000 tons in 1904, to 6,000 in 1906, and to 10,000 in 1913, mostly as a result of technical improvements in the

[70] DALES, *Hydroelectricity and Industrial Development*, p. 62.
[71] J.E. ALDRED, Speech given in Boston, December 6, 1917, cited by DALES, p. 66.
[72] *Ibid.*, p. 69.

furnaces.[73] With the outbreak of war, carbide was in much demand as was acetone made from acetylene gas for the manufacture of cordite. By the end of the war, the Shawinigan chemical industry had been well launched and has continued to grow ever since.

The Northern Aluminum Company (later The Aluminum Company of Canada)

In 1886, Charles Hall had discovered how to produce aluminum by electrolytic reduction, thus making the commercial sale of aluminum products feasible. When Hall's associates were unable to obtain electricity at Niagara in the quantities and at the prices they required, Aldred invited this company, the Pittsburgh Reduction Company, to come to Shawinigan. A contract was signed in May 1899 for 5,000 mechanical horsepower, and in October of the same year the new company was producing the first industrial electricity at Shawinigan. They were in production by November 1901, and in December were already making shipments of aluminum to Nova Scotia and Japan.[74] With rapid expansion and big gains in productivity, output rose from 283,737 lbs. in 1901 to 18,368,524 in 1914, at which time they were regularly employing about 600 men. Much of the aluminum was fabricated on the spot into electrical conductor cable and sold directly to the Shawinigan Company, and about 1910 Northern Aluminum began to specialize in cable made of aluminum strands plaited round a steel core.

In 1906, the new plant was reputed to be the largest of its kind in the world.[75] The rapid progress suffered only two setbacks. Just when the fourth line of pots was completed in 1907, the tenuous world market, on which this new product was partly dependent, gave way, and the plant had to shut down completely from November until June of the following year. And in 1910, when they attempted to finally put their fourth pot-line into production, they found they were short of electricity. This problem could only be solved by buying additional electric power directly from the Shawinigan Company. Like the other industries on the river, the aluminum plant was handicapped by the uneven flow of the river until the Gouin storage dam was completed.

---

[73] For these and other details, see A.F.C. CADENHEAD, "The History of Shawinigan Chemicals Ltd: 1916-1946" (unpublished manuscript, 1947. Private copy of J.S. Whyte, Shawinigan).

[74] For these and other details, see M.E. GOODING, "The History of Reduction Plants at Shawinigan Falls," private history circulated in the company, 1947.

[75] FILTEAU, *L'Épopée de Shawinigan*, p. 128.

The Canadian Belgo Pulp and Paper Company

Just as the aluminum industry began and long remained
dependent on American capital and direction, so the pulp and
paper industry was in the beginning a totally Belgian undertaking.   Aldred had interested La Banque d'Outremer in the
site and they supplied the first capital.   But it had already
decided to liquidate in 1901, when all its capital was spent and
no pulp was yet produced.[76]   The situation was saved by Hubert
Biermans, who already had a reputation as an international
railroad builder in Africa.   He was sent by the Bank to liquidate
the project, but instead undertook to obtain additional capital
and by 1902 the new mill was producing 85 tons of pulp daily.
As in the case of the Laurentide, however, he soon discovered
that to make substantial profits he would have to integrate
paper with pulp production.   This he did, and by 1907 he had
remodelled the groundwood mill and added three paper machines,
which now gave the company a daily capacity of 150 tons of
mechanical pulp and 86 tons of paper, not counting the lumber
production of its big sawmill.

Until 1913, the Belgo continued to buy sulphite pulp from
the Laurentide, but in that year built its own plant.   In 1914,
it was producing 120 tons of newsprint daily.[77]   This industry
had been hit less hard by the recession of 1907-1908 than the
aluminum and carbide industries, and seems to have continued to
produce 80 tons of newsprint daily during that period.[78]

The other important industry to come to Shawinigan was the
spinning factory, an affiliate of the Wabasso Cotton Co. of Trois-
Rivières, which settled here in 1909, to profit from the cheap
power and cheap female labour.   It supplied thread to the parent
company in Trois-Rivières.

But the industrial development of Shawinigan and of the
hydroelectric potential of the valley remains essentially the
handiwork of one enterprising company.   What Dales wrote of
this company years later in 1940, could have been written of it in
1914, just a decade after its founding.   He writes,

> From the point of view of industry itself, the Shawinigan enterprise
> has been an exemplary technological leader, an imaginative and
> aggressive business concern, and the main source of electrical supply
> for the province.   From the point of view of Quebec, Shawinigan's

---

[76] *Ibid.*, pp. 105, 128.   For these and other details see also CARRUTHERS, *Paper in the
Making*, p. 659, and *Newsprint in the Making*, a brochure published by the Belgo Canadian
Pulp and Paper Co. Ltd., 1919.
[77] *Pulp and Paper Magazine*, May 1, 1914, p. 269.
[78] *Ibid.*, May 1908, p. 148.

impact has been felt in various ways. Indirectly, by supplying power to Montreal Light, Heat and Power Company, Shawinigan has supported the growth of the metropolis and main manufacturing center of Quebec. More directly, it has organized a power supply of a large part of the province and provided electricity for general purposes, either by retail sales to final consumers or through whole-sale deliveries to distributing companies. Finally, the most striking aspect of the Shawinigan enterprise has been its direct promotion of manufacturing development in the province. It brought the aluminum reduction and carbide industries to Shawinigan Falls, built up a large chemical industry, encouraged the pulp and paper, textile, chemical, and other industries to locate in the St. Maurice Valley, and has been instrumental in bringing many smaller factories to its territory along the banks of the St. Lawrence.[79]

The Town and the Church

When we turn to the organization of the new town of Sha-winigan, we find some resemblances to that of Grand'Mère, and some striking differences. Shawinigan was destined from the beginning to be a bigger city, and by 1914 it had well over 7,000 residents.[80] As at Grand'Mère, industry here preceded the organization of the municipality, which was incorporated as a village in April 1901, and the very next year had already received its charter as a town.[81] The population grew rapidly until 1907, when the aluminum and carbide industries were hit by recession, and then within a few months the population at the industrial site dropped by more than 1,000, from 4,697 to 3,457.[82] For a few months there was a genuine flight back to the land, but, in 1908, things were back to normal and Shawin-igan continued to expand.

What was the role of the Church during this economic spurt at Shawinigan ? As elsewhere in Canada, missionaries preceded both settlers and industry. The Jesuit, Father Buteux, the first white man known to have penetrated the valley, passed by these falls in 1651, and the crest next to the falls had been named "Portage des Prêtres" because of the frequent passage of the missionaries that way.[83] In 1891, Bishop Laflèche blessed a cross erected to commemorate the spot, and in his address to the people on this occasion expressed his great confidence that the immense resources of the region would be developed in the near future, recalling, doubtless, what he had just seen happen up-stream at Grand'Mère.

---

[79] *Op.cit.*, pp. 99-100.
[80] *Canada ecclésiastique*, 1914, p. 92.
[81] FILTEAU, *op.cit.*, pp. 114, 138.
[82] *Ibid.*, pp. 170-171.
[83] *Ibid.*, p. 55.

The population of Shawinigan has always been more than 80 per cent French Canadian, but the personnel and directors of the companies have been almost exclusively American, Belgian, English, and English Canadian, and ordinarily Protestant. There have been short-lived invasions of Italians, Poles, Ukrainians, and others during construction booms, and it usually fell to them to man the hot "pot-rooms" of the Aluminum Company and the carbide furnaces, but the town has remained essentially French Canadian. The French Canadian labourer initially avoided these unpleasant jobs just as he consistently avoided pick-and-shovel jobs and work on the roadbed of railways. He was an expert woodsman and land-clearer, but seems, like his classically trained brother in the professions, to have had a definite scale of values by which he judged which types of work were worthy of him and which were not.

The foreign industrialists seemed, in the beginning, to have felt clearly independent of any local forces, and to have intended to organize both the town and the industry according to their own plans. They bought up whatever land they could, surrounded it with a fence, and even charged an admission fee for entrance. Aldred had already drawn up a map of the new town, which was later by and large followed, though the fence was removed once the village was incorporated.[84] Nevertheless, the *closed-gate* remained a symbol of the feeling of independence of these industrialists.

Here, as at Grand'Mère, there was the expected hedging on the part both of the companies and of many French Canadians on the matter of taxes, both groups wanting to build a town and neither willing to pay taxes. And, as at Grand'Mère, the eventual solution came only with the acceptance of a town manager by both parties. It was clear that these "foreign" companies did not want to be at the mercy of local French Canadian politics. And the small property owners on their side were still wary lest the tax-exempt companies try to use their high capital valuation to exert pressure in the town's elections.[85] However, Shawinigan was blessed with three competent local men, who seem to have played a key role in those early days, two local French Canadian engineers, Beaudry Leman and Henri Dessaulles, and a local Irish businessman, Vivian Burrill, who supplied the new companies with timber.

---

[84] FILTEAU, *op.cit.*, p. 99.
[85] José CADEN, *L'an 1 de Shawinigan*, p. 114.

Beaudry Leman, a young man of twenty-four, was named town engineer in 1901, and drew up the plans for most of the public works as soon as the village was incorporated. The following year he was elected mayor and remained in office until 1908, when he became director of the Banque Canadienne nationale in Montreal.[86] He was succeeded by Burrill who remained mayor until 1913. These two men, because they were competent and had the confidence of the companies, gave Shawinigan a solid and efficient municipal organization much faster than most other new boom towns. Henri Dessaulles, a graduate of the Montreal polytechnical school in the employ of the Shawinigan company, was an invaluable agent and intermediary for the companies with the French Canadian workers and the population. He was elected a member of the town council. With such competent laymen available and a certain reserve on the part of the companies towards the Church, it was to be expected that the role of the curé here would be less marked than in Grand'Mère. For example, it is significant that we do not find him among the delegation that met with Premier Gouin to discuss the new road to Trois-Rivières.[87]

It was Abbé H. Brousseau who represented the Church in the early days at Shawinigan. It is difficult to discover exactly what this curé's role was in Shawinigan at that time. Most old-timers describe him as "very broad-minded," as a devotee of horse racing, and as very friendly with everyone. They likewise suggest that he was removed for a time from the local scene because his involvement in local politics did not sit well with some of the politicians. His relations with the companies seem to have been friendly. They gave him the land on which to build the church and presbytery, and at least the Belgo Company collected the *dîme* for him from the workers in their plant.[88] But we do not find him or his successors playing as open a role in labour relations as Curé Laflèche at Grand'Mère. Even when the Belgo declared an open-shop policy in 1908 and again in 1910, when the local of the AFL struck on the issue of Sunday work, we find no explicit mention of the local curé's being involved.[89]

---

[86] FILTEAU, *op.cit.*, p. 143.
[87] *Ibid.*, p. 174.
[88] The *dîme* was the 25 cents collected twice a month to pay for the building of the church. All the older workers interviewed agreed about this method of collection; some say it was also done in the other plants.
[89] Cf. GREENING, *Paper Makers in Canada*, p. 38.

In the organization of the schools, too, the curé is not visible.
He was not among the school commissioners.   And it is interesting that here the bishop deals with the Mayor, Beaudry Leman,
and not directly with the companies, when he wishes to acquire
land for the convent school in 1904.[90]   It was only when a bitter
quarrel broke out over where the new convent school was to be
built and when work on the building had come to a stop that
the new curé, François Boulay, was elected President of the
School Commission.[91]   Under him the Commission managed to
enjoy sufficient agreement to open two boys' schools conducted
by the Christian Brothers, and finally, in 1907, the much fought-
over convent school was opened for the girls.   Filteau, himself
a school inspector, observes that it was only with the introduction
of the Brothers and the Sisters that the school system found
some stability and made progress.   His observations seem to be
confirmed by the Inspectors' reports which rated Shawinigan's
schools as "inferior" in 1900, as "very good" in 1905, and finally
as "excellent" a few years later.[92]

Under the presidency of Curé Boulay, the School Commission began to demand seriously that the companies pay school
taxes on their properties.   In 1905, the Commission threatened
the company with a lawsuit, only to have it in return seek an
injunction against the Commission, when the latter wished to
borrow money to build the new boys' college.[93]   The Commission won its case but not without creating a certain amount

---

[90] EATR, copy of letter of Mgr F.-X. CLOUTIER to Beaudry Leman, July 10, 1904.

[91] FILTEAU, *op.cit.*, pp. 147-8.

[92] "Reports of School Inspectors," *Sessional Papers*, XXXIII (1900), Part II, No. 5,
p. 9; XXXVIII (1905), Part II, No. 5, p. 9; XLIII (1910), Part II, No. 8, p. 6; XLVIII
(1915), Part III, No. 8, p. 5.   Each volume of the *Sessional Papers* contains three or four
separately bound Parts.   Each Part usually contains several sessional papers with numerous
supplements and appendices, often with their own independent pagination.   In the interest
of brevity references will not include the lengthy title of the particular sessional paper in
each reference, but only its number and the title or number of the supplement or appendix
referred to together with its proper page numbers.

Since these sessional papers are frequently referred to, the following general guidelines
may prove helpful.   All references to matters of education are to the sessional paper which
contains the annual *Report of the Superintendent of Public Instruction*.   The "Reports of
School Inspectors" are ordinarily included as Appendix I of this report.   All references
to agriculture, agricultural clubs, etc., are to the sessional paper which contains the annual
Report of the Minister of Agriculture, under which the "Annual Report of the Dairymen's
Association" is included as a supplement.   And all references to colonization, colonization
roads and bridges, etc. are to the sessional paper which contains the annual *Report of the
Commissioner of Agriculture and Colonization*.   In 1900, this becomes the *Report of the
Commissioner of Colonization;* in 1901, the *General Report of the Minister of Colonization
and Public Works;* and, in 1910, *Report of the Minister of Colonization, Mines, and Fisheries.*

All translations are the official translations appearing in the English edition of the
Sessional Papers.

[93] FILTEAU, *op.cit.*, p. 175.

of hard feelings.[94]   It was the old problem found so often in the province: neither the French Canadians nor the English and American companies wanted to pay taxes, the former because of deep ingrained tradition, the latter because they considered themselves great benefactors of the local people by simply locating their plants in the province, since thereby they gave people work and brought them prosperity.   However, in Shawinigan they did take the initiative, with the aid of the provincial government, in opening and in financing generously a technical institute.   In the period 1912–1914, its attendance rose to 146 and then fell off to 122 with the falling off of business activity in 1913-1914.   In 1914, about 82 per cent of the students were French Canadians.[95]   From conversations with old-timers one gathers the impression that in the early years the greatest effort was made to teach the French workers English and mathematics—although on paper the program was much more ambitious.

I have been unable to find any direct evidence of either a favourable or a negative reaction on the part of the Church to this first sally, on the part of outsiders, into her traditional field of education, except that somewhat later, in 1919, the committee of the Institute organized a meeting with Brother Charles to propose that they would send him commerce students if he on his part would send them technical students.[96]   Old-timers are in agreement that there was only one curé—he came much later—who ever opposed attendance at the Institute on the grounds that it was "neutral," and company officials agree with this.   This was Curé Émile Trudel, who was curé from 1927 to 1933.   The fact that the Catholic newspaper, *le Bien public,* announced the opening of the Institute in superlative terms without offering any criticism was definitely in its favour.[97]

There is no evidence of hostility on the part of the Church to the new industry or to its initiators.   And it seems that whenever her aid was sought it was readily offered.   The big difference between Shawinigan and Grand'Mère is that in Shawinigan such aid was less often sought.   However, as elsewhere

---

[94] However, in 1909, *le Bien public* (December 31, 1909) was still lecturing the companies on how grateful they should be for their privilege of not paying taxes.   The paper points out that at that date the companies still paid only 6 cents on $100 evaluation whereas ordinary property owners paid 50 cents on $100 in school taxes.   And in municipal taxes the difference was still greater, 13 cents paid by the companies as compared with $1.00 paid by others.

[95] Technical Institute, Shawinigan, *Minute Book*, p. 55.

[96] *Ibid.*, pp. 93-95.

[97] *Le Bien public*, October 12, 1911.

in the province, when a forest fire threatened to destroy the new town in the summer of 1902, Curé Brousseau was called upon to halt it by his intercession.[98]   The staunch Scotch Protestant, J.C. Smart, who was in charge of laying Shawinigan's transmission lines, though often amused at the French Canadians' religious devotion, nevertheless always refers to the curés as "my friends the Catholic priests,"[99] and recounts how on occasion it was to them he turned for support when he had to get his men to work on Sundays, and especially when local people wanted to make a small fortune at the expense of the company in cases where the transmission lines crossed their property.   For example, he tells how through the intervention of his friend, Father Beaudoin, he got a certain Mr. Lanoraie to reduce his price from $1,000 to about $150.   And he concludes as the moral of his story, "this goes to show what confidence the people of these days had in their priest."[100]

When the Wabasso set up its spinning-mill in Shawinigan, Curé Boulay brought in the Dominican Sisters to open a hostel for the girls coming in from the farms to work there.   It lasted only a few years but it probably did serve to make this transition more acceptable to the population.[101]   Again, we find the curé of the parish of Notre-Dame-du-Mont-Carmel, on the other side of the river, actively supporting the efforts of the local people to organize a regular ferry service to Shawinigan for the convenience of the local workers and also for the farmers, who came to Shawinigan to sell their produce.[102]   And it was sturdy Curé Boucher who saw to the observance of law and order at Shawinigan Bay in the early days.

The only points of difference between the Church and the industrialists that clearly emerge are the school-tax issue, the

---

[98] The versions of his success in this supernatural venture vary according to the recounter.   Where the French Canadians tended to see divine intervention in the fact that the wind soon fell and then took a different direction away from the town (see FILTEAU, p. 142) the more sceptical Scotch Protestant, J.C. Smart, recounts the event in his memoirs as follows: "We had a good laugh often about that bunch of men who went and persuaded the priest to come up on top of the hill and forbid the fire to come any further.   He did so, and I can remember the pleased look on the lot of their faces.   The priest stayed there a little too long, and we had to drag him out, or he would have been a 'gonner'!"   (J.C. SMART, "Notes on the Early Days of the Shawinigan," unpublished manuscript in the Shawinigan Library, Montreal, note 25).

[99] *Ibid.*, notes 30 and 38.

[100] *Ibid.*, note 38.

[101] FILTEAU, *op.cit.*, p. 184.

[102] Abbé D.-O.-S. DE CARUFEL, *Notes sur la paroisse de Notre-Dame-du-Mont-Carmel*, pp. 204-209.   This curé, who writes the history of his parish in 1907, shows no chagrin at the revolution that has hit it because of the big industry on the far side of the river at Shawinigan, but only tries to help his people to share better in the common prosperity thus realized in the region.

interference of the companies in local politics, the abuse of Sunday-work, and a feeble protest against the Aluminum company for lowering wages in 1911. There are echoes of these complaints in the diocesan Catholic paper, *le Bien public*, for which the ordinary local correspondents are the curés or their assistants. But even here the companies are never directly attacked.[103]

The most serious of these differences by far was the Sunday-work issue. Sunday work seems to have been introduced from the United States after 1910, especially in the pulp and paper industry. Here the French Canadian clergy reacted because they saw "American," and usually "non-Catholic," industrialists apparently blatantly violating not only Dominion and provincial law but also one of their most sacred Catholic traditions. For a moment, matters came to a head in 1911: the editors of the Catholic paper protested strongly and the bishop's nephew, Abbé E. Cloutier, preached a sermon, urging the workers of Grand'-Mère and Shawinigan to form Catholic unions to press their demands, and if need be even go out on a legitimate strike to bring the companies to their senses.[104] But, in reality, the Church never pressed the companies hard on this matter in the St. Maurice Valley. In 1914, when Mgr Cloutier was asked for his views on these practices by a government commission, he remarked that he had no complaints to make against Sunday work in the blast furnaces in the aluminum and carbide plants ("il n'a rien à dire"); and, at the moment, he had Bierman's promise to do his best to dispense soon with Sunday work in the pulp mill, if not in the papermill.[105]

The general atmosphere that prevailed was one of harmony and co-operation. There is no evidence whatsoever of the clergy trying to keep their people out of industry, and foreign non-Catholic industrialists, probably a little wary in the beginning, gradually came to regard the curés as their friends and benefactors and in time came to support their institutions generously. The observation of Mr. L.J. Belnap, the chief executive of the Consolidated Paper Corporation, who worked as an engineer at Shawinigan in 1900, seems to be borne out. He is quite categorical. He claims that neither as an engineer nor as an industrialist did he ever experience hostility of any kind on the part of the Church, but rather had always felt that the curés

---

[103] See, for example, *le Bien public*, September 28, 1911; and February 10, 1911.
[104] *Le Bien public*, September 21, 1911; and October 26, 1911.
[105] Félix MAROIS, greffier, conseiller de conciliation et d'arbitrage, *Rapport adressé à l'Honorable L.-A. Taschereau, ministre des travaux publics* (Québec: August 3, 1914), pp. 28-29.

were sincerely interested in industrial progress and encouraged to see so much capital coming into their parishes. And it was always the companies' policy to turn to the curés to help them iron out their problems and misunderstandings with the workers and the local community.[106]

To say the least, the Shawinigan company certainly did not feel that the Church had hindered their pioneering work in the valley. In fact, rightly or wrongly, they attributed the contentment of the French Canadian workers to the guidance of their priests and said so publicly in their literature inviting companies to come and settle in the region. Their common practice in such literature was to praise the rich resources, cheap power, good communications and low taxes in the region, but their trump card was always the favourable labour conditions. The following passage is typical.

> Perhaps nowhere in the world is there to be found a parallel to the favourable labour conditions which exist in the Province of Quebec generally, and the Shawinigan Water and Power district in particular. About 75 per cent of the population of this province are French Canadians. A happier and more contented people probably do not exist anywhere on the face of the earth...

And then after praising their great skills and deft fingers, the article continues to laud the contented disposition of the French Canadian workers.

> The contentment of the French Canadian people is a factor of utmost importance to the employer in the district, and this great asset to human happiness is to be attributed directly to the wise and kindly guidance of their 'father confessor'. For centuries—for this district was first settled more than three hundred years ago—it has been a cardinal principle of the habitant's religion to be contented with his lot.
> International trade unions are practically unknown. The local unions are restrained and reasonable in their demands.[107]

LA TUQUE

With the successful development of the falls at Grand'Mère and Shawinigan, it was only a matter of time before someone would try to harness the next falls upstream at the old fur-trading post of La Tuque, where there was a 114-foot drop in the river-bed. This falls, though less accessible, was still closer to the

---

[106] Interview with Mr. L.J. Belnap, Chief Executive of the Consolidated Paper Corporation, April 1962.
[107] The Shawinigan Water and Power Company, *Industry's New Magnet*, (1930).

timber riches on which a pulp and paper mill might feed almost indefinitely.   In 1904, the Brown Corporation, manufacturing paper at Berlin, New Hampshire, had an affiliate company incorporated under the name of the Quebec and St. Maurice Industrial Company with a capital of $2 million buy the falls and sufficient timber limits in the area.[108]   They engaged themselves to build a pulp mill and to load a minimum of 4,000 freight cars per year for eight years on the Lake St. John Railway on condition the latter would build a 37-mile branch line to the dam site.   They acquired their timber limits from the railway which had been richly subsidized in Crown land by the provincial government.   For the priceless falls, they paid a mere $75,000.[109] The branch line was soon to be abandoned, for the Transcontinental Railway arrived at La Tuque in 1908, before the Browns had begun to build.   La Tuque was a booming railway tent-town before it became a more sober pulp and paper town.

The Browns began to build their sulphate pulp mill in the fall of 1909, and in June 1910 they were already producing 30 tons of pulp daily, shipping most of it to their paper plant in Berlin.   Production rose quickly from 2,080 tons in 1910, to 36,889 tons in 1914.[110]   They also built a big sawmill, and for the moment delayed building the paper mill, for their position was already very profitable and they had an assured market for their pulp at their own paper mill in Berlin.

Because of the feverish railroad activity and the announcement of the Brown project, the organization of the new town of La Tuque was already well underway before the company itself put in an appearance, even though it was destined to be a one-company town.   Two names dominate the early history of La Tuque, that of the industrialist family Brown and that of the legendary Curé Eugène Corbeil.   The latter was born at Clarence, Ontario, in 1877, and was completely bilingual.   After being ordained priest he taught for a time at Collège L'Assomption and had been a pioneering curé in the parish of the Ascension in the settlement project north of Montreal before being sent as curé to La Tuque in 1908.   He was a huge muscular man, weighing over 300 pounds, utterly fearless, a born leader of men. Before the Royal Commission on Colonization he had strongly rebuked the government for failing to take seriously its responsibility of seeing that the law was obeyed by wood speculators,

[108] *Pulp and Paper Magazine*, May 1905, p. 144.
[109] *Ibid.*, February 1907, p. 30.
[110] Private Archives of the Canadian International Paper Company, La Tuque.

who were the ruin of sincere settlers and big timber merchants alike.[111]   It was Mgr Lorrain of Pembroke who named Corbeil as curé in 1908 to care for the thousands of men working on the railway as well as to see to the establishment of the Church at La Tuque.[112]   Thereafter, for the rest of his life, Curé Corbeil identified himself with the religious, civil, and economic development of La Tuque.   In the pre-war years, at least, it would be practically impossible to discover an initiative in any field of development or progress to which he was not party—if not chief.

He began by being priest and often judge, coroner and policeman to the thousands of migrant workers of every nationality working on the Transcontinental, where fights, accidents, and even violent deaths were an everyday occurrence.   When not travelling the railway or visiting the lumber camps, the Curé was building the new church.   But he did not have things all his own way.   Here, as in the organization of the village, there was soon a deep split among the newcomers.   As Albert Plouffe remarks in *le Nouvelliste*, "Les Canadiens ont rarement pu accepter la désignation du site d'une nouvelle église sans se diviser, souvent même en poussant leur manière de voir jusqu'au schisme."[113]   In fact, the site of the church has more than a religious significance in new towns and villages, since its location almost infallibly determined the site of the future commercial section as well as the value of the surrounding properties.   However, Corbeil faced the opposition, borrowed $10,000 from Bishop Lorrain and built on the plateau as soon as he discovered that the Browns planned to locate their mill there.   The new church was blessed on the occasion of the visit of three bishops on December 13, 1908.

Political division in the organization of the town lasted longer, and despite the Curé's initiatives in convoking meetings and visiting Quebec City to deal directly with Premier Gouin, in 1910, La Tuque soon found itself divided into two village municipalities, La Tuque and La Tuque Falls, each wasting money and energy duplicating public works and surreptitiously dynamiting each other's waterworks.   Happily the feud was of short duration, for, when La Tuque Falls discovered that it was unable to expand further, it was reconciled with La Tuque and the new town was incorporated on March 24, 1911.[114]

---

[111] Colonization Commission, *Report*, Annex, *Enquête à Montréal*, p. 111.

[112] Almost immediately afterwards, La Tuque was re-allocated into the new Apostolic Vicariate of Temiscaming, before finally becoming part of the diocese of Trois-Rivières at the death of Curé Corbeil, in 1939.

[113] *Le Nouvelliste* (Trois-Rivières), July 31, 1935.

[114] Lucien DESBIENS, *Au cœur de la Mauricie (La Tuque)*, pp. 28-30.

From the *Livre des Délibérations* of the School Commission, of which the Curé was elected president in July 1908, it is clear that it was he who was consistently delegated to carry on the business of the Commission.   Already in 1908 he invited in the Sisters of the Assumption to conduct the convent school, and in 1911 he brought in the Marist Brothers to open a "collège" for the boys.   With the railroad supervisors he was immediately popular and they spent whole nights playing cards with him.[115] Soon too the Brown family came under his spell.   Archie Bilodeau, a French Canadian whom the Browns brought back with them from Berlin in 1909 and who lived with the Brown family for years "comme un fils," is categoric: "Les Browns ne faisaient rien sans consulter Corbeil."   Bilodeau also characterizes Abbé Corbeil as mixed up in everything, active with the workers, towns people, and employers!

> C'était un "politiqueur"–il négociait, faisait des plans, bâtissait, dépensait, à la façon du présent gouvernement–un grand joueur de cartes,—bien bon pour les ouvriers; il envoyait souvent chez Brown les hommes qui étaient dans le besoin pour trouver une "job"; il savait tout, voyait tout, il n'avait pas d'ennemis; il s'intéressait à tout et puis il s'y mêlait—dans la construction des rues, des chemins, des écoles, de l'hôpital; c'était un grand penseur, un dépensier, toujours en bons termes avec les Browns.[116]

It is clear that the Brown family helped to finance many of his projects, and in later years it was commonly believed that he had a bargain with the Browns that if they did not maintain satisfactory labour conditions he would invite in the Catholic unions to organize their plant.

The Curé reveals his deep satisfaction in the rapid progress of La Tuque again and again in his correspondence with Bishop Lorrain.   Here we learn that in October 1911 the population was already almost 4,000 and that more than 450 men were working at the pulp mill.[117]   The following passages from this correspondence reveal its general theme.   The first was written on January 7, 1910, just after the new convent school had been destroyed by fire in 1909.

---

[115] *Le Nouvelliste,* July 31, 1935.   In an interview at La Tuque in May 1962, Lucien Desbiens told the author that Curé Corbeil introduced "contract bridge" into La Tuque, when it was still scarcely known elsewhere in the province.

[116] Interview with Archie Bilodeau of La Tuque, May 1962.

[117] Letter of Curé Eugène CORBEIL to Mgr N.-Z. Lorrain, October 2, 1911, Episcopal Archives of Pembroke.   See other interesting letters of October 2, 1909; August 1, 1909; August 12, 1910.   The Curé's optimism and enthusiasm, however, make him rather prone to exaggeration.

> Maintenant cet incendie sera pour nous le commencement d'un état
> meilleur, car nous allons rebâtir plus beau, plus confortable, et plus
> en rapport avec la situation qui nous est faite.
>
> Car La Tuque se développe rapidement.—Déjà les MM. Brown
> achèvent la construction d'une immense manufacture de pulpe, et
> ils projettent pour l'an prochain la construction de grands moulins
> à papier.—Ils emploient actuellement pour la construction plus de
> 250 ouvriers.—Toutes les compagnies de bois s'organisent pour
> placer ici leurs offices pour l'exploitation forestière. De sorte qu'il
> est probable que nous aurons l'été prochain, ici, environ six à sept
> cents familles catholiques.—Quand le Transcontinental aura cons-
> truit ses usines, La Tuque sera comme vous l'avez prévu, une ville
> très considérable.

And on September 30, 1912, he writes,

> La Tuque se développe toujours et réalise pleinement les espérances
> que vous m'exprimiez quand vous m'avez nommé à ce poste.—La
> construction de l'hôpital avance assez rapidement, celle du collège
> des Frères s'achève, ce sera deux beaux monuments.
>
> J'espère, Monseigneur, que vous pourrez me faire l'honneur et
> la joie de venir voir bientôt tous ces progrès.

In 1914, their Excellencies Mgrs Latulippe, Bruneault, and
Roy came for the big occasion of the blessing of the new convent
school, boys' college, hospital, town hall, and church bell.[118]

The Browns, on their part, took a keen and generous interest
in all these local projects and always left at least one member of
their family at La Tuque. They contributed generously, for
example, to the schools, the hospital, a sanitary dairy, a community centre, etc. Their reward was outspoken gratitude on
the part of the people and harmony in their relations with both
their workers and the local community. This spirit of harmony
was recalled publicly by the Curé on the occasion of the opening
of the Community Club in glowing terms:

> Industry, here, has not for its master an anonymous capital, that is
> to say, men who have no other care but that of touching revenues,
> of making a profit of large dividends; men who are not acquainted
> with their workmen, who do not mind to know them, who are stran-
> gers to them. Industry, here, is in the hands of a brave and generous
> family, who knows and loves us, and desires our welfare and happiness
> and it explains the good spirit and mentality of our population.
>
> The patron and workman, here, know, love and help one another,
> for this reason there is and will be order in the city, prosperity in the
> homes, and peace in the hearts.[119]

---

[118] L. DESBIENS, *Au cœur de la Mauricie*, p. 33.
[119] Speech given by Curé Corbeil, January 1922 (Private Archives of the Presbytery
at La Tuque).

If two names stand out in the history of La Tuque, that of the industrialist family Brown and the Curé Corbeil, as the Lieutenant Governor remarked on the occasion of the town's 25th Anniversary, [120] it was the popular figure of the latter with his keen intelligence who dominated the scene, and led and pushed this hastily fashioned community forward towards the fulfilment of his dreams of their becoming an educated, cultured, and prosperous people.[121]   Industry, it seems, could not have asked from the Church a more suitable atmosphere in which to grow and prosper than prevailed at La Tuque.

---

[120] *Le Nouvelliste*, August 5, 1935.
[121] Cf. DESBIENS, *op.cit.*, p. 43.

CHAPTER III

THE ST. MAURICE RIVER VALLEY: DEVELOPMENTS DOWNSTREAM

TROIS-RIVIÈRES AND CAP-DE-LA-MADELEINE

Economic Development

We now turn to the oldest city in the St. Maurice Valley, the cathedral city of Trois-Rivières situated on the St. Lawrence about halfway between Montreal and Quebec at the mouth of the St. Maurice River. Its geographic position makes it the natural port of the whole region. Discussion of it is appropriate only at this point, however, because the new wave of industrialization hit it last, spreading downstream from the other newly born industrial towns. Being the cathedral city of the region, Trois-Rivières provides a special opportunity for studying not only the more direct relations of the Church with industry, but also those more indirect relations such as are found in the general orientations given by the bishop to the clergy and people of the whole region. The discussion will include reference to the town of Cap-de-la-Madeleine, located on the north shore of the St. Maurice and separated from Trois-Rivières only by a bridge.

First, a rapid survey of the history and economic development of Trois-Rivières. In 1634, Trois-Rivières was founded by Laviolette as a fort, a fur-trading post, and a religious mission. But it grew very slowly since it was too exposed to the constant attacks of the Iroquois. The little village slept for almost two centuries (1660–1852), and was only awakened by the sound of the axe felling timber up the valley. The only exceptions to this general history of lack of industry were the intermittent periods of economic activity at the Vieilles Forges a few miles away, which had been opened first in 1732, had passed into the hands of the Crown in 1763, and were finally closed in 1883.

But when the timber merchants turned their attention to the pines of the valley in the 1830's and especially when the government constructed piles and sluices to facilitate the log-drives in the 1850's the old town of Trois-Rivières was quickly transformed into a sizable commercial and sawmill city, and its population grew from 4,900 to 8,600 in the period 1851–1881.[1]   And at the latter date it finally had direct railway connections with Mont-real and Quebec, and with Les Piles up the valley.

But the economic life of the city was still not sufficiently diversified, and, when the sawmill industry fell on hard days in the 1880's owing to slow markets and the exhaustion of the best pines, hundreds of citizens were compelled to take the well-worn route to the New England textile mills.   In spite of a heavy birth rate, the population of the city fell by 300 in the decade 1881–1891.   The decline was stopped and slowly reversed in the ensu-ing years by the introduction of a biscuit factory, several wood-working shops, an ironworks in 1889 to use the pig-iron produced at Radnor, and a shoe industry in 1903.[2]   The population rose to 9,981 in 1900, but it was only after 1906 that the rate of change increased.   In that year, as a result of local initiative backed by the companies at Shawinigan, Trois-Rivières was directly connected by rail with Shawinigan and, in 1910, with Grand'-Mère.   At about the same time, her harbour facilities were improved.   Still more important, in 1906, the Shawinigan company built a transmission line to Trois-Rivières and extended its first submarine line across the St. Lawrence.   Trois-Rivières had had electricity since 1890, first developed by a local steam plant, and then from the falls at Saint-Narcisse.   But the latter development was soon taken over by the North Shore Company, which itself was absorbed by the Shawinigan in 1907.   There-after abundant industrial electricity was assured, even though the Shawinigan, like other electrical companies at the time, continued to show a certain disdain for household consumption, and several times came under the wrath of the editors of the Catholic paper, *le Bien public*, for this negligence.[3]

In 1907, through the intermediary of the Liberal deputy, Jacques Bureau, the city invited the successful textile industri-alist, C.R. Whitehead, to open a cotton mill, offering him a bonus and relief on municipal and school taxes.   The happy result was that he built his cotton mill in 1908, the very year when the rest of the textile industry was crying "depression."[4]

---

[1] Yvon THÉRIAULT, *Trois-Rivières: ville de reflet*, pp. 40ff.

[2] R. BLANCHARD, *La Mauricie*, pp. 130–32.

[3] See *le Bien public*, for example, October 5, 1909; October 15, 1909; November 23, 1911; February 29, 1912.   J. DALES (*Hydroelectricity and Industrial Development*, p. 179) suggests that the power companies in Quebec did not appreciate electricity sufficiently as a consumption good that unleashes the economic and social forces that make for economic growth and hence "may fairly be said to have restricted, though no doubt unwittingly, the economic development of the province."

[4] W.L. Mackenzie KING, Deputy Minister of Labour, Commissioner, *Report of the Royal Commission to Inquire into Industrial Disputes in the Cotton Factories of the Province of Quebec* (Ottawa: King's Printer, 1909), p. 7.

The industry expanded rapidly and in 1913 had an average employment of over 1,000 and had invested about $3 million in its plants in Trois-Rivières and Shawinigan.[5]

In 1908, a disastrous fire completely destroyed much of the central section of the old city, and its reconstruction was the signal for a period of rapid growth centred round the bigger pulp and paper, ironworks, and cotton industries.

As mentioned above, the Vieilles Forges of Saint-Maurice were finally closed in 1883. But already a local group under the name of Larue and Company had set up another ironworks at Radnor, which was to include furnaces and rolling mills combined with a carwheel factory in Trois-Rivières. Though the capital to be invested exceeded $1 million, the group went bankrupt owing to disastrous fires and the lack of suitable transportation facilities, since the branch line to Les Piles was still not in operation. In 1889, the Canada Iron Furnace Company, an English Canadian group, took over the ironworks. And in 1892 the local curé blessed the new furnace which was reputed to be the largest in Canada, with a potential daily capacity of 40 tons and promising soon to employ about 1,000 men.[6] But as local ore bodies became scarcer and wood more expensive their charcoal pig-iron was being undersold by the new American imports, and the forges were closed in 1909. Some years earlier the same group took over the ironworks in Trois-Rivières, which had originally been established by Belgian money, but had changed hands many times since. In 1908, they were employing about 800 men and were producing 40,000 car wheels (for trains) and 20,000 tons of pipe. After a severe fire in 1909, the company was encouraged to rebuild and expand by the favourable tax concessions offered it by the city, and later it branched out into the production of machinery, especially for the pulp and paper industry.

Trois-Rivières was destined to be one day the pulp and paper city of the world. C.R. Whitehead, with the aid of Rodolphe Forget and others, took the initiative in organizing the first big "kraft" paper mill on the Isle de la Potherie in 1910, to replace the old Baptist sawmill, which until that time had continued to

---

[5] *Standard Rates of Wages and Hours of Labour in Canada 1900–1913* (Ottawa: The Public Archives, No. 042135, "The Wabasso Co., Ltd."). See also *Annual Reports of the Wabasso Cotton Company*, "Corporation Records Collection," Baker Library, Harvard Business School.

[6] *Montreal Gazette*, March 25, 1892, cited by H.N. MOLESWORTH, "Canada Iron Foundries Limited" (unpublished manuscript, Files of the Canada Iron Foundry, Trois-Rivières). This latter document is also the source of other details on the industry given here. See also, *le Nouvelliste*, January 5, 1948.

employ about 300 men and had regularly shipped 15,000,000 feet of lumber to England each year. The sawmills had experienced a resurgence at the turn of the century with the wave of urban construction; but now much of the money and timber which had been tied up in that industry passed into the new pulp and paper industry.[7] The new company sought a federal charter under the name of the Wayagamack Pulp and Paper Company and issued $6 million in bonds and $5 million in regular stock in 1911. They bought out the old sawmill and the Baptist timber limits and were soon producing 75–100 tons of pulp and 50 tons of kraft paper daily, and continued to expand their daily capacity to 200 tons. In 1912, they earned $151,773 net profits and, in the following year, $193,903. At that time they continued to run the old sawmill and in all had a maximum employment of 2,000 men.[8]

During the same period, the Union Bag and Paper Company built a new pulp mill at Cap-de-la-Madeleine with American capital, and in 1912 was producing 130 tons of pulp daily and would soon integrate this with a paper mill. The new industry changed the cape almost overnight from a small agricultural and sawmill village into a new boom town whose growth rivalled that of its bigger neighbour.[9]

Several other smaller industries such as textiles, gloves, clothing, woodwork, bottling works etc., were attracted to the region by the favourable tax and bonus system and the cheap industrial power provided by the Shawinigan Company, which offered electricity at a 35 per cent reduction to big industry and at a 20 per cent reduction to smaller industries.[10] By 1914, the population had reached about 19,000, which represented a 25 per cent increase in four years and a 50 per cent increase since the turn of the century; and the city was busy discussing the introduction of a gasworks and tramway. It had developed more in the six years since the fire of 1908 than it had since its foundation in 1634, and it was still on the eve of even more spectacular developments in the pulp and paper industry.

---

[7] In 1910, there were still several big sawmills in the region, the biggest of which were the Grès Falls Co. and the St. Maurice Co., which together cut over 100 million feet of timber annually and gave employment in the woods and in the mills to almost 6,000 men. See CITIZENS ASSOCIATION OF THREE RIVERS, *The City of Three Rivers* (Three Rivers, 1910), p. 16.
[8] *Pulp and Paper Magazine*, November 1910, p. 276; July 1911, pp. 266-68; November, 1911, p. 389; August 1, 1914, p. 462. See also *le Bien public*, November 9, 1911.
[9] *Pulp and Paper Magazine*, July 1911, p. 278; July 1912, p. 230.
[10] CITIZENS ASSOCIATION OF THREE RIVERS, *The City of Three Rivers.*

Today the city of Trois-Rivières is the most French city in the world, having a population 95.93 per cent French Canadian, and 97.68 per cent Catholic.[11] This is not a new situation. In 1914 the diocese of Trois-Rivières was already about 94 per cent French Canadian and about 98 per cent Catholic, with a Catholic population of 93,518, and a non-Catholic population of 1,464.[12] On the other hand, at least in all the big industries in the valley which have been discussed, if we except the two great promoters and financiers, Senator L.-J. Forget and his nephew, Sir Rodolphe Forget, the French-Canadian Catholic population had had no major role in either their financing or their organization. They provided the bulk of the unskilled and some of the skilled labour, although usually in the beginning, except in the case of textiles, skilled labourers had had to be brought in from outside, since the demand was for new skills in industries new to Canada.

The Church

The diocese of Trois-Rivières was erected in 1852, but in 1885 it was divided and retained only 30 parishes on the north shore of the St. Lawrence in what might be called the greater St. Maurice Valley. The fiery old ultramontane bishop, Mgr Louis-François Laflèche, who had spent several years as a missionary in the Canadian West, held office at the time, and was succeeded at his death, in 1898, by the milder, more scholarly seminary professor, Mgr François-Xavier Cloutier. The rapid growth of the diocese reflected the new era of industrial progress. Whereas in the 26-year period, 1870–1896, the number of parishes was only increased by 7, in the following shorter 18-year period, 1896–1914, 30 new parishes were created.[13]

Mgr L.-F. Laflèche. First a word on the controversial figure of Mgr Laflèche, who continued as bishop until his death in July 1898 at the age of eighty-one. He, along with Mgr Bourget of Montreal, had been the champion of the ultramontane and conservative wing of the French Canadian Church and an ardent adversary of Archbishop Taschereau of Quebec and of Université Laval which he believed to be the stronghold of the so-called "Catholic Liberalism" Masonic influences were surrep-

---

[11] Y. THÉRIAULT, *Trois-Rivières, ville de reflet*, p. 49.
[12] *Canada ecclésiastique*, 1914, pp. 88-89.
[13] For these and other details on the diocese, see Chanoine Georges PANNETON and Abbé A. MAGNAN, *Le diocèse de Trois-Rivières 1852-1952*, p. 337.

titiously spreading everywhere in the province.[14] He was likewise the most outspoken opponent of the Liberal party and its leader, Wilfrid Laurier, who came to office in 1896. For him, Laurier and his associates were "Liberals" in the sense condemned by the Church. He was firmly convinced of the ultramontane doctrine of the supremacy of the Church over the State and felt that Confederation, by guaranteeing Quebec's provincial autonomy, had also guaranteed the Church a very special position therein. What he feared most was the repetition in Catholic Quebec of what had already happened in Catholic Europe. He reported his deep misgivings on the local situation in the conclusion to his famous memorandum to Rome in 1882 on religious troubles in Canada.

> Aussi tous les esprits les plus clairvoyants, tant dans le clergé que parmi les laïcs, en sont-ils effrayés et tous s'accordent à dire qu'à moins d'un secours providentiel qui nous permette d'enrayer ce fatal mouvement, nous avançons rapidement dans les voies révolutionnaires de la France et de la Belgique, et que nous tomberons plus tôt qu'on ne le pense dans le même abîme.[15]

However, under Pope Leo XIII, Mgr Laflèche's ideas gradually lost favour in Rome; Université Laval was exonerated, the "Liberal" Archbishop Taschereau was named Canada's first Cardinal, and the Church was finally reconciled with Laurier's "Liberalism" by the encyclical *Affari Vos* of 1897, even though Laurier had failed to obtain equal treatment for the French Catholic schools in Manitoba, which French Canadians held to be their clear right under the British North America Act.

Undoubtedly, it was in this general field of controversy that Laflèche spent his best efforts and his pastoral letters reveal this preoccupation to the end of his life. The "liberal" remains for him the monster who "arrachera l'enfant à l'autorité de la famille et de l'Église pour lui donner dans des écoles sans Dieu, et aux dépens des contribuables, une instruction obligatoire, gratuite et laïque."[16] This was the suspicion that dogged every

---

[14] See M. WADE, *The French Canadians*, pp. 346-83 *passim;* and Laurier-L. LAPIERRE, "Joseph-Israël Tarte: Relations between the French Canadian Episcopacy and a French Canadian Politician (1874-1896)," *Reports of the Canadian Catholic Historical Association* (1957-1958), pp. 23-38.

[15] *Mémoire de l'Évêque des Trois-Rivières sur les Difficultés religieuses au Canada* (Trois-Rivières, 1882), p. 49. (ASTR, printed copy.)

[16] Mgr L.-F. LAFLÈCHE, "Lettre pastorale concernant les dangers auxquels la foi catholique est exposée en ce pays," *Mandements, Lettres pastorales, Circulaires* (Trois-Rivières, February 25, 1895), p. 108. Because references to these volumes of *Mandements* are frequent, they will be referred to hereafter simply by their initial letters MLPC, with the date and diocese involved. Since the use of volume numbers is not always consistent, and since many of these letters and circulars have their own independent pagination, the most reliable reference is the date of the particular document.

attempt to "reform" the education system in Quebec since Confederation.

Mgr Laflèche, as was noted earlier, has also been proposed by certain authors as the typical prophet of "agriculturalism" in the province of Quebec.[17]   And certainly it is easy to find texts that testify to this bent in his thinking.   For example, in 1895, when this seventy-nine-year-old pioneer of the western frontier was asked to address a Congrès des missionnaires agricoles at the Trappist Monastery of Oka, he indeed revealed his predilection for agriculture.   He extolled the pioneer work of the Trappists in scientific farming, using this as an example of the affinity which he believed to exist between religion and agriculture. And, he continues, agriculture, the normal state of man, is most fitted to develop his faculties:

> Or, je n'hésite pas à dire que le travail agricole est celui de l'état normal de l'homme ici-bas, et celui auquel est appelée la masse du genre humain.   C'est aussi celui qui est le plus favorable au développement de ses facultés physiques, morales et intellectuelles, et surtout qui le met le plus directement en rapport avec Dieu...
>
> Efforcez-vous donc, Messieurs les missionnaires agricoles, de faire aimer à notre jeunesse le travail de l'agriculture, et continuez avec persévérance à perfectionner les méthodes...[18]

This might be thought a special occasion on which he was expected to make an oratorical tour-de-force in favour of agriculture.   However, a few months later, he comes back to this same theme in a pastoral letter to his people concerning the use of temporal goods.[19]   He develops the idea that there are three fundamental laws that guide us in our use of temporal goods: (1) the law of work, (2) the law of economy (or thrift), and (3) the law of justice.   Here again he revels in the vocation of the farmer, who like the priest has God for his working companion.   He does not feel he need insist too much on the law of work, for the Canadian people are truly "industrious" but not "thrifty."   He deplores their intemperance in drink and the women's flair for new fashions and for the products of "foreign" industry, and recommends that they continue to feed and clothe themselves by their own efforts as much as possible, and not put themselves at the mercy of industrial crises.   It is intemperance in drink and fashions that have forced people to

---

[17] See, for example, M. BRUNET, "Trois dominantes de la pensée canadienne-française..."

[18] "Discours de Mgr L.-F. Laflèche au congrès des missionnaires agricoles à Oka, le 9 août 1895." (ASTR, typed report.)

[19] Mgr L.-F. LAFLÈCHE, "Lettre pastorale concernant les biens temporels et les œuvres diocésaines," *MLPC* (Trois-Rivières, October 24, 1895), pp. 163-202.

emigrate to the United States. He has a word of praise for those patriots who are founding new parishes in the forest and thus making new land, and he insists on the duty of parents to educate their children. He warns workers against leaders who would provoke them to strike, but he feels that the real areas of injustice in French Canadian life are not to be found here, but rather in electoral corruption and in a certain mania for lawsuits. He likewise reacts against dishonesty and injustice in commerce and industry which harm the buyer and compromise the value of the province's trade.[20]

In 1896, he sent a special directive to all his clergy urging them to encourage the improvement of agriculture especially by promoting agricultural clubs and education.

> J'ai déjà eu l'occasion, en diverses circonstances, de vous faire connaître mon opinion au sujet des cercles agricoles établis dans un bon nombre de paroisses de ce diocèse, et de vous dire que j'y attache une grande importance au point de vue de la prospérité de nos cultivateurs. En effet ces associations, au témoignage d'hommes compétents, rendent partout de grands services à la classe agricole, et en conséquence, comme père de la famille paroissiale, il est convenable que le curé n'y reste pas étranger. Je profite donc de la présente pour vous engager à les favoriser, à les soutenir et à les encourager de votre autorité et de vos conseils chaque fois que vous aurez une occasion de le faire. Je souhaite même que là où ces cercles n'existent pas encore, M. le Curé porte le zèle jusqu'à conseiller à ses paroissiens d'avoir au milieu d'eux cette association agricole, qui ne manquera pas de leur être utile comme partout ailleurs, pourvu que l'on y apporte du zèle, de l'entente et de la bonne volonté. L'encouragement que je désire voir donner aux cercles agricoles, je le désire également pour les écoles d'agriculture, auxquelles le gouvernement a fait subir d'importantes améliorations, en vue de pouvoir y recevoir un plus grand nombre d'élèves, et pour qu'ils y soient plus confortablement.
>
> Messieurs les Curés feraient bien d'user de leur influence auprès des parents pour que leur paroisse soit représentée dans ces écoles au moins par un élève. L'avantage qui en résulterait serait non seulement pour ce dernier, mais aussi pour toute la paroisse, qui bénéficierait des notions utiles et pratiques que le jeune homme, à son retour, serait en mesure de donner à ses co-paroissiens sur l'agriculture.[21]

This very special encouragement which Mgr Laflèche heaped on agriculture can scarcely be interpreted, given the local circumstances of his diocese, as an attempt to dissuade his people from other forms of economic activity and progress. He was,

---

[20] *Ibid.*, pp. 173, 190-91, 177, 185, 196. These pastoral letters are, as a general rule, read to the people and commented on by the local curé, they are often taken later as the matter for sermons over several weeks.

[21] Mgr L.-F. LAFLÈCHE, "Circulaire au clergé, No. 211," *MLPC* (Trois-Rivières, December 23, 1896), pp. 320-321.

in 1895, speaking to an essentially agricultural people, still suffering from the effects of the depression in the sawmill industry and the local ironworks, a period during which he had witnessed some 5,000 of his people compelled to take the route to American industry. In encouraging agriculture he was encouraging his people to increase productivity in an industry in which all but a small minority of them were at least partially engaged, in an industry which was, even allowing for the poor quality of the soil, still very inefficient. As other industries appeared, he gave them likewise his encouragement and blessing—even if not his preference. He was on hand to bless and encourage the power installation at Saint-Narcisse in 1893. He visited the new pulp mill under construction at Grand'Mère in 1887, and returned to bless it when it was completed and to encourage both the workers and the entrepreneurs. About the same time, as noted earlier, he publicly expressed his high hopes for similar developments at Shawinigan in the near future.

Thus, as bishop of a diocese which still had at that time only a few parishes that were not agricultural, he urged his people to improve their agriculture, but when industry began to appear it likewise received his blessing even though it was in the hands of foreign, non-Catholic capitalists.[22] Interestingly enough, this pioneer of the settlement movement in the West, this lover of agriculture, who had long been bishop of a diocese almost totally agricultural before his best agricultural parishes were re-allocated into the new diocese of Nicolet in 1885, was, in his old age, still realist enough not only not to undertake a serious effort at land settlement in the valley, which he regarded as largely unsuitable for agricultural settlement, but, as we have already seen, to resist the enthusiasm of the Curé Labelle and others who urged him to do so. Thus, unlike some other dioceses in the province, we do not find a diocesan colonization society organized in Trois-Rivières in spite of constant heavy emigration from this region to the United States.

Mason Wade has suggested another quite plausible reason for this phenomenon. It seems that, unlike other bishops in Quebec, Mgr Laflèche did not see emigration to New England as an unqualified disaster. Rather he seems to have harboured

---

[22] Mgr Laflèche seems to have entertained a somewhat "Marxian" explanation for the conflict existing between capital and labour. He attributes it to the fact that as the division of labour progresses further, the labourer receives less and less of the product of his labour. However, he concludes that provided the worker is paid a wage sufficient to sustain this family—a wage to which he has a right by natural law—he cannot thereafter violate the employer's right and exact a wage that would ruin his business. See ASTR, "Discours de Mgr L.-F. Laflèche, au congrès des missionnaires agricoles à Oka."

dreams of one day seeing the establishment of an independent French Canadian state which would also embrace those areas overrun by their demographic expansion.   New England Yankees naturally did not relish this idea, and we find echoes in the newspapers of the time revealing the terror that it aroused in them.   For example, an editorial in the *Boston British and American Citizen* of December 28, 1899 sounded the alarm:

> Reflect American Patriots, the French Jesuits have conceived the project of forming a Catholic nation out of the Province of Quebec and New England, and this project of making New England French Catholic has already taken proportions capable of alarming the most optimistic...   Soon, united with the Irish they will govern you, Americans; or rather the Pope will govern you, for these masses recognize him as master.[23]

Similar warnings were aired by the United States Consul at Trois-Rivières in his reports to the State Department.[24]   However, there was a certain tone of fantasy in the whole affair and it is not without significance that this same consul was later removed from Trois-Rivières for having insulted the local people by his grossly exaggerated reports on the poor sanitary conditions existing in the city.   Whatever dreams Mgr Laflèche may have cherished on this subject, they remained dreams—the vast majority of French Canadians, laymen and clergy alike, continued to consider emigration to New England as a "forced exile" from which they would one day return.

Mgr F.-X. Cloutier and le Bien public.   Mgr Cloutier was consecrated bishop just as the diocese entered on an era of solid progress in both industry and agriculture.   For the story of how he and his clergy met this challenge of rapid change, the primary documentation continues to be the bishop's official pastoral letters, directives to his clergy, reported sermons, and private correspondence: as bishop he is exercising his authoritative powers of teaching and interpreting Catholic doctrine in local circumstances.   But Mgr Cloutier also founded a Catholic newspaper, *le Bien public*, to better direct, inform and educate the Catholic population, and this paper can be relied on heavily as a source of valid documentation for his activities.   The bishop founded this paper as an independent Catholic paper,

----

[23] Cited by WADE, *The French Canadians*, p. 434.   Wade has a good discussion of the whole matter.
[24] Nicholas SMITH, American Consul at Three Rivers, "The Fecundity of the French Canadians," *Despatches from U.S. Consuls in Three Rivers: 1881-1906* (Washington: National Archives, Microcopy No. T691, Roll No. 2), October 10, 1890.

assigned it its goals, and submitted its editors directly to the "Comité de la Bonne Presse" over which he himself presided.[25]

His editor, Joseph Barnard, clearly stated the goals of the newspaper to a meeting of the clergy and representatives of the laity at the first Congrès d'action sociale held in 1912: it was to stimulate interest in economic and social progress in the diocese.

> Fondé non seulement pour promouvoir l'intérêt moral, mais aussi l'intérêt matériel de notre district, *le Bien public* a à cœur de seconder tous les efforts, et toutes les idées généreuses; il combat en autant qu'il le peut le préjugé et l'esprit de parti, ces deux principes morbides que nous trouvons au tournant de toutes les routes et qui se dressent en face de chaque effort comme pour décourager toutes les initiatives...
>
> Nous formons partie d'un centre commercial et industriel de premier ordre; notre cité entourée de cinq petites villes et de paroisses importantes qui ne demandent qu'à grandir; en travaillant de toutes ses forces au progrès de notre région *le Bien public* s'efforce de détruire la légende qui veut que les titres de catholique et de français soient synonymes d'incurie dans les affaires et de stagnation dans les choses de l'industrie. Cette légende est stupide et fausse, ici comme ailleurs. Pour le prouver, *le Bien public* s'applique à seconder et à faire connaître tous les bons mouvements, individuels et collectifs; car, avec Mgr notre Évêque, nous pouvons dire: "Combien d'actions louables, d'initiatives généreuses, d'expériences fécondes, de mesures progressives, se produisent sans cesse au milieu de nous, qui deviendraient des sujets d'édification et d'émulation pour peu qu'ils fussent connus au dehors." (Mgr F.-X. CLOUTIER, "Le Bien public," *Mandements, lettres pastorales, circulaires* [Circulaire n⁰ 92, le 7 janvier 1911] p. 221.)[26]

The bishop himself continually expressed his satisfaction with this paper and urged his clergy to promote its sales as a regional paper; he even named the curés or their assistants as the local correspondents in each parish and sent them topics to discuss and models of how to draw up their news column. Since these directions perhaps better than anything else reveal the bishop's and the clergy's attitude towards economic development in all its different phases, they are given extensive quotation here. The topics to be covered were the following:

VIE MATÉRIELLE:

Agriculture. — Semailles. — Moissons. — Vente des produits. — Méthodes de culture.—Culture améliorée, intensive.—Rendement de foin, de grains, de légumes.—Engrais chimiques.—Expériences inté-

[25] Besides, the Procurator of the diocese, Mgr J.-E. Paquin, was president of La Compagnie 'Le Bien public' Incorporée, and, in 1913, the editor, Joseph Barnard, was still the only layman among the stockholders (see ASTR file No. E2:J87).

[26] Joseph BARNARD, "La bonne presse," *Compte rendu du premier congrès d'action sociale du diocèse des Trois-Rivières*, 1912, p. 52.

ressantes.—Succès remportés.—Cercle agricole.—Syndicat agricole (services qu'ils rendent).—Chantiers, leur influence sur l'agriculture. —Dépopulation des campagnes.—Émigration.

Industrie laitière.—Avantages.—Étude comparée du rendement obtenu et des profits réalisés.—Soins à donner aux troupeaux.— Diverses races.—Moyens de les améliorer.—Troupeaux remarquables.—Succès aux expositions.—Méthodes de fabrication du beurre et du fromage.—Bonnes ventes.—Comparaison entre diverses fabriques.—Fromageries et beurreries coopératives.

Commerce et industrie.—1. Activité.—Prospérité.—Décadence.— Causes.—Conditions de la production.—Débouchés.—Communications.—Main-d'œuvre.—Initiatives heureuses ou infructueuses.

2. Conditions du commerce local.—Va-t-on acheter à l'extérieur ? —Pourquoi ?—Y a-t-il trop de négociants ?—La paroisse est-elle fréquentée par les Juifs ou les Syriens ?—Achète-t-on à crédit ?— Y a-t-il des usuriers ?—Caisse populaire d'épargne et de crédit.— Sociétés mutuelles.

Vie intellectuelle :

École.—Conditions matérielles, hygiéniques.—Sollicitude des parents.—Surveillance des commissaires.—Salaire des institutrices.— Choix judicieux.—Fréquentation scolaire.—Visite des écoles.— Succès des instituteurs et des élèves.—Gratifications particulières.— Concours.—Écoles modèles.—Couvents et pensionnats.

Culture générale.—Bibliothèque paroissiale.—Est-elle florissante ?— Fonctionnement, moyens dont elle dispose, diffusion et circulation des livres.—Lit-on de mauvais livres ?—D'où viennent-ils ?—Journaux.—Y a-t-il de mauvais journaux ?—Les bons journaux gagnent-ils du terrain ?—Bonnes revues, pieuses, sociales, littéraires.—Propagande des bonnes lectures.—Cercles d'étude : agricoles, sociaux, mutualistes.

Vie sociale et civile.—Affaires municipales.—Entreprises utiles et progressives.—Union et bonne entente.—Dissensions et chicanes.— Politique municipale et esprit de parti.—Mouvement de la population vers les centres industriels, vers l'Ouest, les États-Unis.— Retours.—Succès, insuccès.—Restons chez nous, vivons simplement, économisons, cultivons bien.

Vie morale :

Religion.—Fêtes et cérémonies notables.—Confréries pieuses : bien qu'elles font, leur activité, leur progrès.—Pratique religieuse.—Communion fréquente : ses effets.—Esprit de foi.—Respect du prêtre.— Désordres, amusements dangereux.—Avis, réprimandes, défenses de l'autorité religieuse.

Mœurs et traditions.—Tempérance.—Luxe.—Abandon des vieilles coutumes qu'il faudrait conserver : simplicité des mœurs.—Vertus et traditions familiales.—Dignité et fermeté des parents.—Respect et soumissions des enfants.—Cordialité des relations.—Hospitalité.— Générosité.—Aide mutuelle.—Fêtes populaires : la Saint-Jean-Baptiste.

The following are typical examples of models suggested for reporting:

> Notre paroisse entre dans une ère de progrès.   Notre Caisse popu-
> laire a déjà fait beaucoup de bien parmi nous.   On est très content
> aussi du Syndicat agricole fondé pour l'achat en commun des grains
> de semence, des engrais et des machines agricoles.   On parle mainte-
> nant d'une fromagerie coopérative: l'expérience a été tentée ailleurs
> et paraît avoir donné d'excellents résultats.
> L'industrie laitière a donné un bon rendement.   C'est toujours ce
> qui arrive d'ailleurs, quand on a de bonnes vaches et de l'herbe à
> leur donner.
> Les journaux jaunes et neutres perdent tous les jours du terrain.
> Tant mieux!
> Madame Joseph X... vient de faire baptiser son 17e enfant.   Hon-
> neur à la femme canadienne!
> ... nos hommes se disposent maintenant à partir pour les chantiers.
> C'est nécessaire, à ce qu'on dit, si l'on veut attacher les deux bouts
> au printemps.   Triste nécessité tout de même.[27]

Quite obviously the paper was meant to educate as well as provide local news.   If we can accept the circulation figures claimed by *le Bien public*—5,000 copies in a diocese of less than 90,000 at the end of 1910, with the energetic promotion work just at its beginning—and take into consideration the large size of the average family, this newspaper must have been available to the majority of the Catholics in the diocese, especially in the later years.[28]

On the day of his consecration, July 28, 1899, the new bishop stated clearly when addressing the mayor and the citizens of Trois-Rivières what his attitude towards temporal progress in the diocese would be.

> Les chefs spirituels, en effet, occupés par état des intérêts éternels,
> ne sont pas pour cela indifférents à ceux du temps présent.   Avec
> quelle sollicitude, au contraire, ils suivent du regard ceux qui sont
> spécialement chargés de ces intérêts matériels!   Comme ils savent
> dans l'occasion applaudir à leurs succès!   Comme ils admirent les
> étonnantes productions de leur intelligence et de leur génie, les res-
> sources inépuisables de leur habilité artistique, les merveilles de
> leur industrie, leurs découvertes toujours progressives et tendant à
> améliorer la condition humaine!

Nevertheless, he has reservations.   He will only applaud progress that does not nail men down to earth.   But,

---

[27] Mgr F.-X. CLOUTIER, "Le Bien public," *MLPC* (Trois-Rivières, Circular No. 92, January 7, 1911), pp. 224-25.
[28] See *le Bien public.* On successive copies the circulation stated rises from 2,950 (March 18, 1910) to 5,000 (December 16, 1910).

... Aussi longtemps donc que les évolutions de l'activité humaine au milieu des choses terrestres ne blessent en rien la volonté suprême de Dieu, ceux qui sont chargés des âmes et des intérêts éternels n'ont qu'à admirer et approuver.[29]

And he concludes by promising the mayor and the people that with their aid he will assure them, as far as it is in his power, of happy days here below and of constant progress towards the eternal country.

In practice, how did the Church under this bishop use her influence in the various areas of economic development during the period ?

Land settlement. Mgr Cloutier was preoccupied even less than his predecessor with promoting land settlement in the valley, and he never touches on it in his official letters or directives. *Le Bien public* seldom raises the question of land settlement, and when it does it is to criticize the provincial government's lack of a serious, rational and methodical program for promoting agriculture, colonization, and road-building. For its editors, this is the real cause of emigration—and not drunkenness, an exaggerated taste for travel, and ignorance, as others so often alleged. They suggest that the provincial government spend on this project the millions that it was currently losing through its inefficient administration of public lands. Likewise, the federal government would do well to spend less on military arms and more on agriculture.[30] Only on two occasions do we find the farmers urged not to abandon their land for the cities. And then it is argued that thier lack of prosperity is due to unscientific agriculture, and that concentration in the cities causes the birthrate to fall.[31] A single editorial warns that Montreal is growing more rapidly than is healthy—and the forebodings of Napoléon, Mirabeau, Colbert, and Charles V concerning Paris are recalled.[32] But, at the same time, the editors bewail the fact that the population of Trois-Rivières has dropped in 1910, and in the following year they rejoice at the rapid growth of the city:

Cet accroissement subit est une bonne fortune pour tout le monde, pour le commerce de la ville et pour celui de la campagne, car nos cultivateurs reçoivent aussi leur large part de profits.[33]

---

[29] *Le Trifluvien*, July 29, 1899, ASTR.
[30] *Le Bien public*, December 21, 1901; April 5, 1910.
[31] *Ibid.*, May 30, 1912.
[32] *Ibid.*, April 12, 1910.
[33] *Ibid.*, October 25, 1910; November 9, 1911. This copy of November 9, 1911, available in the Archives of the Séminaire de Trois-Rivières, is marked in blue pencil "Édition Supprimée." I have been unable to verify the truth of this remark or to find a plausible reason why this particular copy might have been suppressed.

Agriculture. In 1914, about 42 out of a total of 53 parishes in the diocese were still primarily agricultural, though the parishioners added a few dollars to their subsistence farm-income by selling wood cut on their land or by working for the wood merchants during the winter months. In 1905, Mgr Cloutier reduced the *dîme* which the farmers were obliged to pay annually for the support of their curé.[34] The bishop was seriously preoccupied with encouraging increases of productivity in agriculture in his diocese, but in terms of space devoted to urgent matters, if we except the *caisses populaires*, it receives less attention in the paper than education, Catholic trade unions, and other industrial and city problems. And *le Bien public* follows the same pattern of emphasis. However, as time passes the editors increased the space devoted to agriculture. It is interesting to observe that only in his pastoral letter of January 1914, when industry is in recession, does the bishop return to the time-worn theme:

> Chez tous les peuples, la terre est la plus solide assise de la prospérité publique, et chez nous, plus qu'ailleurs peut-être, c'est là, au sein de la classe agricole, que se trouve le plus puissant facteur de la richesse nationale, en même temps que le plus ferme soutien de nos précieuses traditions.[35]

It is clear nevertheless that here, as elsewhere in the province, it is in the improvement of agriculture that the Church has had its most direct economic impact. The clergy are everywhere directly involved in working towards this goal. For example, they are urged by the bishop to announce from the pulpit and to attend personally the conventions of the dairy industry, so that they can later repeat the lessons thus learned for the profit of their own parishioners.[36] But the bishop's biggest single initiative in this area seems to have been that of throwing his full weight and influence behind the movement to foster the *caisse populaire* in each parish.

---

[34] Mgr F.-X. CLOUTIER, "Lettre pastorale apportant certaines modifications à la dîme," *MLPC* (Trois-Rivières, April 20, 1905), pp. 86-90. The farmers will continue to give 1/26 of all grain, and instead of paying 75 cents on each thousand bundles of hay over the first thousand, they will now be taxed only on bundles of hay over the first two thousand. However, they must make up the difference if this tax does not reach a minimum of $2. Property owners with holdings worth $500 or less pay $2 per family and 50 cents per $1,000 thereafter, up to a maximum of $10. Single individuals pay $1, but if poor only 50 cents.

[35] Mgr F.-X. CLOUTIER, "Lettre pastorale sur l'action catholique," *MLPC* (Trois-Rivières January 1, 1914), p. 566.

[36] Mgr F.-X. CLOUTIER, *MLPC* (Trois-Rivières, Circular No. 69, January 27, 1908), p. 502.

This popular movement launched in Quebec by Alphonse Desjardins at the turn of the century had the same general objectives and organization as the Credit Union movement encouraged elsewhere by the Church.   It will be discussed later (Chapter VI) at length as a genuine form of education in private saving and thrift fostered among the French Canadians.   For the moment, we need only observe how the regional clergy were involved in its organization and promotion in the St. Maurice Valley.

In 1911, the bishop addressed a special directive to his clergy on this matter.   He writes of the encouragement to thrift and to local industry which these *caisses* would be:

> Bien pourvues des organismes nécessaires à la vie religieuse et civile, nos paroisses manquent d'organisation au point de vue économique. C'est une lacune que les caisses populaires vont heureusement combler.   Le moment me paraît venu d'en établir dans chacune de nos paroisses.   Plusieurs d'entre vous l'ont déjà fait, du reste, et ils n'ont eu qu'à s'en féliciter.   La caisse populaire est devenue chez eux une école d'économie et de prévoyance; elle sert à combattre l'usure, le luxe, l'intempérance, ainsi que le crédit ruineux dont nos gens abusent tant; elle aide au développement de l'agriculture et de l'industrie locale en faisant fructifier sur place l'argent produit dans la paroisse.   Elle donne enfin toute la mesure de son utilité par l'établissement de la caisse scolaire.   Celle-ci constitue certainement un puissant facteur éducationnel, et elle obtient de ce chef une telle portée morale que nous ne serions pas justifiables de nous en désintéresser.[37]

And he tells his curés that he and the other bishops have asked Rome for permission for them to hold positions of an administrative and supervisory nature in the *caisses*, although Rome has forbidden this in the past.   In the same letter, he urges his clergy to promote the establishment of parish libraries to furnish good reading material as well as technical literature on agriculture, domestic economy, etc.   Finally, he includes a personal copy of A. Desjardins' *Catéchisme des caisses populaires*, for each curé's use.[38]

On another occasion, Mgr Cloutier stoutly defends the priest's role in fostering all forms of mutual aid such as the *caisses populaires* and co-operatives which aim at improving the economic conditions of their people within the limits of justice and charity—thus following the example of Christ himself who took

---

[37] Mgr F.-X. CLOUTIER, *MLPC* (Trois-Rivières, Circular No. 93, February 15, 1911), p. 253.

[38] *Ibid.*, pp. 254-57.   In reality, this catechism was written for Desjardins by his friend Father Grondin. (See Yves ROBY, *Alphonse Desjardins et les caisses populaires, 1854-1920*, p. 110.)

pity on the multitude when he saw them hungry in the desert.[39] And, in 1914, he was happy to report that 15 *caisses populaires* were now in operation covering the territory of 20 parishes.[40]

Over this same period, *le Bien public* undertakes the task of educating the people in the use of the *caisse populaire*, carrying a column in almost every issue and keeping them abreast of the progress achieved. For example, in the issue of August 10, 1909, we are told about the *caisse* at Saint-Maurice, of which Curé Caron is president and Bishop Cloutier himself honorary president, that it is steadily working to give the French Canadians economic power and independence.[41] Likewise, at the First Congress of Social Action organized by the bishop for the Curés as well as lay representatives of all 54 parishes, Mgr Cloutier's nephew, Abbé Émile Cloutier, was assigned the role of promoting the *caisses* and reporting on the success thus far achieved.[42]

Le Bien public began, in 1909, by publishing only occasional articles on agriculture, mostly reprints from other papers, and no editorials. But in 1910 it began to heed the readers' demands for more articles on agriculture, and it seems that as the bishop tried to make the paper more truly a regional paper, more space was devoted to agricultural interests; a little later a large section entitled "Agriculture," which dealt with the state of the markets, local successes, new ideas, etc., was included regularly.

A glance at the village level reveals that the bishop's efforts were being generously seconded there.[43] For example, we find that in the new parish at Lac-à-la-Tortue, Curé Pierre Boulay had succeeded in getting his parishioners to switch from cereals to specialization in potatoes, hay, and cattle-raising, which were more suitable to the sandy soil, provided it was well manured. And soon, through the organization of a co-operative, their potatoes were rapidly gaining a "national" reputation and some of the farmers were making $1,000 annually on potatoes alone.[44] At Saint-Justin, Curé Denis Gérin not only preached better agriculture, but himself cultivated 16 acres to give an example of how to increase productivity. He was also known province-

---

[39] Mgr F.-X. CLOUTIER, "Lettre pastorale sur l'action catholique," p. 562.

[40] *Ibid.*, p. 563.

[41] *Le Bien public*, August 10, 1909. If we are tempted to smile at this ambitious goal, we should note that at the present time there exist in the province over 1,200 such *caisses* with receipts exceeding $1 billion. (See *Statistical Year Book*, XLVI [1963], 569.)

[42] *Compte rendu du premier congrès d'action sociale*, pp. 64–69.

[43] These few examples merely serve to complement the earlier discussion on the role of the curé in the local villages.

[44] *Le Bien public*, December 31, 1909; January 7, 1910.

wide as a promoter of the dairy industry and represented the
region on the executive of the provincial Dairymen's Association.
He had organized the local agricultural club and it was one of his
disciples who opened the first local cheese factory.   Finally,
he had provided his parish with a local library.[45]

Industry and City Organization.   Mgr Cloutier carried out
his promise, made on the day of his consecration, that he would
support and encourage everything that he recognized as "true"
progress in the city and the diocese.   From the beginning, it
was clear that he considered the greatest obstacle to such progress
to be the excessive "party spirit" that divided the community
into the two entrenched camps of the "bleus" and the "rouges,"
who seemed incapable of any team work to promote the common
good.   He attacked this evil in a major sermon and asked the
citizens to give their hearty support to two local papers, *le Nouveau Trois-Rivières*, which promoted the "industrial and commercial progress of our city," and his own *le Bien public*, which
was concerned with both the moral and the material progress
of the city.   And he publicly deplores the party spirit which
has systematically paralysed "City-Hall" and consequently the
city's industrial, commercial, and social progress.   He concludes
with the plea, "Abattons donc enfin cette funeste barrière qui
barre la porte au progrès de notre ville."[46]

The editors of *le Bien public* take up this theme, and, except
for brief intervals when major religious or national interests are
at stake, the city's rapid economic development remains the
dominant theme of the paper's front-page editorials.   The City
Council and the Chamber of Commerce are the paper's favourite whipping boys: they are, it alleges, paralysed by partisan
politics.[47]

Once the editors take up the pursuit of a local question, they
are merciless.   The case of the city's inadequate fire protection
is typical.   After the city had been almost completely destroyed
by fire in 1908, the Council got around to buying a new pump—
but they still had no mechanic![48]   And when they do get a

---

[45] Léon GÉRIN, *Le type économique et social des Canadiens*, p. 103.   It might also be
noted that a few years earlier, the curé's best cow, "La Major" was listed among the prize-
winners of the province, having given 271 pounds of milk per week.   Later the clergy seem
to have dropped out of such competition ("Supplement to the Twentieth Annual Report
of the Dairymen's Association," *Sessional Papers* XXXVI [1903], Part I, No. 3, p. 206).
[46] *Le Bien public*, January 7, 1910.
[47] See for example, the issues of January 21, 1910 and October 15, 1909.   Little wonder
if partisan politics was on the upswing.   This was the period when Henri Bourassa's campaign against the Liberals reached its height, and the very bitter and crucial election of 1911
was being prepared on such major issues as nationalism, the naval bill, and reciprocity.
[48] *Ibid.*, July 12, 1909.

mechanic, either he is a "political" appointment and "incompetent," or else the vaunted pump is no good.[49] The *coup de grâce* comes when the city hall burns down the following year even though it is located right beside the new fire station—as if to confirm the paper's allegations![50] The paper pleads with the Council finally to hire a competent civil engineer and leave him free to get on with the job.

One of the major preoccupations of *le Bien public* is the improvement of the transportation and commercial facilities of the city's market area. It fights the tolls on bridges which keep farmers from coming to buy and sell in the city.[51] It publishes a lengthy series of front-page articles and editorials on the inefficiency of the railway connections of the Grand Trunk with Trois-Rivières and the inadequate ferry-service provided across the St. Lawrence, both of which hamper farmers and businessmen and thus reduce the market area served by the city.[52] It likewise keeps insisting that the Shawinigan Company provide better domestic service in Trois-Rivières, as we have already noted.

For a time, *le Bien public* becomes totally disenchanted with the inefficiency of both the City Council and the Chamber of Commerce and urges the formation of a citizens' association to clean house in the city's affairs and to promote its interests.[53] The issue of April 5, 1910, is devoted almost entirely to the promotion of such an association:

> Le but que l'on se propose est le bien général de la ville, de nous faire mieux connaître à l'étranger, d'amener ici les touristes, et les capitalistes, de favoriser l'établissement de nombreuses manufactures, l'embellissement, et l'assainissement de la cité.[54]

A few months later the editors credit the newly formed association with having co-operated with Mr. Whitehead to obtain a $25,000 bonus for the new Diamond Textile Company, which will soon employ 200 workers.[55] And later the paper follows the association's attempts to get improvements on the main highway connecting the city with Quebec and Montreal.[56] This citizens' group seems to have lasted only about a year.

[49] *Le Bien public*, August 27, September 10, 1909.
[50] *Ibid.*, October 4, 1910.
[51] *Ibid.*, June 18, 1909.
[52] *Ibid.*, July 2, September 3, September 10, September 21, October 1, October 12, 1909; January 14, April 8, April 22, June 24, 1910; January 13, 1911.
[53] *Ibid.*, January 18, 1910.
[54] *Ibid.*, April 5, 1910.
[55] *Ibid.*, June 3, 1910.
[56] *Ibid.*, December 23, 1910.

And its major achievement seems to have been the promotion of new industry by publishing the brochure, *The City of Three Rivers*, to show how attractive the city was to new industry, with its cheap electric power, generous tax remittances, good harbour and railway facilities, and its large labour force, that has never been known to strike![57]

Thereafter, *le Bien public* goes back to sermonizing the City Council and the Chamber of Commerce, reprinting their election promises, and telling them to get on with the job.[58] It later enters on a campaign to promote the installation of a gas works and a tramway system and publishes full-page advertisements on the exceptional advantages which the city offers to new industry.[59] But, apparently despairing once more of overcoming the partisan roadblocks, it again turns to promoting an independent civic organization in July 1914.[60]

Particular industries have a friend in *le Bien public*. It campaigned for a generous tax concession to the Canada Iron Foundry, which threatened to leave the city after its disastrous fire in 1909.[61] It urged a loan to a needy glove company.[62] If it insists that the Wayagamack get rid of its foul odour, it, nevertheless, rejoices at the company's announcement that it is earning substantial profits.[63] Likewise, it encourages the efforts made by the curé of Cap-de-la-Madeleine to found a citizens' association, similar to that of Trois-Rivières, to improve the town's services and to invite in new industry.[64]

Finally, *le Bien public* wholeheartedly backs Mgr Cloutier's direct intervention in the city's fair, and undertakes a systematic campaign to make the annual fair an occasion for the citizens and farmers to become acquainted with the latest agricultural and industrial machinery, and not merely a circus providing drink and amusement.[65] In brief, it is quite evident that *le Bien public* is delighted with the new era of progress and keeps urging the City Council and the Chamber of Commerce on to greater things. Perhaps its front-page editorial of September 12, 1912,

---

[57] It is interesting to note that in their brochure they invite not only capitalists but also labourers to come to their city.

[58] *Ibid.*, November 23, 1911.

[59] For example, see *ibid.*, September 19, 1912; July 24, August 7 and 21, 1913; July 23, 1914.

[60] *Ibid.*, July 30, 1914.

[61] *Le Bien public*, issues July–December 1909.

[62] *Ibid.*, July 1, 1910.

[63] *Ibid.*, September 26, 1912; July 31, 1913.

[64] *Ibid.*, November 30, 1911; April 11, 1912.

[65] *Ibid.*, several issues during the months of July 1909 and August 1910.

entitled "Trois-Rivières Agrandi," best sums up the general attitude of its editors—and hence of Mgr Cloutier and his close associates:

> Notre ville prend un développement si intense et si rapide que pour peu que cela continue, avant deux ans le chiffre de notre population aura doublé...
> Les grandes industries établies ici récemment font un commerce si prospère que toutes travaillent à prendre de plus en plus d'extension. La Canada Iron a doublé et triplé son personnel, la Wabasso donne à son usine des proportions phénoménales, et la Diamond Whitewear double la longueur de sa manufacture, et construit un étage de plus. C'est-à-dire que tous ces agrandissements signifient une nécessité de main-d'œuvre de plus en plus considérable; et un regain extra-ordinaire de prospérité pour notre ville des Trois-Rivières. D'un autre côté, le développement qui s'opère au Cap-de-la-Madeleine est lui-même tout à fait étonnant; c'est une véritable petite ville qui se construit là.[66]

The editor goes on to say that he is not one to envy the growth at the Cape; rather he urges that the promised tramway be immediately built to link the two cities and that the toll collected on the bridge which separates the two cities be abolished.

Relations with Industry. But however favourable he was to the new era of progress—and he went out of his way to declare publicly on several occasions that neither he nor the Church were hostile to it—Mgr Cloutier did have some definite reservations about it.[67] He rejected that part of progress that led to "déca-dence morale" and to an uncontrolled passion for gain on the part of employers, who would make men slaves to "ces terribles machines tueuses d'hommes."[68] In April 1907, he condemned out of hand all Sunday work that was pursued merely out of the

---

[66] *Ibid.*, September 12, 1912.
[67] For example, see his sermon, "Le progrès véritable" as reported in *le Bien public*, January 3, 1911.
[68] *Ibid.* It is quite clear also that the clergy, as is reflected in the articles and editorials in *le Bien public* from time to time, did have reservations on what they considered the "American" drive for material gain and progress. Perhaps better than most others, Father Lalande, in a conference which he gave at this time at Trois-Rivières on "L'Argent" succeeds in giving the correct nuance of this reservation (*le Bien public*, November 30, 1909). He begins by vigorously denying that the Church forbids the faithful to acquire riches and that there is any truth in the adage "pays catholique, pays pauvre." He likewise refuses to admit that any upper limit should be set to French Canadians in their pursuit of riches, "car, là, comme ailleurs, il n'est jamais bon de rester volontairement au second rang quand on peut être au premier." On the other hand, French Canadians must ever be mindful of the nobility of their beginnings in America, and not let utilitarian preoccupations replace their spiritual ones. When he thinks of French Canada, he conjures up a vivid memory of Cartier, immediately after landing, standing there before a cross just planted in New France, surrounded by his men all with eyes raised to heaven in prayer. When he thinks of the United States, he paints a picture of a ship just landed in Pennsylvania; the men are already busy making a comfortable camp and the soup is boiling away merrily. He says these American pioneers also had faith—nevertheless, the first idea that came to their minds on embarking was to have a good meal!

desire for added profits at the expense of ruining the human organisms of the workers. And in a directive accompanying this pastoral letter he warned curés against letting Sunday work gain a hold in their parishes. However, he added that in applying his letter to the local situation, they should not do so in a puritan way, seeing all in black and white.[69] But, as a rule, the bishop seems to have dealt personally with the employers concerning interference with Sunday, not pushing the question unduly either through *le Bien public* or through the Catholic trade unions. For example, we find in his correspondence copies of letters addressed to Mr. C. Whitehead on this matter. On one occasion, we find him graciously granting permission for his men to work on the Catholic feast of the Epiphany; on another occasion the bishop regretfully but firmly informs Whitehead that after consulting with his fellow bishops he cannot authorize him to expect work regularly at the Wayagamack on Sundays and feast days, giving as his reason that the necessity is not clearly proven, since Mr. Dubuc, a French Canadian, runs a very profitable pulp mill at Chicoutimi without working on Sundays and feast days.[70] And in 1912, the pulp mill at Cap-de-la-Madeleine seems to have stopped Sunday work on the energetic instance of the bishop, backed up by the workers' resistance to such work.[71]

When Mgr Cloutier was asked to report on the conditions of Sunday work in his diocese before a government commission which was set up in 1914 to investigate this matter, he pointed out that he had no objections to the necessary work on the blast furnaces at Shawinigan; that, for the moment, Mr. Biermans of the Belgo had promised him to do all he could to cease work in his pulp mill on Sunday if not in the paper mill; and that he had authorized Mr. Chahoon to continue such work for another eight months with the assurance it would then end. And as for Mr. Whitehead, for the moment, he accepted his explanation that he was preparing French Canadians to replace the Swedish and Norwegian workers. (The implication seems to be that as soon as he has a sufficient number of French Canadian specialized

---

[69] Mgr F.-X. CLOUTIER, *MLPC* (Trois-Rivières, Circular No. 62, April 10, 1907), pp. 381-84.

[70] EATR, copies of letters from Mgr F.-X. CLOUTIER to Mr. C.R. Whitehead, Manager of the Wayagamack Pulp and Paper Company, December 12, 1913, and May 15, 1913. It might be noted that in the diocese of Trois-Rivières, as elsewhere in the province, the bishops took measures to reduce the number of purely Catholic holidays. For example, in 1893, the feasts of the Apostles Peter and Paul, Corpus Christi, and the Annunciation of the Virgin were suppressed as public holidays in the diocese. (See G. PANNETON, *Le diocèse de Trois-Rivières*, p. 291.)

[71] *Le Bien public*, March 5, 1914.

workers he will fire the foreigners, who want to work on Sunday to earn higher wages.) However, he asks the government to strengthen the law and thus effectively protect the companies themselves from their competitors.[72]

It seems evident that Mgr Cloutier was on personal and friendly terms with all the industrialists in the valley, and though there were disagreements over Sunday work there was never any semblance of a clash or of bad feelings between the Church and industry. In Trois-Rivières, however, we find no evidence of the *dîme* being collected in the factories, or of the new factories being officially blessed, although old-timers recall occasional visits by the bishop to the plants. Since these employers and managers were neither French nor Catholic they inevitably remained outside French Canadian parish life. It was not because they were industrialists. In this regard, it is interesting to note that the one big French Canadian financier and promoter, Sir Rodolphe Forget, who played a role in the area's development, had easy access to high honours in the Church. For example, we find Mgr Cloutier writing to him in 1912, praising the "œuvres colossales" that he along with others have undertaken in the region, and warmly inviting him to be the sponsor of the new Cathedral bells, which are to be publicly blessed in a few weeks.[73]

The Catholic Trade Unions. Mgr Cloutier took much more vigorous action to protect the French Canadian workers from the dangers to which he considered them to be exposed in the national and especially in the international (AFL) labour unions. In 1909 *le Bien public* warned against labour leaders who were openly attacking the Church's role in education and especially her religious teachers.[74] And in 1912 when the AFL began seriously to organize the rapidly growing labour force in the valley, Mgr Cloutier, foreseeing the inevitable clash between capital and labour, determined to head it off by supplanting the international unions with Catholic unions in line with the recent teaching of Popes Leo XIII and Pius X.[75] In December 1912, he gave two major sermons on the labour question, vigorously defending the right of the workers to unionize to protect

---

[72] Félix MAROIS, *op.cit.*, pp. 28-29.

[73] EATR, copy of letter of Mgr F.-X. CLOUTIER to Sir Rodolphe Forget, M.P., August 5, 1912.

[74] *Le Bien public*, several issues from September to December, 1909.

[75] See for details *le Bien public*, and especially the excellent study by Michel TÊTU, "Les premiers syndicats catholiques canadiens (1900-1921)" (unpublished Ph.D. dissertation, Université Laval, 1961), 562 pp.

themselves against the excesses of monopolies and of capitalism.[76]
But since the existing unions seemed to him to have abused
their trust, he proposed to endow (*doter*) the city with a Catholic
workers' organization.   *Le Bien public* undertook the publicity,
huge rallies were organized, and within a year the bishop could
claim that the new union had a membership of 1,000 workers.[77]

The mutual agreement proposed by the clergy was that the
employers should give their preference to the new unions and in
time of trouble have recourse to conciliation and arbitration
rather than to a lock-out, while the unions, for their part, would
furnish competent workers, and submit their problems to conciliation rather than strike or join the "foreign" unions.[78]

These unions were entirely the creation of the clergy, and
though lay officers were elected, it was the chaplain, Abbé
J. Massicotte, who seems to have taken most of the initiative.
The local employers did not seem to object to the new unions,
and some of them, for example the Tebbutt Shoe Company,
warmly invited them into their shops.   There seems to be no
evidence, however, that they negotiated wage agreements with
the new unions at this time.

These unions were probably a net gain for the employers.
The aggressive international unions were ruled out of court for
the time being, and the Church all but assured the employers
peaceful, competent, sober labourers, for only these were accepted
into the Catholic unions.[79]   One suspects that the clergy hoped
through these unions to encourage the employers to get rid of
the foreign specialized labourers and to replace them with French
Canadians.   It is not by accident that *le Bien public*, on several
occasions, holds up Curé Laflèche of Grand'Mère as the champion
of the French-Canadian workers, for it was he who had successfully counselled getting rid of the foreign workers who were out
on strike and replacing them by French Canadians.   It also
maintains that the manager Chahoon was most satisfied with
the exchange, and that the immediate result was a 20 per cent
increase in productivity![80]

It was likewise to the eventual advantage of economic
development that Mgr Cloutier carried on a systematic campaign
against the excessive number of open bars as well as against the

[76] *Le Bien public*, December 26, 1912.
[77] Mgr F.-X. CLOUTIER, "Lettre pastorale sur l'action catholique," p. 567.
[78] TÊTU, *op.cit.*, p. 151.
[79] See TÊTU, p. 158.
[80] *Le Bien public*, for example the issues of May 29, July 10 and July 17, 1913.   Since
all the participants in this incident were still alive and active in the region, there must be
at least a semblance of truth in these claims.

causes of tuberculosis. Both matters were seriously studied
at the Diocesan Congress of Social Action in 1912, and thoroughly aired over the years by *le Bien public*.[81]

   Education. This section merely takes up the role which the
Church played in education in this region. A later chapter will
provide a more complete discussion of the bearing which this
education had on the economic development of Quebec at this
time.

   Mgr Cloutier, like his predecessor, was very alarmed by the
attempts of certain members of the Liberal party to increase the
government's control over education in Quebec. In a sermon
in 1905, he admits that the present system of education is not
perfect, but he fears that the critics are proposing reforms that
would cast the State in an exaggerated role as the ideal educator
—a role which he believes it lacks the stability to undertake.[82]
In 1912, he brands as a monstrous error the State's desire to
substitute its own for the Church's control in education by
promoting free, neutral, and obligatory education. For him,
this would be to walk in the footsteps of the French revolution
and to accept the reform fostered by the Free Masons, who were
at present in power in France. Still another reason for rejecting
the neutral school is that it would attempt to fuse the races and
would be little concerned with the future of our race, and the
maintenance of our national traditions.[83]

   On the other hand, the bishop throws his full weight behind
the improvement of education in his diocese. The level of
education, however low it still was at the turn of the century,
was already vastly superior to what it had been a few decades
earlier. School enrolment for the age bracket 5–15 years had
increased from 38 per cent in 1851 to 80 per cent in 1901, and
the duration of the average student's stay in school had increased
from less than 3 years to between 6½ and 7 years.[84] In 1900,
the teaching personnel in the region's 300 schools consisted of
about 50 priests and brothers, 150 religious sisters, 250 school
mistresses, and only 6 lay instructors. In his official report for
1896, the inspector, E. Béland, found "too large a number of
schools given to incompetent teachers," since competent teachers
were driven from the field by the excessively low salaries paid

---

[81] See *Compte rendu du premier congrès d'action sociale.* In 1914, the bishop could
rejoice at the fact that there was no longer a single license left in the rural parishes. (See
"Lettre pastorale sur l'action catholique," p. 569.)
   [82] *La Croix* (Montréal), April 15, 1905.
   [83] *Le Bien public*, February 1, 1912.
   [84] Gérard FILTEAU, "L'éducation en Mauricie, 1634-1852," *La Société canadienne de
l'Église catholique* (1951-1952), p. 77.

by the local school commissions. He also thanked the local
curés for visiting the schools with him and for seconding his
recommendations.[85]

The Church accepted the challenge of trying to keep pace
with the wave of urbanization that was taking place. Thirty
additional schools were staffed with brothers or sisters in the
period 1896–1914, with the aim of providing these communities
with cheap, stable, competent, religious educators.[86] In 1903,
the bishop introduced a French congregation of sisters, called
the "Filles de Jésus," who had recently been expelled from their
teaching occupation in France, and assigned them the task of
teaching in the local rural parish schools. He gives notice that
they are to receive a minimum wage of $100 annually, and to be
provided with heat and decent lodging; and he urges the curés
to show their people that this is an occasion for them to have
not only the best education available, but also the cheapest,
hence one more within the reach of their people.[87] By 1914,
these sisters were teaching in 15 rural communities.

We have already seen how, in the new industrial parishes,
it is usually the curé, as president of the school commission, who
manages to provide them in short order with schools meriting
the rating of "excellent." Any praise the inspectors deign to
give is usually reserved for the religious educators. Typical
is the remark of Inspector Béland in 1897—even before the
Church started her concerted drive for improvement. He
reports, "the religious bodies who teach under control [i.e.
under the School Commission] evince much zeal in the fulfillment
of their duties, and their work is always crowned with success."[88]
This was to be expected, for however poorly the brothers and
sisters were paid, the lay mistresses were usually paid less and
rarely stayed longer than a single year.[89] In 1908, Mgr Cloutier
obtained government aid for a diocesan Normal School to be
conducted by the Ursulines, and he ordered his clergy to do all

[85] "Reports of School Inspectors," *Sessional Papers*, XXX (1896), Part II, No. 5, p. 7.
[86] See G. PANNETON, *Le diocèse de Trois-Rivières*, pp. 261-62.
[87] See Mgr F.-X. CLOUTIER, "Lettre pastorale faisant connaître l'admission dans le diocèse de religieuses françaises sous le nom de 'Filles de Jésus'"; and Circular No. 31, *MLPC* (Trois-Rivières, March 25, 1903), pp. 421-28.
[88] *Sessional Papers*, XXXI (1897), Part II, No. 5, Appendix I, p. 8. Needless to say, the independent or private schools were always more successful. For example, in 1910, their average attendance was 92 per cent as compared with 77.45 per cent in other schools. About 10 per cent of the students attended these schools directed by religious. (See *Sessional Papers*, XLIII (1910), Part II, No. 8, Appendix I, p. 3.)
[89] *Sessional Papers*, XLIII (1910), Part II, No. 8, Appendix I, p. 3. Here we are told that, in 1910, the average wage for the sisters was $165, as compared with $117.50 for lay mistresses. The bishop seems to have succeeded better in protecting the former than the latter from the miserly school boards in rural areas.

in their power to encourage it and to furnish it with apt pupils so that finally the diocese would be blessed with qualified teachers.

Again, in 1913, the bishop, in an effort to push the rural school commissions to raise the salaries paid to teachers as well as to promote other educational standards, assembled a Congress of the School Commissioners at Trois-Rivières, at which all the weaknesses of the system were fully aired and firm resolutions taken to remove them.   The bishop himself presided and reminded the congress of Pope Leo XIII's directive to the Canadian bishops in 1897, in the encyclical *Affari Vos*, "It is fitting that Catholic schools be able to rival the very best in both the excellence of their methods of formation and by the brilliance of their teaching." He stated his opposition to excessive decentralization, on the grounds that too many schools meant poor schools, and urged the commissioners to pay their teachers better, to organize school libraries, to put their students on guard against the abuse of alcohol, and to reduce the length of the vacations. The mayor, in his turn, deplored how, as in other areas of French Canadian civil life, the relations between parents and school commissioners were still plagued with disgraceful and ruinous lawsuits.[90]   It seems always to have remained very difficult to raise school taxes in French Canadian communities!   Filteau, himself a school inspector, sums up the topics of this congress:

> On discuta franchement de la situation, sans farder les lacunes et les faiblesses.   On reconnut particulièrement que la grande misère était le manque de stabilité du personnel enseignant.   Les changements annuels atteignaient une proportion fantastique, surtout chez les laïques: 63% en 1911, 66% en 1912.   Ajoutons à cela l'incompétence de plusieurs titulaires, l'encombrement des classes, surtout chez les petits, les nombreuses absences des élèves, surtout dans les écoles des campagnes.   De là le peu d'efficacité de l'école: 10% des élèves seulement dépassaient le niveau du cours élémentaire.   A force de rester dans les mêmes classes, les élèves se dégoûtaient de l'école et la quittaient le plus tôt possible.   Les garçons, pour lesquels le diocèse ne comprenait que dix collèges, devaient fréquenter les écoles mixtes presque partout.   Ils abandonnaient la classe à douze ou treize ans, parfois à onze.   La communion solennelle était le signal du départ pour un grand nombre.   De tout cela, il résultait une scolarité écourtée.   En tenant compte des institutions de toute catégorie, on établissait que moins de 20% des élèves fréquentaient plus ou moins l'école après l'âge de treize ans.[91]

Filteau concludes that the congress did bear fruit, for shortly thereafter the level of salaries was raised and a new surge in school-building launched.

---

[90] *Le Bien public*, September 4, 1913.
[91] FILTEAU, *op.cit.*, p. 82.

So much for the elementary school. The institution of higher education in the region was the Séminaire de Trois-Rivières, which was at once a commercial school, a classical college, and a seminary. As far as one can determine by studying the prospectus, its organization remained unmodified throughout this period of industrial change.[92] The program provided for a 3-year "commercial" course to precede the strictly classical course. It included courses in grammar, arithmetic, letter-writing, mental arithmetic, stenography, book-keeping, English and French translations—all of which would have the advantage "de faciliter l'accès aux carrières commerciales ou industrielles" for a great number of students, who otherwise would not be able to enter on them. But it is quite clear that this is primarily a classical college; if a commercial course is taught it is done in such a way as not to hinder the more serious study of classics. In fact, one is left with the impression that if any of the graduates of the classical course later turned out to be successful businessmen or enterprising priests promoting the economic betterment of their parishes, it was surely not because of their classical education. This classical college seems, at least in its program of studies, to have remained aloof successfully from the feverish economic activity that swirled around it in Trois-Rivières during these years of progress. But of course this was not merely a local problem.

As for technical education, the Church in general was favourably disposed towards it, but looked rather to the government for initiative in this field. Mgr Cloutier, in one of his sermons, takes occasion to express his admiration for American technical schools, which, he believes, have contributed much towards making the United States the most powerful industrial nation in the world. And he praises the provincial government for its initiatives in this field.[93] *Le Bien public*, in its turn, frequently encourages workers to attend night school in order to become more competent and so earn higher wages.[94] Its editors were also very enthusiastic about the federal Royal Commission on Technical Training, and praise the efforts on the part of the industrialists, priests, and teachers who met to prepare the agenda for the Commissioners.[95] But their enthusiasm turned to disillusionment and anger a week later when

---

[92] See ASTR, *L'année académique du séminaire Saint-Joseph aux Trois-Rivières*, 1896-1897; 1913-1914.
[93] *Le Bien public*, February 1, 1912.
[94] *Ibid.*, see also, among others, the issue of October 8, 1909.
[95] *Ibid.*, February 3, 1911.

the Commissioners finally appeared. First, the witnesses had
to give testimony in English or through an interpreter "qui ne
sait pas le français." And when the Commissioners left the
field of technical education and started to ask searching questions
on how the Séminaire was run, its fees, the preparation of its
professors, etc., the editors saw in this an open breach of provincial autonomy in education, an inquisition which would merely
provide the detractors of Quebec with more ammunition. As
they write: "Ceux qui font métier de jongler avec les chiffres
et de cuisiner les statistiques auront beau jeu pour cribler de
leurs projectiles préférés les châteaux forts de 'l'obscurantisme'
ou les fenêtres closes du 'dark Quebec'."[96] Gone is their enthusiasm for aid from this Commission; they simply reject the
whole project and tell the federal government to mind its own
business.

But the editors continue to foster local initiatives in technical education, and while favourable to the new schools opened
in Montreal and Quebec by the Gouin government they do not
feel that the government has sufficiently prepared the ground for
them. They are persuaded that the French Canadians will not
spend the money to attend them.

> Ici comme ailleurs du reste, quand il s'agit d'instruction, notre
> population est assez réfractaire à l'effort; le déplacement lui répugne,
> et le surcroît de dépense, si minime soit-il, et pour le peuple surtout,
> lui est impossible. Le peu de succès de nos écoles d'agriculture le
> démontre surabondamment.[97]

They favour rather the proposal of Brother Quintal that a
technical school be opened in Trois-Rivières. It would better
prepare the people for such technical education and be of more
immediate service at the local level than the new institutions
in Quebec and Montreal. Their final solution seems to be that
the employers should be able to require such technical education
of their workers as a condition of employment, for that seems to
be the only way to get more of the people to take it.

We will come back to this problem of technical education in
the general discussion of the relationship between education and
the economic development that took place in the period 1896–
1914.

---

[96] *Le Bien public*, February 10, 1911.
[97] *Ibid.*, February 3, 1911.

CHAPTER IV

THE CHICOUTIMI-LAKE ST. JOHN REGION

"The Kingdom of the Saguenay"

A study of this area is useful not primarily because of the importance in quantitative terms either of the size of its population or of its total agricultural and manufacturing output, but rather because here we can watch land settlement, agriculture, and the beginnings of industry all taking place at the same time and in the same diocese. In the St. Maurice Valley there was really no serious possibility of promoting extensive agriculture, but here especially in the valley of the Saguenay river and of Lake St. John there was such a possibility, and so it is possible to study how this new element in the situation affects the attitude of the Church towards industrialization. Professor A.R.M. Lower, a well-known student of the settlement movement in eastern Canada, claims that in regions of Quebec where agriculture has preceded industry, the Church has not welcomed the latter too warmly. For example, he writes,

> In Quebec, notably in the Lake St. John District, the industry has invaded an area in which agricultural settlement has preceded it. It has not been welcomed too heartily by the Church, which has been loath to see a disturbing force entering its self-contained agricultural colonies and by employment under semi-urban conditions giving the habitant new and materialistic conceptions of what comprises the 'good life.' But the companies know how to make their peace with the local curés and they are consistent contributors to the upkeep of the local church.[1]

Here we find another striking difference from the St. Maurice Valley in that French Canadian initiatives in industry are numerous and some of them successful, so that the Church is involved in a quite different economic situation than in the former region where major French Canadian initiatives were striking only by their absence.

This region has an interest and a charm of its own, for no region in Quebec has been the subject of so many grandiose

---

[1] A.R.M. LOWER, *Settlement and the Forest Frontier*, Vol. IX of *Canadian Frontiers of Settlement*, ed. W.A. Mackintosh and W.L.G. Joerg, p. 133. Lower may well write with later experience in mind; our interest here is to observe the nature of the original confrontation between the pulp and paper industry and agriculture.

dreams and promises as the "Kingdom of the Saguenay," as it was named by the Indians.   This is also "the Lake St. John Country," which provided the setting for Louis Hémon's *Maria Chapdelaine.*   Hémon spent several months here, at Saint-Gédéon, Roberval, and Péribonka in 1912, and completed his novel the following year in Montreal, shortly before being killed accidentally by a train in Northern Ontario.   Hémon emphasizes the more austere side of life in the Saguenay, but there were also those at the turn of the century who considered it the future gateway to the north and foresaw the day when Chicoutimi might eclipse even the proud city of New York.

In this study of the region, we will take a rapid survey of its economic history and devote our attention particularly to the period 1896–1914 and to what were then the two more important counties of Chicoutimi and Lake St. John.   Particular attention will be paid to Roberval, the chief urban centre in the county of Lake St. John, the various pulp and paper villages and towns, and especially Chicoutimi, the cathedral town and the largest urban centre north of Quebec City.

DESCRIPTION

The Chicoutimi-Lake St. John region coincides roughly with the drainage basin of Lake St. John and the upper section of the valley of the Saguenay River.   It includes an area of about 41,000 square miles, or 7.9 per cent of the area of the province of Quebec.[2]   The basin, which was originally gouged out of the Canadian Shield by glaciers, now drains all the surrounding region into Lake St. John and forms a 400-square mile reservoir feeding the Saguenay River.   The river drops 320 feet in its first 30 miles before meeting the tide-water which gives the area access to the sea through the lower St. Lawrence. The area is heavily wooded and much of the soil on the shores of Lake St. John and in certain areas along the Saguenay is good for agriculture.   Though over a hundred miles north of Quebec City, this region has a climate only slightly more extreme, and its inconvenient remoteness from other markets and industrial areas of the province is somewhat reduced by its easy access to the sea via the Saguenay fjord and the St. Lawrence.

<hr/>

[2] For an excellent geographic study of the region, see Raoul BLANCHARD, *L'est du Canada français* (Montréal: Librairie Beauchemin, 1935), II, Part IV, 7-155. The bulk of the documentation for my own study was made available through the kind offices of la Société historique du Saguenay at Chicoutimi.   Hereafter, its archives will be referred to by the abbreviation ASHS.

Here, forming an attraction for industry, is one of the most concentrated hydraulic power potentials of the world with 3,860,600 horsepower developed in 1959, as compared with the estimated potential for the whole river basin of 698,760 horsepower in 1915. At the present time this represents almost one third of the hydro power developed in the province of Quebec and one seventh of the Canadian total.[3] However, despite the many grandiose projects rumoured, discussed, and even launched at the turn of the century to harness this mighty hydroelectric potential to furnish cheap electricity for vast projected electric railways and the reduction of carbide, as well as to provide motive power for pulp and paper mills, the dozen or so electrical stations installed in the whole area prior to World War I were nearly all quite small and used primarily for lighting rather than industrial use. Among the bigger installations was that developed by the Price Brothers Company at Murdock Falls on the Shipshaw River with a capacity of 10,000 horsepower, to furnish power for the pulp and paper industry. In 1914, the plans were completed by men capable of doing the job—Sir William Price of the Price Brothers Company and James B. Duke, the president of the American Tobacco Company—and only the intervention of the war delayed still further the day when this tremendous hydroelectric potential would be harnessed and spawn one of the largest aluminum reduction plants in the world. For the time being, the abundant waterpower was harnessed in smaller doses and used to drive the turbines of the sawmills, flour mills, and the big new pulp and paper mills.[4]

HISTORY

As early as 1672, the Jesuit missionaries among the Indians had drawn attention to the agricultural possibilities of the Lake St. John region and proved them by cultivating for their own use a corner of their mission station at Métabetchouan.[5] But the monopoly of the fur traders, first of the Northwest Company and then of the Hudson's Bay Company, succeeded in excluding settlement officially until 1842, when the latter's lease was

[3] Cf. THE ECONOMIC RESEARCH CORPORATION, *La Région Saguenay-Lac Saint-Jean,* étude économique préparée pour le Ministère de l'Industrie et du Commerce (Québec: 1961) pp. 20-21, and the *Statistical Year Book,* II (1915), 519.

[4] Cf. Rossel VIEN, *Histoire de Roberval, cœur du Lac Saint-Jean, 1855-1955,* pp. 317-18.

[5] R.G. THWAITES, *The Jesuit Relations and Allied Documents, Travels and Explorations of the Jesuit Missionaries in New France, 1610-1791,* ed. R.G. THWAITES (Cleveland: Burrows Bros., 1896-1901), Vol. LVI, p. 154, cited by R. BLANCHARD, p. 66.

renewed only on condition that it would permit agricultural settlement.[6]

However, a few years earlier a group of adventurous French Canadians from la Malbaie, in the county of Charlevoix above Quebec City, formed "la Société des Vingt-et-Un" under the leadership of Alexis Tremblay, their resolve being to penetrate the Saguenay, set up sawmills, and thus indirectly open the area to settlement. In the years 1838 and 1839, they founded eight little centres along the Saguenay fjord each provided with its own sawmill. They had raised on their own about $25,000, but were ably seconded by the English timber merchant, William Price, who was in constant contact with them and furnished them with equipment, supplies, and men, and bought up their produce.[7] He did more; in 1840 he proceeded to buy out 9 of the 21 shareholders and later, in 1842, he bought out the rest. It is not perfectly clear why these French Canadians sold out to this enterprising Englishman so quickly. They may have been in trouble due to lack of experience and hardship—they had lost many logs through booms breaking and had suffered a disastrous forest fire in 1841—yet, as Mgr Maheux notes, Price's accounts indicate that he made immediate and substantial profit on these newly acquired shares.[8] Whatever the full reasons, thereafter Price rapidly gained control of the timber industry of the entire region, and consolidated his monopoly power in 1852 on the death of Peter McLeod, a métis-Scotsman, who had earlier opened mills in the Chicoutimi area. From the government investigation on monopoly charges, it is clear that in 1849 Price personally or Price and Company owned 28 mills in

[6] BLANCHARD, p. 67.

[7] *L'Histoire du Saguenay depuis l'origine jusqu'à 1870* (Chicoutimi: la Société historique du Saguenay, 1938) pp. 181-82. See also, Mgr Arthur MAHEUX, "William Price et la Compagnie Price, 1810-1954," (unpublished manuscript, Price Brothers' Archives, Quebec, 1954), pp. 124-25.

[8] MAHEUX, p. 125. The reason given by William Price himself in his defence against a charge of monopolizing the timber industry of the Saguenay in January 1849 was their lack of technical knowledge of how to hold the booms in rough waters and their fear of the risks involved in the industry. If we can fully accept Price's sober testimony on this occasion, many of the mills he took over were by no means financial bargains (see Document No. 899, Price Brothers' Archives, cited by Mgr MAHEUX, pp. 197–218). Among others, Mgr Victor Tremblay, director of la Société historique du Saguenay, maintains that the real interest of the "Twenty-One" was not to operate sawmills but to cultivate the land, the building of sawmills being merely a pretext to gain entrance to the Saguenay. Mrs. Louise Miville-Dechène has recently formulated the hypothesis that the "Twenty-One" had never been anything other than a creation of William Price to obtain a permit to cut timber in the Saguenay and to monopolize this industry there (Mme Louis MIVILLE-DECHÈNE, "William Price, 1810-1850" [unpublished licentiate thesis at the Institut d'histoire, université Laval, 1964]). According to this interpretation, Price's design happily coincided perfectly with the French Canadians' enthusiastic desire to open this new region to settlement as quickly as possible.

the region and sold the produce of the other 24 mills which they did not own.[9] For the next half-century the "Kingdom of the Saguenay" had its "King" in William Price, and his three sons were to be his heirs. If settlers came, they came under the aegis of the timber industry. However, since before 1860 there was no sluice to enable the wood merchants to float logs over the high falls and jagged rapids at the head of the Saguenay river, the Lake St. John region was reserved primarily for agricultural settlement, a movement which was largely promoted and carried out by the Catholic clergy in an attempt to stay the mighty wave of emigration to the United States.[10]

Typical was the initiative of Abbé N.-T. Hébert, curé of the parish of Saint-Pascal-de-Kamouraska, who founded the first settlement in this new region at Hébertville, in 1849. Of him and his colonization society Blanchard writes, "Le véritable créateur du lac Saint-Jean fut la société de l'Islet-Kamouraska, et surtout celui qui en était l'âme, l'abbé F.-N. Hébert."[11] Under his supervision, between 1849 and 1851, his settlers cut a road through the wilderness from the lower Saguenay settlement at Laterrière to Lake Kénogami, and from the north end of that lake to the new settlement at Hébertville. By 1861, the new parish had about 500 members and had its own sawmill and flourmill.[12] Likewise, by 1851, another priest, Curé Boucher had with great difficulty founded another settlement some distance above Hébertville at the mouth of the Belle-Rivière and had already cleared 60 acres.[13] Thereafter, settlement was more rapid and the timber industry entered the region once a sluice had been constructed at the head of the Saguenay river to enable the logs to be floated down over the falls and rapids undamaged to the sawmills farther downstream. By 1896, 15 parishes were established in the Lake St. John region besides many small mission outposts, and in the Chicoutimi or Saguenay River district there were 10 parishes, not counting the smaller mission outposts. Later, the history of a few of them will be given to provide some general idea of how they developed.

From the point of view of ecclesiastical jurisdiction, this whole region belonged to the diocese of Chicoutimi, which was constituted in May 1878, with its bishopric in the town of Chi-

---

[9] MAHEUX, pp. 197-218.

[10] BLANCHARD, *L'est du Canada français*, p. 76.

[11] *Ibid.*, p. 74.

[12] Abbé F. PILOTE, *Le Saguenay en 1851: Histoire du passé, du présent et de l'avenir probable du haut Saguenay au point de vue de la colonisation.* (Québec: A. Côté, 1852), pp. 88-93; cited by BLANCHARD, pp. 74-75.

[13] BLANCHARD, p. 74.

TABLE V

Percentage Increases of Population over the Decade by Region and County; and Percentage of Population that is Urban and Rural*

Year	Region		Chicoutimi County				Lake St. John County			
	Population	Increase over decade	Population	Increase over decade	Urban	Rural	Population	Increase over decade	Urban	Rural
1844	1,590					100				100
1851	5,364	237	5,214	228		100	150			100
1861	10,478	95	8,955	72		100	1,523	913		100
1871	17,493	65	11,812	33	12	88	5,681	273		100
1881	23,530	26	13,801	17	17	83	9,729	71		100
1891	28,726	22	14,244	3	20	80	14,048	44	10	90
1901	37,028	30	16,872	18	38	62	20,156	43	11	89
1911	50,486	36	23,375	40	48	52	27,111	35	18	82
1921	73,117	44	35,578	60	62	38	35,539	31	25	75

* Claire M. Johnston, "The Historical Geography of the Saguenay Valley" (unpublished Master's dissertation, McGill University, Montreal, 1950), p. 75, based on the decennial census estimates.

coutimi. Besides the parishes mentioned earlier, the diocese contained six small parishes on the north shore of the St. Lawrence above the mouth of the Saguenay fjord and twelve older parishes in the county of Charlevoix on the St. Lawrence below the Saguenay basin.[14] The parish statistics indicate that the six parishes above the Saguenay doubled their Catholic population from 2,645 to 5,165, in the period 1897–1914; but that of Charlevoix, in spite of some gains in industry especially in lumber and dairy industries, increased in the same period by only 2,833, from 17,944 to 20,777, and five of its twelve parishes suffered a decrease in population.[15] In fact, many of the new settlers in the Chicoutimi-Lake St. John region came from Charlevoix. Though part of the diocese of Chicoutimi, these 18 parishes on the shores of the St. Lawrence do not properly belong to Chicoutimi-Lake St. John region and here they will therefore be given only incidental attention.

In 1890, the Saguenay river basin was divided into the counties of Chicoutimi—the region along the Saguenay river—and of Lake St. John—the region around Lake St. John. The former, as we saw, was populated largely under the aegis of the timber industry, but the latter was populated initially as an independent agricultural area. Hence it is not surprising to find the population movements in Chicoutimi county patterned on the booms and crises in the timber industry while the county of Lake St. John largely escapes this influence. Claire M. Johnston provides a clear picture of the population movements in both regions for the period 1844–1921, which is reproduced in Table V. It will receive closer attention later.

It should always be borne in mind that here we are dealing with an essentially Catholic population. The parish census of 1914 estimates the Catholic population of the diocese at 74,200, and the Protestant population at 100 (see Table V).

COMMUNICATIONS

In the early days, settlers and timber alike were transported by water. A steamer service was provided to Grande-Baie in 1849, and to Chicoutimi in 1869. In 1879, the river channel was dredged to permit steamers to come into Chicoutimi at low tide. The number of such steamer voyages increased from 2 in 1840 to 84 in 1870, but so long as ice gripped the Saguenay fjord

[14] *Canada ecclésiastique*, 1897, pp. 48–50.
[15] *Ibid.*, and 1914, pp. 117–28.

during the winter months all navigation was inevitably interrupt-ed.[16] Travelling overland was still more inconvenient. By 1850, two wagon roads had been cut through the forest from Grande-Baie to the county of Charlevoix to provide access to the outside world during the winter months. Of the roads in the interior Abbé Hébert's "Kénogami road" long remained the most important. Finally, in 1887, the provincial government opened a 140-mile road joining Lake St. John to Quebec City.[17] But these roads, although passable in winter, remained impass-able in spring, and passable only with difficulty even in mid-summer. The usually enthusiastic journalist, Arthur Buies, when visiting the region in 1880, wrote of the new government road to Lake St. John, "il est simplement passable; l'hiver, on met entre trois et quatre jours à le parcourir d'une extrémité à l'autre (140 milles, 225 km.); mais il se passera encore quelque temps avant qu'on puisse l'utiliser pendant la belle saison."[18] In 1894, a bridge was at long last built over the Grande-Décharge at the mouth of Lake St. John to permit easy access to the north shore of the lake and the Saguenay River. But it was quite evident that without a railway the region had little economic future, for people here were either too far from or entirely cut off from the industrial and agricultural markets of the province.

As early as 1854, a company had been formed to undertake the task of building a railway, but nothing came of it. For lack of capital, an American entrepreneur was engaged in 1871 to build a railway with wooden rails from Quebec City, but the project was abandoned after it had reached Gosford, about 26 miles from Quebec City, because it quickly became clear that only iron or steel rails could stand up to the extremes of the Quebec winter.[19] Later, in 1874, the Quebec-Lake St. John Railway Company was incorporated. Work finally got under-way in 1880, and the first train arrived at the Chambord junction in 1888, and a few months later at Roberval on Lake St. John. The branch line from Chambord to Chicoutimi was inaugurated in the summer of 1893. In 1908, Chicoutimi was connected with the closest deepwater seaport on Ha Ha Bay. Other branches were added later, but they were not as essential to the district. The arrival of the railway inaugurated a new era of progress for these regions.[20]

---

[16] *L'Histoire du Saguenay depuis l'origine jusqu'à 1870*, pp. 299-300.
[17] R. BLANCHARD, *L'est du Canada français*, pp. 85-86.
[18] A. BUIES, *Le Saguenay et le bassin du Lac Saint-Jean*, p. 287.
[19] R. VIEN, *Histoire de Roberval*, p. 108.
[20] *Ibid.*, pp. 155ff.

Politicians, businessmen, and churchmen all had their role in the coming of the railroads, the latter, like others, using their powerful influence with the first two groups. Two names especially stand out at the achieving end of this long sought project, the Scot, James B. Guthrie Scott, the secretary of the Quebec-Lake St. John Railway Company, and the enterprising American engineer, Horace Jansen Beemer of Philadelphia, whose aim in completing the project was to open Lake St. John to tourism as well as industry. But behind these men were those who fought day after day for the government and municipal subsidies without which the railway would never have been built, as is clear from the fact that work stopped each time the subsidies ran out.[21] All the evidence points to the fact that the clergy engaged their full influence, bargaining power, and enthusiasm in each new railway project—sometimes, undoubtedly, in a paralysingly parochial spirit to win for their own parishes benefits that would probably have otherwise gone elsewhere, but more often for projects that benefited the whole region or diocese. And the bishop's or the curé's enthusiasm for a railway was always very contagious. I cite only a few of the better documented examples. During the years when the local people were agitating for a railway the curés often took far-reaching initiatives. In 1873, we find the curés of the five villages of Roberval, Chambord, Saint-Prime, Saint-Jérôme, and Hébert-ville strongly endorsing a series of articles written by J.-C. Langelier which first appeared in the newspaper *le Canadien* and were later reproduced in pamphlet form. The purpose of these articles was to promote the new railway and "faire disparaître la mauvaise impression que l'insuccès de la compagnie du chemin de fer de Québec et Gosford a laissée dans l'esprit des personnes qui s'intéressent à la colonisation de la vallée du Lac Saint-Jean."[22] In fact, even so ardent a promoter of farm settlement in the region as the Oblate, Father Lacasse, directed prospective settlers not to consider the valley until there was a railroad:

> Je vous conseille... de ne pas vous établir au Lac-Saint-Jean avant d'avoir reçu l'assurance qu'un chemin de fer y sera construit, à moins toutefois que vous ayez assez d'épargnes pour faire face à tous les imprévus. Dans l'état actuel des choses, celui qui s'endette au Lac-Saint-Jean signe un contrat de départ pour la terre étrangère. *Il n'y a pas de marché*, par conséquent, pas d'argent.[23]

---

[21] *Ibid.*

[22] *Ibid.* p. 110. Vien cites the author without giving a complete reference.

[23] Le Père LACASSE, O.M.I., *Une mine produisant l'or et l'argent*, p. 156. He refers here to the necessity of going to the United States to earn money to pay one's debts.

In 1885, we find Curé Lizotte of Roberval along with the surveyor, Horace Dumais, and Euloge Ménard undertaking a sensational trip by canoe and foot over the projected route of the new railway to meet the directors of the railway company at the other end and assure them of the feasibility of their project.[24] Curé Lizotte was the known champion of Roberval as the terminus of the railway, and we find his name again and again at the head of lists of delegations to the provincial government, rubbing shoulders with Premier Mercier at Roberval on special occasions, and organizing excursions and briefings for journalists visiting the region in 1887 in order to promote the completion of the railway.[25]

But more significant than these initiatives undertaken by the curés usually at the parish level were the direct interventions of the successive bishops of Chicoutimi: Mgr D. Racine, who was named first bishop of Chicoutimi in May 1878; Mgr L.-N. Bégin, who succeeded him in October 1888; and Mgr M.-T. Labrecque, who became bishop in April 1892, when Mgr Bégin was named auxiliary bishop of the archdiocese of Quebec.

Initially, Mgr Racine advocated strenuously the construction of a railway with its terminus in the "lower Saguenay." If the choice had to be between Roberval and Métabetchouan, he favoured the latter on the grounds that it was closer to Chicoutimi. And when it was decided to make a junction at Chambord with one line running north to Lake St. John and a second line south to Chicoutimi, he used all his influence at Ottawa and Quebec to have the Chicoutimi line constructed first. However, once Premier Mercier decided that Roberval would have its railway first, and invited the people of the region to take full part in a provincial fair at Quebec, in September 1887, to acquaint the province with its produce and so strengthen the Premier's hand, Mgr Racine enthusiastically wrote a special pastoral letter urging his people not to miss this opportunity to prove they merited government subsidies for their railway.[26] The result was that some 270 farmers, accompanied by their curés, the more brilliant students of the Ursuline Convent School, their choice farm animals and produce, and even a race horse, arrived in Quebec City in September to convince the province once and for all of the existence of the "Kingdom of the Saguenay."

[24] R. VIEN, *Histoire de Roberval*, p. 113.
[25] *Ibid.*, pp. 116-18.
[26] *Ibid.*, p. 118.

But in those days it was far easier to dream and talk of a new railroad through the Laurentians than to build one, as Vien and Hémon graphically remind us. Vien describes the rugged life and hardships of the workers.

> L'exploration, le défrichement, le déblayage, le minage, le transport et la pose de l'acier, tous les travaux et la lutte que représentait la construction d'une voie de 190 milles, de Québec à Roberval, à travers la rugueuse nature des Laurentides, créèrent une épopée, rappelant *l'épopée du rail* de l'Ouest. Les travailleurs étaient soumis à un régime d'esclaves. L'armée qui s'avança dans les bois durant cinq ans vivait de lard, de farine et de patates, couchait dans des huttes provisoires ou sous des tentes, en toute saison, et obéissait tant bien que mal aux consignes sévères édictées par les chefs de l'entreprise. Conformément au triste cliché, des étrangers occupaient les postes de commande tandis que les Canadiens français formaient le plus grand nombre des hommes de peine, parmi lesquels se trouvaient aussi des individus d'autres nationalités. Beemer avait favorisé d'abord les siens, Américains compétents et précis, dont les procédés étaient clairs, sinon courtois. Les boissons enivrantes étaient strictement interdites aux ouvriers. Ceux-ci touchaient une piastre par jour, en général. On raconte que si quelqu'un se faisait tuer par accident, chaque travailleur fournissait $0.50 à la veuve.[27]

Edwige Légaré, one of Hémon's characters in his *Maria Chapdelaine*, recalls his own experience of these hardships vividly,

> Thirty years ago, when the railway from Quebec was built, I was there; that was something like hardship, I can tell you! I was only sixteen years of age but I chopped with the rest of them to clear the right of way, always twenty-five miles ahead of the steel, and for fourteen months I never clapped eye on a house. We had no tents, summer or winter, only shelters of boughs that we made for ourselves, and from morning till night it was chop, chop, chop,—eaten by the flies, and in the course of the same day soaked with rain and roasted by the sun.
>
> Every Monday morning they opened a sack of flour and we made ourselves a bucketful of pancakes, and all the rest of the week three times a day, one dug into that pail for something to eat. By Wednesday, no longer any pancakes, because they were all stuck together; nothing there but a mass of dough. One cut off a big chunk of dough with one's knife, put that in his belly, and then chopped and chopped again!
>
> When we got to Chicoutimi where provisions could reach us by water we were worse off than Indians, pretty nearly naked, all scratched and torn, and I well remember some who began to cry when told they could go home, because they thought they would find all their people dead, so long had the time seemed to them. Hardship! That was hardship if you like.[28]

---

[27] *Ibid.*, p. 114.
[28] Louis HÉMON, *Maria Chapdelaine: A Tale of the Lake St. John Country*, pp. 83-84.

But Beemer finally led his weary army triumphantly into Roberval just as the first snow began to fly in 1888.   Lake St. John had finally been put on the map!   Needless to add, when the first train arrived at Roberval the following year, the new bishop, Mgr Bégin, along with all the celebrities of the Church, the State, and the railway company were on hand for the public blessing and celebration, for now at long last the reputed "Granary of the Province" had an outlet to the province's markets. The stimulus to settlement and development was immediately felt.   *Le Progrès du Saguenay* of Chicoutimi reported on December 6 that in a single month the population of the town almost doubled.

It is not without interest to see in more detail how the bishops went about exercising their influence to promote railway construction in the region.   The normal pattern seems to have been that the secretary of the railway company, the Scotch Protestant, J.G. Scott, kept the bishops fully briefed on all the projects and progress of his company and suggested to them when and from whom to demand subsidies for the region's railways.[29]   For example, we find Scott writing to Mgr Racine in May 1887, recalling the company's promise to him to construct the railway as far as the Métabetchouan at the same time as the line to Roberval and asking him to "bien prêter le concours de votre influence à Ottawa."[30]   Scott, it seems, had good reason to believe in the weightiness of Mgr Racine's intervention with the federal politicians, for the previous year we find the Canadian Prime Minister, John A. Macdonald, writing to the bishop promising him that the government will give a grant to the projected railway: "I write you this information in consequence of the great earnestness with which you have pressed this enterprise so important to the part of the country where you reside and preside."[31]

Once the railway to Lake St. John was completed in 1888, the new bishop, Mgr Bégin, took up the cause of his predecessor and frequented Ottawa and Quebec with equal zeal in the interest of the railway company and his own people.   At the suggestion of Scott, he turned his attention successively to the federal, to

[29] A whole collection of this correspondence is to be found in the Episcopal Archives of Chicoutimi under the title "Chemins de fer."   Most of this correspondence dates from the period 1885–1902, and thus involves all three of the bishops mentioned.   Hereafter these archives will be referred to by the abbreviation EAC with an indication of the reference number or date found on these documents.

[30] Letter from J.G. SCOTT, Secrétaire de la Cie du Chemin de Fer de Québec et du Lac Saint-Jean, May 30, 1887, EAC, 3-191-7.

[31] Letter from John A. MACDONALD, Prime Minister, to Mgr Racine, July 2, 1886, EAC, 3-191-4-14.

the provincial, and to the local political leaders; in fact few influential politicians seem to have escaped his pleas for subsidies for the construction of the railroad to Chicoutimi and beyond to Ha Ha Bay, the nearest deepwater harbour.[32]   In February 1889, he assures the local mayor and town councillors that he fully supports their plan to send a delegation to Ottawa.

> Je suis bien sûr... que si nous restons tranquillement chez nous, les Ministres et les députés resteront tranquillement chez eux, bien contents de voir que nous n'avons besoin de rien et que nous les laissons en paix.[33]

And he precedes this delegation to Ottawa by personal letters to certain powerful members of the federal Cabinet to assure that the local delegation will be well received.   For example, to the Minister of Public Works, the Honourable Sir Hector Langevin, he writes, in part,

> Aussi longtemps que durera l'isolement dans lequel se trouve ma patrie d'adoption, tant qu'elle n'aura pas, en toutes les saisons de l'année, des communications faciles avec le reste du monde, sa prospérité matérielle ne pourra être que fort restreinte; l'activité de nos braves colons, leur énergie bien connue et la richesse du sol ne suffiront pas à répandre ici cette aisance générale qu'on admire en tant d'autres localités.   Il faut un chemin de fer qui nous relie avec les grands centres commerciaux et qui nous permette d'écouler ailleurs les abondants produits agricoles de notre Saguenay...[34]

And a few months later he turns his attention to the Premier of the province, the Honourable Honoré Mercier, and urges on him the same arguments, reminding him too of his promise to the Chicoutimi delegation that he would do something for them if the federal government first did its share.   Now the latter has voted a subsidy for 20 additional miles and he has a formal assurance that it will do still more the following year.[35]   Mercier replies to the bishop, "J'ai le plaisir de vous informer que vos espérances sont enfin réalisées," and promises to ask the legislature for the necessary subsidies.[36]

Little wonder then that when the railway was inaugurated at Chicoutimi, in August 1893, the formal invitation sent out

---

[32] Even industrialists did not escape his web. For example, in 1890, we find Evan John Price assuring the bishop that he will do all he can in Ottawa to secure the necessary subsidies (see letter from E.J. PRICE to Mgr Bégin, February, 1890, EAC 3-191-5-15).

[33] Copy of the letter sent by Mgr BÉGIN to the Mayor and Town Councillors of Chicoutimi, February 2, 1889, EAC 3-191-5-4.

[34] Copy of the letter sent by Mgr BÉGIN to the Honourable Sir Hector Langevin, Minister of Public Works, February 14, 1889, EAC 3-191-5-5.

[35] Copy of the letter from Mgr BÉGIN to the Honourable Honoré Mercier, Premier of Quebec, September 7, 1889, EAC, 3-191-5-3.

[36] Letter from the Honourable Honoré MERCIER, Premier of Quebec, to Mgr Bégin, May 26, 1890, EAC, 3-191-4-23.

by the railway company invited the visitors to assist at the joint blessing of the new railway and of the Cathedral's new bells. It had indeed been a combined effort of railway builders, politicians, and Churchmen!

Mgr Labrecque continued in the same tradition but apparently with less vigour now that the essential railways were in place; no doubt, this relaxation was also because the governments were becoming less generous with such subsidies, and the bishop was not particularly known for his warm sentiments towards the new Liberal governments which dominated the scene after 1896.   Nevertheless, we find him, in 1895, seeking further subsidies for the new railway which was at that time in financial difficulty,[37] and in 1902 writing enthusiastically to the Liberal Prime Minister, Sir Wilfrid Laurier, to urge him to support the project of the Trans-Canada railway, which would have "une immense influence, notamment sur le développement du Nord de la Province de Québec et des autres provinces."[38] Laurier's reply seems to lack the warmth of sentiment of those of his predecessors, but, nevertheless, he assures the bishop that his representations "recevront en temps et lieux toute la considération qui est due à votre autorité."[39]   Thereafter, there is no written evidence of the bishop's direct hand in promoting railways at this top level, but the local curés carry on as usual. For example, it is the name of Curé Henri Cimon of Saint-Alphonse on Ha Ha Bay which appears at every turn in the promotion of the railway to this deepwater seaport. With the approval of the bishop, he leases some of his parish's land to the Compagnie Générale du Port de Chicoutimi and gives it first right of purchase, but on express condition that the company agrees to load its ships at the new port.[40]   In 1904, he enlists the support of the federal representative, Joseph Girard, and his name appears first on the list of those who worked for a subsidy from the provincial government in 1908.[41]   Nevertheless, the bishop himself is on hand for the solemn blessing of the new Ha Ha Bay railway, in December 1910, and takes

[37] Copy of the letter from Mgr LABRECQUE to the Honourable Mackenzie Bowell, Prime Minister of Canada, December 6, 1895, EAC, 3-191-5-7.

[38] Copy of the letter from Mgr LABRECQUE to Sir Wilfrid Laurier, Prime Minister of Canada, March 10, 1902, EAC.

[39] Letter from Sir Wilfrid LAURIER, Prime Minister of Canada, to Mgr Labrecque, March 17, 1902, EAS, 3-191-5-9.

[40] Damase POTVIN, *La Baie des Hahas* (Beauceville: La chambre de commerce de la Baie des Hahas, 1957), p. 184.   He also discusses Curé Cimon's role in promoting the new railroad.

[41] Letter of Curé H. CIMON to Joseph Girard, January 12, 1904, Document No. 356, ASHS; *Le Soleil* (Québec), May 29, 1926.

occasion to praise this project as an example of how parishes should work together for the progress of the whole region. For him, there is genuine progress and prosperity for a region when harmony of spirits and abundance of capital work together, and he elicits the hope that soon another railway will pass north and east of Lake St. John to bring prosperity and new settlers to that region whose development is still hampered by lack of an adequate system of communications.[42]

There are many other examples,[43] but these are sufficient to show how keenly aware the clergy were of the need to provide the settlers with better access to markets if the new settlements were to prosper. In this whole history of railroad building in the region one need only scratch the surface of the available documentation to find the name of a curé or even a bishop who was deeply involved—and the same is true of other forms of communication and transportation, especially of road building.

NEW SETTLEMENT

We have already seen how the leadership of the clergy was almost synonymous with agricultural settlement in the region, and even if in some areas settlers came in under the aegis of the timber industry, nevertheless, it usually fell to the clergy to sustain and encourage them. And this continued to be the pattern even later when less heroic courage and endurance were required of the new settler who now arrived by train. In the period 1888–1914, after the arrival of the railway, twenty new parishes were founded, five of them being primarily industrial parishes and the others agricultural.[44] The type of initiative that might be undertaken by a curé at this time is well illustrated by that of Curé Lizotte of Roberval in the founding of the parish of Sainte-Hedwidge. The early history of this mission is recorded in a *Notebook* kept by the curé in the parish archives. It runs as follows, from the first clearings in 1887 and then the first settlings, until a bridge in 1899 gave communication with Roberval:

---

[42] *Le Progrès du Saguenay*, December 15, 1910.

[43] Two other important railway apostles were Mgr Calixte Marquis and Mgr Eugène Lapointe. The former made continual efforts to get Scott to continue the railway around Lake St. John (see "Papiers Marquis," Archives of the Séminaire de Nicolet, cited by J.-E. Laforce, "Mgr Calixte Marquis, Colonisateur," *Rapports de la Société canadienne d'histoire de l'Église catholique* [1943-1944], p. 131). Mgr Lapointe lent great encouragement to Alfred Dubuc in his project to build a railway around Lake St. John and to Sir Rodolphe Forget in his project to build a railway from Quebec to Tadoussac and eventually to Labrador (see, for example, letter from Mgr E. Lapointe to J.-E.-A. Dubuc, January 3, 1915, and Mgr E. Lapointe, "Recueil de souvenirs," p. 35, Archives of the Séminaire de Chicoutimi. Hereafter, these archives will be cited by their initial letters ASC).

[44] *Canada ecclésiastique*, 1914, pp. 117-28.

> Les premiers défrichements furent faits vers 1887, par Mr. J.-J.
> Guértin, ... maintenant [1900] banquier à Willow City, Dakota du
> Nord... le succès ne couronna pas les essais de Mr. Guértin, à
> cause du manque de chemin et de route, et Mr. Guértin vendit
> ses lots.
>
> Une couple d'années plus tard, ayant réussi à obtenir quel-
> qu'argent pour faire ouvrir la route actuelle jusqu'au fronteau entre
> les 5ième et 6ième Rang, je sollicitai et obtins l'octroi d'un demi lot
> en faveur de la future mission, et M. le Grand-Vicar Leclerc alors
> curé de Notre Dame d'Hébert-ville, fut chargé par feu Mgr D.
> Racine, alors Évêque de Chicoutimi, de se fixer le site de la future
> paroisse. Il donna à la future mission le nom de Ste-Hedwidge,
> en souvenir de la fête de Ste-Hedwidge que nous célébrions ce jour-là
> (17 octobre) (qui ne comptait pas encore une âme).
>
> Plusieurs avaient pris des terres dans les deux Rangs (5 & 6);
> quelques ouvrages avaient été faits. Mais la difficulté était de
> décider quelqu'un à y établir domicile. J'avais acheté un lot, à
> côté de celui de la chapelle: je l'offrais gratuitement à un pauvre
> homme vivotant du travail de sa journée, tout en élevant une nom-
> breuse famille, et je lui donnai le grain de la première semence, et
> du pain pour lui faire attendre sa première récolte; il accepta, et
> alla bâtir son log-house dans le printemps de 1892 sur le Lot 12
> du 6ième Rang de Roberval: c'était le premier colon: il s'appelle
> *Jean Baptiste St. Pierre*, et il est devenu un cultivateur à l'aise,
> et a récolté l'an dernier près de 300 minots de grain...
>
> Un pont était nécessaire pour mettre ce canton en communica-
> tion avec celui de Roberval: je sollicitai et obtins sa construction
> qui fut faite dans l'automne de 1899.

He concludes his story proudly by noting that in 1900 there
were 187 parishioners.[45]

In 1889, Mgr Calixte Marquis was named colonization
agent for the Lake St. John region by Mgr Labelle, the deputy
minister of agriculture, on a government salary. The description of the task assigned him by the local bishop, Mgr Bégin,
although perhaps overstated by his enthusiastic biographer,
Ernest Laforce, is still substantially correct in that Mgr Marquis
did take initiatives in all the areas mentioned:

> Mgr Bégin le charge de s'occuper de la construction d'un chemin
> de fer, d'un monastère, d'une école d'agriculture, de combler les
> vides dans les paroisses récemment ouvertes... et d'en fonder de
> nouvelles.[46]

However, Marquis' chief success seems to have been finally
to have persuaded—with the aid of the persuasive powers of

---

[45] ASHS, Dossier 187, copy of this notebook of the mission of Saint-Hedwidge, pp. 1–3.
Lizotte's successor, Curé Joseph-G. Paradis, adds a sour note a few months later to show
that all was still not easy. "Nous avons constaté avec chagrin que les patates et le sarrasin
ont été détruits par la gelée du 12 au 13 courant. Gens découragés." The month referred
to was July.
[46] E.-J. LAFORCE, "Mgr Calixte Marquis, Colonisateur," p. 131.

Premier Mercier and a grant of 6,000 acres of land—the Trappists to open a monastery in the wilderness to the north of Lake St. John at Mistassini to promote rapid settlement and good agriculture in this area by their successful example.   Mgr Labrecque welcomed the French monks into his diocese by issuing a special pastoral letter, in which he writes in part:

> C'est avec raison que la fondation d'un monastère de Trappistes est accueillie avec joie par le clergé, le peuple et son premier Pasteur, car elle répond aux besoins particuliers de notre diocèse, d'un diocèse dont l'avenir repose sur le progrès de l'agriculture et de la colonisation.[47]

It is evident from the testimony of the Trappist Abbot Father Pacome before the Colonization Commission, in 1904, that the beginnings of settlement in the region of Mistassini were extremely difficult for the monks.   He claims that they had been "trop bons" to the new settlers, who rapidly became indebted to them and seldom if ever paid them back and often finished by abandoning their land.   Their Mother House at Oka had to advance them between $30,000 and $40,000, and the monks had to beg besides to cover their expenses.   The waterfall granted to them by the government to indemnify their construction and operation of a flourmill for the settlers seldom provided sufficient waterpower for its task.   In fact, they had thought of leaving, but neither the Mother House nor the bishop would allow it.   However, all is not black in Father Pacome's report, for in 1903 the monks had harvested 17,000 bundles of hay and 1,100 minots of grain and had been able to pay their labour at $1.25 a day.   A second Trappist, in his turn, insists that, in spite of some claims to the contrary, if the Trappists had not come here in the first place, there would have been no colonization, and further that the moment the Trappists leave, all the settlers will also go away.[48]

For all their troubles the Trappists did succeed in opening up their area to colonization.   By 1914, the parish of Mistassini had 775 parishioners all anxiously awaiting the construction of a railway around the north shore of Lake St. John to bring them finally closer to a market.   Among the many extravagantly

[47] Mgr M.-T. LABRECQUE, "Lettre pastorale annonçant l'établissement du monastère de Notre-Dame de la Trappe de Mistassini, Lac Saint-Jean," *MLPC* (Chicoutimi, November 21, 1892), p. 52.

[48] The Colonisation Commission, *Report*, Annex, *Enquête au Lac Saint-Jean*, pp. 115-17. It might be added that in 1897, the Trappists after only five years in the region won 13 out of a total of 24 prizes at the exposition at Chicoutimi, and 7 out of a total of 14 prizes at the provincial exposition at Quebec City (J.-C. CHAPAIS, "Religion, agriculture, colonisation." *Courrier du Canada*, December 23, 1898, reprinted in *Rapport du congrès de la colonisation tenu à Montréal les 22-24 novembre 1898*, p. 244).

laudatory reports on the solid work accomplished by the monks
for settlement and agriculture in this area, an editorial in *le
Progrès du Saguenay* of March 2, 1911, is especially interesting
for its detail about the agricultural methods of the monks:

> Avec un invincible courage ils s'établissaient en pleine forêt-vierge,
> dans un endroit où tout, par conséquent, était à créer, et où tout
> était rendu plus difficile par les difficultés de communications.   Aussi
> les débuts furent-ils un peu lents et bien pénibles.   Mais ces hommes
> de sacrifice s'étaient mis à l'œuvre et ils se sont montrés à la hauteur
> de la tâche.   Tout en défrichant la terre, ils élevaient les construc-
> tions nécessaires, granges et étables, moulin, forge, scieries, etc.
>   Ils ne négligèrent pas l'agriculture.   L'intention du gouverne-
> ment, appelant les Trappistes au Lac Saint-Jean, n'avait nullement
> été de les placer sur les terres les plus fertiles, et l'emplacement
> choisi ne l'exposait pas à recevoir ce reproche des futurs colons.
> Mais ces habiles agronomes 'se rendent maîtres du sol partout où
> ils s'établissent', a dit Mgr notre évêque, ... et sa prophétie s'est
> réalisée.   Par un travail énergique et soutenu, grâce à une culture
> rationnelle, les Révérends Pères ont réussi à améliorer un sol assez
> pauvre et à en tirer des récoltes qui font l'admiration des colons
> établis partout sur les excellentes terres avoisinantes.   Ils continuent
> à travailler à l'amélioration du sol par l'établissement d'un bon
> système de rotation, par des sélections, et des importations de grains
> de semence, etc.
>   Ce qui n'a pas peu contribué à la prompte occupation des lots
> voisins et au rapide succès des colons, c'est l'encouragement donné
> par les RR. PP. Trappistes à l'industrie laitière.   Ils ont établi
> chez eux une beurrerie et une fromagerie et ont donné tout le soin
> possible à l'amélioration des vaches laitières, ne reculant pas devant
> les frais énormes pour se procurer des animaux de race pure; et, de
> fait, ils ont aujourd'hui un excellent troupeau.
>   Il nous faut passer sous silence... nombre de grands travaux
> d'utilité publique, accomplis par ces moines, tels que construction
> de quais, ouverture de chemins, établissement de lignes télépho-
> niques, etc.
>   Depuis 18 ans les RR. PP. Trappistes se sont dévoués, sans
> compter, à leur grande œuvre.   Ils ont été tout à la fois bûcherons
> et agronomes, curés et médecins, notaires et agents de colonisation.
> Ils ont été surtout la Providence des colons qui venaient s'établir
> autour d'eux et qu'ils ont soutenus à leurs dépens.   Qui dira jamais
> tout ce qu'ils ont donné, les avances qu'ils ont faites, les familles
> qu'ils ont secourues, sans espoir de retour!

Still another very important initiative undertaken by the
Church at the turn of the century as an encouragement to new
settlement was to promote the founding and to become part of
"La Société de Repatriement et de Colonisation du Lac Saint-
Jean" a joint venture sponsored by the Quebec-Lake St. John
Railway and the Church and seconded by certain government
grants.   The purpose was to people the area, especially with

French Canadians brought back from the United States, and to promote industry in order to increase the freight on the new railway. Railway and Church had a common interest, for the railway company was thereby assuring its future prosperity and the Church was re-establishing French Canadian Catholics on their native soil.

In October 1889 the railway company had sought the clergy's support of its own efforts to settle the region more quickly by sending a circular to all the priests of the province asking them to send two delegates to examine the land at Lake St. John and report to their respective parishes.[49] Later, the new colonization society was founded under the patronage of the Lieutenant Governor of Quebec and the honorary presidency of the Honourable J.-I. Tarte, Minister of Public Works of Canada, the Abbot of the Trappists, and Mr. Frank Ross, President of the Quebec and Lake St. John Railway. It did good work. In fact, it was one of the few such societies to be wholeheartly endorsed and praised by the Colonization Commission of 1904.[50] From the annual reports of the society, it is clear that the more usual method of recruiting settlers was for the curés of the older parishes to come to visit the region at the railway's expense and then to return to encourage the more needy of their parishioners to settle in these new parishes; often the curés would later return to see how their former parishioners were succeeding. The propaganda literature of the society praises not only the fertile soil and the successful farmers of the region, but also the new pulp industry, which now provides another source of revenue for the settlers.[51]

Over the period 1897–1905, the society directed 17,523 settlers into the region.[52] Almost half of them were French Canadians returning from the United States, several hundred were Europeans, especially Belgians and Frenchmen, and the rest were Canadians, mostly from the province of Quebec.[53] As the president of the Society admits, many did not stay. Some, like M. Guértin at Sainte-Hedwidge, were quickly dis-

---

[49] Letter of J.-G. SCOTT, Secrétaire de la Cie du Chemin de Fer de Québec et du Lac Saint-Jean, to Mgr Bégin, October 10, 1889, EAC, 3-191-1-27.

[50] *Report*, pp. 49, 64.

[51] See, for example, La Société de Repatriement et de Colonisation du Lac Saint-Jean, *Rapports annuels*, 1899, 1901,1902, 1905; available in ASHS.

[52] Letter of Jules TESSIER, Président de La Société de Repatriement et de Colonisation du Lac Saint-Jean, to *le Progrès du Saguenay*, September 13, 1906. The federal government had granted the society subsidies amounting to $18,000, and the provincial government had subsidized it only to the amount of $4,000.

[53] *Rapports annuels*. For example, in 1903, of 2,891 settlers registered, 1,129 came from United States; 1,171 from Quebec; 190 were Finns; 142 French; and 72 Belgians.

couraged; many, unlike Hémon's Maria Chapdelaine, could not resist the temptation to seek an easier, more comfortable life in New England's textile towns—for the words put by Hémon in the mouth of Éphrem Surprenant to comfort the emigrant Parisians of Péribonka, "It is rough here, rough and hard!" were often literally true.[54]   Besides, this region was like others plagued with "bogus" settlers—often seconded by the operators of sawmills and other wood merchants—who came in to make a quick profit by cutting the timber on their lots with no intention of settling.[55]   For these several reasons there was a considerable turnover of settlers and it is not surprising that Brother E.C. Stackler of the Orphelinat Agricole de Vauvert reports that in his travels, in 1914, he saw an average of one out of four farms abandoned.[56]

Blanchard has discounted the importance of immigration into this region except for the directors and personnel of the new industry, on the grounds that natural increase alone accounted for about 30 per cent growth in the population per decade.[57] The percentage increases in population per decade for the counties of Chicoutimi and Lake St. John are indicated in Table VI.

TABLE VI

Percentage Increases in Population per Decade in Each County*

Decade	Chicoutimi County	Lake St. John County
1871–1881	17	71
1881–1891	3	44
1891–1901	18	43
1901–1911	40	35
1911–1921	61	31

* Taken from Table V above.

[54] Louis HÉMON, *Maria Chapdelaine*, p. 192.
[55] The Colonization Commission, *Report*, p. 60, where reference is made to the fact that the colonization society of Lake St. John had been asking for the cancellation of the licenses of hundred of such "bogus" settlers at a time.
[56] *Le Progrès du Saguenay*, March 19, 1914.
[57] R. BLANCHARD, *L'est du Canada français*, p. 148.

When the logging industry fell into a depression in the 1870's, there was much emigration from the region, especially from Chicoutimi county, but, as we shall see, this trend was reversed by the arrival of the pulp and paper industry at the turn of the century. As for Lake St. John county, being more independent of the logging industry, it managed to grow steadily over the whole period. One suspects from indications on the local scene that there was really much more population movement than is suggested by these percentage increases. The efforts of the colonization society and other such efforts on the part of the Church, the railway company, and the government, did not so much create villages and towns overnight as succeed admirably in more than balancing the counter movement of emigrants and "failures" in a task that was initially both herculean and heroic in its demands, as Hémon has so well shown.

The colonization society fell on hard days in 1906, when the political winds blew adversely and the society's subsidies were cut off on various unproven charges of corruption and scandal. Perhaps it is not an exaggeration to suggest that reality had finally caught up with it. Of its colourful publications, including those prepared by the government and the railway, Rossel Vien observes that they were perforce illusory.

> Ces imprimés étaient rédigés habilement, contenaient toutes sortes de renseignements et montraient des scènes champêtres, des édifices de Roberval, etc. Ils étaient forcément mensongers. On y affichait, par exemple, une liste de colons 'prospères' avec la valeur de leur exploitation: tant de mille dollars qui n'étaient que la richesse conditionnelle de leur travail. L'annonce qu'on lisait partout était ainsi formulée: 'La région du Lac Saint-Jean:—20,000,000 d'acres d'excellentes terres à blé à 20 centins l'acre.—Un pays abondant en bon bois et en excellente eau.—Un pays pour les industries de toutes sortes...—Beau climat et communications faciles.' Singulier cadre pour *Maria Chapdelaine*! Ces vingt millions d'acres sont l'étendue approximative du bassin hydrographique du lac, alors que son territoire cultivable n'en comprend qu'un million et demi environ. Bref, notre Société répandait une image fortement embellie de la terre promise.[58]

---

[58] R. Vien, *Histoire de Roberval*, p. 183. In fairness to the colonization society, it must be added that even surveyors' reports at the time were often written in the same glowing terms. For example, we find the government surveyor, Henry O'Sullivan, describing the region between Lake St. John and James Bay as "le cœur même de la portion la plus productrice du Territoire nouvellement acquise par la province de Québec." (See Henry O'Sullivan, "Rapport préliminaire d'une exploration de l'étendue du pays comprise entre le lac Saint-Jean et la baie James," *Régions de Québec, du Lac St-Jean, de Chicoutimi et de la côte nord du Saint-Laurent: Description des cantons arpentés, exploration de territoires et arpentage des rivières et des lacs de 1889 à 1908* [Québec: Ministère des Terres et Forêts, 1908], p. 117). And the Colonization Commission likewise claimed that the future of industry and agriculture lay in regions to the north and west of Lake St. John (see *Report*, p. 92).

And yet one wonders how many Chapdelaine families would have come to Lake St. John and stayed to prosper instead of ending up in the textiles of New England if no such mystique of a promised land had been offered.

AGRICULTURE

The Church's interest in the promotion of settlement in this new region was closely related to an effort to improve agriculture. This was one of the stated reasons for introducing the Trappists into Lake St. John: to teach by their example.   This was also Mgr Bégin's concern when he urged Mgr Marquis to organize an agricultural school at Chicoutimi—a project he did not succeed in carrying out at this time.   Nevertheless, the region had had its agricultural school of sorts since 1881, when Curé Lizotte had taken the initiative to get the Ursuline Sisters to open a convent school at Roberval.   These sisters soon founded an "école ménagère," which was to be the model of similar schools throughout the province in later years.   In addition to giving girls a solid education this school aimed at training them to become efficient and thrifty housekeepers especially in what concerned the domestic arts and agriculture.   Mother St. Raphael, who was the inspiration of this work, soon came to be known throughout the province, especially after 1895 when her work won for her monastery the silver medal of the "Ordre du Mérite Agricole."   This in turn soon led to the school's being subsidized by the government.[59]   Thereafter, some of her annual reports to the minister of agriculture are included in the government's *Sessional Papers*.   For example, in 1896, she reports on the increased yield of butter achieved by introducing the new small Danish centrifugal separator, on the improvement of fodder for the cattle, on the school's experimentation in the culture of fruit trees, etc.[60]   Successive school inspectors continually turn in a glowing report on the progress achieved in the school's educational programme.[61]   However, the greatest tribute to this initiative of the Ursuline Sisters was that, in 1914, there were 43 more such domestic science schools in the province with a total student body of 4,477.[62]

---

[59] VIEN, p. 145.
[60] "Report of Ursuline Farm at Roberval and of the School of Housekeeping in Connection with the Secondary School for the year 1896," *Sessional Papers* XXX (1896), Part I No. 5, p. 24.
[61] For example, see "Report of School Inspectors," *Sessional Papers*, XLVIII (1915), Part III, No. 8, p. 14; and XXXVIII (1905), Part II, No. 5, p. 91.
[62] *Statistical Year Book*, II (1915), 315.

In his first years as bishop, Mgr Labrecque threw his full weight and influence behind the movement to improve local agriculture. In May 1893, he issued a directive to his clergy telling them to see to it that all the agricultural clubs affiliate with the new provincial association founded to promote better agriculture and settlement in the province, the Syndicat des cultivateurs de la Province de Québec, of which Cardinal Taschereau is honorary president and Mgr Bégin active president. The fair cause of agriculture must be encouraged, he writes, as on it depends the prosperity of the region:

> Ne restons pas inactifs au milieu du mouvement général qui se produit en faveur de la belle cause agricole.—N'oublions pas que la prospérité de notre région en particulier repose presque exclusivement sur le progrès de l'agriculture et de la colonisation. Rendons, par tous les moyens, l'agriculture payante, et, non seulement nous retiendrons au milieu de nous les enfants de nos cultivateurs, mais nous verrons nos compatriotes exilés revenir au pays prendre leur place aux foyers de la grande famille canadienne...

And after urging the curés to direct the young people to settle in the new area opened up by the Trappists at Mistassini, he continues in a rare rhetorical outburst:

> Encouragez les parents chrétiens, surtout les cultivateurs, à donner leurs enfants à l'agriculture, et à la colonisation, leur rappelant qu'en agissant ainsi, c'est les donner à la patrie, à la religion, à Dieu même.[63]

The following year, 1894, Mgr Labrecque joins with the other bishops of the province in issuing a joint pastoral letter establishing the work of the "missionnaires agricoles."[64] Since this important document concerns the whole province, only its key points will be mentioned here and further discussion will be left to chapter V. Its purpose was to lend the full influence of the Church to the efforts being undertaken by the government to improve the defective state of agriculture in the province, which had been one of the major reasons for mass emigration to the United States over the previous decades. The bishops want to take advantage of the temporary lull in emigration to remove its causes and to make agriculture more successful. They urge the curés to encourage parents to send at least one boy from each parish to an agricultural school so that on his return he can show his neighbours by his example how to farm

[63] Mgr M.-T. LABRECQUE, "Circulaire au clergé," *MLPC* (Chicoutimi, May 4, 1893). In reality, he is only repeating the eloquent language used by Mgr Turgeon in 1850 (see Pierre TRUDELLE, *L'Abitibi d'autrefois, d'hier, d'aujourd'hui*, p. 51).
[64] "Lettre pastorale de Nos Seigneurs les Archevêques et Évêques des provinces ecclésiastiques de Québec, de Montréal, d'Ottawa, établissant l'œuvre des Missionnaires agricoles," *MLPC* (Chicoutimi, January 6, 1894), pp. 95-101.

more profitably. But their major innovation is to provide
for the naming in each diocese of certain priests as *missionnaires
agricoles* who would popularize and spread without delay both
a theoretical and a practical knowledge of agriculture by visits
to each parish at least twice yearly. The bishops feel that they
are only confirming initiatives already widespread among their
clergy:

> Nous avons constaté avec bonheur que la plus grande partie des
> cercles agricoles sont dirigés par des prêtres; nous en avons conclu
> que les sentiments que nous exprimons aujourd'hui sont partagés
> par la masse du clergé, et nous trouvons dans ce fait une grande
> consolation et comme un gage de prospérité future pour nos pa-
> roisses.

Bishop Labrecque followed up this pastoral by naming
eleven such *missionnaires agricoles* in his diocese and urged them
to carry out this task "avec zèle et dévouement pour le plus
grand bien du pays et l'honneur de la religion."[65]

It is interesting to notice how closely this initiative of the
bishops was co-ordinated with the plans of provincial government officials. For example, we find the Minister of Agriculture
addressing a confidential document to the bishops in January
1894 to the effect that their directive will mark the beginning
of a new era in agriculture:

> Le mandement concernant les missionnaires agricoles sera lu, sans
> doute, dans toutes les églises de la province dimanche prochain, Sa
> Grâce Monseigneur l'Archevêque de Cyrène me disait qu'il est
> maintenant distribué. Permettez-moi, Monseigneur, en mon nom,
> et je pourrais dire aussi au nom de la Province de remercier Votre
> Grandeur du puissant secours qu'Elle veut bien nous accorder en
> ce moment. Ce mandement va marquer le commencement d'une
> ère nouvelle: une ère de succès agricoles semblables à ceux que nous
> avons obtenus dans l'instruction classique.

The Minister ends with the shrewd recommendation that the
curés not take up a special collection to promote the movement until after the visit and the lecture of the agricultural
missionary in each parish.[66] A few years later we find the
federal representative, Joseph Girard, requesting and obtaining
from the bishop a priest to serve as an agricultural lecturer.[67]

---

[65] Mgr M.-T. LABRECQUE, *MLPC* (Chicoutimi, Circular No. 19, October 12, 1894),
p. 160.

[66] Polycopied confidential letter from the Honourable Louis BEAUBIEN, Minister of
Agriculture of Quebec, to Mgr Labrecque, January 26, 1894, EAC, 3-23-1-66.

[67] EAC, letter of Joseph GIRARD, federal representative, to Mgr Labrecque, August
25, 1906.

In 1899, Mgr Labrecque accedes to the request that he
allow Sunday work in the butter and cheese factories when
necessary to complete batches started the preceding evening.[68]
But, for the most part, after 1894, the initiative in promoting
agriculture is left to the local curés, the agricultural missionaries,
and the priests who serve in government employ as colonization
agents, such as Mgr C. Marquis and the Abbé Louis Tremblay.
One of the more sustained methods employed by the clergy to
promote better agriculture and more rapid settlement was the
local press.   In 1897, the Curé Lizotte with the help of
L.-P. Bilodeau founded a weekly newspaper called *le Lac Saint-
Jean*, whose purpose was clearly indicated in its sub-title "Coloni-
sation-Agriculture-Repatriement."   It was the first regular
newspaper in the region of Lake St. John, and though it lasted
less than a year its successors preached the same theme.[69]   In
1898, the future Vicar General and Superior of the Séminaire de
Chicoutimi, Mgr Eugène Lapointe, founded a newspaper, *la
Défense*, edited by laymen.   It lasted for six years and strenuously promoted progress in both agriculture and industry
in the region.[70]   And finally, a few years later when the industrialist, J.-E.-A. Dubuc, bought out the most influential
newspaper in the district, *le Progrès du Saguenay*, his close friend,
Mgr Lapointe, managed gradually but noticeably to convert
the wrangling partisan spirit of this paper into one committed
to the Catholic, agricultural, and industrial interests of the
region.   In 1912 it began to feature regularly a special section
for the farmers which was both educational and informative.[71]

Sufficient has now been said to indicate the whole-hearted
support which the Church lent both to colonization and to
agriculture in the Saguenay.   We shall later have occasion to
relate this attitude to that shown by the Church towards the
blossoming of new industry in the valley.

INDUSTRY

We have already seen that by 1852 William Price controlled
the timber industry in the entire Saguenay region, even if he

---

[68] Mgr LABRECQUE, *MLPC* (Chicoutimi, Circular No. 38, February 27, 1897), p. 294.
[69] R. VIEN, *Histoire de Roberval*, p. 242-43.   *Le Lac Saint-Jean* is on file at the Archives
of la Société historique du Saguenay.
[70] ASHS, *La Défense*. See Dossier No. 168, where in a confidential letter to the clergy of
the diocese Mgr Lapointe recalls how *"la Défense* naquit, sous le haut et bienveillant patronage de Mgr Labrecque.   Avec deux ou trois laïques, j'en portai le poids durant huit ans."
[71] Cf. ASHS, Dossier, No. 168, where Mgr Lapointe recounts the story of this transformation.   Lapointe himself often writes in the paper under the pseudonym "John Black."
Finally, in 1915, a professor of the Séminaire, Abbé Calixte Tremblay, becomes editor.

did not actually own all the sawmills.   He retained this control until almost the turn of the century.   Over the years, the Price family won the esteem and respect of both Church officials and French Canadians generally—so much so, in fact, that the title "Père du Saguenay" was inscribed under the name of the elder Price on the huge Price monument erected at Chicoutimi.   The frontier villages along the Saguenay looked on him, and among his sons especially on William Edward, not as collaborators but as benefactors, who often stood between them and starvation. This is easily understandable since their region had an economy of company labour, company money, and company stores, with the people living in almost complete dependence on their employers.   Mgr Arthur Maheux, an ardent and enthusiastic admirer of William Price, recounts in his biography of this intrepid entrepreneur how generous he was to the local curés, often supplying both land and wood for the construction of their churches and presbyteries, contributing to their favourite charities, and stocking in his stores all the articles of Catholic devotion.[72]

Price was also a gentleman farmer, and owned a large efficient 800-acre farm at Saint-Alexis de Grande-Baie which supplied his camps with food and at the same time served as a model for farmers in the region.   In 1860, Curé Martel reported that Price harvested as much grain as all his parishioners together and produced excellent butter, pork, wheat, beef, cattle, and sugar beets.   At times, as many as 100 men worked this farm for him.[73]

William Price was succeeded in his "kingdom" in 1867, by his three bachelor sons, William Edward, David Edward, and John Evan.   William Edward particularly endeared himself to the people of the Saguenay in 1870, by his immense generosity, when a disastrous forest fire swept the region leaving more than a third of the population, some 5,000 in all, hungry and homeless. Five hundred and fifty families were totally ruined and another 146 lost either their homes or other buildings.[74]   On this occasion the Price brothers opened their stores and provided food, wood, and money to second the efforts of the clergy and the government to stave off complete disaster.   William Edward supported them in other areas besides.   Astute politician that he was, he is reported even to have made a public commitment:

[72] Mgr A. Maheux, "William Price et la Compagnie Price," p. 301.

[73] Abbé L.-Eugène Otis, *Saint-Alexis de Grande-Baie, 1838–1938*, p. 38.

[74] *L'histoire du Saguenay depuis l'origine jusqu'à 1870*, p. 320.

> Je n'hésite pas à le déclarer publiquement, et je vous en donne ma
> parole, que je serai toujours en faveur de toutes les demandes que
> Messeigneurs vos Évêques feront dans l'intérêt de la religion catho-
> lique romaine. *Je vous déclare de plus publiquement, que je suivrai*
> *toujours et avant tout, en politique* [sic], les conseils de vos Évêques
> et prêtres. Quant aux écoles catholiques, je les soutiendrai de toute
> mon influence, et je les protégerai de toutes manières. Je travaille-
> rai pour tous vos intérêts! Je protégerai en tout et partout votre
> religion et votre nationalité canadienne-française![75]

When William Edward died, the French Canadians and
their clergy readily took up the suggestion of his friend,
J.G. Scott, to erect a huge monument at Chicoutimi to his and his
father's memory. The enthusiastic tribute paid to the company
on this occasion by the Abbé Ambroise Fafard, superior of the
seminary and curé of Chicoutimi, has remained for the Price
family telling proof that they were beloved by the people of the
Saguenay. Fafard's praise for what that family had done for
the development of the region is unstinted, and his economic
reasoning is both sound and revealing:

> Messieurs, ce qui manque bien souvent à une colonie naissante comme
> celle du Saguenay, éloignée des grands centres commerciaux, privée
> de voies ferrées, composée surtout de pauvres colons dont l'unique
> capital consiste dans un courage invincible servi par des bras vigou-
> reux, ce qui manque à une telle colonie, dis-je, ce sont des capitalistes
> entreprenants, disposés à employer leur fortune au développement
> industriel d'une colonie semblable, capables d'établir au centre même
> de cette colonie un marché facile où ces nouveaux colons pourront
> vendre leurs produits, et réaliser l'argent qui leur est indispensable
> pour faire honneur à leurs affaires.[76]

It is his thesis that neither agriculture nor industry is self
sufficient; both are necessary to ensure the prosperity of a country. And he concludes that without the Prices' courageous
industrial initiatives, the Saguenay would have developed
much more slowly. That is why, Fafard says, William Price I
is rightly named "Père du Saguenay."

During all this period, Price certainly found no hostility
to his endeavours on the part of the Church and could have
whatever co-operation he desired. It is not clear that he particularly needed it. And no doubt Curé Fafard for all his oratory
was shrewd enough to realize how completely his people depended
at this time on Price's industrial activities in Chicoutimi.

When deep crisis hit the logging industry in the 1870's and
1880's, faith in industry in the Saguenay was badly shaken.

---

[75] MAHEUX, "William Price et la Compagnie Price," p. 330.
    [76] *Inauguration du Monument Price* (Québec: Brousseau, 1882), cited by MAHEUX,
ibid., pp. 328–34.

There was necessarily much emigration, for, as we saw, despite a natural increase of about 30 per cent per decade, the population of Chicoutimi county increased 17 per cent in the decade 1871–1881 and only 3 per cent in the following decade. It was in this period, 1883–1898, under the management of Evan John Price, that the Prices began to lose some of their monopoly and prestige in the Saguenay and especially in the town of Chicoutimi. In fact, John Price tried unsuccessfully in 1894 to sell the mills at Chicoutimi along with their forest reserves to John Ross of Quebec for the sum of $225,000.[77] In 1899, the Price Brothers Company was in bankruptcy but continued to earn substantial profits under the direction of Mr. Ritchie of the Bank of Montreal, for the Price "kingdom" was too rich to know sudden ruin. Its assets at this time were evaluated at $4,317,500 and included 10 sawmills with their equipment, 100,000 acres of freehold and seigneurial land, and over 6,000 square miles of limits operated under licence, of which 3,800 were in the Saguenay.[78]

The nephew of Evan John, William Price II,[79] who had been born and raised in Chile and educated in England, now took over the management of the Price holdings. In 1902, he began to orientate the old company towards the relatively new pulp and paper industry. And in 1904 he reorganized the Price Brothers Company Limited as a joint stock company, obtaining the greater share of the new capital from England with the aid of Isaac Walton Killam.[80]

But, in the meantime, the people of the Saguenay had had to fall back more than ever before on their own resources and it was only the introduction of the dairy industry together with easier access to the province's markets both by railway and by water that had saved them. In 1895, five years after its inauguration, the railway carried 1,318,965 pounds of cheese to market; four years later, in 1899, this figure had risen to 2,149,981 pounds.[81] It is during this period, while the logging industry was still in difficulty, that the agriculturalist theme is quite frequently heard. We have already seen that Mgr Labrecque, on two important occasions in 1892 and 1893, without mentioning

---

[77] MAHEUX, *ibid.*, p. 350A.

[78] Price Brothers and Company Limited, "Status as of Montreal," June 26, 1905, "Corporation Records Collection," Baker Library, Harvard Business School. The average profit for the five years 1899–1904 was $246,277.09.

[79] Though William I's eldest son was named William Edward, he seems to have been called Edward rather than William.

[80] MAHEUX, "William Price et la Compagnie Price," p. 391.

[81] La Société de Repatriement et de Colonisation du Lac Saint-Jean, *Rapport annuel pour l'année 1899*, p. 2.

industry seemed to entrust to agriculture the future prosperity of the Saguenay and to show for it a particular predilection; it is a theme which he seems to drop deliberately once industry revives in the valley, for there is not a single example of a similar statement again prior to World War I.   However, even earlier when he is preaching that for Christian parents to give their children to colonization and agriculture is to give them "à la patrie, à la religion, à Dieu même,"[82] he is already encouraging local industry.   For example, in 1894, he addresses a directive to the curés of Lake St. John asking them to favour the new woolen manufacture which Mr. Wells proposes to establish at Chicoutimi, for it will permit the wool of the region to be made into clothing locally.   He also asks them to encourage local industry:

> Veuillez, en même temps, leur recommander d'encourager avant tout l'industrie locale qui pourra, avant peu, leur donner des produits d'égale valeur et à des conditions plus avantageuses que les industries étrangères.   C'est d'ailleurs l'avantage général de nos localités de retenir ici des capitaux qui iraient favoriser la prospérité de centres éloignés au détriment de nos propres paroisses. [83]

The popular little journal of the seminary, *l'Oiseau Mouche*, edited by the priest professors, echoes at this time the same agriculturist theme.   Typical is an editorial which appeared in 1895, on the occasion of the convention of the province's dairy association at Chicoutimi, hymning the blade of grass:

> Oui, saluons... le brin d'herbe!   En dépit des apparences, c'est l'un des fermes piliers de notre existence.
>   Nous avons été et nous sommes une race agricole.   La prospérité de l'agriculture, c'est la richesse de notre Province, c'est le maintien de notre nationalité.   Or, dans les conditions présentes, l'industrie laitière est l'instrument principal de notre progrès agricole.   Et l'industrie laitière, qu'est-ce autre chose que le brin d'herbe ? Le brin d'herbe de nos prairies, qui se fait beurre et fromage, s'en va sous d'autres cieux, et nous revient or et argent...
>   Ici, encore plus qu'ailleurs, c'est la victoire du brin d'herbe sur le pin géant!   Vive le brin d'herbe du Saguenay![84]

And, in the same issue, the editors heartily approve the three-hour speech of the great promoter of agriculture, J.C. Chapais, and conclude with him that "toute la question sociale est dans la culture des champs.   Une population agricole est florissante

---

[82] Mgr M.-T. LABRECQUE, "Circulaire au clergé," May 4, 1893.
[83] Letter from Mgr LABRECQUE to the curés of the Lake St. John region, May 1, 1894, EAC, 2-313-1-22.
[84] *L'Oiseau Mouche*, March 2, 1895.   This journal is on file in the Archives of la Société historique du Saguenay.

et morale, tandis que celle qui déserte les campagnes pour en-
combrer les villes, est en pleine décadence et renferme les germes
de sa ruine." With rare and unimportant exceptions this
theme seems to have come to an abrupt end after 1895, when
the pulp industry was born in the Saguenay under French
Canadian auspices, and the urban movement began to accelerate.
Yet even if the new towns are relatively small they still entice
especially the younger people to leave the land.   From 1891 to
1911, Chicoutimi county's "urban" population jumped from 17
to 48 per cent of the total population, and by 1921, to 60 per
cent.

Before turning to the pulp and paper towns, we may look
briefly at Roberval, the largest urban centre in Lake St. John
county.   As we have seen, the curé of Roberval, the indomitable
Lizotte, was an ardent and bold promoter of the railway and
colonization and agriculture in this region.   He was likewise
deeply involved in every new project to promote the organization and development of the town, once it had become the
northern terminus of the railway.   While he was curé, he saw
Roberval grow from a small village of 300 to the commercial
town of the entire region with a population of about 3,000.[85]
One of his contemporaries wrote in 1914 of his fascination with
development:

> M. Lizotte a laissé un souvenir ineffaçable dans la population de
> Roberval.   Curé jusqu'en 1900, il prit une part active au développe-
> ment de Roberval: son presbytère était le rendez-vous de tous les
> principaux hommes d'affaires non seulement de Roberval mais de
> toute la région et même de la ville de Québec.   Il y aurait tout un
> chapitre important à écrire sur le rôle qu'a joué l'abbé Lizotte durant
> cette période du développement de Roberval, qui a vu arriver la
> première locomotive du chemin de fer, la construction de l'établisse-
> ment d'une manufacture de lainage, le développement des moulins
> Scott et du Tremblay, l'installation de la lumière électrique, du
> téléphone, etc.... Ajoutons à ces qualités, une charité ardente pour
> ses paroissiens dans l'exercice de son ministère...
>   M. l'abbé Joseph Paradis, son successeur, se confina à l'exercice
> de son ministère.[86]

In fact, Lizotte's enthusiasm for material development became
so boundless that the bishop began to feel that the curé was
over-extending himself in temporal affairs, and in 1899 wrote
to him rebuking him for being so often outside the diocese in
delegations to the government, and recommending that he show
as much zeal for the spiritual care of his parish as for its temporal

---

[85] R. Vien, *Histoire de Roberval*, especially pp. 95–154.
[86] *Le Progrès du Saguenay*, June 18, 1914.

affairs, "qui ne sont pas de votre ressort, mais de celui des laïques."[87] No doubt, this admonition helped to restrain the temporal activities of his more studious successor, Curé Paradis. But the pattern had been set and it was not by accident that the biggest industrialist of Roberval, J.B. Scott, a Scotch Protestant, was warmly welcomed in audience by Pope Pius X while on a visit to Rome.[88]

The star of Roberval soon began to pale before the rising star of the old fur-trading post of Chicoutimi, where, in 1896, the first pulp mill in the region was built by French Canadian initiative—a successful enterprise which was to spark similar undertakings throughout the Saguenay. The hero of the piece—for he was just that to all French Canadians—was the manager of the local bank, a youth of twenty-five, J.-E.-Alfred Dubuc, who without either personal capital or business experience successfully built the Compagnie de Pulpe de Chicoutimi into the largest single producer of pulp in the world during the pre-war period, and won for himself acclaim as a financial genius who could literally build without money.[89]

Alfred Dubuc entered the employ of La Banque Nationale of Sherbrooke, in 1887, at the age of sixteen, with a diploma in commerce from Séminaire Saint-Charles of Sherbrooke which really qualified him for little more than bookkeeping. In 1892, he was sent to open a branch bank at Chicoutimi. And, as is evident from his first *Letter Copying Book*, which covers the period 1893–1898, he began at once with unbridled enthusiasm to promote every conceivable form of economic development in the region. He started by obtaining a lower rate of interest for the bishop's development loans,[90] and then investigated the feasibility of obtaining a long-term loan for a group of 25 or 30 farmers with the collateral of first mortgage on all their properties.[91] He organizes a local chamber of commerce and is elected its first secretary.[92] He tries to interest a certain

[87] Letter of Mgr LABRECQUE to Abbé Joseph Lizotte, February 23, 1899, EAC.

[88] VIEN, *Histoire de Roberval*, p. 276.

[89] The source of the information to be given is chiefly the Dubuc Archives in the personal possession of his son, Antoine Dubuc of Chicoutimi. The author is indebted to him and to members of his family for graciously allowing him access to these private documents and through personal interviews helping him to interpret them. Hereafter these archives will be referred to by the abbreviation DA.

[90] Copy of a letter of A.-E.-J. DUBUC to R. LaRoche, Quebec, March 23, 1893, *Letter Copying Book*, DA. And letter of A.-E.-J. DUBUC to M.M. Hanson Bros., Montreal, June 6, 1896, DA.

[91] Copy of a letter of J.-E.-A. DUBUC to M.M. Hanson Brothers, Montreal, August 8, 1896, DA.

[92] Copy of a letter of J.-E.-A. DUBUC to Mr. Levasseur, Secrétaire, Chambre de Commerce, Québec, June 13, 1895; also the formal declaration constituting the Chambre de Commerce of the District of Chicoutimi with A. Dubuc as Secretary, February 19, 1897, DA.

A. Steward in the iron mines of the district,[93] and D.H. Holt, President of the Montreal Gas Company, in the manufacture of carbide of calcium by employing the abundant local water-power resources to develop electricity.[94] He tries to convince Alex Wendler of Zchopan, Germany, to invest in a waterpower development and in the pulp industry in the region and guarantees him river and railway communications with Tadoussac.[95] With F.F. Cole of Toronto he discusses this latter project of building an electric railway from James Bay to Roberval and Chicoutimi, and finally to the "winter seaport" of Tadoussac.[96] He urges the town councillors of Saint-Alphonse to work for a federal subsidy for a Ha Ha Bay railway.[97] He invites the Glen Falls Paper Mill Company to open a pulp and paper mill in the region,[98] and asks William Kennedy of Montreal to submit his terms for providing a complete pulp plant producing 20–25 tons daily.[99] He arranges for markets for butter and cheese and pulp with Carter Wilkinson Company in Liverpool, tries to interest them in investing in the pulp industry of the region and in marketing Canadian-made cardboard.[100] He likewise endeavours to get French capital into the Saguenay.[101]

The Mayor of Chicoutimi, J.-E. Guay, a close friend of Dubuc and owner of the local newspaper, *le Progrès du Saguenay*, eagerly seconded Dubuc's efforts, and himself undertook many similar initiatives to get new industry into the region. A few other enthusiastic French Canadians associated themselves with these hardy promoters and they soon bought out the major hotel in Chicoutimi, erected a hydroelectric station and power dam to provide the city with electricity, organized the water-works and sewage system, and, when they did not succeed in attracting outside industrialists, finally decided to found their own pulp industry in the city. It was not long before the Pres-

---

[93] Copy of a letter of J.-E.-A. DUBUC to A. Steward, undated, DA.

[94] Copy of a letter of J.-E.-A. DUBUC to H.D. Holt, President of Montreal Gas Company, August 7, 1897, DA.

[95] Copies of letters of J.-E.-A. DUBUC to Alex Wendler, Zchopan, Germany, September 16, 1897; September 30, 1897; February 23, 1898, DA.

[96] Copy of a letter of J.-E.-A. DUBUC to F.F. Cole, Toronto, January 12, 1898, DA.

[97] Copy of a letter of J.-E.-A. DUBUC to the councillors of the parish of St. Alphonse, February 7, 1898, DA.

[98] Copy of a letter of J.-E.-A. DUBUC to Glen Falls Paper Mill Company, Glen Falls, New York, March 19, 1896, DA.

[99] Copy of a letter of J.-E.-A. DUBUC to William Kennedy, Montreal, August 8, 1896, DA.

[100] Copies of letters of J.-E.-A. DUBUC to Wm. Stark, Liverpool, and to Carter Wilkinson & Company, Liverpool, March 16, 1897; June 9, 1897; September 22, 1897, DA.

[101] Copy of a letter of J.-E.-A. DUBUC to A. Bodard, Paris, February 23, 1898, *ibid*. This enumeration by no means exhausts the long list of initiatives undertaken by the young bank manager but rather presents a good sample of their variety and scope.

ident of La Banque Nationale, Napoléon Lavoie, began to have some misgivings about the rumours of the wild financial adventures of his young bank manager, but Dubuc was able to reassure him:

> C'est moi qui ai fait toute la correspondance tendant à la réussite du projet à Chicoutimi, je travaille la chose depuis deux ans. L'automne dernier, voyant que toutes ces démarches restaient encore sans résultats pratiques, j'ai proposé à quelques Chicoutimiens entreprenants d'y mettre de l'argent eux-mêmes afin de prouver aux étrangers que vous avez confiance dans la réussite de la chose. L'idée a été bonne puisque deux compagnies américaines se disputent une partie du stock de la future compagnie de Chicoutimi...
>
> Je ne suis pas personnellement intéressé dans cette compagnie de pulpe pour une raison incontrôlable, je n'ai pas d'argent. La moitié du stock est entre les mains de J.-D. Guay, Jos. Gagnon, Jean Guay, F.-X. Gosselin, Ovide Bossé et l'autre moitié entre les mains des Américains . . .

He goes on to tell how he learned to promote such enterprises from William Farwell, the bank manager at Sherbrooke, who taught him to understand that "dans toutes entreprises industrielles les Banques en retirent leur large part et les quelques petites frictions qui se produisent ne sont rien à comparer aux profits qu'elles nous apportent." He assures Lavoie,

> J'ai à cœur la réussite de la Banque Nationale et je paye de ma personne à chaque fois que je puis trouver une occasion, même au besoin en faire naître, et il est facile de constater que la succursale de Chicoutimi ne serait pas ce qu'elle est sans ce travail.[102]

The new Compagnie de Pulpe was incorporated in May 1897, with an authorized capital of $50,000. A single American, Frilez Shilde, a manufacturer of Carthage, New York, was among the directors. He seems to have been quickly bought out, for Joseph Gagnon replaces him on the board of directors the following September. However, an English Canadian with some experience in the pulp industry, O.E. Porritt, invests his savings for a time in the company and becomes the mill superintendent. Nevertheless, it is Alfred Dubuc, director general with the powers of treasurer and secretary, who dominates the scene from beginning to end.[103]

The first mill started with 6 grinders in 1898, had a daily capacity of 30 tons of dry mechanical pulp, and employed about 150 workers in the mill. With the completion of the second mill

---

[102] Copy of a letter of J.-E.-A. Dubuc to Napoléon Lavoie, Président de la Banque Nationale, March 8, 1897, DA.

[103] For these and many other details I am indebted to unpublished notes of one of the directors, F.-X. Gosselin, who seems to have been the unofficial historian of the company (DA).

in 1903, the capacity was increased to about 120 tons daily and the company now employed about 300 men in the mill and about 800 in the woods.   By 1913, the combined capacity of the mills at Chicoutimi and Val-Jalbert was about 285 tons, and this was raised to 325 tons in 1915.[104]   When in May of that year, the company became part of a merger with two American companies, the Tidewater Paper Mills Company of Brooklyn and the St. Lawrence Pulp and Lumber Corporation in Gaspé under the new name, North American Pulp and Paper Companies, with Dubuc as President, the Compagnie de Pulpe de Chicoutimi claimed to have assets worth $4,250,000 "not counting timber holdings, undeveloped water power, and equity in its underlying securities"; it had an annual capacity of 90,000 tons of pulp and boasted "this is the largest single capacity in the world and nearly one-quarter of the entire mechanical pulp shipped from the Dominion of Canada."[105]

The company tended to operate "on a shoe string" and was only protected from the cyclical swings in the mechanical pulp market by having secured long-term contracts for markets in England.   It is not clear why Dubuc, who talked about producing paper and cardboard at Chicoutimi as early as 1896, never succeeded in integrating his mills with a paper industry before the merger of 1915 unless the reason was the all too evident lack of capital.   But although he continually walked a financial tight-rope, Dubuc also consistently managed to keep the company profitable.   It paid a 6 per cent dividend in its first year of production, declared a 10 per cent dividend the following year, and, in January 1900, earned a capital gain of 50 per cent by selling out its holdings to the reorganized company for $375,000.[106]   The threat of bankruptcy in that year due to the bursting of one of the flumes was somewhat compensated for by the winning of a gold medal at the Paris Exposition for the quality of the company's pulp.   The second mill, completed in 1903, was claimed to be the best of its day, and, in fact, embodied the latest equipment and engineering which enabled the company to make a profit of $7 per ton in comparison with their

[104] "Who's Who in the Canadian Pulp and Paper Industry," *Pulp and Paper Magazine*, June 1, 1915, pp. 323-24.
[105] *Description of the Manufacture of Pulp and Paper of the North American Pulp and Paper Companies*.   Publication on the occasion of the issuance of new shares on the market in 1916.   The actual average production of the Companie de Pulpe de Chicoutimi, 1910–1913, was 36,841 tons.   The 90,000 ton capacity was obtained by taking over the mill at Val-Jalbert and by increasing the capacity of both plants.
[106] F.-X. GOSSELIN, unpublished notes, DA.   He admits that the record is not clear on whether or not the 10 per cent dividend declared in 1899 was in addition to the 4 per cent dividend declared paid earlier.

former profit of $5.60 per ton in the old mill.[107]   The incomplete
records available indicate new profits of $49,902.32 in 1902-
1903,[108] rising to $136,988.16 in 1908, in what was considered in
many places a recession year, and to $258,000 in 1916.[109]   These
same sources indicate that in spite of a considerable programme
of expansion a dividend of at least 4 per cent seems to have been
paid each year, in some years one of 6 per cent, and occasionally
one of 8 per cent.   But we enter the land of fairy-tales when
we find the *Paper Maker and British Paper Trade Journal* talking
in 1903 of the high hopes of the directors of the company to
obtain "an increase on their regular monotonous 8 per cent
dividend."[110] The object of the article on Dubuc's recent successes was probably more to promote the company's pulp on
the English market than to write history, for the company was
only then recovering from a close shave with bankruptcy.

But much more important than its total production and
profitability was the fact that this new French Canadian company ushered an era of industrial prosperity into this region
where industry had long been synonymous with the name Price.
And this fact had many notable consequences.   The reaction
was almost immediate; we hear no more talk in the region either
by Church officials or by the newspapers about French Canadians being "une race agricole."   Already in January 1898,
when Mgr Lapointe founded his[111] newspaper *la Défense*, the
editor notes in the "Prospectus," "L'élan de la prospérité, de
l'avancement, du progrès dans le domaine de l'agriculture et de
l'industrie vient d'être donné.   Il va s'accentuer encore."   He
lists among the interests to be pursued by the paper not only
agriculture and colonization but also industry and social economy, and promises an honest attempt to do all he can to quell
local wrangling and "acrimonies stériles qui ont trop longtemps
divisé nos concitoyens et paralysé le développement de notre
ville."[112]

The first ton of pulp had scarcely emerged from the mill
when Abbé Alfred Tremblay, professor at the seminary, boldly

---

[107] LA CIE DE PULPE DE CHICOUTIMI, *Rapports mensuels*, DA.
[108] LA CIE DE PULPE DE CHICOUTIMI, *Rapport aux actionnaires*, Chicoutimi, August 19,
1903, DA.
[109] *Description of the Manufacture of Pulp and Paper of the North American Pulp and
Paper Companies.*
[110] *Paper Maker and British Paper Trade Journal*, December 1903, pp. 3-4.
[111] "His" because the paper was initiated, financed, and supervised by Mgr Lapointe.
However, it was not the bishop's official organ, as he was careful to inform Mgr Racicot of
Montreal, when he complained about some of its articles.   (See copy of letter of Mgr LA-
BRECQUE to Mgr Racicot, Vicar General of Montreal diocese, May 18, 1899, EAC).
[112] *La Défense*, January 18, 1898.

committed to print in *l'Oiseau Mouche* the dreams that were beginning of the rosy industrial future of Chicoutimi and the Saguenay. As the population moves northward, he foresees, the main route in Canada will pass through Winnipeg, Abitibi, Lake St. John and Chicoutimi, and then continue on to Tadoussac—the winter-port of the region—and finally to Labrador. He concludes enthusiastically about Chicoutimi's large future:

> Chicoutimi attirerait ainsi à lui une partie du commerce des villes de New-York, Boston, Montréal et Québec; il serait le centre du plus vaste commerce du bois, de pulpe, et de papier du continent; il vendrait presque autant de blé que Winnipeg, plus de beurre et de fromage que Montréal, autant de fourrures que Nijni-Novgorod. Il deviendrait une ville énorme, éclipsant New-York, et je vous laisse à penser s'il serait fier.[113]

For the moment, all thought of the decadence of big cities seems to be forgotten in the excitement of believing that one day Chicoutimi will itself be a big city! The inspiration had been given, and French Canadian enthusiasm knew no bounds. *La Défense* in its issue of February 3, 1898, hails the growth in pulp:

> Le mouvement est à la pulpe dans notre région. C'est l'industrie du jour et l'élan est donné dans ce sens... Les regards des capitalistes qui s'intéressent à cette industrie sont fixés sur notre région... La Compagnie de Pulpe de Chicoutimi fait maintenant des projets grandioses, audacieux... Une compagnie s'est formée au Lac-Bouchette; on construira bientôt. A Roberval, on parle d'utiliser les chutes de la rivière Ouiatchouan. Une autre compagnie puissante est en train de se former pour établir l'industrie à Alma... Tout cela est d'excellent augure.

Many of these projects got no further than their announcement. Nevertheless, we will briefly review the actual results achieved in this first fervour of enthusiasm for the pulp industry as well as the role which the Church played in it, before returning to take a closer look at the intimate relationship which existed between the Compagnie de Pulpe de Chicoutimi and the Church, for which there is more documentation.

Perhaps the most striking initiative was that undertaken at Jonquière, for here a pulp mill was constructed and financed by a group of local farmers under the guidance of a self-made engineer, Joseph Perron, who had gained some experience in pulp-making while working at the Chicoutimi mill. The little village granted the new company tax exemption for 25 years, but refused to

---

[113] *L'Oiseau Mouche*, February 12, 1898. Abbé Alfred Tremblay writes under the pseudonyme of "Derfla," his middle name spelled backwards.

approve an outright grant.[114] Perron raised about $35,000 locally from French Canadians and was producing pulp by November 1900. For the moment, the mill produced only 20–25 tons of pulp per day, but its charter authorized a capital of $1 million to construct hydroelectric installations and saw-mills as well as pulp mills.[115] The enthusiasm of the two cler-ically inspired newspapers, *l'Oiseau Mouche* and *la Défense*, knew no bounds. The latter gives a long description of the new enterprise and urges the public to invest in it.[116] And on the occasion of its solemn public blessing by the Vicar General, F.-X. Belley, taking the place of the absent bishop, *l'Oiseau Mouche* gives a glowing account of all the proceedings and concludes with a proud boast about local initiative:

> Qu'on vienne *brailler* maintenant que le cultivateur canadien est routinier et en arrière de son siècle. En trouverez-vous beaucoup d'habitants dans les autres provinces qui, sans capital, n'ayant que la ferme qui fournit chaque année le pain de leur famille, se lance-ront dans une telle entreprise? Si l'on voulait faire le bilan des Canadiens français, comparer ce qu'ils étaient à ce qu'ils sont, ce qu'ils avaient à ce qu'ils ont, je crois que le dividende de leur pro-grès, à tous les points de vue, ferait pâlir celui de n'importe quelle nationalité.[117]

But the boasting came too soon. History was to repeat itself. By the end of the year, the young William Price had bought out the majority of the shares at par—which was above their market price at the time. And soon all but the most stubborn of the French Canadians had taken back their money and unmortgaged their farms. Price's readily available timber limits and rich sources of working capital assured the success of his enterprise. In 1903, he installed cardboard production and thereafter raised the capacity of the mill. In fact, this mill of Jonquière was the only one of these early pulp mills destined to have a long and prosperous future. It continued in production until 1962.

In 1901, another French Canadian pulp mill was launched by the Compagnie de Pulpe de Métabetchouan formed by Charles Paquet, a Quebec merchant and an unnamed local farmer from Saint-Jérôme, at Saint-André on the Métabet-

[114] Mgr Victor TREMBLAY, "La pulperie de Jonquière," *Centenaire de Jonquière*, 1847–1947, pp. 69–73.
[115] MAHEUX, "William Price et la Compagnie Price," pp. 384-85.
[116] *La Défense*, August 30, 1900.
[117] *L'Oiseau Mouche*, March 2, 1901.

chouan River. But it was burnt out, as were its forest limits before it came into production, having begot the little parish of Saint-André which survived it.[118]

A similar French Canadian initiative was undertaken by the Compagnie de Pulpe de Péribonka formed by a local group from Roberval under the leadership of Thomas Du Tremblay aided by some Quebec businessmen. They built at the last falls on the Petite Péribonka above Lake St. John where they founded the parish of Saint-Amédée. They were soon producing 20 tons of pulp a day, but they lacked sufficient waterpower and transportation facilities to ship their pulp. In 1906, they went into bankruptcy and soon thereafter the mill was destroyed by fire. Their "incompetence" merited them a knowing sermon on the part of the editors of the *Pulp and Paper Magazine:*

> ... the worst of it was that the management of the mill was in the hands of men who did not understand the business, and who had not even competency in mechanical engineering. The site was not fit for a pulpmill, and the power was quite deficient, but the persons invited to subscribe the capital evidently did not give the matter much consideration, and did not seem to realize that it takes experience to run any business even under the best circumstances.[119]

The successor to the Compagnie de Pulpe de Péribonka, the Compagnie de Pulpe Dalmas, rebuilt the mill in 1909, and continued to produce about 4,500 tons of pulp annually until it was destroyed by a second fire. The mill later followed the lot of many such French Canadian projects by eventually ending up in the hands of the Price Brothers Company in 1917.[120]

The Compagnie de Pulpe Ouiatchouan, founded with a capital of $150,000 in 1901 by a group of French Canadians on the initiative of Damase Jalbert, was more successful. The new village, first called Ouiatchouan, was later named Val-Jalbert, after its founder. However, in 1908, the finances of the company had to be strengthened with the aid of American money and Alfred Dubuc became supervisor of the company.[121] At that time it was incorporated with an authorized capital of $600,000 and had a capacity of 50 tons of pulp per day. There-

---

[118] BLANCHARD, p. 93; Document No. 254, ASHS; *Le Colon du Lac Saint-Jean,* February 28, 1901, ASHS. I am unable to account for the 15,000 tons of pulp estimated by Girard to have been produced by this company in 1905; see Alex GIRARD, *La Province de Québec* (Québec: Dussault & Proulx, 1905), p. 124.

[119] *Pulp and Paper Magazine,* June 1906, pp. 151-52. However merited this little sermon may have been, it is not to the credit of this English Canadian publication that only French Canadian failures seem to have been subjected to such bitter post-mortems.

[120] VIEN, *op.cit.,* p. 286.

[121] *Pulp and Paper Magazine,* April 1908, p. 99; July 1908, p. 173.

after, it was gradually absorbed by the Compagnie de Pulpe de Chicoutimi. And though Dubuc talked of integrating it with newsprint production in 1909 he never did so.[122]

For Val-Jalbert there is more documented evidence of a relationship with the Church. For example, on the occasion of the opening of the mill, in August 1902, Mgr Labrecque was on hand for the solemn blessing and took the opportunity to thank the promoters of the industry profusely. He explained to the settlers that they should be grateful to the industry for furnishing them with a source of employment and money, and he asked the industrialists not to tolerate either blasphemy or drunkenness in their new mill. He argued that industry is necessary to promote the settlement movement, but on this occasion left the impression that he still considers it as merely an adjunct to agriculture:

> Nous devons nous réjouir de ce courant industriel qui se porte vers notre région, car nous en avons besoin. Nous habitons un beau pays, une région extraordinairement fertile, cette grande fertilité du sol promet aux colons courageux l'aisance à courte échéance. Mais avant d'en arriver là, pendant qu'il abat les arbres de la forêt pour y jeter la semence qui doit pourvoir à sa subsistance, il lui faut du secours, s'il n'est pas fortuné; il lui faut travailler ailleurs que sur sa terre pour se procurer de l'argent; c'est à l'industrie qu'il a recours. L'industrie est donc nécessaire au colon.[123]

The bishop's presence on this occasion brought him the warm thanks of the new pulp company as well as that of the railway company. They were in full agreement that "Monseigneur a toujours été un bon ami du progrès du pays."[124]

It is at once amusing and significant to find Curé Delage of Chambord, the nearest village, complaining to the bishop a few months later that the curé and the people of Roberval are encroaching on the territory of the new pulp mill, which he and his people consider their very own. As he says, "les gens de Roberval, *peut-être le curé avec*, se vantent de pouvoir dire *notre manufacture* [his emphasis] au détriment de Chambord."[125] Another incident that occurred much later in this industrial parish gives us a good insight into the role which the local curé

---

[122] *Ibid.*, July 1908, p. 173; September 1909, p. 257.

[123] *Le Progrès du Saguenay*, August 21, 1902; a report of what he said, not his actual words. The reasoning of the bishop is better understood when we recall that this was the first pulp mill to be built in a farming area. Moreover, it was just beginning to be commonly realized that trees, like crops, could be raised and harvested and that the cutting down of a virgin forest was not a once-for-all proposition as the settlers had long thought.

[124] Letter of the secretary of the Compagnie de Pulpe de Ouiatchouan to Mgr Labrecque, August 22, 1902, EAC, 59-5-1-3.

[125] Letter of Curé F.-X. DELAGE to Mgr Labrecque, August 4, 1903, EAC, 26-71-1-41.

often played in these new industrial parishes—a role seldom
revealed in the available documents.   After this pulp mill was
merged with the Compagnie de Pulpe de Chicoutimi and its
capacity increased, the latter, under the supervision of Dubuc,
was lavish in its generosity to the little town, the Church, and
the schools.   The new curé, Joseph-Edmond Tremblay, was
very active—too active it would seem, for when matters finally
came to a head much later, in 1924, the local manager, Adolphe
Lapointe, made the accusation that "Monsieur le curé veut
être le maître dans les bureaux et les usines de la compagnie
comme il est le maître spirituel de sa paroisse."[126]   Mgr Labrecque made a thorough investigation of the matter and gave
his decision.   He admitted that Curé Tremblay was guilty of
some "très légères imprudences," but his general observations
reveal that this was not an unusual situation in his diocese:

> En tenant compte du rôle que joue le curé dans les petites paroisses,
> surtout à leurs débuts, de la collaboration étroite, souvent sollicitée
> autrefois, du curé dans les affaires de l'usine, en y mettant de la bonne
> foi et de la bienveillance, on ne voit vraiment rien de bien sérieux à
> reprocher au curé en tout cela...

And he later adds,

> L'impression nette et la conviction générale qui résultent chez les
> ouvriers de Val-Jalbert de la conduite générale de leur curé, est que
> celui-ci est très favorable, trop favorable, à leur gré, à M. Lapointe
> et à la Cie.

Quite evidently the Church had warmly embraced the new
pulp and paper industry in the Saguenay, and the clerical editors
continued to dream dreams of the region's brilliant economic
future, for we continue to find such titles in *l'Oiseau Mouche* as
"Rêves Saguenéens" and "Le Royaume de Saguenay" where
"l'agriculture et l'industrie vont ... faire des merveilles."[127]
However, these priest editors, like the bishop himself, have
some reservations.   When in 1901 a certain Mr. Nordin proposed
a project which would bring both Finns and Finnish capital
into the region, the clergy balked.   They are all in favour of the
foreign capital, but not of the foreign people:

> Dans l'encouragement de l'industrie en notre région, il nous semble
> qu'il y a deux choses qu'il ne faudrait pas perdre de vue: assurer le
> progrès de la colonisation et sauvegarder les intérêts matériels et
> religieux de la race canadienne-française qui a ici des droits acquis.[128]

---

[126] "Litige de Val-Jalbert"; Collection of relevant documents by Mgr LAPOINTE, ASC.
[127] *L'Oiseau Mouche*, April 26, 1902; June 7, 1902.
[128] *Ibid.*, December 7, 1901.

They want the newly created French Canadian industries protected against a wave of immigration. They are afraid their very success, which has made known the resources of their region, will be the cause of their own ruin.[129] Mgr Lapointe's paper, *la Défense*, while favouring the Nordin plan inasmuch as it will provide foreign capital to open the Saguenay to ocean traffic, still fears the "Protestant" invasion and sees some danger of a second "Yankee Cuba." The slogan of his paper remains "Ours First."[130] The argument used by the railway company and the colonization society to persuade the bishop, namely, that there was a great shortage of labour in the region, was far from convincing in a province that had fought emigration for over half a century and was still fighting it.[131] The real reason for their enthusiasm seems to have been, as is admitted by the secretary of the colonization society, that this project of immigration meant additional federal subsidies for them.[132] Initially, a compromise seems to have been reached. The Finns would be settled in groups of not more than ten, would learn French, be instructed in the Catholic faith, and eventually become integrated into French Canadian society. But when this agreement was violated in 1902 the bishop directed the federal representative, Joseph Girard, to fight the project, which he now considered "un danger national et religieux."[133] The alarm of the clergy seems to have been quite unnecessary, for neither Finns nor Finnish capital were to play an important role in the Saguenay.

In all this controversy, the "French Canadian" or "national" interest seems to get equal or even more than equal attention compared with the religious interest. This impression finds some confirmation in the fact that the bishop likewise refuses to accept into his diocese a compact group of Welsh Catholics accompanied by their own priest.[134] However, the bishop always remains primarily a pastor of souls supporting

---

[129] *Ibid.*, November 23, 1901.
[130] *La Défense*, November 21, 1901.
[131] Letters of J.G. SCOTT, Secrétaire de la Cie du Chemin de Fer de Québec et du Lac Saint-Jean, and of R. DUPONT, Secrétaire de la Société de Repatriement et de Colonisation du Lac Saint-Jean, to Mgr Labrecque of April 16 and 12, 1902, EAC, 3-191-1-42 and 3-235-1-35.
[132] Letter of R. DUPONT, *supra*.
[133] Letter of Mgr LABRECQUE to Joseph Girard, federal representative, April 6, 1902, ASHS, Document No. 356.
[134] Letter of Mgr LABRECQUE to Rev. J. Brunel, priest, Swansea, Wales, March 10, 1903, EAC. The reason given by the bishop for refusing, namely that the missions were already established and provided with chapels and priests, however valid from the point of good order in the diocese, was probably less than convincing to these would-be Welsh immigrants.

and controlling the initiatives of his clergy in temporal affairs in the interest of keeping an orderly diocese. For him even the settling of French Canadians in the region should not be allowed to upset this good order substantially. On occasion he reveals both his enthusiasm and his reservations about this popular patriotic cause. For example, in 1899, when J.G. Scott, secretary of the railway company, wrote to ask him for a priest for a new settlement opened by the railway, the bishop warmly thanked him for all his interest in the colonization of the region. Nevertheless, he wearily added, probably wondering where he would find a priest available, "Je vous avouerai sans détour que cette colonisation en masse paraît m'offrir beaucoup d'inconvénients; même au point de vue religieux."[135]

Returning to Chicoutimi, which was rapidly becoming the industrial centre of the Saguenay, we find there unprecedented harmony and co-operation between the Church and the French Canadian Chicoutimi Pulp Company. The occasion of the solemn blessing of their second mill, in November 1903, was a combined religious and civic holiday and provided the theme of local and Quebec newspapers for days on end. The key to all the excitement seems to have been that now the French Canadian flag is flying over a truly modern and well-equipped factory giving proof that "le génie canadien-français peut accomplir de grandes choses sans l'aide de gros capitaux."[136]

During the blessing ceremony, the Vicar General Belley, taking the place of the bishop who was absent in Rome and sent a congratulatory message to the company, explained that the purpose of this ceremony was to invoke God's blessing upon the enterprise, to ask Him to keep it from all accident and to bless everyone connected with it. Before proceeding to the blessing itself he urged the workers ever to be loyal to their work and their masters and to avoid all strikes.[137] Father Crechman, the French Eudist serving in the workers' parish, in his sermon at the special solemn Mass celebrated for the occasion ridiculed the lies of those who claim that the Church with her unchangeable dogmas and moral teachings is incompatible with progress. He noted how the Church revels in the masterpieces conceived by

---

[135] Letter of Mgr Labrecque to J.G. Scott, secrétaire de la Cie du Chemin de Fer de Québec et du Lac Saint-Jean, April 4, 1899, EAC.

[136] *La Défense*, October 29, 1903. In actual fact, most of the engineers and the equipment installed were American and Norwegian; they were, however, in the employ of French Canadians (cf. also *Le Soleil*, November 29, December 1 and 2, 1903; *L'Événement*, November 21, 1903).

[137] *The Chronicle* (Quebec), November 31, 1903, which also refers to the mill as "the largest pulp mill in the world."

the human intelligence and how her ministers hasten with their prayers and blessings when new ships are to be launched and new trains dispatched. Far from condemning the man who seeks to unveil the secrets of nature to better the lot of human society, the Church encourages his projects with all her power. Crechman exulted in the completion of the new "usines gigantesques," paid tribute to the men whose intelligence conceived them, and praised all these men had already done for the region.[138]

As time passed, the relations between the Company and the Church seem to have become increasingly intimate. Only a few of the more striking incidents will be mentioned here. In 1904, Dubuc was knighted by the Pope at the request of Mgr Labrecque. Though the papal brief does not explicitly mention his role of entrepreneur, in his letter of thanks, Dubuc assured the Pope that this honour "sera pour moi un puissant encouragement à travailler avec plus d'ardeur que jamais à promouvoir les intérêts temporels et moraux de la population qui m'est soumise."[139] Likewise, in 1904, the bishop himself addressed a letter to the president of the company, N. Garneau, wherein he writes of his wish to co-operate with it:

> Vous témoigner de l'intérêt, ce n'est de ma part qu'un acte de justice et un acte de légitime reconnaissance. La prospérité actuelle de Chicoutimi, nous la devons à la Cie de Pulpe. Aussi, me ferai-je toujours un devoir de témoigner, en toute occasion, ma reconnaissance aux Directeurs de cette compagnie dont j'apprécie, comme ils le méritent, l'esprit de progrès bien entendu, et surtout profondément chrétien. Nous travaillerons ensemble pour conserver à la population ouvrière les sentiments chrétiens qui la distinguent, pour son plus grand bien personnel et pour le succès de votre industrie à laquelle je souhaite la plus grande prospérité.[140]

Yet it is not the bishop personally but rather his Vicar General, Mgr E. Lapointe, who seems to dominate the diocese in all that relates to its material progress and organization.[141] A close friend of Alfred Dubuc, twice Superior of the seminary during this period, founder and promoter of the newspaper *la Défense*, Mgr Lapointe soon became the guiding spirit in the founding and organization of the first Catholic labour unions in

---

[138] *Le Soleil*, December 1, 1903.
[139] Copy of the letter of J.-E.-A. DUBUC to Pope Pius X; DA, Personal Scrapbook of Mrs. Dubuc, p. 71.
[140] Letter of Mgr LABRECQUE to N. Garneau, president of the Cie de Pulpe de Chicoutimi, February 5, 1904, cited in *le Progrès du Saguenay*, January 24, 1907.
[141] In fact, on one occasion, the bishop had to remind Mgr Lapointe that he was still Superior of the seminary and would have to cut down his frequent absences (see letter of Mgr LABRECQUE to Mgr E. Lapointe, August 22, 1910, ASC).

America at the Chicoutimi pulp mill.   His, like Dubuc's, was a vision which at once encompassed the whole future history of the French Canadian race in the Saguenay.   Much later he would write in his memoirs,

> Nous ne fûmes cependant pas lents [Dubuc and Lapointe] à nous comprendre, et sans nous le confesser, nous entretenions sur l'avenir de la région du Saguenay, par exemple, les mêmes pensées, les mêmes ambitions.   Il était né homme d'affaires; j'étais éducateur par vocation.   Nous vîmes que notre effort commun, chacun dans son domaine, devait tendre à donner aux Canadiens-français en héritage et dans son intégrité le domaine saguenéen.[142]

Mgr Lapointe had already through his newspaper *la Défense* often championed better education, adult education through night school, professional training for the workers, saving, temperance, etc., but in 1903 he took more direct action by founding La Fédération Ouvrière.   At first it brought together only a few dozen workers and its major accomplishment seems to have been a small mutual savings bank, "une caisse d'économie."[143]   Plans were already afoot in 1905 to do more, and finally, in 1907, he founded La Fédération Ouvrière de Chicoutimi over the opposition of several political and municipal leaders and even of some of the "piliers du temple."[144]   Perhaps his strongest opposition came from the federal representative, Joseph Girard, who objected to Lapointe's exclusion of all political influence in the movement while he at the same time allowed for some "membres honoraires," among them employers and capitalists, who could thereby control the union at their pleasure.   Lapointe's reply to Girard is at once blunt and realistic,

> En fait, Monsieur Girard, toutes les sociétés ouvrières sont menées en dernier ressort par des hommes qui n'appartiennent pas à la profession ouvrière.
> Prenez par exemple, le Congrès des Métiers et du Travail du Canada, ce vaste syndicat de presque toutes nos sociétés ouvrières, qui n'est au fond qu'une organisation politique et monstrueuse exploitation, qui est-ce qui mène là?   Des ouvriers?
> Les ouvriers sont toujours menés par quelqu'un, vous le savez bien.
> Toute la question est de savoir s'ils doivent être menés par des gens éclairés et consciencieux, qui soient en même temps des hommes d'œuvres, ou bien par des exploiteurs ignorants et malfaisants.[145]

[142] Mgr E. LAPOINTE, "Recueil de Souvenirs," p. 44, ASC.
[143] M. TÊTU, "Les premiers syndicats catholiques canadiens," p. 89.
[144] Letter of Mgr LAPOINTE to Joseph Girard, federal representative, April 18, 1907, ASHS.
[145] Letter of Mgr LAPOINTE to Joseph Girard, federal representative, December 11, 1907, ASHS.

Nevertheless, despite all his guarantees that he would not permit his union to be exploited by employers he later had to drop them as honorary members since the workers were distrustful of them. The Constitution written at this time spells out the excessively idealistic and overambitious purpose of the new union which was to be essentially Catholic and fully independent of all political and municipal influences. It reads in part:

> La Fédération Ouvrière de Chicoutimi a pour objet d'étude, la protection et le développement des intérêts moraux et matériels de ses membres.
>
> Elle s'occupera spécialement d'améliorer la situation économique des ouvriers dans les limites de sa circonciption, en encourageant, dans la mesure de ses moyens, la mutualité catholique et nationale; en favorisant la création, en dehors d'elle, de sociétés coopératives de consommation et de crédit, d'une bourse de travail qui garantira le travailleur honnête contre le chômage et assurera à l'employeur des ouvriers honnêtes et compétents; d'une caisse d'économie populaire, d'unions professionnelles, d'écoles spéciales, où les jeunes gens qui ont fait leur cours modèle ou commercial dans les institutions déjà établies, acquerront, avant leur entrée en apprentissage, les connaissances techniques qui leur seront indispensables dans l'exercice de leur profession; en organisant en un mot, le travail suivant les principes de la justice, de l'équité et de la charité, en conformité des lois du pays et en parfaite soumission aux directions de l'Église, notamment à celles données par les papes Léon XIII et Pie X.[146]

If this is the more sober official rationalization of the new Catholic unions, it is enlightening to catch Mgr Lapointe off guard as it were when he is explaining on another occasion the founding of the Fédération. His remarks on this occasion leave one with a strong suspicion that at the beginning, at least, the religious motivation was quite secondary to the economic and nationalist one:

> La grande industrie canadienne-française de la pâte à papier venait de naître au bord du Saguenay. C'était, à nos yeux,—nous étions peut-être naïfs,—un commencement de conquête économique, une première digue dressée contre le flot envahissant du capital étranger en train de nous submerger. Nous eûmes l'intuition qu'une telle tentative, cependant, était probablement vouée à l'avortement si le travail, dans nos usines, n'était pas de son côté libéré de la tyrannie d'une direction étrangère omnipotente.

And he goes on to admit that the Fédération's first programme between 1907 and 1912 was too idealistic and vast to be successful. What really saved the union was the war undertaken by

---

[146] M. TÊTU, "Les premiers syndicats," p. 92.

the international unions to dispose of this new union: the workers like a fight! He concludes, "Ce fut définitivement le salut."[147]

The minute book of the Fédération clearly reveals that prior to 1912 this union was primarily preoccupied with the promotion of mutual insurance, "caisses d'économie," adult education, etc.; but by that year, it had won preference in all the local companies under the management of Alfred Dubuc.[148] Mgr Lapointe, as chaplain, secretary, and general organizer of the Fédération, set up branches in the surrounding mills at Jonquière, Bagotville, Saint-Fulgence, Val-Jalbert, Kénogami, etc., in an attempt to prevent further inroads by the international unions. By 1914, the new Fédération had a membership of about 3,000.[149] Much of its success in this latter period was due to the full backing lent to the movement by Mgr Labrecque in a directive addressed to all the clergy in March, 1912.

In this directive he assigns the Fédération the task of improving the social and economic situation of the workers and of preventing the introduction of the international unions into the diocese, for they are of socialist tendencies or "entachées du vice de la neutralité." He energetically defends the right of the workers to associate to protect their rights and promote "le développement progressif de leur bien-être matériel et moral." And he names Mgr Lapointe to head a committee to help the workers "dans la création et l'organisation matérielle d'organismes sociaux et économiques." The bishop indicates no sign of alarm, but is rather satisfied with what has already been done by both industry and the Church and now tries to foresee the economic, social, and moral needs of the thousands of industrial workers who will soon be established in his diocese. He here seems to accept industrial society on its own merits with no reference to either agriculture or settlement, and if he does not talk of industrial workers having a special vocation as he earlier did of farmers and settlers, yet his whole preoccupation is to study the situation of the workers and see "Ce qu'on a fait jusqu'ici et ce qui reste à faire de notre part pour le bien religieux, moral, et même matériel de cette portion si intéressante de la population de ce diocèse."[150]

---

[147] Mgr E. Lapointe, undated conference on the history of the Fédération, ASC·

[148] La Fédération Ouvrière de Chicoutimi, "Procès verbaux des assemblées générales et des assemblées du conseil de direction de la Fédération Ouvrière de Chicoutimi et histoire de sa fondation," unpublished manuscript, 1907–1914, p. 78, ASC.

[149] M. Têtu, "Les premiers syndicats," p. 110.

[150] Mgr Labrecque, "Circulaire au Clergé sur la Question ouvrière," *MLPC* (Chicoutimi, March 19, 1912), pp. 309, 312, 314, 315.

From the minutes of its meetings, it is clear that without the initiative of Mgr Lapointe the Fédération would have come to nothing. He himself remarked ruefully at one of the meetings, "Je me demande ce que vous feriez sans union et sans prêtre à votre tête..."[151] For example, they gladly and unanimously voted that he should meet with Dubuc to get him to introduce the 3-shift system and the 8-hour day.[152] It is to Lapointe's credit that he continually pushed them to take the initiative themselves and to do their own bargaining. And their demands were usually granted.[153]

There is little doubt that the pulp company was indebted to the Church and especially to Mgr Lapointe for providing it with peaceful, honest, patient labourers during this period, for the company being often short of working capital did not have the reputation of keeping a regular pay-day schedule. In fact, Dr. J.-A. Couture, one of its directors and the most enthusiastic of Dubuc's biographers, interprets it as a tribute to his hero that on one extraordinary occasion when he was in particular trouble he managed o keep his work force intact for a period of six months without their receiving a cent of their wages.[154] And we find a similar, better documented case reported in the Fédération's minute book in 1914. On this occasion, Mgr Lapointe engaged all his personal prestige and influence to win Dubuc a respite from a threatening strike for several weeks while the latter scoured Europe for the necessary funds to pay his workers.[155]

Yet the Fédération did obtain solid gains at this time in wages, hours, conditions, and a more regular pay-schedule. And when the company was not in financial straits it was generous to the workers, paying an additional 3 per cent interest on all savings in *la caisse de petite économie*, organizing feast and sports days, banquets for their foremen and department heads, etc.

The initiative of the pulp company, in fact, the initiatives of all industrialists in the region including William Price, received encouragement and glowing praise in the monthly parish bulletin which was edited by the Eudist Fathers in charge of the workers' parish.[156] Perhaps never has an industrialist had more faithful

---

[151] "Procès verbaux," March 22, 1914, p. 260.
[152] *Ibid.*, April 3, 1913, p. 63.
[153] *Ibid.*, June 30, 1913, p. 188.
[154] ALEXIS (Dr J.-A. Couture), "Le roman d'un Canadien français," *l'Événement* (Québec), December 30, 1916 and January 3, 1917; reproduced in *le Progrès du Saguenay*, January 10, 1917 and August 16, 1942.
[155] "Procès verbaux", March 15, 18 and 22; May 9, 1914, pp. 249–62.
[156] *L'Écho paroissial du Sacré-Cœur*, monthly bulletin, ASHS.

and favourable chroniclers of all his undertakings than had Dubuc in these enthusiastic priests. They likewise supported in their parish bulletin all the efforts undertaken by the bishop and Mgr Lapointe to foster the *caisses populaires*, temperance, adult education, professional training, Catholic trade unions, etc. Perhaps symbolic of their enthusiasm is their whole-hearted approval of the acceptance by the Société de Géographie of the local suggestion that the two new townships in the county be named Lapointe and Dubuc respectively, the former to honour Mgr Lapointe, the latter J.-E.-A. Dubuc, "gérant de la Compagnie de Pulpe de Chicoutimi et l'une des personnalités les plus marquantes du monde industriel."[157]

One of the most important changes in the Saguenay district during this period, but one to which only passing reference can be made, is that the rising star of the French Canadian, Dubuc, began to dim somewhat the lustre of the former "kings" of the Saguenay, the members of the Price family, and particularly that of William Price II. Unfortunately, this period was marked by an endless series of bitter lawsuits carried on between the two interests and their representatives. For years a most acrimonious name-calling battle was waged between *le Progrès du Saguenay*, owned by the directors of the Compagnie de Pulpe de Chicoutimi, and *le Travailleur*, the local French Canadian defender of the Price interests and especially of their lawyer, L.-G. Belley.[158] It does honour to neither side that their partisan efforts often crippled Chicoutimi's political life and thwarted many bold initiatives. Dubuc seems to have gained a Pyrrhic victory in 1909, when the Privy Council in England finally awarded him the ownership of a valuable strip of land bordering on the river at Chicoutimi over which he and Price had fought in the courts for over a decade.[159] This defeat in the courts seems to have been one of the principal reasons why William Price built his big new paper mill at Kénogami instead of Chicoutimi. By 1914, this new mill was producing about 50,000 tons of newsprint annually and its success marked the beginning of the Price Brothers' economic re-conquest of the Saguenay.

---

[157] *Ibid.*, April 1914.

[158] At times these partisan newspapers carried attacks on the persons of Dubuc and Price. For example, see *le Progrès du Saguenay*, November 11, 1904; August 23, 1906. And, in 1909, Dubuc won three cases against *le Travailleur* involving libellous attacks on himself and the company; one of them dealt with an attempt to undermine the company's credit and solvability (see *le Progrès du Saguenay*, October 28, 1909).

[159] The higher Church officials kept a strict neutrality on these quarrels but at least on one occasion the Eudist Fathers did not. In 1907, they hailed one of Dubuc's victories in the courts by flying the flag publicly (see *le Progrès du Saguenay*, February 21, 1907).

By 1951, this company would be producing 452,617 tons of newsprint in the region, when the name of Dubuc would be merely a cherished memory—the embodiment of what might have been.[160] In his memoirs, Mgr Lapointe recalls that dream which he and many a priest shared with Alfred Dubuc:

> Il ambitionna de prendre pour lui-même et de donner à ceux de sa race et de sa foi, dans la grande industrie, la place qui semblait réservée jusque là aux Anglo-Canadiens et aux Américains. Et il y réussit. On put croire un moment que la partie était définitivement gagnée.[161]

In speaking of how Dubuc lost out in the twenties to more powerful financial interests, Lapointe asks himself the question, Who was responsible? He answers, "La puissance financière Anglo-Canadienne centrée sur la Banque de Montréal, l'explique bien peut-être pour la large part." But in considering the matter further, he concludes: "Mais notre individualisme foncier et incorrigible, à nous Canadiens-français, en fut sans doute la cause principale."[162]

But, for a quarter of a century before disappearing from big business into federal politics, Dubuc was held in esteem and respect by the English and American financial world, and for the French Canadians was a conquering hero capable of proving that a French Canadian could compete successfully in the world of big business. His renown reached its peak during World War I, when in addition to being managing director of the Compagnie de Pulpe de Chicoutimi and having formed and controlled some half dozen smaller local utility and railway companies, he was elected president of the new 30 million dollar merger of his own pulp company with the two big American companies, the Tidewater Paper Mills of Brooklyn and the St. Lawrence Pulp and Paper Lumber Corporation of Gaspé. He was also invited to reorganize the St. Lawrence Corporation which had been losing money. At the same time he undertook to build a new chemical pulp company for English interests on Ha Ha Bay, at Port-Alfred, which was named "Alfred" after him. Needless to say, he was, at this time, the subject of extravagant biographies published under such colourful titles as

---

[160] PRICE BROTHERS' SALES CORPORATION, "Production Records," Price Brothers Archives, Quebec.

[161] Mgr E. LAPOINTE, "Recueil de souvenirs", p. 42.

[162] See *ibid.*, p. 28. He had discussed earlier in his "Recueil" how such growing financial powers as Dubuc and Forget had refused to work together, though together, prior to World War I, they were capable of controlling the whole Saguenay region and more. He is also thinking of the perpetual wrangling among French Canadians that had brought many a bold initiative to nought.

"Le roman d'un Canadien-français," and *Une industrie; une région; un homme*, the former written by one of the directors of the Compagnie de Pulpe, Dr. J.-A. Couture as "Alexis," and the latter by a member of the Royal Society of Canada, the Honourable Rodolphe Lemieux.

If Dubuc had been most generous to the Church and her institutions, the Church had also lent him and his associates every conceivable form of public and private aid and encouragement. He was not only knighted by the Pope and publicly supported in all his initiatives by the bishop and Mgr Lapointe, the Vicar General of the diocese; we even find the bishop helping him on a more humble and practical level by refusing to let a curé take legal action against him for damage sustained through the fault of his company,[163] and advising the Mother Superior of the Hôtel-Dieu de Saint-Vallier to make a gift of a certain piece of land required by Dubuc for his work and to rely simply on his generosity.[164]

But did the Church by wholeheartedly endorsing Dubuc's efforts give short shrift to or damage the industrial interests of the Price family in the region? It does not seem so, although here harmony was at times less than perfect. Certainly Mgr Labrecque was most solicitous that the Church's relations with this important family be as friendly as they were in the past. In 1902, he took quick action to correct the situation when a visiting priest wrote an article prejudicial to William Price. He asked the federal representative, Joseph Girard, to assure Price that these were not his sentiments,[165] and on his own initiative he arranged a personal meeting with William Price to assure him that this was so. As he told Girard on March 1, "Je suis en bons termes avec M. Price qui a toute ma confiance et je ne voudrais pour rien au monde lui créer aucun embarras; ce serait ingratitude de ma part." However, if Price mistook Labrecque for a weak man, he was soon to discover his mistake, when he tried to exercise pressure on the bishop on the alleged grounds that he had supported the Nordin project to settle Finns in the Saguenay against Price's personal interests. Mgr Labrecque denied the allegation and reminded him that to supply a chapel and a priest for his workers at L'Anse Sainte-

---

[163] Letter of Mgr LABRECQUE to the curé of Saint-Fidèle, M. O. Larouche, November 29, 1908, EAC. He gives the additional reason that the clergy should not give bad example to the faithful in this matter of indulging in lawsuits.

[164] Copy of the letter of Mgr LABRECQUE to Révérende Mère St-Gabriel, Superior of the Hôtel-Dieu de Saint-Vallier, July 26, 1912, EAC.

[165] Letters of Mgr LABRECQUE to Joseph Girard, federal representative, January 28; March 1 and 23, 1902, ASHS.

Catherine is not a favour he has to ask of Mr. Price, and that if the latter does not concern himself with the matter neither will he. He wrote bluntly,

> Si vous croyez justifiable de vous désintéresser d'un projet sollicité par vos agents dans l'intérêt de votre établissement, vous admettrez facilement que je serai aussi justifiable de ne rien faire et de laisser peser sur vous toute la responsabilité de cet état de choses. Je doute fort que la population ouvrière de Sainte-Catherine aime à se voir condamnée soit à aller à Tadoussac pour ses besoins religieux, soit à vivre sans religion.—Si vous tentez l'épreuve, vous pourriez bien avant longtemps revenir à la pratique de vos prédécesseurs qui ont toujours favorisé les intérêts religieux de leurs ouvriers comme la plus sûre garantie de leurs intérêts temporels.

He ended by saying that if the local curé was not adequately supported by the company and the workers, he would simply remove him.[166]

This open disagreement seems to be very much the exception at this time. Nevertheless, when Price took over the pulp mill at Jonquière in 1903 and started to produce cardboard he unwittingly sowed the seeds of future trouble with the Church. At first, the new company cut out Sunday work at the request of Church officials, but pleaded to be allowed to work until 6 a.m. on Sunday morning. Among other reasons the most important mentioned is the fact that certain key "foreign" workers on the cardboard machine belong to the international union and refuse to begin work at midnight on Sunday.[167] The same problem came up again in 1906, and reached a crisis in December 1912, when the bishop, who had from the beginning vigorously fought this blatant violation of a sacred French Canadian Catholic tradition, wrote a pastoral letter on the matter, obviously aimed at the Sunday work being carried on by the Price Brothers and other companies in his diocese.[168]

He argues that such work is illegal both in dominion and provincial law. He claims that complete Sunday rest cannot harm the prosperity of industry because it provides it with workers enjoying physical, intellectual, and moral superiority. He enlists the authority of unnamed economists to give irrefutable proof that Sunday-working countries produce at much higher costs than Sunday-resting countries because of the vigour

---

[166] Copy of a letter of Mgr LABRECQUE to William Price, February 17, 1903, EAC.

[167] Letter from LA CIE DE PULPE DE JONQUIÈRE to the Vicar General Belley, March 9, 1903, EAC, 21-5-4-3.

[168] Mgr LABRECQUE, "Lettre pastorale sur la sanctification du dimanche et le repos dominical," *MLPC* (Chicoutimi, December 15, 1912), pp. 330–40.

and capability of the latter's workers.   On the other hand, the Church is the enemy of "tout rigorisme pharisaïque."   When urgent or necessary work must be done he will readily permit it, but what he is absolutely against is the *habit* of Sunday work, "la coutume de traiter le saint jour du dimanche comme un jour ordinaire."   And he concludes by reminding both employers and workers that no one can compel such Sunday work, which violates both the dictates of conscience and the laws of the country.

Mr. Price seems to have accepted this directive of the bishop willingly enough, for he promises him that he will do everything possible to discontinue Sunday work in the near future.[169]   Unfortunately, this exercise of moral pressure on the part of the bishop to stop all Sunday work in the Saguenay coincided with Mgr Lapointe's vigorous efforts to organize the Price Brothers' plants and to dislodge the internationals.   The company, under pressure from its competitors—the majority of paper mills in the province did some Sunday work and the pulp mill of Dubuc was one of the very few pulp mills which did not—and under pressure from his unionized paper makers, who had been accustomed to Sunday work elsewhere in the province, seems to have finally chosen against the Church and the Catholic unions.

Earlier, Mgr Lapointe had gone out of his way to assure the French Canadian workers at Kénogami that the Price Brothers Company was directed by "des hommes honorables," who would listen to the demands of the workers to cease Sunday work and discrimination against French Canadian in favour of Anglo-Saxon workers.   He singled out Price himself for special praise: "M. Price ... est l'héritier des traditions de gentilhommerie de ses oncles, qui furent les pionniers de l'industrie dans le Saguenay, et dont le souvenir vit encore parmi nous.   Je suis en mesure de vous affirmer que M. Price est animé des intentions les plus bienveillantes à votre égard et qu'il ne tardera pas à faire les réformes que vous réclamez à juste titre."[170]   But Mgr Lapointe's hopes were premature.   Sunday work was in fact stopped for a while at the Jonquière plant, but it was soon resumed.   Clearly Price was not interested in joining forces with Mgr Lapointe to oust the international union in favour of the Catholic union by rejecting the demands of the former to continue Sunday

---

[169] Letter of William PRICE to Mgr Labrecque, January 28, 1913; February 1, 1913, EAC, 62-11-1-3 and 62-11-1-5.
[170] *Le Progrès du Saguenay*, April 10, 1913.   This is not a direct quotation but only a report of what he said on this occasion.

work.[171] The new Catholic union did not interest the Price Brothers in the least, and these men, like many other Quebec employers, were quite disillusioned to find their former great ally, the Church, now becoming directly involved in the labour unions.

Matters came suddenly to a head in April 1914. The Company did the unforgivable: it fired some Catholic workers who had refused to appear for Sunday work at the Jonquière plant on the express advice of Mgr Lapointe and the officials of the Catholic union.[172] As Vicar General, and in the bishop's absence, Mgr Lapointe retaliated by refusing to allow Curé Lavoie to bless the Price Brothers' new mill at Saint-Gédéon to the great consternation of the company, the workers, and the local clergy.[173]

Apparently Price suspected that his old enemy Dubuc and his associates at Chicoutimi were behind the whole affair.[174] And, in fact, Dubuc was an easy target for their suspicions. Since his appearance as a successful French Canadian entrepreneur in the Saguenay, the two companies had been locked in perpetual bitter lawsuits in the courts; Dubuc's paper, *le Progrès du Saguenay*, was the most severe critic of Price Brothers and had carried all Mgr Lapointe's thundering condemnations of the Sunday work carried on in their plants; Dubuc had eagerly given work to the employees fired by Price for refusing to work on Sunday; it was under Dubuc's benign auspices that the Catholic union had gained power, and its inspirer, Mgr Lapointe, was known to be his dear friend; finally, and most galling of all, Dubuc was for the bishops and the government the model employer who did not work Sundays and so gave "proof" that such work was not necessary for a company to be profitable—at least in the pulp industry.[175]

[171] Copy of a letter from Mgr E. LAPOINTE to William Price, January 12, 1912, ASC. In this whole controversy it is difficult to distinguish the role of William Price from that of the Price Brothers' Company. Here we use these names interchangeably.

[172] Letter of the FÉDÉRATION OUVRIÈRE to the local at Jonquière, April 23, 1914; and the official notice asking the workers not to appear for Sunday work, April 27, 1914, ASC.

[173] Letter of Curé Joseph LAPOINTE of Kénogami to Mgr Lapointe, June 16, 1914. ASC.

[174] *Ibid.*, where the Curé Lapointe tells Mgr Lapointe that the local manager, Mr. McCarthy, as well as William Price believe "que c'était Dubuc qui était en dessous de toute cette affaire."

[175] Nor was it any consolation for Price Brothers that the editor of the *Pulp and Paper Magazine* wholeheartedly endorsed the stand of Dubuc's *Progrès du Saguenay*. He writes of this Sunday work (March 1914, p. 125), "As pointed out recently in the columns of the *Pulp and Paper Magazine*, this is not necessary, and a mill can earn more money by eliminating entirely any regular Sunday work. The report of efficiency engineers of the American Paper and Pulp Assoc. states that mill paper can be made by doing repairs on a Saturday shut-down. We heartily agree with *le Progrès du Saguenay* that Sunday work is unnecessary."

In the government investigation into Sunday work that followed, the Price Brothers chose to overlook all the private correspondence which William Price and his agents had carried on with the bishop, Mgr Lapointe, and the Fédération Ouvrière and simply stated:

> Comme nous n'avons pas reçu de plaintes de la part de nos gens et que d'après ce que nous en connaissons la meilleure entente existe entre nous,... C'est notre intention d'exploiter notre fabrique comme par le passé, comme 'Atelier libre', et quand se produiront des grèves, de congédier tous les grévistes et de les remplacer par d'autres.[176]

What emerges from this unfortunate confrontation is that neither the bishop, nor the Catholic union, nor the weak temporizing provincial government could bring a strong obstinate English Canadian company into line on this matter of Sunday work, although all were agreed that the company was in the wrong; it must also be recognized that the company rightly felt that the government should not make it the whipping boy while it allowed other pulp and paper makers to continue to work Sundays with impunity. The end result was that Sunday work continued in these Saguenay plants until after the tragic drowning of William Price in a landslide at his Jonquière mill in 1924—an accident which many local people considered "an act of God" even though the Catholic press of the province took the occasion to praise Price as one of the great benefactors of both the province and the French Canadian race.[177]

If the Church, through its Catholic unions, could exclude and even at times dislodge the international unions, calm the spirits of Catholic workers, and thus initially render an encouragement and service to local employers, she was soon to learn that few in number are the employers who will heed the arguments of sweet reasonableness and charity on the part of unions, even Catholic unions, unless they are backed by a sizeable strike fund. It is clear from this open disagreement with the Price Brothers that they were much more concerned by the fact that a local curé had refused to bless one of their mills at Saint-Gédéon than by the fact that they had incurred the displeasure of the bishop, the government, and the Catholic union, for before the investigating committee they angrily stated:

> Cette fabrique de Saint-Gédéon est l'un des deux nouveaux établissements qui ont été ouverts cette année, et nous nous permettrons de dire que c'est un étrange encouragement à nous donner pour établir

[176] Price Brothers Company, "Rapport re: travail du dimanche aux ateliers de Kénogami," in F. MAROIS, *Rapport adressé à l'Honorable L.-A. Taschereau*, p. 20.
[177] See letter of Mgr LAPOINTE to Jules Dorion, Director of *l'Action Catholique*, October 13, 1924, complaining of this fact. ASC.

de nouvelles industries dans le district du Saguenay, surtout si l'on considère que voilà maintenant plus d'un siècle que nous travaillons dans ce district en harmonie et en relations amicales avec nos employés.[178]

And yet Price, or any other English or American industrialist, could have all the encouragement and blessings of the Church—if not the warm effusive admiration which her ministers reserved for a French Canadian Dubuc—and could have them even though he violated openly sacred local customs under the pressure of competition or of small groups of specialized "foreign" workers. Such disagreements were usually aired at a high level and their echoes caused only consternation for the local curé who was inevitably indebted to the local company officials, even as they were to him. As is clear from weekly announcement books, the curé of neither Jonquière nor Kénogami attacked the Price Brothers Company on the Sunday work issue even though they clearly set forth the Church's position on this matter.[179]

But rising French Canadian nationalism and the Sunday-work issue would take their toll over time. It was all too easy to cast Price as the villain and Dubuc as the hero; and that is what happened in the postwar period. For example, at the provincial Catholic Action Congress held in Chicoutimi in 1919, Dubuc is introduced as a truly progressive industrialist, and at his appearance the whole assembly took up the chant "Il a gagné ses épaulettes!" On the other hand, one of the *missionnaires agricoles*, Abbé Jean Bergeron, took occasion to stigmatize the "pierre menteuse" (the Price monument in Chicoutimi) which calls William Price "le père du Saguenay" although, in reality, he was "la cause des causes qui ont retardé de vingt-cinq ans le développement de notre région."[180] But there continued to be as always many a French Canadian worker, who, as one old Scot put it, ardently believed like his father before him that "it was an honour to work for Price in the Saguenay, even if it was only to shovel manure. For Price looked after his men and their families."[181]

---

[178] MAROIS, *op. cit.*, p. 20.
[179] See "Cahiers de prône et d'annonce de la paroisse de Sainte-Famille de Kénogami," Presbytery Archives of Kénogami; "Cahier d'annonce de la paroisse St. Dominique de Jonquière," Presbytery Archives, Jonquière. This same concern on the part of the local curés not to offend the company is expressed in the letter of Curé Joseph LAPOINTE of Kénogami to Mgr Lapointe, June 16, 1914, ASC.
[180] L'ASSOCIATION CATHOLIQUE DE LA JEUNESSE CANADIENNE-FRANÇAISE, *Le problème de la colonisation au Canada français*, report of the Congress held in Chicoutimi, June 29-July 2, 1919, pp. 244, 161.
[181] Interview with Mr. Charles F. Louthood of Jonquière, August, 1962. He has lived and worked at Jonquière since 1902.

EDUCATION

The pattern for education follows closely that found in the St. Maurice Valley, and the description here will be brief. We find the local curé at every turn pushing for improvements in primary education and bringing some stability into the teaching profession by introducing brothers and sisters into his parish schools. For example, at Roberval it is Curé Lizotte who, as we have seen, invited in the Ursulines in 1881.[182] Some years later, we find him writing to the bishop to inform him that he has arranged to bring in the Frères du Sacré-Cœur "en conformité avec vos désirs ... Leur cours est très bien adapté pour une bonne éducation commerciale en rapport avec les exigences modernes."[183] Nor was the bishop himself inactive. In 1893, he informed his clergy that henceforward authorization to employ teachers without diplomas would be accorded only in exceptional and urgent cases and on the recommendation of the school inspector of the district.[184] In 1897 he warmly congratulated the Inspector J.-E. Savard for the zeal he had shown in giving pedagogical lectures to the local teachers at which the bishop himself had been present.[185] He rebuked his clergy for not carrying out more diligently his directive to organize parish libraries to accustom the people to good reading.[186]

The inspectors' official reports leave no doubt that whatever progress was achieved in the region was largely due to the efforts of the local clergy and religious brothers and sisters. Their direct work in teaching invariably merited a eulogy. Typical are the following excerpts from the 1905 report of Inspector Savard, who has some 194 local schools under his supervision:

> Teachers are becoming scarcer and scarcer in this district. Fortunately, several of the model schools are now entrusted to the Sisters of Le Bon Conseil, who are really doing much good and this good movement seems to continue, for at Sainte-Anne, and Saint-Alexis-de-la-Grande-Baie, there will also be, next September, a school directed by the same Sisters of Le Bon Conseil...
> The Chicoutimi Seminary ever maintains its high renown...
> The Ursuline Academy of Lake St. John, directed by the Ursuline nuns, so creditably known throughout the country, goes from

[182] R. Vien, *L'Histoire de Roberval*, p. 134.
[183] Letter of Curé Joseph Lizotte of Roberval to Mgr Labrecque, May 5, 1896, EAC, 17-11-7-29.
[184] Mgr Labrecque, *MLPC* (Chicoutimi, Circular No. 11, October 1, 1893), p. 86.
[185] Copy of letter of Mgr Labrecque to J.-E. Savard, school inspector, December 11, 1897, EAC.
[186] Mgr Labrecque, *MLPC* (Chicoutimi, Circular No. 80, October 7, 1905), p. 383.

one success to another and the number of pupils is increasing so that an annex is now being built to open upon the re-opening of schools in September...

The Marist Brothers of Chicoutimi, Roberval, and Saint-Alphonse, are doing much good in those places. Their schools show marked progress each year.[187]

Typical also are the remarks of Inspector A.-H. Simard concerning another more remote area of the diocese, the western portion of Saguenay County. He wrote in 1910 in his official report: "They who assert that the Canadian clergy are not helping on elementary education, have only to visit those districts to become convinced of the contrary. In all fairness, I must attribute this substantial progress to the priest in each parish."[188]

There is constant progress. The number of teachers without diplomas of any kind dropped from 43 to 1, in the short period 1895–1897,[189] regular pedagogical congresses were organized for the teachers, a normal school conducted by religious sisters was opened in Chicoutimi in 1906 to train local teachers, and, in 1914, a regional meeting of the school commissioners was held at Roberval in which the clergy and especially Mgr Lapointe played a major role.[190] Nevertheless, school attendance still remained as low as 75 per cent in 1914, particularly because of the youngsters 5–7 years old who often stayed home from November to April.[191] The turnover among teachers, due particularly to poor pay, still ran as high as one third of the total annually, with some 78 out of 189 teachers leaving their positions in 1914.[192] Rural Quebec especially was slow to learn the lesson that in education one cannot expect marvels without paying something for them. Ironically, the harshness of the lesson was often softened by the devotedness of priests, religious brothers and sisters who did not compel the people to pay adequately for their services even when they became able to do so. Nevertheless, the general impression one has of this remote area is that the Church threw her full energies and resources into educating a people who often still did not sufficiently value education.

The Séminaire de Chicoutimi merits particular attention. It was the chief centre of higher education in the region and the

---

[187] "Reports of School Inspectors," *Sessional Papers*, XXXVIII (1905), Part II, No. 5, pp. 90-91.

[188] *Ibid.*, XLIII (1910), Part II, No. 8, p. 115.

[189] *Ibid.*, XXXI (1897), Part II, No. 5, p. 93.

[190] *Ibid.*, XLVIII (1915), Part I, No. 8, p. 13.

[191] *Ibid.*, p. 18.

[192] *Ibid.*, pp. 133-34.

constant object of unstinted praise on the part of the government school inspectors. It was a combined commercial and classical college, whose primary purpose, as the bishop clearly stated, was to provide the diocese with young priests, but whose task was also to form "la classe dirigeante de la société."[193] It was economically viable by means of a nominal annual salary of $100 paid to the priest professors, an annual tax on all the clergy of the diocese, the donations of benefactors,[194] the ridiculously low fees of the students,[195] and an annual grant of $1,000 from the provincial government. In a typical year, 1913-1914, it had 364 students of whom 246 were in the commercial course; and the operating expenses for the year amounted to $36,313.[196]

The classical course might go on virtually unchanged, but there are some notable changes in the Séminaire at this time. Already in 1894, and probably much earlier, there was a "Banque du Séminaire de Chicoutimi" operated by the students to initiate them in business practices and a course in bookkeeping was carried on in English.[197] With the arrival of the pulp industry in the Saguenay, in 1897, the Séminaire had two priests specially prepared to teach a fifth year in the commercial course, the so-called "classe d'affaires." Its purpose and content are described in the prospectus with naive optimism:

> L'enseignement s'y donne en anglais. Toutes les matières commerciales y sont enseignées avec soin, au point de vue pratique, de manière à mettre les élèves qui auront suivi cette classe en état de remplir avantageusement tous les postes commerciaux qu'on pourra leur confier.[198]

The Séminaire won the warm congratulations of the inspector for this initiative. He wrote in his official report:

> The Minor Seminary of Chicoutimi will add to its commercial course a "business class." This important addition to the curriculum of this

[193] Mgr LABRECQUE, *MLPC* (Chicoutimi, Circular No. 89, August 15, 1907), p. 20.

[194] Alfred Dubuc was a most generous benefactor and on the occasion of the building of the new seminary, in 1911, contributed $90,000 to foster priestly vocations, so that this education could be carried on exclusively by priests, and to promote besides this classical education, for those capable, "cette éducation moyenne, commerciale ou autre, qui en fera des ouvriers plus ouverts, partant plus compétents, mieux élevés, et donc des Catholiques plus éclairés et formés et des citoyens plus honnêtes. "(Copy of a letter of J.-E.-A. DUBUC to the superior of the Séminaire, Personal Scrapbook of Mrs. Dubuc, p. 110, DA). Dubuc, perhaps at that time French Canada's shrewdest businessman and industrialist, reveals a sense of inferiority because he did not have the good fortune to have a classical education. In the letter mentioned above he writes, "Nous savons par expérience ce que vaut à l'homme d'affaire comme à l'homme de profession la haute culture intellectuelle puisée dans un cours classique, aussi bien que ce qui manque à celui qui ne l'a pas reçue..."

[195] See *Annuaire du séminaire de Chicoutimi* (1894-1895), p. 297, where the total fees for a boarder are given as $100 per year and those of a day student as $1.50 per month.

[196] *Statistical Year Book*, II (1915), 308-309.

[197] *Annuaire du séminaire* (1894-1895), p. 314.

[198] *Ibid.*, 1897-1898, p. 502.

establishment will doubtless be appreciated by the business men of our parts, and the town of Chicoutimi in particular; the starting of large business firms and new manufactures, the impetus lately given to already established industries in the neighborhood, require the services of young people speaking English and French correctly and sufficiently initiated into business ways. The Seminary has not hesitated to make fresh sacrifices to respond to the legitimate aspirations of fathers of families by forming this fifth class, which will be a worthy crown of the commercial class.[199]

These professors of classics show a continued concern, both in the Séminaire's paper, the little *Oiseau Mouche*, and in Mgr Lapointe's *la Défense*, for practical education and the very complex problem of reconciling intellectual culture with attachment to the manual professions.[200] They even see it as a mistake for the government and others to promote the liberal arts rather than manual labour.[201] Moreover, as we have already seen, Mgr Lapointe, himself twice superior of the Séminaire, is an ardent promoter of adult education through night school. He takes every occasion, as does Alfred Dubuc, to urge French Canadian day-labourers to strive to become skilled workers. In one of his typical lectures to the workers he insisted on the fact that they can only escape from the category of labourer by means of further education:

> Si vous ne tenez pas à demeurer toute votre vie de simples manœuvres il faut que l'éducation technique pénètre chez vous. Elle y est déjà, mais il en faut plus. Voyez-en les résultats par les travaux qui ont été exécutés dernièrement au vieux moulin de la Cie de Pulpe.
>
> Il y a 10 ans, il aurait fallu amener d'ailleurs des hommes compétents pour conduire le grand travail de reconstruction du moulin. Mais qu'avez-vous constaté? Seuls les ouvriers de Chicoutimi, dirigés par des contremaîtres et des ingénieurs de Chicoutimi, formés ici à l'école de l'expérience, ont exécuté ces mêmes travaux.

He went on to tell them that they are not an inferior race; they have only to study, save their earnings, and put off their timidity.[202]

However, every now and then some evidence emerges to indicate that the clergy are not all of one mind in these matters. For example, in January 1914, an old *missionnaire agricole*

---

[199] "Report of School Inspectors," *Sessional Papers*, XXXI (1897), Part II, No. 5, pp. 94-95. These priest professors were sure they would get quick results. One of them, expressing his hopes in *l'Oiseau Mouche* (June 19, 1897), was optimistic that one of the rich businessmen to be prepared at the seminary would later endow it with a chapel which they needed badly.

[200] "Trop de collèges," *La Défense*, May 12, 1898.

[201] For example, see "L'éducation pratique," *L'Oiseau Mouche*, November 5, 1898; "Le travail des mains et la culture intellectuelle," and "L'agriculture et la science," *La Défense*, May 18, 1898. At this time there was considerable criticism of the classical colleges for their failure to give "une éducation pratique."

[202] *Le Progrès du Saguenay*, May 19, 1909.

took up his pen to thunder against the proliferation of classical
and commercial colleges in the province which he saw as taking
the people off the land in to the cities.   He is particularly vehe-
ment against the commercial schools run by religious brothers,
not to mention priests:

> Je prétends... que la cause principale de la déviation de notre sens
> canadien et catholique, c'est le collège commercial...
>   En effet, quel est le but du cours commercial ?   Faire des
> hommes d'affaires avant tout...

And he is revolted by the fact that it is religious men vowed
to poverty who teach the children the principle denounced by
Christ himself, "Il faut faire de l'argent ...   Et, dans l'esprit
de ces jeunes gens cette maxime sera article de foi vu *que ce sont
de bons religieux qui les ont surtout outillés pour le commerce et
très peu pour le reste* [sic]."   As for himself, he claims for the
French Canadians as Latins a heritage in the things of the spirit;
indeed, an Anglo-Saxon commercial education is "contre nature
pour nos Canadiens."[203]

His provocative article did not go long unanswered.   In a
letter to the editor written by a former superior of the Séminaire
—doubtless, Mgr Lapointe—the old missionary and his kind
were commended for their zeal and good intentions in promoting
settlement and agriculture, but were decisively ruled out of
order for generalizing about matters in which they lack both the
necessary information and the competence to make sound judg-
ments.   The paper is rebuked for publishing the missionary's
letter without comment and further discussion of the issue in the
columns of the paper is discouraged.[204]

The classical course at the Séminaire de Chicoutimi certainly
did not promote, even if it did not actually discourage, the
formation of an economic elite or one of technical experts.   But
its commercial course aspired, perhaps naively, to do just that.
What is perhaps most striking in the whole development is the
number of these clerical classical scholars, including superiors
of the Séminaire, who are deeply preoccupied with the economic
progress of the region.   Among the most outstanding examples
are Abbé Ambroise Fafard, the great admirer of the Price Brothers' industrial achievements, who ended his days pioneering a
company for the generation and distribution of electricity at

---

[203] *Le Progrès du Saguenay*, January 15, 1914.
[204] *Ibid.*, February 12, 1914.

Baie-Saint-Paul;[205] and Mgr Lapointe, who tried by every means to assist the efforts of the French Canadian entrepreneur Dubuc to conquer an industrial kingdom for members of his race and religion in the Saguenay. The dichotomy between a classical education and economic alertness may not always be as sharp as we have been led to believe in the past. We will return to this subject in a later chapter.

[205] Nérée Tremblay, *Saint-Pierre et Saint-Paul de la Baie-Saint-Paul* (Québec: La-flamme, 1956), p. 277. At the death of Curé Fafard, in 1899, *l'Oiseau Mouche* (September 9, 1899), noting how "sous son impulsion puissante" the quiet village of Baie-Saint-Paul had suddenly sprung to life with all the modern utilities, concluded, "S'il était resté dans le monde, M. Fafard aurait probablement joué un rôle de premier ordre dans les affaires et dans la politique."

CHAPTER V

THE CHURCH'S ROLE IN NEW SETTLEMENT, COMMUNICATIONS, AND AGRICULTURE

The preceding chapters have given a picture of the scope and nature of the Church's economic attitudes and initiatives in two important regions of French Canada, the St. Maurice Valley and the Chicoutimi-Lake St. John region. How typical are they of the Church's attitudes and initiatives elsewhere in the province? The following chapters will provide a rapid survey of other major areas of the province, without, however, entering into detailed study of them. These more general findings will be compared with those already reported and similarities as well as differences in substance, nuance, or emphasis will be pointed out. In the present chapter, the attitude towards economic activity and initiatives in the areas of colonization or new settlement, communications, and agriculture will be considered. These three areas of economic endeavour tend, as we have seen, to be elements in the same over-all programme. In French Canada, "le colon est un agriculteur en puissance," as Esdras Minville has observed.[1] Without adhering to a hard and fast division, in the following two chapters we shall examine the Church's attitudes towards industry and education with particular emphasis given to the urban industrial scene.

For such a survey a number of general sources can be used:

(1) Parish and regional histories. Published histories have been collected together by the provincial archivist into one section at the Provincial Archives in Quebec City. This author has consulted 194 volumes of the collection, each of which touches on the history of at least one parish during the period 1896–1914. However, as earlier in this book the initial date has been left rather flexible so as to permit us to note whether there was any marked change in the Church's economic role at or about this key date. All regions are represented in this collection, some better than others according to their good fortune in finding historians to tell their particular story.

---

[1] Esdras MINVILLE, "La Colonisation," *L'agriculture*, in the collection *Études sur notre milieu*, ed., Esdras Minville, p. 276.

(2) The directives and pastoral letters of the bishops to the clergy and to the Catholic people during this period. Those of the more important dioceses of Montreal and Quebec are especially useful. So also are the bishops' more important public statements and initiatives, their private correspondence with the Premier of Quebec, and other relevant private initiatives where known.

(3) Official Catholic publications, especially *la Semaine religieuse* of both Montreal and Quebec, and the only major official Catholic daily newspaper, *l'Action sociale*. *La Semaine religieuse* is a weekly news bulletin issued in the two major dioceses to keep the clergy and others abreast of religious happenings. It is ordinarily religious in its content, but occasionally it indicates the clergy's position on particular economic issues. *L'Action sociale* was founded by Cardinal Bégin in 1907, with the warm commendation of Pope Pius X, and has been endorsed and actively promoted by several bishops of the province. The Cardinal wanted to have a Catholic paper, free of political attachments, supporting "avec les vrais intérêts de la patrie, la cause de Dieu, de la religion et des âmes."[2] Abbé Paul-E. Roy, whom the Cardinal named director of the Catholic press and of the works of Catholic Action, spelled out the programme of both in more detail. They were to educate the Catholic conscience, fight selfish individualism, study social questions, popularize the social sciences, organize Catholic workers in their own professional associations and so supplant or forestall the organization of their socialist counterparts, and, finally, promote various other kinds of economic association. He wrote,

> Il s'agit ici des œuvres suivantes: *Caisses* de chômage, d'épargne, de retraite, caisses rurales; *Coopératives* d'achat, de production, de consommation, de construction, de crédit; *Syndicats* agricoles et industriels; *Cercles* ruraux; *Secrétariats* du peuple; *Banques*, etc. Notre pays est très pauvre en institutions de ce genre, qui fleurissent partout en Europe, et produisent de merveilleux résultats. Il est pourtant bon partout et toujours de stimuler l'épargne, de la protéger, et de soustraire efficacement le peuple des villes et celui des campagnes à la tyrannie ruineuse et immorale des prêts usuriers. Si on l'eût fait plutôt, ici, on aurait fait disparaître l'une des causes de l'émigration qui a dépeuplé notre province. Il entre dans le programme de l'Action sociale catholique de travailler à acclimatiser

---

[2] Mgr L.-N. Bégin, "Lettre pastorale sur l'action sociale catholique et en particulier de la presse catholique," *MLPC* (Quebec, March 31, 1907), p. 63. It seems that initially Bishop Émard of Valleyfield and Archbishop Bruchési of Montreal were uneasy lest the new paper might unduly foster French Canadian nationalism, then on the rise (see Mason Wade, *The French Canadians*, p. 551).

ici, en les adaptant aux conditions économiques du pays, ces œuvres
essentielles au bien-être matériel d'un peuple.[3]

The new Catholic paper had a certain Quebec City bias, since
it was published there. That city was not experiencing the
same phenomenal surge of industrialization and urbanization
as Montreal. This Quebec City bias is unfortunate for our
study since the editors inevitably follow that city's economic
development with greater sympathy than that of their booming
rival, Montreal. However, the paper circulated in both cities
as the official Catholic paper and was quoted everywhere as such.
A measure of its influence is that Premier Gouin himself had a
special notebook in which he kept track of various articles and
editorials which were not favourable to certain policies, members,
and publications of his Liberal party.[4]   On one dramatic occasion
he even resorted to an open attack on the ultramontane editor-
in-chief, the Abbé d'Amours, on the floor of the Assembly,
calling him a bad journalist.[5]   The only indication we have of
the circulation of *l'Action sociale* is a remark made by Mgr
E. Lapointe to Joseph Girard in which he says that one may
adopt whatever opinion one likes concerning "Action sociale,"
but, he adds, "une chose est certaine, c'est que c'est une organisation avec laquelle il faudra compter. Le journal qui est son
organe, sort avec une liste d'abonnés de plus de 35,000."[6]

Its influential sister paper in Montreal, *le Devoir*, which was
founded by the great nationalist leader, Henri Bourassa, was
not an officially Catholic paper, although in many outside circles
it was considered as such.   Bourassa himself held that his paper
was Catholic in its ideas, because its founders and editors were
convinced Catholics, "Mais *le Devoir* n'est ni l'organe de la
'hiérarchie', ni celui du clergé, ni celui d'aucun groupe de religieux ou de prêtres."   According to Bourassa, it took full
responsibility for its opinions and reserved the right to differ
from the bishops in free matters.   However, Bourassa accepted
unquestionably and was one of the great promoters of the principle held by the vast majority if not all of the clergy, namely,
that "nous ne resterons catholiques qu'à condition de rester
Français et nous ne resterons Français qu'à condition de rester
catholiques."[7]

---

[3] *L'Action sociale catholique et l'œuvre de la presse catholique, motifs—programme—
organisation—ressources*, p. 38.
[4] Public Archives of Canada, Gouin Papers, Nos. 006612-34.
[5] *L'Action sociale*, May 29, 1912.
[6] Letter of Mgr LAPOINTE to Joseph Girard, federal representative, December 11,
1907, ASHS.   It is not improbable that this impressive figure is exaggerated.
[7] Henri BOURASSA, *Le Devoir, son origine, son passé, son avenir.*   Speech given at the
National Monument, January 14, 1915, (Montréal: *Le Devoir*, 1915), p. 43.

In reality, on all major issues of the day the ideas and opinions of this paper were very similar to those found in *l'Action sociale*. Some of the chief editors and writers had worked for both papers and it became increasingly evident that, as the mood of the province swung more and more to French Canadian nationalism, Bourassa had much influence on the ideas expressed in *l'Action sociale*. For practically all economic and social questions it makes little difference whether one reads one paper or the other—these are the voices of urban intellectual French Canadian Catholics.

Another unofficial, independent Catholic weekly, *la Croix*, began publication in Montreal in April 1903 under the direction of J.-U. Bégin. This paper seems to have had a small circulation and relatively little influence. Though under lay direction, it enjoyed the occasional collaboration of individual members of the clergy. Unlike *l'Action sociale*, it did not follow closely the economic developments taking place in the city, and its discussion on strikes, education, etc., tends to remain on the level of lofty principle. It might be characterized as a "prenons-garde" paper ever ready to sound an alarm. Since, as already indicated, we shall leave out of consideration the dozens of unofficial Catholic papers that circulated in the province on the grounds that their link with the Church is too tenuous for our purpose, we are without an official Catholic newspaper in Montreal in which we might follow the Church's reaction to new local economic developments more closely.

(4) The *Sessional Papers* of the Quebec Legislature; the printed reports of Royal Commissions, congresses, and conventions of importance in which the clergy play a role; published books and pamphlets.[8]

The Church's interest in colonization and agriculture is not of recent origin. In 1850 the bishops of the province wrote a joint pastoral letter deploring the loss of "des milliers de compatriotes qui gémissent sur la terre étrangère où ils allaient chercher fortune." They pointed to the reaches of land which might benefit from settlers:

> ... cependant des milliers d'acres d'excellente terre, près de vos portes, n'attendent que des bras forts et vigoureux pour se dépouiller des antiques forêts qui les ombragent, et pour récompenser au centuple

---

[8] There is a particularly rich collection of thousands of Canadian pamphlets in the Archives of Collège Sainte-Marie in Montreal, which the Archivist kindly put at my disposal.

la main industrieuse qui voudra les cultiver. Il importe donc de diriger de ce côté-là ceux de nos frères qui seraient tentés d'émigrer, et de les retenir ainsi dans le sein de notre patrie, assez vaste et assez riche pour renfermer et nourrir une population beaucoup plus nombreuse.[9]

And in the same year, 1850, Bishop Bourget of Montreal sent a directive to his clergy about education in farming:

Je crois devoir vous suggérer de former une Association d'agriculture dans votre paroisse et recommander à vos paroissiens de profiter des longues soirées d'hiver, pour acquérir toutes les connaissances agricoles qui leur sont nécessaires. La bibliothèque paroissiale pourra fournir les livres ou les journaux qui les aideront à passer agréablement et utilement un temps qui est souvent perdu à des entretiens frivoles.[10]

The following year, 1851, a committee was organized by the government to investigate the causes that were retarding the settlement movement in the Eastern Townships. They based their report largely on the findings gathered by twelve missionary priests during the preceding years and edited by Abbé Antoine Racine, later to become first bishop of the region. The report recommended: (1) the taxing of the uncultivated acreage of large landowners, (2) the establishment of a system of secondary roads more in harmony with local needs, and (3) the opening and keeping under repair of essential arteries of communication in the region.[11] The action subsequently taken on the committee's recommendations was largely responsible for the fact that less than twenty-five years later a prosperous French Canadian diocese had been carved out of the wilderness—the new diocese of Sherbrooke with Mgr A. Racine as its bishop.[12]

All the evidence in later years points in the same direction. The initiatives undertaken by the clergy of every rank to advance the national and religious causes of colonization and improved agriculture seem almost numberless, and their purpose is always the same: to prevent the French Canadians from being forced through poverty or need to emigrate to the United States. Indeed, without accepting as proven the unqualified thesis, enthusiastically espoused in 1899 by a former cabinet minister,

---

[9] "Lettre pastorale des évêques de la province ecclésiastique de Québec," *MLPC* (Montreal, May 11, 1850), p. 81.

[10] Mgr Ignace BOURGET, "Lettre pastorale," *MLPC* (Montreal, November 26, 1850), p. 161.

[11] *Premier et second rapport du comité spécial, nommé pour s'enquérir des causes qui retardent la colonisation des townships de l'est du Bas Canada*, pp. 47-48 and 21. The missionaries also published their finding under the title *Le Canadien émigrant* (Québec: Côté et Cie, 1851), p. 46.

[12] See Mgr Maurice O'BREADY, "Jean ou John Holmes 1799–1852," (unpublished manuscript, Université de Sherbrooke, date not specified), pp. 156ff.

J.-C. Chapais, that "dans notre province, tout ce qui s'est fait de beau, de grand, de bon, en agriculture et en colonisation, comme, d'ailleurs, en bien d'autre chose, s'est fait par l'influence, sous la direction et l'initiative de la religion," we can, nevertheless, accept his general survey of the available evidence as reliable.[13]   Taking his inspiration from the work accomplished by the Trappist monks in five short years at Mistassini in the Lake St. John region, he leads his reader on a tour across the province to establish the correctness of his assertion.   His tour provides us with an excellent summary description of the Church's direct involvement in these two movements at the turn of the century.

> Dans cette excursion, je lui [the reader] ferai voir tous nos grands centres de colonisation, dans lesquels, soit le prêtre, soit le religieux, soit le moine, ont toujours précédé, ou, du moins, accompagné le colon, lui ont ouvert la voie, lui ont donné l'exemple, l'ont encouragé. Je lui montrerai, dans nos régions agricoles les plus prospères, le nom du prêtre attaché à tous les grands progrès réalisés...

He begins his excursion at the extreme west of the province where

> nous trouvons les RR. PP. Oblats, défrichant les premiers lots dérobés à la forêt, en étant, actuellement, les meilleurs cultivateurs de cette région.   Si nous allons sur la rivière Gatineau, ce sont encore les Pères Oblats, que l'on rencontre, les premiers établis à Maniwaki. Dans la direction du lac Nominingue, sont venus au lac même, d'abord les Révérends Pères Jésuites, qui ont accompagné les premiers colons, puis, les Chanoines Réguliers de l'Immaculée-Conception, qui leur ont succédé.   Partant de là, en descendant dans la vallée de la rivière du Nord, nous trouvons les traces des travaux et le souvenir du véritable type colonisateur, Mgr Labelle, le roi du nord, comme on l'a, à bon droit, appelé.   Puis, à Montfort et à Arundel, encore des religieux, les Pères de la compagnie de Marie, qui sont à la tête d'orphelinats agricoles.   Descendant de là vers Montréal, nous passons par la Trappe de Notre-Dame-du-Lac, à Oka, où les austères moines cisterciens cultivent un domaine servant, aujourd'hui, de modèle de bonne culture à toute la province de Québec, qui y envoie des enfants étudier le noble art agricole, à l'école d'agriculture, qui y est ouverte depuis six ans déjà.   Suivant la rive nord du fleuve Saint-Laurent, à l'Assomption, nous avons une autre école d'agriculture qui doit son existence à des prêtres, messieurs les directeurs du collège classique de l'Assomption.

---

[13] J.-C. CHAPAIS, "Religion, agriculture, colonisation," *Courrier du Canada,* December 23, 1899.   Incorporated into *Rapport du congrès de la colonisation, tenu à Montréal les 22–24 novembre 1898,* p. 243.   Chapais also held several positions directly related to the promotion of better agriculture; at the time he wrote this article he was assistant superintendent of the experimental farm in Ottawa.   He was, therefore, in a position to be well informed.

Then he leads us through the northern settlements spread out between Ottawa and Quebec City where

> nous trouvons, parmi les populations agricoles, le souvenir encore vivace, ou bien nous contemplons les travaux actuels de prêtres colonisateurs et agriculteurs tels que les Lacasse, les Paradis, les Tassé, les Théberge, les Desmarais, les Paré, les Brassard, les Prévost, les Turgeon, les Guérin, les Bédard. Si l'on jette un regard au sud du Saint-Laurent, on trouve, gravés dans la mémoire des cultivateurs et des colons des comtés à l'ouest de Lévis, des Cantons de l'Est, et du nord de Montréal, les noms des Abbés Holmes, O'Reilly, Racine (mort évêque de Sherbrooke), Trudel, Bélanger, le martyr de la colonisation des Bois-Francs, Provencher, Leclerc, Marquis (Monseigneur), Champeau, Côté, Durocher, des Abbés Pilote, fondateurs de la première école d'agriculture du Dominion, à Sainte-Anne-de-la-Pocatière, Brosseau, fondateur de l'orphelinat agricole de Saint-Damien de Bellechasse, Mailloux, Marquis, Morrisset, Pelletier, Brillant, Gagné, pour la partie est et sud de la province; des Abbés Hébert, Beaudry, Boucher, Tremblay et des Révérends Pères Oblats qui, tous, ont tant fait pour la colonisation du Saguenay et du Lac St-Jean. Et de combien d'autres noms, omis ici, pourrait s'allonger cette liste des prêtres bienfaiteurs du colon et du cultivateur! Dans cette excursion, partout nous voyons la trace du bien accompli par les cercles agricoles, dont M. l'Abbé Montmigny s'est fait l'un des premiers champions et qui, presque tous, sont patronnés ou présidés par des prêtres; du grand progrès réalisé au moyen de l'œuvre des missionnaires agricoles, qui a été l'objet de l'attention et de la sollicitude toute particulière de Nos Seigneurs les évêques, qui l'ont instituée en 1894; des efforts couronnés de succès de nos sociétés provinciales de colonisation, dont des prêtres zélés sont les plus vaillants sociétaires et qui se soutiennent au moyen de quêtes ordonnées par l'épiscopat dans tous les diocèses de la province.[14]

After giving a detailed account of the work accomplished recently by the Trappists at Mistassini, he concludes by proposing the triad "Religion, Agriculture, et Colonisation" as the slogan for the whole agricultural movement.

Of the "Curé Labelle," the idol of dozens of these colonizing priests, we must say a word. He was publicly credited by English and French politicians and businessmen with opening the area north of Montreal to settlement, obtaining the railroad which gave it access to the markets of the metropolis, and within a few short years peopling it with over 10,000 new settlers.[15] After having served briefly as Deputy Minister of Agriculture under Premier Mercier in the Quebec Cabinet, a few days before his death in December 1890 he could write in his letter of resignation about what had been accomplished:

[14] *Ibid.*, pp. 240-41.
[15] See, for example, Canada, House of Commons, *Debates*, Session of 1883, May 17, pp. 1254-1279. Here several of the ministers publicly commend his achievements and vote funds to extend "his" railway still further.

Monsieur le premier ministre—Je suis venu à Québec en qualité de député-ministre de l'Agriculture et de la Colonisation pour un temps déterminé par les circonstances et sujet à l'approbation de mes supérieurs ecclésiastiques. Je crois que l'objet de ma mission est maintenant rempli, et, en conséquence, je vous donne ma démission. L'organisation du ministère de l'Agriculture, l'amélioration des lois des Terres de la Couronne, l'augmentation des octrois pour la colonisation, la construction de chemins de fer dans l'intérieur de la province, la diffusion de renseignements sur notre province en pays étrangers pour amener chez nous une saine immigration et élever notre crédit sur le marché financier du monde, la bonne entente des rapports de l'Église et de l'État, un nouvel élan donné à l'agriculture, la création du mérite agricole, voilà des divers points du vaste champ où je me suis efforcé d'exercer mon modeste zèle et mon sincère dévouement pour le pays.[16]

For the Curé Labelle, "Il y a bien des manières d'offenser Dieu, mais une des plus communes et des plus graves, c'est de ne pas tirer parti des ressources que la Providence a mises à notre disposition."[17] For him, undeveloped resources are a source of scandal. He is always impatient at the lethargy of his fellow countrymen. His ambition for them is that they one day rival the English and Americans, as he stated clearly in his speech at the Jacques Cartier Hotel in Montreal, in January 1872,

L'émigration aux États Unis nous dévore. Nos ressources restent inertes dans les entrailles de la terre. Notre bois pourrit sur le sol. Allons-nous périr au milieu de l'abondance? Non, Messieurs. Pour développer notre pays, il nous faut des industries, il nous faut des chemins de fer. Qui veut la fin doit vouloir les moyens...

Nous sommes aussi intelligents et aussi industrieux que les habitants du sud. Qu'on nous donne les mêmes moyens d'action et nous le prouverons. C'est ainsi que nous pourrons devenir plus tard les rivaux des Anglais et des Américains dans le commerce et dans l'industrie.[18]

---

[16] Abbé Élie-J. AUCLAIR, *Le Curé Labelle*, p. 101. The agricultural merit consisted in a program of bestowing medals and special honours on particularly progressive farmers.

[17] Cited by Beckles WILLSON, *Quebec: The Laurentide Province*, pp. 136, 262.

[18] AUCLAIR, *Le Curé Labelle*, p. 113. Joseph-J. GRIGNON, who was one of the Curé's altar boys, claims that the Curé was so taken up with railroad building that one day in the confessional he mistakenly imposed as penance on his penitent to "faire un chemin de fer" instead of "un chemin de croix," (*Le vieux temps* [Saint-Jérôme: 1921], p. 76). Likewise, his biographer, Abbé E.-J. AUCLAIR, cites letters of Sir Hugh Allan and Honourable M. Abbot, promoters of the Canadian Pacific Railway, in which they thank the Curé for all his help in promoting the new trans-Canada railway (pp. 114-15). Unfortunately, it was discovered that they had contributed $350,000 to the government's campaign funds to favour their bid for the contract, and a public scandal resulted. But the railway was built.

It might be noted here in passing that in Canada at this time it seems quite clear that both politicians and businessmen often tried to curry favour with the clergy to further their own particular goals, and vice versa. In such a situation, it is often very difficult to evaluate particular public declarations. However, the overall picture leaves no doubt as to the Church's powerful influence in almost every sphere of life—a fact that politicians and businessmen could only ignore at their own peril.

As for the source of his drive, there is no room for doubt. Curé Labelle, like all other members of the clergy at that time, spent all his energies to find a remedy "à ce cancer de l'émigration qui nous dévore en éparpillant dans les pays étrangers les forces vives de la nation." The economic waste is there for all to see. As he says,

> Élever un enfant, en faire un homme dans la force du mot, et perdre de suite le bénéfice de son intelligence et de son travail, au profit des pays étrangers, c'est un malheur que l'on ne saurait trop déplorer. Que nous a servi d'avoir fait de grandes dépenses pour amener au milieu de nous des émigrants [*sic*], si, pour un qui s'y fixe, deux de nos concitoyens quittent le sol natal ?[19]

Nor was Curé Labelle the last of his kind. Like him his successors were not content merely to promote and influence the building of railroads, they were even actively engaged in the more humble task of building secondary roads and bridges. In the annual reports to the provincial government on "colonization roads and bridges," either already built or recommended to be built shortly, we find under the title "Overseers, Contractors, etc.," the names of priests appearing 44 times, in 1896; 30 times, in 1900; 49 times, in 1905; 40 times, in 1910; and 46 times, in 1914[20]—and these are only a few years selected at random. Some of this work—about one quarter of it—was undertaken in connection with the diocesan colonization societies of Quebec and Sherbrooke whose work was enthusiastically endorsed by the Colonization Commission in 1903,[21] but most of the priests seem to have been under direct contract from the government to carry out this essential work in the more remote settlement areas.

The local curés also remained directly involved in the promotion of more scientific agriculture. In 1896 the names of priests are found as presidents or secretaries of 166 out of a total of 389 agricultural clubs and societies in the province.[22] Nor are these farmer priests concentrated in any particular region of the province, for we find them holding these positions in 46

---

[19] Cited by L.-A. BRUNET, *La famille et ses traditions*, p. 102.
[20] *Sessional Papers*, XXX (1896), Part I, No. 3, pp. 209-312; XXXIII (1900), Part I, No. 14, pp. 1-93: XXXVIII (1905), Part. I, No. 7, pp. 1-122; XLIII (1910), Part II, No. 7, pp. 1-177; XLVIII (1915), Part II, No. 7, pp. 4-129.
[21] *Report*, p. 47.
[22] *Sessional Papers*, XXX (1896), Part I, No. 3, pp. 29-59.

out of the 62 counties.[23]   Thereafter, their number seems to
drop slowly as laymen take over these administrative jobs, but,
as late as 1914, the clergy still held such offices in 114 out of the
total 689 agricultural clubs and societies with a membership of
65,324.[24]

Nor were these priests always content merely to promote the
work of others in agriculture.   Many a local curé made the lot
beside his presbytery into a sort of model farm for his parishioners.   The examples of such diligent curés were often cited
at the public conventions of farmers and dairymen.   For example, in 1895, at the annual convention of the Dairymen's
Association, the editor of the *Journal d'Agriculture*, E.-A. Barnard, praised the work of Curé Dauth of Saint-Léonard as a
model of what intelligent farming could achieve in the brief span
of three years.   By frequent hoeing and the diligent use of
manure this curé had increased the produce of his 14-acre farm
by 1500 per cent to earn an additional income of $4,680. Barnard
concludes:

> There, gentlemen, is what a very modest, though very earnest curé
> has done himself on 16 1/2 arpents of land, without neglecting the
> souls of his parishioners!
> Last spring, Mr. [Father] Dauth wrote me word that his people
> had bought three carloads of Victor fertilizer, at one order, besides
> ashes and lime in great quantities.   See, again, the fruits of ex-
> ample![25]

The agricultural missionaries also continued their work of
popular agricultural education.   For example, in the year
1911-1912 they visited 282 parishes and gave lectures to 50,195
people on some 83 topics, mostly of a technical nature and including improvement in cattle breeding, silage, road repair,
etc.[26]   Some of the bishops had given these missionaries explicit

---

[23] Six of these exceptions were counties where there was a large English-speaking
minority, but in nine other counties where an important English minority existed the
priests still had this role.   These names do not include those of the many priests who were
merely honorary presidents or who simply chose to promote the clubs without taking an
official position.
    To gain a clearer idea of some of the activities in which these clubs and societies were
involved we may take the report of their work for 1905, in which year priests still held
the office of president or secretary in 139 out of a total of 568 clubs and societies.   In that
year the clubs spent $7,753.51 on prizes for competition; $5,707.72 on the purchase of implements; $11,926.97 on the purchase of livestock; and $77,689.39 on the purchase of seed.
And the agricultural societies spent $29,757.34 on prizes at expositions; $1,640.52 on farm
competitions; $4,926.52 on competition for standing crops; $796.36 for ploughing matches;
$7,755.88 on exhibitions; $10,842.81 on the purchase and care of cattle; and $10,020.23
on the purchase of seed, etc.   *Sessional Papers*, XXXVIII (1905), Part I, No. 3, pp. 40–77,
and 120.
    [24] *Sessional Papers*, XLVIII (1914), Part I, No. 3, pp. 211-52.
    [25] The 14th Report of the Dairymen's Association of the Province of Quebec, *Sessional
Papers*, XXX (1896), Part I, No. 3, pp. 83-84.
    [26] *L'Action sociale*, July 11, 1912.

permission to give their agricultural lectures in the local churches when the halls available were inadequate; others advised that the more technical lectures should be given elsewhere.[27] In- cluded here are the very detailed and wise instructions issued to these agricultural missionaries by Bishop Bégin of Quebec in 1894. He seems to have overlooked nothing that his priests might do to improve local agriculture and invokes at once all the persuasion of religion, nationalism, economic reasoning, and good sense:

(1) Le missionnaire agricole devra s'occuper avant tout de donner à sa mission un caractère religieux.

(2) Il s'efforcera de faire aimer l'agriculture, d'en faire ressortir la noblesse, les avantages, la supériorité sur les diverses professions libérales et sur les différents métiers et industries; et cela à divers points de vue: au point de vue matériel, au point de vue de la famille, et au point de vue national.

(3) Il fera connaître et expliquera les avantages des associations agricoles, des cercles, des syndicats. Dans ce but, il en étudiera avec soin les divers statuts et règlements; il tâchera de faire comprendre que ces diverses associations sont le moyen le plus pratique, le plus facile de s'instruire en agriculture et de mieux connaître les mouvements du commerce des produits agricoles.

(4) Il encouragera les cultivateurs à suivre le mouvement qui se porte aujourd'hui vers l'industrie laitière, et il s'appliquera à leur démontrer que, pour arriver au succès, il faut, a) améliorer le sol pour lui faire produire en abondance de bons fourrages et de bons herbages; b) améliorer le bétail et tout particulièrement la race bovine; c) adopter le meilleur système d'alimentation du bétail.

(5) Il s'appliquera tout spécialement à faire comprendre aux cultivateurs la nécessité de l'économie dans les habits, dans la table, dans les voitures, dans les maisons, etc., et à cette occasion il fera de solides instructions sur les trois grands fléaux qui ruinent notre peuple canadien: le luxe, les procès et l'intempérance.

(6) Il fera ressortir l'immense avantage pour les cultivateurs de suivre un bon système de comptabilité agricole, aussi court et aussi simple que possible: il l'expliquera et leur en fera distribuer les formules.

(7) Il encouragera les industries dans les familles afin d'éviter les achats chez le marchand.

(8) Il indiquera les endroits les plus propres à la colonisation et fournira tous les renseignements désirables à ce sujet.

(9) Il laissera aux conférenciers spéciaux la tâche d'expliquer aux cultivateurs l'enseignement technique des divers modes d'amélioration du sol, du choix des grains ou graines, du croisement des

---

[27] See, for example, Mgr Elphège GRAVEL, *MLPC* (Nicolet, Circular No. 52, March 24, 1893), p. 320. Here the bishop advises the curés that they can use the church for agricultural lectures and suggests that they themselves from time to time should give statistics from the pulpit showing the progress accomplished in local agriculture, the possibilities, etc.

races d'animaux, des modes d'alimentation du bétail, de production et de conservation des fumiers et de leur emploi, du choix et de l'utilité des instruments aratoires, etc.

(10) Toutefois le missionnaire agricole pourra traiter ces questions s'il se sent parfaitement renseigné et capable de donner une réponse satisfaisante à toutes les objections routinières qu'on ne manque pas de soulever dans ces causeries.

(11) Il tâchera de trouver dans chaque paroisse un jeune homme qui puisse être envoyé à l'école d'agriculture et y étudier avec profit, de telle sorte que, revenu au milieu de ses coparoissiens, il leur serve de modèle à tous égards.   Le gouvernement aidera, croyons-nous, à défrayer les dépenses de ces étudiants.[28]

Finally, a survey of the parish histories confirms the suspicion that these attitudes and initiatives on the part of the clergy were widespread in the province during this period.   Of the 194 parish and regional histories reviewed by the author, 99 do not touch on this economic role of the clergy.   These histories are, for the most part, either purely religious in character, mere catalogues of the names of past officials and curés of the parish, or they are interested in the family trees of parishioners, or they are histories prepared for tourists or they are written by politicians or manufacturers in the interests of their party or their trade.   Of the 95 histories that touch on the economic role of the curé in the parish, most do so rather modestly.   About 27 of these 95 are not written by members of the clergy, but their manner of treating this apparently delicate subject is not substantially different.   Of these 95 authors, 16 tell of curés "qui ont peuplé la terre" and all this involved; 20, of curés actively promoting communications such as the construction of railways and roads; 29, of curés promoting better agriculture—especially the new dairy industry and better animal husbandry—at times, by personal example; 10, of curés promoting or actively managing the new *caisses populaires*; 37, of curés promoting or being actually involved in the introduction of modern utilities, such as electricity, the telephone, and waterworks, as well as of local industries, into their parishes or regions; 47, of curés being champions of better educational facilities, especially by founding model schools and academies in their parish or by introducing the sisters or brothers into the local parochial schools to overcome the marked instability of the system created by the very high turnover of lay mistresses; 7, of curés talking admiringly of the industrial successes scored in their region, leaving the definite impression that there was a

---

[28] "Notes à l'usage des missionnaires agricoles," *MLPC* (Quebec, August 17, 1894), pp. 177-78.

warm collaboration between the Church and local industry; 1, limits himself to the well-worn phrase, found so often in these histories, that the curé led his parish "dans la voie du progrès."

We have several indications that these parish histories understate rather than exaggerate the economic role of the local curé.[29] We find cases of several histories of the same parish where one author discusses the economic role of the curé while the other does not; where an author totally omits or relegates to a footnote an industrial development around which the whole of the economic life of the parish revolves. Second editions of a history may omit or water down the economic role of a particularly active curé. The criticism levelled against these parish histories by the sociologist Léon Gérin, in 1901, is certainly quite valid for the bulk of them. "En somme toutes ces histoires ont un grave défaut: elles se confinent trop exclusivement dans l'histoire religieuse de la paroisse. Le côté agricole, industriel, économique, social est oublié ou négligé."[30]

And yet despite these valid criticisms of the weakness of this abundant literature from the point of view of economics, they still clearly confirm our suspicion that the clergy were constantly active and involved in local economic endeavours. However incomplete, this evidence is sufficient to indicate why Esdras

---

[29] For example, Abbé E.-J. Auclair, the author of several of these parish histories, manages in the case of the little parish of Les Cèdres to mention only in a footnote the development of a $30 million power project which got underway there in 1912 and undoubtedly determined much of the parish's economic life thereafter (Abbé E.-J. AUCLAIR, *Histoire de la paroisse de Saint-Joseph-de-Soulanges ou Les Cèdres: 1702–1927* [Montréal: Imprimerie des Sourds-Muets, 1927], p. 331 in note).

Still more surprising, we find Abbé Venant Charest, one of the best known agricultural missionaries in the province, writing the history of the parish of Saint-Janvier-de-Weedon without making a single reference to the curés' economic role (Abbé V. CHAREST, *Notes sur la paroisse de Saint-Janvier-de-Weedon* [Sherbrooke: 1891], 87 pp.).

Two of the parish histories written by Abbé A. Gravel have been re-edited to modify considerably or simply omit allusion to the vigorous economic initiatives of the local curés. The second edition of his *Histoire de Coaticook* completely omits mention of Curé Chartier's founding of several local industries (Abbé A. GRAVEL, *Histoire de Coaticook* [Sherbrooke: La Tribune, 1925], 222 pp. The second edition appearing the same year has only 214 pages). And in his history of Mégantic (Abbé A. GRAVEL: *Histoire du lac Mégantic* [Sherbrooke: La Tribune, 1931], p. 97), he makes only passing reference to Curé Choquette's initiative in introducing electricity into the town and remaining the town's electrician until his death in 1918. He recounts these economic activities of Curé Choquette in much greater detail elsewhere (*L'annuaire du Séminaire Charles-Borromée* [Sherbrooke: 1918-1919], pp. 595–608).

[30] Léon GÉRIN, "Notre mouvement intellectuel," *Proceedings and Transactions of the Royal Society of Canada*, VII, Series II (1901), Section I, p. 158.

A bibliography of parish histories published prior to 1938 is to be found in Antoine ROY, "Bibliographie des monographies et histoires de paroisse," *Rapport de l'archiviste de la province de Québec pour 1937-1938* (Québec: 1938), pp. 255–364. Since that time, the newly published parish histories have been added to the collection at the Archives, but, to our knowledge, no comprehensive bibliography has been made of them.

Minville, for long director of l'École des Hautes Études, gives the government little credit for the successes achieved in settling the province.   He is quite categoric,

> Le clergé a été l'instigateur, l'animateur; et si ce mouvement a eu, d'une génération à l'autre, une certaine forme organisée, c'est surtout lui qui la lui donna.   Il la lui donne d'abord par la paroisse dont nous avons déjà indiqué le rôle—un rôle final, de regroupement et d'enca-drement sur le plan social.   Il la lui donne aussi par les sociétés de colonisation qui aident les colons pauvres, recrutent les aspirants-colons et canalisent le mouvement général vers telle ou telle région.[31]

In fact, over the 30-year period 1885–1915 the provincial government spent on grants to colonization roads, colonization, immigration, and publicity, the total sum of only $4,508,857.18, or an average of $150,295.24 each year.   Only after 1908 did it spend more than $200,000 in any one year.   Two decades later, in 1937, massive unemployment would finally force the government to spend $10,571,900 on new settlement in a single year, almost 70 times what it had spent on it in the average year in the heyday of the colonization movement.[32]

Professor Gustave Toupin in his review of the history of agriculture in the province for the period 1882–1912, confirms the role of the curés in its development:

> Pendant trente ans, de 1882 à 1912, les habitants de Québec, poussés par la Société d'industrie laitière et encouragés par leurs curés, ont forgé eux-mêmes, dans les cadres protecteurs de la paroisse, les pre-miers organismes de leur relèvement matériel: les fabriques de beurre ou de fromage et les cercles agricoles.   Vivifiées par l'esprit paroissial, ces deux institutions se sont développées en complétant mutuellement leur action.   C'est au cercle agricole que les habitants ont appris, de la bouche des premiers conférenciers, parfois de la bouche de leurs curés ou de leurs confrères commentant une circu-laire ou un article de journal, les premières leçons d'agriculture ra-tionnelle.   C'est à la fabrique, par ailleurs, dans les comptes rendus présentés aux patrons, qu'ils se sont rendu compte de l'importance d'un bon élevage.
>
> Les cercles agricoles ont été officiellement organisés par un acte de la Législature en 1893.   Pendant longtemps, ils ont exercé, par la part active prise dans l'amélioration des travaux de culture, par l'introduction des bonnes variétés de semences et des reproducteurs de race pure et par leurs concours de tous genres, une influence consi-

---

[31] Esdras MINVILLE, "La Colonisation," p. 300.
[32] *Ibid.*, p. 306.   Our estimates are based on Minville's figures.

dérable sur la classe agricole. On a dit que la Société laitière avait été la mère des cercles agricoles. Ce qu'il y a de certain, c'est qu'elle en a fortement encouragé la formation.[33]

The Church's principal motive in consistently promoting by every means in her power the work of new settlement and of improvement in communications and agriculture remains always the same—it is to stem the wave of emigration of the French Canadians to the United States. We saw that this was the reason alleged by the bishops in their pastoral letter of 1850. Half a century later, in 1894, they offer the same reason for organizing the agricultural missionaries. Here their aim is to render local agriculture sufficiently profitable to keep the French Canadians from deserting the land, for they consider it both "une grave atteinte à la prospérité publique" and "dans l'ordre moral, un véritable désastre."[34] They believe the moment ripe to take advantage of the lull in emigration caused by the industrial recession in New England to accomplish their task.

But if the clergy are generally agreed that emigration must stop, there is certainly no unanimity among them on how or why colonization should go forward. Each of four successive priests to address the provincial Colonization Congress in 1898 presented a slightly different view of the problem. The former colonization missionary of the Northwest, Abbé Georges Dugas, with the aid of many authoritative scriptural quotations, rhapsodizes on the vocation of the French Canadian to be a farmer, since he has neither the taste nor the aspiration to be a businessman; and he invokes the great authority of Sully to prove that agriculture is the true basis of the riches of a state, for the gluts and crises peculiar to industry are unknown to it. Abbé Rouleau, in his

---

[33] Gustave Toupin, "La Production animale," *L'Agriculture* in *Études sur notre milieu* p. 212. Bouchette tells us that the curé of the little parish of Sainte-Marie, J.-P.-A. Chaperon, was one of the nine stockholders who invested to the extent of $300 in la Société de Fabrication de Ste-Marie, which, in 1886, introduced the first Danish centrifugal cream separator into America, and that he preached every Sunday that summer on the importance of the new industry for his people (Errol Bouchette, "Les débuts d'une industrie et notre bourgeoisie," *Proceedings and Transactions of the Royal Society of Canada*, VI, 3rd Series [1912], Section I, pp. 145–48).

It is also clear from the Annual Reports of the Dairymen's Association, published yearly in the *Sessional Papers*, that the clergy were consistently well represented in this group of progressive agriculturists, often reading papers at their conventions, and almost annually receiving a special vote of thanks for their support of the Association's activities. They also provided the Association with its president from 1892 to 1896 in the person of Abbé Théophile Montmigny. And, in 1901, the new president, J.-A. Vaillancourt, remarked as a commonplace in his presidential address, "Many a factory in the parishes owes its success to the curé who aided in starting it." ("Nineteenth Report of the Dairymen's Association," *Sessional Papers*, XXXV [1902], Part I, No. 3, p. 78.)

[34] "Lettre pastorale de Nos Seigneurs les Archevêques et Évêques des provinces ecclésiastiques de Québec, de Montréal, d'Ottawa, établissant l'Œuvre des Missionaires agricoles," p. 97.

turn, is careful to point out that political influence belongs to property owners, and that is why the French Canadians must take hold of the land in the province of Quebec. Fathers A. Bouchette and J. Cottet, being local curés, are more pragmatic in their approach: Bouchette favours agriculture, but his more immediate interest is to obtain a new railway to bring in industry, sawmills, etc., to provide his people with winter work and possibly to open up mica and gold mines in his region of Montfort; Cottet is likewise primarily a railroad promoter, for only by means of improved communication facilities can his region of Nominingue be successfully opened up to the timber, dairy, tourist, and fishing industries.[35]

With the recovery of industry in Quebec in the late 1890's, we find no further formal pronouncements on the part of the bishops in favour of agriculture or colonization; their economic statements now tend to deal almost exclusively with the problems arising out of the new wave of industrialization and urbanization. Even if individual bishops in the more rural dioceses do occasionally come back on this theme, it never dominates their statements as it did earlier. So too, in its first years, agriculture and colonization are not dominant themes in the new official Catholic daily, *l'Action sociale*. In fact, controversies on educational reform, the defence of the French culture and language, religious persecution in Europe, the Masonic menace, the general situation and progress in industry and commerce—all receive more space and more attention. However, at least once each year, on the occasion of the annual convention of the Agricultural Missionaries, French Canadians are dutifully reminded that they are by vocation primarily "une race agricole"; and each time the question of colonization comes up in the legislature, the editors air the complaints of the regions most neglected by the government, and all readers are reminded that colonization is a vital question for their race. For the rest, the actual doings in industry and commerce get better coverage; in particular, the interests of industry and commerce in Quebec City are closely followed, analysed, and promoted, and any French Canadian success is hailed with great éclat.

But, after 1910, as French Canadian nationalism gains in vigour and expression through the new Catholic Action groups, *le Congrès du Bon Parler français*, and the constant instigation of the nationalist champion, Henri Bourassa, and especially as

---

[35] *Rapport du congrès de la colonisation, tenu à Montréal les 22-24 novembre 1898,* pp. 71-79, 84, 113-14, 155.

progress in both industry and agriculture begins to falter in 1913, the themes of colonization and agriculture seem to revive with all the emotional appeal they knew in the early 1890's. One is tempted to suspect that the clergy—like many other French Canadians—had for one brief decade hoped against hope that their race could still win a dominant place in the new industry, but soon began to see this hope as an illusion and a dream, and fell back on their tried economic and political defences of agriculture and colonization. The theme comes to be that expressed earlier by the editors of *l'Action sociale:*

> Il est juste de se réjouir de ce perfectionnement continu de nos méthodes et de notre outillage industriel.
> Sachons, cependant, garder en cela une juste mesure, et n'allons pas, au milieu du bruit assourdissant des machines, oublier que la base de toute prospérité industrielle et commerciale, c'est l'agriculture. Pas de récoltes, pas d'argent; pas d'argent, pas de commerce ...
> Quelles sont en effet les années qu'on appelle les 'mauvaises', ces années où comme disent nos gens, 'l'argent ne rentre pas'? Ce sont *inévitablement* les années de mauvaises récoltes ... Et tout cela est plus vrai encore pour le peuple *canadien-français* que pour aucun autre peuple. Nous sommes essentiellement une race de terriens.

The lesson drawn is that French Canadians must ceaselessly study to improve agriculture, and that at the present time they have more need of *habitants* than of diplomas. "On peut vivre sans électricité; on ne peut vivre sans pain."[36]

As the industrial crisis deepened in 1914, we find the theme of colonization getting more and more attention in *l'Action sociale.* The religious aspect is once again very closely allied to the racial aspect of this endeavour. Colonization is "une œuvre patriotique et religieuse," as first claimed by Mgr Turgeon in 1850.[37]

---

[36] *L'Action sociale*, June 3, 1911.
[37] Cited by *l'Action sociale*, March 13, 1914.

CHAPTER VI

INDUSTRY AND THE CHURCH

TOWNS AND VILLAGES

What was the attitude of the curé towards industry in the smaller towns and villages? In general, he was anxious to have industry come to his parish; it would help the parish grow and become more prosperous, provide better sources of revenue for the schools and the Church, keep his people from emigrating to the United States or the bigger industrial centres of the province.[1] It is not accepted either by custom or by Canon Law that a priest be involved as deeply and personally in industry as he may be in agriculture. Canon No. 142 reads as follows, "Clerics are forbidden to engage either personally or through others in any business or trading, whether for their own benefit or for that of others."[2] Therefore, on principle, we can expect the clergy to play only a marginal role if any in the promotion of industry and commerce. However, such directives seem to have meant restraint rather than personal disinterestedness or hostility towards industry on the part of the clergy. We have found that 37 out of the 88 parish histories that directly mention

---

[1] Even S.D. Clark, who is wont to consider the religious interest as *per se* antagonistic to economic development, has recognized that in prereformation days the Catholic Church by its peculiar involvement in secular institutions could not afford to be "entirely hostile" to economic enterprise; but he seems to consider it as a compromise forced on the Church rather than something consonant with Catholic theology. He writes, "Within the system of ecclesiastical control developed by Roman Catholicism the economic—and political—organization of society was made as far as possible to serve the ends of religion, but the Church was not entirely hostile to economic enterprise. A healthy economic life was essential to a healthy Church life. Thus an effort was made to maintain a balance between man's spiritual and his wordly interests. Ecclesiastical control of such a kind did not make for marked economic progress—there was too little economic freedom permitted—but it did make for economic well-being." (S.D. CLARK, "Religion and Economic Backward Areas," *American Economic Review*, XLII [May, 1951], p. 259).

[2] *Codex Juris Canonici* (Rome: 1918). That this discipline was already in Quebec before the promulgation of the Code of Canon Law, in 1918, is clear from the reminder issued by Bishop Fabre of Montreal to his clergy in 1893. He reminds them that, "Il vous est expressément défendu par nos conciles provinciaux de prendre, sans la permission de l'évêque, des parts dans les compagnies de chemin de fer, de navigation, d'assurance, d'industrie, d'imprimerie, dans les banques, dans les sociétés commerciales, financières, etc. De plus, n'oubliez pas que jamais il ne pourra être permis à un prêtre de devenir directeur d'aucune association de ce genre." (Mgr FABRE, *MLPC* [Montreal, Circular No. 128, April 16, 1893], p. 171). Evidently, the more enthusiastic element of the clergy did not always conform to the letter of this directive—nor did the bishops always take a severe attitude in this matter.

their curé's economic role refer to his initiative in promoting local industry and public utilities, such as the introduction of electricity, the telephone, waterworks, a sewage system, the construction of bridges, and the removal of tolls on both bridges and roads, and that 20 others mention his role as a railway and road promoter.

A survey undertaken in 1913 by Hormisdas Magnan for the Department of Colonization, Mines, and Fisheries to enquire into the economic situation and particular needs of the 270 parishes of the province which were still asking for settlers, confirms this rather general interest of the clergy in local industry. Since he depended on the local curés for his information, this survey provides us with an excellent opportunity to become better acquainted with their preoccupations at this time.[3] The fact that these parishes represent about 29 per cent of the total 942 parishes of the province and are scattered over 42 of its 62 counties gives us sufficient assurance that we are not dealing here with narrowly localized phenomena. The curés interpret the needs and possibilities of their parishes as follows: 155 ask for additional farm settlers; 64 do not ask for additional farm settlers;[4] 116 invite new industries to come into their parishes, 5 specifying that they want pulp or paper mills, 42 remarking on the sources of water power available locally to furnish power for industry, several not indicating exactly what kind of industry they want, but those who do specifying a very wide range including sawmills, flour mills, woollen and cotton mills, clothing and shirt factories, wood industries of all kinds (especially furniture factories), foundries, tanneries, brickyards, cheese and butter factories, food preserving industries, etc.; 22 remark on the mineral resources available in their parishes, and 7 invite companies to come in to exploit them; 17 ask for factory workers; the majority ask for additional doctors, notaries, tinsmiths, shoemakers, plumbers, tailors, etc.; 7 invite banks into their parish; and many comment on the touristic attractions of their region, especially on its natural beauty and hunting and fishing facilities.

The type of direct initiative undertaken by the clergy varied greatly from place to place as it had in the previous decades. Bold undertakings were rare: the exceptions are the intrepid Curé

---

[3] Hormisdas MAGNAN, *Monographies paroissiales*, p. 3.
[4] In many of the other parishes, it is not clear whether or not they are excluding farm settlers from the settlers they ask for; in any case, they do not formally ask for them.

Labelle, who had not only arranged for local industries such as the Rolland Paper Company to locate under favourable tax conditions at Saint-Jérôme but had even been commissioned by the government to visit France to invite French industrialists and capitalists to Canada,[5] and the less successful Curé Chartier of Coaticook, who had personally organized a laundry business, a general store, a sawmill, opened several new streets and built houses for his workers in the parish to promote the French Canadians in industry, only to fall into bankruptcy and have his church, presbytery, and convent seized by Montreal financiers.[6] More typical were Curé Plamondon of East Angus, who worked diligently for industrial peace, and succeeded for several years in keeping the disturbing influence of the international unions at a minimum in the mills of Brompton Pulp and Paper Company,[7] and Curé Choquette of Lac Mégantic, who pioneered and directed the town's first electrical station and remained the town's electrician until his death in 1918,[8] to say nothing of the dozens of curés who either personally organized or directly promoted the organization of the local cheese and butter factories during this period. We find such initiatives in the stagnant parishes as well as in the new, booming parishes. For example, in 1911, in the little parish of Wotton, whose population had increased by only 112 (from 1,825 to 1,937) over the twelve-year period 1901–1913, Curé Brassard enthusiastically endorsed the proposal of H. Charland to build a factory to provide work for

---

[5] Abbé Proulx, his travelling companion, quotes Curé Labelle's address to his European audiences in part as follows, "Ce n'est pas seulement aux agriculteurs, que nous nous adressons, maix aux capitalistes également. A ceux qui hésitent à exposer leurs fonds sur le marché monétaire de l'Europe actuellement si craintif, notre Canada offre des placements sûrs et rémunérateurs dans l'exploitation de ses forêts inépuisables; dans les opérations d'un commerce qui a à son service la quatrième flotte du monde et un réseau de chemin de fer de plus de trois mille ligues; dans l'achat de débentures gouvernementales ou municipales et de parts de banque tout à fait solides; dans la construction de lignes de chemin de fer subventionnées par l'État; dans la mise en valeur de nos mines de phosphate, de fer, de cuivre, d'argent, d'or, d'amiante ou de charbon; dans nos sociétés de colonisation, qui émettent des parts." He goes on to point out that this latter type of society not only settles the land but "elle s'occupe des industries—chemins, moulins, manufactures ou maisons de commerce—que fait naître nécessairement la création d'un village nouveau." (L'Abbé J.-B. PROULX, *Le Canada, le Curé Labelle, et la colonisation*, pp. 61-62.)

The Curé brought back a delegation of about 60 Belgians and Frenchmen, who wished to look into the situation for themselves (*Ibid.*, p. 163). But subsequently neither French nor Belgian capital or immigration played more than a very marginal role in Quebec's economic development.

[6] Abbé A. GRAVEL, *Histoire de Coaticook*, p. 89.

[7] *Notes historiques sur East Angus: description de l'église et compte rendu des fêtes civiles et religieuses* (Québec: 1924), pp. 34-35.

[8] "Le Curé Choquette," *Annuaire du Séminaire Charles-Borromée* (Sherbrooke: 1918-1919), p. 600.

the local people.[9]   The Curé's selection of the man best equipped
to organize it was accepted and many of the townspeople took
out shares in the new Wotton Chair and Toy Company.   After
a few bright months, the new business fell into bankruptcy,
with an estimated loss of $200,000 to the community.[10]   As in
the Saguenay, it was often not enthusiasm for industry that was
lacking among the French Canadians and their curés; it seems
much oftener to have been lack of experience.

In the cities, and most strikingly in Montreal, we find a
somewhat different pattern.   As in the case of Trois-Rivières, so
too in Quebec and Montreal we find no evidence of the clergy
having a direct role in industry and even the blessing of a new
factory seems to have been a rather rare occurrence.   The
relatively few available histories of Montreal parishes seem to
indicate that the curé's sphere of economic activity did not at
this time extend much beyond the building of churches and
schools for the rapidly growing population.   In the big city,
the effects of industry tend to transcend the parish boundaries
and insofar as there are contacts between it and the Church
they tend to take place on a higher level, through the bishops,
the press, the diocesan or regional organizations and associations.[11]   The special cases of the cities of Quebec and Montreal
will be considered here briefly, but only in sufficient detail to
highlight their more striking differences.

QUEBEC CITY

From early days the Church had fostered industry here for
the same reasons as she had fostered colonization and agriculture
elsewhere: to stem the tide of emigration to the United States.
For this reason, the first trade unions were no more welcomed by
the clergy than they were by businessmen.   Cardinal Taschereau
had condemned the unions in the wood industry, in 1871, for
preventing other men from working.   He wrote, "elles [the
unions] tendent à ruiner le commerce déjà si peu florissant de
notre cité, pour le porter ailleurs, et par conséquent à forcer

---

[9] Mgr Maurice O'Bready, *Histoire de Wotton, Comté de Wolfe, 1848-1948*, Appendix.
In fact, this population figure gives no evidence of the actual population movements that
were taking place in this little village.   In the period, 1901-1913, 282 families left the
village and 339 returned to the village; 114 families left for the United States and 88 returned from the United States.

[10] *Ibid.*, pp. 290-96.

[11] However, there is some evidence to warrant a suspicion that further research might
discover that, in such industrial suburbs as Saint-Henri and Lachine, the curé had an economic role not substantially different from that in towns elsewhere in the province.

un grand nombre de bons ouvriers et journaliers à aller à l'étranger, pour gagner leur subsistance et celle de leur famille."[12] He repeated his condemnation, for the same reasons, in 1880[13] and in 1885 he condemned the new Knights of Labour—a condemnation which the American Cardinal Gibbons later had rescinded by the Pope.[14]

The shoe industry remained Quebec's big industry after the decline in ship-building, and it was one of the few industries where French Canadian entrepreneurship flourished. In 1900, when a major strike, involving 21 firms and about 5,000 workers, had almost totally tied up the industry for a period of six weeks, costing the city an estimated loss of $750,000 in sales and $200,000 in wages, and several manufacturers were seriously considering leaving the city, Cardinal Bégin, like Cardinal Manning in London in 1889, took the unprecedented step of agreeing to arbitrate the case. He had a committee of three priests investigate the situation thoroughly and then insisted that the industry accept the workers' right to associate and form unions, in harmony with the teachings of Pope Leo XIII. However, the unions, on their part, had to agree to remove from their constitutions some of the more offensive "socialist" language, exclude the closed-shop clause, remove articles concerning strike action in favour of obligatory arbitration, and, finally, accept chaplains who would have the right to assist at and participate in their meetings.[15]

His decision was accepted by both parties. Hailed as a personal triumph for the Cardinal, it was destined to set the pattern in the province for years to come for both bishops and local curés, who would continue to try to settle the differences between capital and labour peacefully and thus avoid wasteful and bitter strikes. The Cardinal himself, who, as Bishop of Chicoutimi, had earlier been a great promoter of the Saguenay-Lake St. John Railway, now turned his attention to improving industrial relations in Quebec City. This new preoccupation is evident in the letter which he wrote to the Franciscan, Father Alexis, asking him to become chaplain of the labour unions in Quebec. He writes,

---

[12] Mgr Taschereau, *MLPC* (Quebec, June 5, 1871), pp. 51-52.
[13] *Ibid.* (May 14, 1880), pp. 204-205.
[14] *Ibid.* (February 2, 1885), pp. 454-55.
[15] "Sentence arbitrale de Monseigneur L.-N. Bégin, dans la cause des fabricants de chaussures de Québec et de leurs ouvriers, le 10 janvier, 1901," cited by Michel Têtu, "Les premiers syndicats catholiques canadiens," pp. 51-55.

> La question ouvrière est celle qui intéresse davantage la société à
> l'heure actuelle. De sa solution pacifique et juste dépendent le
> bien-être des familles, la prospérité d'un pays et même la paix so-
> ciale.[16]

Father Alexis not only accepted, but succeeded over the years
in sowing the seed for the eventual transformation of these
unions into Catholic unions.

It is evident from their writings that what had most concerned the Cardinal and the investigating commission of priests in the
shoe industry dispute was the interference of American labour
organizers in Quebec affairs and the fact that if the production
costs of Quebec shoes were driven up by demands for wages equal
to those paid in Montreal, in spite of the lower cost of living
prevailing in Quebec, the industry would leave the city, since
it was already inconvenienced by higher transportation costs.[17]
The Cardinal also felt there was a great work of education to be
done if what he considered socialist tendencies were not to
prevail among the workers of an industry vital to Quebec's
prosperity. It is not surprising, therefore, that a few months
later he recommended that his priests circulate the "excellent"
little *Catéchisme du Travail*, written by Abbé Nunesvais, among
the workers.[18]

Thereafter, the Cardinal seems to have reduced his direct
intervention in economic matters to that of waging a strenuous
campaign in favour of temperance, of encouraging la Société
d'Économie sociale et politique de Québec, whose purpose was to
promote the study of current economic and social problems, and
of zealously espousing the cause of *caisses populaires*. Otherwise, his influence seems to have been channelled primarily
through the new Catholic daily, *l'Action sociale*, which he founded in 1907.

L'Action sociale naturally supported all the economic works
in which the Church was directly involved, such as colonization,
improvement of agriculture, the *caisses populaires*, temperance
crusades, and good labour relations. Its attitude towards
industry and commerce was almost invariably favourable, but
its editors became genuinely excited only when a French Canadian entrepreneur such as Dubuc or Amyot was involved.   The

---

[16] Copy of letter of Mgr Bégin to Révérend Père Alexis, F.M.C., August 24, 1902,
cited by Têtu, pp. 80-81.
[17] See, for example, Abbé Stanislaus Lortie, *Compositeur typographe de Québec: la question ouvrière à Québec en 1903* (Paris: La Société d'Économie sociale, 1903), p. 101, cited
by M. Têtu, p. 229.
[18] Mgr Bégin, *MLPC* (Quebec, Circular No. 23, February 8, 1902), pp. 249-50.

latter, the Honourable Georges-E. Amyot, was one of the few
French Canadians—two others were Alfred Dubuc and Sir Rodolphe Forget—who proved the exception to the rule that big
business was a domain reserved to the Anglo-Saxons. Like
the others, he could have whatever Church honours he sought,
whether it was a private audience with the Pope or a solemn
blessing of his new corset factory with full front-page coverage
in *l'Action sociale* under the headline "Un grand événement
industriel à Québec—vingt-cinq ans de progrès."[19]

To mention only a few of dozens of other possible examples,
the editors of *l'Action sociale* also commend the French Canadian
banks; for instance they praise La Banque Provinciale for its
good record and recommends it to the people; and even the Bank
of Montreal commands the admiration of the editors by its
ability to earn 13 per cent profit in a depression year.[20] They
try to reason with the dockworkers whose "unreasonableness,"
they fear, will drive ships to other ports and hurt the prosperity
of the city.[21] They give detailed coverage to all the progress
achieved in the pulp and paper industry in the different towns
throughout the province.[22] They reprint in full all the confer-
ences organized by Université Laval under the auspices of la
Société d'Économie sociale et politique de Québec, whose purpose
was to study economic and social problems objectively and
without political bias. They consistently urge Quebecers to
stop wrangling among themselves and get on with the job of
bringing the new transcontinental railway into the city, urging
individuals to sacrifice their personal convenience in the interest of general progress; they likewise urge that the railway
shops be installed as near as possible to the city.[23] They take
great pride in the completion of the Quebec bridge, which finally
connects the city with the south shore of the St. Lawrence
River.[24] They continually urge the city to equip the harbour
better in order to attract ships which now continue on to Montreal; they urge the construction of a dry dock.[25] They try to
persuade the public to take measures to retain the leather industry in the city.[26] They are enthusiastic promoters of the

[19] *L'Action sociale*, December 18, 1911.
[20] *Ibid.*, May 21, 1910; December 12, 1908.
[21] *Ibid.*, February 20, and April 21, 1908.
[22] *Ibid.*, January 31, February 1 and 3, 1908. Here they carry in full a long lecture given by Honourable N. Garneau on "L'industrie de la pulpe."
[23] *Ibid.*, May 22 and May 24, 1913.
[24] *Ibid.*, June 24, 1910.
[25] *Ibid.*, November 13, 1908; August 3, 1909; March 27 and July 30, 1912.
[26] *Ibid.*, December 7, 1908.

projected Georgian Bay Canal which would allow more of the
western wheat to be shipped via the St. Lawrence, and they want
Tadoussac to be made into Canada's winter seaport. They
recount all the notable progress achieved in local industry and
encourage such new arrivals as the Abbatoir Company by
favouring certain monopoly and tax privileges that have been
proposed.[27]

After the trouble concerning Sunday work in the pulp and
paper mills began in the Saguenay, in 1913, *l'Action sociale*
undertook again and again to warn the English Canadian and
American employers that they were only building hate and
trouble for themselves, and that it was not in their long-run
economic interest to work worn-out men seven days a week.[28]
As in the Saguenay, their disillusionment reached its peak when
more and more reports came in that Catholics were being fired
for refusing to work under such conditions and were even being
mocked by their foremen for losing their jobs because of their
priests. In July 1914, the editor warned that the Church was
the most tolerant of societies and would permit all necessary
work, but the "capitalistes étrangers" should not think that
they could do in French Catholic Quebec what they were not
permitted to do in English Protestant Ontario. And he ended
with the futile question, "Est-ce qu'il suffirait d'être capitaliste
et souvent étranger au pays pour fouler impunément nos lois,
nos coutumes et nos croyances?"[29] But the cup of bitterness
was still not filled to the brim; employers knew full well that they
could do as they pleased with impunity as long as laissez-
faire prevailed and the government, like most French Canadians, continued to consider industrialists primarily as their
benefactors.

MONTREAL

As we saw, by 1913 about one half of the province's total
manufacturing output and almost one quarter of its total population was concentrated in this metropolis. In fact, the city's
population had doubled in the previous twelve years. Little
wonder then that when Mgr Bruchési became bishop of Montreal
in 1897, his official letters and circulars which dealt with the
economic aspect of Catholic life were devoted almost exclusively

---

[27] *Ibid.*, August 18, 1909; October 8 and December 24, 1913.
[28] *Ibid.*, February 27, 1914.
[29] *Ibid.*, June 19, 1914.

to new urban problems. The Sunday-sermon plans to be followed by the priests of the diocese reveal this new concern. For
example, in 1902, the sermon outlines stressed the law of work
and the dangers consequent on leisure and idleness from the
Christian point of view.[30] In 1903 and 1911, the theme was
the obligation of parents to send their children to school regularly
and not to take them out of school too early, and to develop in
them, even in those of wealthy families, a taste for work.[31] And
in 1904, a whole series of sermons was devoted to the labour
question, insisting on the duties of workers to work conscien-
tiously, to make only reasonable demands, to respect others'
liberty to work, to consider their duty to their masters, etc.
Other topics that kept recurring were warnings against extrava-
gance, intemperance, injustice, the contraction of debts, speculation, and the desire to get rich quickly.[32]

The choice of these Sunday sermons in 1904 was not an
accident. The preceding year, 1903, had been for Montreal
perhaps its worst year for major strikes, and the bishop felt
obliged to write a special pastoral letter on the question. He
urged the workers to patience and moderation in their demands
and the employers to pay wages corresponding to the true value
of the work rendered in harmony with the current cost of living.
He rejected as erroneous the idea that only labour contributes
to the fortune of nations, and maintained that provided a just
wage is paid, a strike initiated by the workers reveals a lack of
both Christian spirit and patriotism, for it paralyzes the general
prosperity of the whole of society. He also warned the workers
of their imprudence in committing their vital interests to the
hands of foreigners, who demand large sums of money for their
services, and he offered both himself and his curés as interme-
diaries for conciliation and arbitration to help avoid strikes.
Strikes can only be the last resort of workers for a strike has,
as he says,

> pour résultat presque inévitable d'appeler dans les villes une nouvelle
> immigration d'ouvriers, qui viennent augmenter le nombre des
> travailleurs et occasionner une offre de labeur au rabais. Une autre
> conséquence désastreuse de la grève, c'est la dépression du commerce
> et de l'industrie; c'est l'exode en contrées étrangères, ou l'enfouisse-
> ment dans les banques, des capitaux et des épargnes qui, sans cela,
> circuleraient parmi le public et activeraient le mouvement des af-
> faires pour le plus grand bien de tous.[33]

[30] Mgr Bruchési, *MLPC* (Montreal, 1902), p. 441.
[31] *Ibid.* (1903), p. 589; (1911), p. 474.
[32] *Ibid.* (1904), pp. 595-97.
[33] Mgr Bruchési, "Lettre pastorale sur la question ouvrière," *MLPC* (Montreal,
April 23, 1903), pp. 525-37.

This letter was followed up by the series of sermons already mentioned. And thereafter the bishop personally promoted and usually attended the special religious services organized for the Catholic workers of Montreal on Labour Day, at which they were instructed on the Church's attitude to work as well as her interest in their problems.[34]

The bishop's intervention in his pastoral letter bore at least some immediate fruit. The curés undertook a concerted effort to convince French Canadians to abandon the international unions which had successfully tied up the Montreal tramways in 1903, and the strike was soon settled.[35] And, in later years, Mgr Bruchési himself arbitrated or served on boards of arbitration in attempts to settle strikes among such diverse groups as the dock workers, the plasterers and carpenters, and the shoemakers, at times making detailed investigations by visiting the factories involved in person.[36]

It is obvious that the bishop and his clergy were still at a loss as to how to confront the new problems arising out of rapid industrialization and urbanization. In 1908 they decided to make a careful study of the whole situation. The work was begun in study circles, and then, in 1911, all the bishops were asked to submit reports on the situation of the workers in their respective dioceses and to send representatives to a general meeting to be held in Montreal.[37] In the reports submitted by the bishops, it appears that all the bishops except Mgr Émard of Valleyfield and Mgr Labrecque of Chicoutimi were quite concerned at the present situation, especially at the sight of organizers of the international unions going from centre to centre spreading among the workers distrust of the directors of industry and particularly of the clergy. They were alarmed at the fact that the leaders of both international and national unions were openly attacking the Church's jurisdiction in education and that some of them were known Freemasons.[38] On Mgr Bruchési's initiative it was decided that the best solution was to organize Catholic labour unions and to begin by first providing social education for the clergy as well as for the other groups of society. This task fell primarily to the newly organized École sociale

[34] Mgr Bruchési, "Lettre aux ouvriers," *MLPC* (Montreal, August 15, 1904), pp. 675-78.

[35] Robert Rumilly, *Histoire de la province de Québec*, X, 218.

[36] For example, see *la Semaine religieuse de Montréal*, July 7, 1907, pp. 393-400; March 19, 1906, pp. 185-95; and R. Rumilly, *op.cit.*, XII, 74.

[37] M. Têtu, "Les premiers syndicats catholiques," pp. 274-78. He reproduces in appendix (pp. 539-41) the report submitted to the bishops by the meeting held January 25-26, 1911.

[38] *Ibid.*, p. 278.

populaire. It was to bring together specialists and to popularize social teachings and studies. Its programme was very broad, but its general aim was eventually to organize Catholic associations as

> le meilleur moyen de conserver et de rétablir la paix sociale et d'améliorer le sort des travailleurs dans les villes; d'augmenter le bien-être de nos populations dans les campagnes et d'arrêter l'exode rural;...

It would foster the *caisses populaires*, all forms of economic co-operation, and particularly legislation to improve working conditions in the factories and to prescribe a maximum workday and Sunday rest. It would also work to prevent the State from further restricting the authority of parents and the Church over education in its own favour.[39] During the first few years, apart from continually striving for labour peace, its work was chiefly educational; by the end of 1914, it had already published some 40 studies in pamphlet form—all devoted to such urban problems as labour conditions, temperance, mutual insurance, education, workers' and children's health, socialism. But this education of its very nature was a long-run investment and in the pre-war period probably achieved few concrete results in Montreal other than preparing the ground for the future Catholic labour unions.

It seems clear, therefore, that in Montreal more than elsewhere the Church's direct role in industry was very marginal, though she did consistently lend all her moral force to providing management with a sober, hardworking, peaceful labour force. Since the metropolis did not have its own official Catholic newspaper sponsored by the hierarchy, we find less evidence of the Church's day-to-day attitudes and involvement in the industrial developments of the city—if, in fact, they did exist. *L'Action sociale* took less interest in Montreal's economic development, which it tended to consider as in competition with that of Quebec City; but when it does remark on Montreal's achievements, it is usually to compare the industriousness of its city officials and Chamber of Commerce with the sluggishness of Quebec City's organizations.[40] We know too that Mgr Bruchési was an ardent promoter of peace and harmony between all the groups represented in the city, and was a personal friend not only of the Liberal Prime Minister, Sir Wilfrid Laurier, and Premier Gouin of Quebec, but also of such business giants as Thomas Shaughnessy, president of the powerful Canadian Pacific Railway.[41] How-

---

[39] "La Constitution de l'École sociale populaire," *Institut social populaire*, No. 1 (1911), p. 17. French Canada's first trained economist, Professor Édouard Montpetit, was its first vice-president.

[40] For example, see *l'Action sociale*, November 13, 1908.

[41] R. RUMILLY, *Histoire de la province de Québec*, X, 188.

ever small its contribution, the Church was doing what it could to make Montreal an agreeable setting for Anglo-Saxon industrialists and capitalists, who controlled big business in this metropolis.[42]   It is not surprising that here the Church's attitude, even when most favourable, was not coloured by the exuberant enthusiasm that characterized her warm welcome of French Canadian industry in the Saguenay.

---

[42] It may be suspected that both the bishop and his curés were much more active in local affairs than this evidence indicates.   The bishop's letter to Premier Gouin commending the work of "La Ligue de progrès et d'embellissement de Montréal," which grouped all the interested parties in the city, is probably typical of a whole sphere of activity that had at least some marginal bearing on the city's industrial development.   (See letter of Mgr BRUCHÉSI to Sir Lomer Gouin, January 31, 1912, Gouin Papers, Document No. 008842).

CHAPTER VII

EDUCATION AND THE CHURCH

The exact nature of the relationship between education and economic development is still far from clear. Indeed it is only in recent times that education has come to be considered seriously as an investment as well as consumption good, and economists have only begun to try to determine the return on capital invested in different kinds of education, since obviously education is anything but a standardized commodity. However, most economists would agree with Denison's findings that as time passes education tends to contribute to economic productivity at an increasing rate. His research indicates that its contribution to the growth of real national income in the United States in the period 1929–1957 was almost double its contribution in the earlier period 1909–1929.[1] There is thus good reason to suspect that the relationship between formal education and economic development was not as intimate during Quebec's economic spurt in the period 1896–1914 as it seems to be today. Nevertheless, awareness of this relationship was not entirely foreign to the clergy in Quebec at the turn of the century. In 1892, Abbé F.-A. Baillairgé, professor of philosophy and political economy at the classical college of Joliette, in what was the first economics text-book written in Canada for Canadians, *Traité classique d'économie politique selon la doctrine de Léon XIII, avec applications au Canada*, insisted that education has a great influence on the productivity of labour. And he makes applications to Quebec in question-and-answer form:

> Les écoles élémentaires, les académies et les collèges classiques suffisent-ils pour donner à un peuple la somme de connaissances dont il a besoin? Non.
> Les écoles primaires donnent les premiers éléments de la science; les académies développent ces éléments; les collèges classiques ajoutent à cela, avec un plus fort développement des facultés, l'ensemble des connaissances nécessaires dans les diverses professions.
> Ces institutions sont donc d'absolue nécessité. Pour les compléter avantageusement, dans l'intérêt de la société, il faut des écoles

---

[1] Edward F. DENISON, "United States Economic Growth," *Economic Growth: An American Problem*, ed. Peter M. Gutmann (Englewood Cliffs: Prentice Hall, 1964), p. 87. Denison found that education contributed 0.67 per cent annually to the growth rate of real national income in the period 1929–1957, and only 0.35 per cent in the earlier period 1909–1929. His estimates did not take into account the different kinds and qualities of education.

spéciales: écoles d'agriculture, écoles industrielles, écoles des arts et métiers, écoles des mines, tout comme il y a des écoles de droit, de médecine, etc.[2]

ATMOSPHERE

As indicated earlier, the French Canadian Church, however missionary in spirit in many foreign countries, consistently chose at home a policy of cultural isolation, believing herself in this way able to protect her flock from dangers thought to be threatening on every side—from English "Protestantism," American "materialism" and "socialism," French "anti-clericalism" and "free-masonry," Irish Catholic "compromise," as well as from the anti-French bias of the federal government and the anti-Church bias of a minority of radicals in the provincial Liberal government. No protective walls were built higher and none were more strenuously garrisoned that those that encircled the Catholic school system. The clergy watched with foreboding the overthrow of the Church's influence in education in Europe, especially in "Catholic" France, and were ever ready to interpret this history as a forecast of their own, taking little account of the basic differences that existed between the two situations. There were just sufficient omens on the horizon to rouse their suspicions anew at every turn of the road. Vianney Décarie has summed up the situation aptly:

> Pour tout dire en un mot, c'est la crainte de l'État, tel qu'il se constitue en Europe à ce moment, État qui désire prendre ses responsabilités dans son propre domaine et qui, en réaction contre le quasi-monopole exercé par les Églises sur l'éducation, tend lui-même à devenir monopolisateur. Je pense tout particulièrement ici à l'évolution de la situation en France et en Italie, pays traditionnellement catholiques, et où l'Église avait assumé, avec des privilèges considérables, toutes les obligations de l'enseignement. Il semble bien qu'on ait appliqué ici, dans une Province où les catholiques représentaient plus de 90% de la population sur qui, donc, la hiérarchie avait une influence directe, des considérations qui valaient pour des peuples à moitié ou aux trois-quarts déchristianisés...[3]

In 1875, under the Conservative government of de Boucher-ville, a bill was passed by the legislature introducing two major

---

[2] Abbé F.-A. Baillairgé, *Traité classique d'économie politique selon la doctrine de Léon XIII, avec applications au Canada* (Joliette: 1892), pp. 31-32. He follows the classical economists rather dutifully, but he refuses to accept the pessimistic conclusions of Malthus and Ricardo, which he cannot reconcile with his ideas on Divine Providence. See also Craufurd D.W. Goodwin, *Canadian Economic Thought: The Political Economy of a Developing Nation 1814-1914*, pp. 193-94, 200.

[3] Vianney Décarie, "Réflexions sur les rapports de la société canadienne-française et de l'Église dans le domaine de l'éducation," in Vincent Harvey, O.P., *et al.*, *L'Église et le Québec*, p. 119.

reforms in education with the purpose "de mettre l'école hors de la politique et assurer à tout le système plus de stabilité et plus de liberté," namely, the entrance of the bishops *ex officio* into the Council of Public Instruction and the abolition of the office of Minister of Education.[4] The Superintendent of Public Instruction, appointed by the government, became *ex officio* president of the Council of Public Instruction and was responsible for carrying out the Education Act in accordance with the intentions of the Council, although he was obliged to report annually to the legislature and to request from it the subsidies required.[5]

All attempts of later governments to restore the Minister of Education, to impose uniform school books throughout the province, or free and compulsory education, were considered as so many efforts to repeat the experience of France in Quebec. This was not, in brief, an atmosphere conducive to great changes in the educational system. Suspicion was rampant; calm, charitable, objective discussion almost unknown. The writings of such men as Kentucky-born Jules-Paul Tardivel, who a decade earlier had sought diligently to ferret out freemasonry and liberalism even in the ranks of the clergy, in Université Laval, and in the archbishop's palace itself, had their progeny.[6] Extreme called forth extreme. The pleas for reform often came from a small but very vocal group of anti-clericals and radical liberals, using the medium of the press, and pamphlets, often written anonymously.[7] They formed such groups as La Ligue de l'Enseignement in Montreal, which was soon discovered to be affiliated to the society with the same name in France which had

[4] Louis-Philippe AUDET, "Le centenaire du système scolaire de la province de Québec," *Cahiers du service extérieur d'éducation sociale*, IV (Faculté des Sciences sociales de l'université Laval, No 8, 1947), 41.
[5] Catholic and Protestant laymen equal in number to the bishops were likewise appointed by the government, as were the school inspectors. The Council was made up of two separate committees, a Catholic and a Protestant committee, each with exclusive jurisdiction over its own schools. However, regulations adopted by them required the sanction of the government. The system permitted equal treatment to both the Catholic majority and the Protestant minority—a fact not called into question in almost a century of application (*ibid.*, p. 41).
[6] Séraphin MARION, "Jules-Paul Tardivel, pionnier de la presse indépendante et catholique au Canada français," *Rapports de la Société canadienne d'histoire de l'Église catholique*, (1954-1955), p. 15.
[7] Typical of the more extreme element in this anti-clerical literature was an anonymous pamphlet published in Montreal in 1896, under the title, *Le cléricalisme au Canada*, vol. II of *Saintes comédies*. It is a diatribe against the Church in which bishops, priests, brothers, and sisters are all accused of the grossest of crimes and of every imaginable form of sin (for example, see *ibid.*, p. 21). Such attacks were quite obviously not circulated in the hope of winning the Church's co-operation to improve the system of education, but to work for her complete overthrow through means fair or foul.

wreaked havoc with Catholic education.[8]   And such happenings
as the discovery, in 1910, that a teacher long in the employ
of the Catholic school system in Montreal was secretly the
secretary of the local masonic lodge only served to give credence
to popular myths fostered by emigrant clergymen recently
expelled from France and by extremists such as Tardivel, who,
in 1895, had written a novel entitled *Pour la Patrie*, in which an
anti-Catholic secret society plots to seize power in the federal
government and subsequently to exterminate French Canada and
Catholicism.[9]

The fact that the constitutional rights of French Canadians
in the Canadian West to have their own French Catholic schools
were being either entirely denied or substantially modified by
the English majority and were being seriously questioned in
Ontario only helped to heighten the atmosphere of foreboding.
When the English Canadian press gleefully picked up the already
exaggerated and purely negative criticisms of the French anti-
clerical "reformers"—which found their way into *le Soleil* and
le Canada, the organs of the Liberal party—and added not a few
innuendos of its own, the Church and even the local government
was thrown on the defensive.   For the *Ottawa Journal*, a province which spent so little on education was a "national dis-
grace."[10]   The *Toronto Globe* could only feel pity for a province
where

> the children of the poor people either do not go to school at all,
> or else are taught in the common schools by untrained and un-
> qualified teachers, who are under the domination of the Church.   The
> pupils are given three or four hours a day of religious instruction,
> and are forced to attend chapel and prayer for more hours in the
> day.   There is, therefore, little or no time left for instruction in the
> elementary branches, or what is understood as common school
> matters.[11]

Thus even the constructive criticism of those who seriously
wanted to improve the province's education now became ammunition in the hands of the "enemy."   A further hindrance to
change remained in a group of laymen and clergy for whom
educational reform had already gone too far.   For example, the
chagrined chaplain of the Bon Pasteur reported to the Papal

---

    [8] *L'Enseignement primaire* (1910-1911), p. 131.
    [9] John HARE, "Nationalism in French Canada and Tardivel's Novel *Pour la Patrie*,"
Culture, XXII (December, 1961), pp. 403–12.
    [10] Cited by *la Semaine religieuse de Montréal*, February 2, 1903, p. 75.
    [11] *Globe* (Toronto), May 13, 1913.

delegate in 1904 that religious instruction was having to give way to teaching concerned with the more material side of life:

> A l'heure présente même, notre Conseil de l'Instruction publique, sans en avoir parfaite conscience probablement, agit trop au gré de nos libéraux impies. En effet, sous prétexte qu'on ne donne pas aux enfants de la Province de Québec une éducation pratique aussi parfaite que dans les écoles d'Ontario et des États-Unis, ils sont de temps à autre à crier et à demander des réformes qui mettent mieux l'enfant en contact avec les exigences du progrès moderne. Ils ne l'avouent pas, mais ils veulent que l'enseignement, en se tournant davantage vers le côté matériel de la vie, perde de plus en plus son caractère religieux. Pour leur avoir prêté l'oreille, on a obtenu ce résultat: les leçons de catéchisme sont devenues forcément très courtes, se rattachant fort mal aux autres matières; puis, les excellents livres de lecture qui enseignaient la religion, ses dogmes, sa morale et son histoire *ex professo*, ont été mis de côté pour faire place à différents manuels, traitant du soin à donner aux animaux, du jardinage, de l'agriculture, de la botanique, etc. Enfin, on veut mettre de tout dans les écoles, et cette surcharge, qui nuit beaucoup à tout enseignement, est surtout infiniment préjudiciable à l'enseignement religieux...

The chaplain also sees it as a grave error to overload the professions with mediocre students who thus come to despise agriculture and abandon it. "On pousse aux écoles commerciales, aux académies, aux collèges une foule de jeunes gens qui ne sont aptes qu'à recevoir une bonne éducation élémentaire."[12]

In this atmosphere, it proved impossible for the government to pass a measure introducing a minister of education or free and compulsory education, for these had come to be considered by the majority of the people as of masonic inspiration, and, by many serious educators, as quite unnecessary in Quebec. In 1912, Premier Gouin felt obliged to reject emphatically a proposal introduced by members of his own party to make education compulsory at least for Protestants. He argued that it was not at all necessary, for "chez nous, nous avons une population tout aussi intelligente et tout aussi instruite que la population de n'importe quelle autre province de la Confédération." And he

---

[12] ANON. [the chaplain of the Bon Pasteur], *Mémoire succinct et confidentiel sur la situation religieuse du Canada, et spécialement de la province de Québec* (Montreal: September 3, 1904), Archives of Collège Sainte-Marie, pp. 28-29. He signs it merely "xx". That his thinking was not shared generally by the hierarchy is clear from the fact that he takes occasion to claim that Cardinal Taschereau, Canada's only cardinal, had long been "victime et très docile instrument des prêtres libéraux de sa maison et de son séminaire" and that the forces working behind all these liberals is freemasonry (*ibid.*, p. 23).

proceeded to spin out pages of official statistics to ridicule those who said that Quebec was backward in educational progress.[13]

In a field so pitted with rhetoric, even in official documents, one must tread with care. "Progress," "practical," "technical," and "scientific" education can often merely mean a system of "neutral" or "lay" education without any ecclesiastical control or supervision, on the simple unproved assumption that a state monopoly of education is inevitably more "progressive."[14] And, on the other hand, there is the equally unproved and unprovable assumption on which the clergy and the vast majority of French Canadian thinkers spoke and acted at the time, an assumption clearly revealed in the statements of the Inspector General, C.-J. Magnan,

> ... l'histoire nous l'apprend, *l'instruction obligatoire*, puis *l'école obligatoire* ont été inventées dans les loges maçonniques et sont devenues aux mains des ennemis des traditions catholiques de la France des armes perfides et puissantes.[15]

He manages to conclude on weighty authority that free masonry will play the same role in the province of Quebec. Magnan is merely repeating his catechism, which taught that free education is inevitably linked with compulsory and neutral education and so with "God-less" education.[16] As the great French Canadian authority on Church-State relations, Abbé Paquet (later Monsignor) of Université Laval wrote,

> La gratuité est un anneau de la chaîne forgée par les sectes pour étouffer la foi chrétienne et assujettir à leurs doctrines l'esprit de l'enfance. Fût-elle en elle-même absolument inoffensive que son alliance avec la neutralité, la laïcité et la contrainte scolaire serait suffisante pour nous la rendre suspecte et nous engager à la rejeter comme un présent funeste.[17]

---

[13] *Résumé d'un discours sur un projet de loi concernant la fréquentation obligatoire des écoles chez les protestants*, November 26, 1912, pp. 8, 23. As we shall later see, not all his statistics bear close examination. For example, he makes much of the fact that only 14 per cent of the children are not enrolled in school in Quebec as compared with 23 per cent in Ontario; but he seems to pass over as unimportant the fact that his estimates are based on a school age of 5–16 years in Quebec and of 5–21 years in Ontario. Likewise, he makes much of the fact that 19 per cent of Quebec's population is in school as compared with 18 per cent of Ontario's; but is was a well-known fact that, because of to bigger families and emigration of people of work age, Quebec had a higher percentage of children of school age.

[14] RUMILLY, *Histoire de la province de Québec*, IX, 237-38.

[15] C.-J. MAGNAN, *Éclairons la route*, p. 175. See also L.-P. AUDET, "La querelle de l'instruction obligatoire," *Les Cahiers des Dix*, XXIV (1959), 146.

[16] Abbé Léonce BOIVIN, *Le catéchisme social*, pp. 71-72.

[17] Mgr PAQUET, *Droit public de l'Église: l'organisation religieuse et le pouvoir civil*, p. 250. In reality, over this whole period, the average fees paid by parents only once amounted to one dollar per child per year, and usually were considerably less (*Statistical Year Book*, II (1915), 293). The Church seemed to regard it as her prerogative to provide "free" education for those who were unable to pay; and she did so frequently, as is clear from the sample studies made by *l'Action sociale* (October 23, 1909; November 6, 1909). Nor do children ever seem to have been turned away from local schools for not paying the nominal fee.

Nevertheless, the bishops were committed, as they had been in the past, to fight illiteracy. In 1894, when the educational system was under general criticism, they issued a joint pastoral letter renewing this commitment. Here again they refuse to accept reforms that would substantially change the intellectual training provided by the classical colleges or that would turn them into specialized schools, but they maintain that the Church wishes to assist progress in all fields provided it has the true well-being of men as its aim:

> L'Église catholique n'est pas opposée au vrai progrès; elle le désire au contraire, elle l'appelle de tous ses vœux non seulement dans les sciences et les lettres, mais encore dans l'industrie, le commerce, l'agriculture, en tout ce qui peut améliorer le sort de l'homme. Elle voit d'un œil favorable la fondation d'écoles spéciales destinées à promouvoir nos intérêts matériels; elle fait même tout ce qu'elle peut pour perfectionner ce genre d'études, pourvu que ce ne soit pas au détriment d'études supérieures plus importantes et nécessaires; elle bénit le savant, chercheur infatigable, qui, après avoir arraché à la nature ses secrets et ses trésors de fécondité, les fait servir à son avantage et à celui de ses semblables.[18]

In 1897, Pope Leo XIII, in his encyclical letter *Affari Vos*, charged the Canadian bishops with the task of developing education to even higher levels:

> It is fitting that the Catholic schools be able to compete with the most flourishing by the excellence of their methods of formation and by the brilliance of their teaching. From the point of view of intellectual culture and of the progress of civilization, one can only qualify as fine and noble the design conceived by the Canadian provinces to develop public education, to raise it to an even higher level and thus make it an even higher and more perfect thing.[19]

PRIMARY EDUCATION

In Quebec, primary education was at the turn of the century an 8-year course made up of 4 years in elementary, 2 years in model or intermediate schools, and 2 years in academies or "écoles supérieures." In what was called "le cours commercial" the last 5 of these 8 years were devoted to commercial studies, bookkeeping, mathematics, etc. The Church was inevitably deeply involved in primary education, since the bishops sat

---

[18] "Lettre de Nos Seigneurs les Archevêques des provinces ecclésiastiques de Québec, de Montréal et d'Ottawa," *MLPC* (Montreal, March 19, 1894), pp. 689-90.
[19] Pope Leo XIII, *Affari Vos*, in *MLPC* (Montreal, December 8, 1897), p. 75. Author's translation.

on the provincial Council of Public Instruction and the local curé had the right to supervise the local schools from the moral and religious viewpoint.

In fact, what education existed and what improvements took place prior to World War I, were more the work of the Church than of the State. A Liberal government, which as late as 1908 was spending annually less than 50 cents per child enrolled in the primary schools, and which gave as its excuse for not increasing this meagre expenditure its duty first to balance the budget, appeared in a rather beggarly position to demand major changes in the system, especially when such changes involved adding a link or two in the "inevitable chain" that led to the "God-less" school.[20] But the bishops and the clergy, on their part, were determined to co-operate with the State to make the educational system as good as any in Canada, without, however, engaging the coercive powers of the latter. It would be easy to multiply evidence of the Church's efforts to improve the quality of education and to get parents to send their children to school and keep them there. In their joint pastoral letter of 1894, the bishops had repeated and substantially strengthened their teaching on this obligation of parents, which had already been insisted on by the 4th Council of Quebec in 1868. Of primary education, they write:

> Or, pour bien former l'homme et le conduire, s'il est besoin, par différentes étapes jusqu'aux sommets de l'instruction supérieure, il importe tout d'abord d'asseoir sur une base solide l'édifice de ses connaissances. Cette base, c'est l'instruction primaire dispensée indistinctement à tous les enfants, parce que tous, à quelques états de vie que la Providence les destine, peuvent avoir besoin, surtout

---

[20] *Statistical Year Book* II (1915), 282, 295. In that year, the grant to public schools was $160,000 and the total enrollment 352,944 children. If grants to normal schools, poor schools, teachers' pensions, etc. were included they would only raise this average figure by several cents.

See also l'Honorable F.-G. MARCHAND, premier ministre, *Discours sur la loi de l'instruction publique.* A speech addressed to the Legislature, December 28, 1897 (Quebec: 1897), p. 5.

For a very general idea of the financial role of the Church in education at this time, we have the estimate of the official provincial statistician, G.-E. Marquis, made for the school year 1910-1911. He estimated that in her private schools the Church spent a total of $3,222,000 as compared with the total of $1,065,279 spent by the provincial government on education of all kinds in that year. Even if his estimates may be a little exaggerated—for his purpose was to indicate the largest possible total spent in the province on education and thus make Quebec appear more favourable in interprovincial comparisons—nevertheless, had he imputed a fair salary to the hundreds of priests, brothers, and sisters engaged in teaching, in both the private and the public school system, instead of the nominal pittance which they actually received, his estimate would rather err on the side of understatement (*L'Enseignement primaire* [1912-1913] p. 395).

dans les conditions économiques de l'âge moderne, des premiers éléments des connaissances humaines. C'est pourquoi, N.T.C.F., Nous ne saurions trop vous exhorter à prendre tous les moyens et à faire tous les sacrifices possibles pour assurer à vos enfants cette première éducation qui peut leur être si utile et pour laquelle ils vous garderont une éternelle reconnaissance. "Sans doute," écrivaient les Pères du Quatrième Concile de Québec, "vous n'êtes pas tenus à ce qui serait au-dessus de vos moyens; mais prenez garde d'exagérer à vos yeux votre propre indigence, et d'avoir un jour, mais trop tard, à gémir sur la négligence d'un devoir aussi important que celui de l'instruction de vos enfants." Nous considérons que c'est pour les parents une obligation essentielle qu'ils doivent avoir à cœur de remplir.[21]

The faithful were continually reminded both in sermons and in the Catholic press of the seriousness of this duty to ensure primary education for their children.

Equally important was the improvement in the quality of the education offered, and in this the clergy were not less diligent for there was much to be done in non-controversial areas. The pastoral letters of individual bishops, the reports of the proceedings of the Catholic Committee that formed part of the Council of Public Instruction, the parish histories, the official records, and the school inspectors' reports all confirm the substantial truth of a statement made in a letter to Premier Gouin by Abbé Émile Roy, the Vicar General of the diocese of Montreal, in November 1912. He congratulates the Premier on having scornfully rejected the bill that would have instituted compulsory education for the Protestants, and he goes on to praise the diligence of the clergy in urging both diffusion and progress in education:

Certes, le clergé tient énergiquement à ce que la religion soit sauvegardée à l'école et qu'on écarte tout ce qui pourrait dans l'avenir la compromettre. Mais quand ce principe supérieur est mis en sûreté, il est pour tout ce qui peut véritablement promouvoir la diffusion et le progrès de l'instruction.

Pour moi, qui suis en relation constante avec les prêtres, je sais ce qu'ils font, par exemple, pour la fréquentation scolaire: exhortations en chaire, conseils particuliers aux parents, encouragements aux enfants, action sur les commissaires, visites des écoles, etc. Ce qui a fait notre force jusqu'ici au point de vue national comme au point de vue religieux, c'est la vie paroissiale. C'est certainement

---

[21] "Lettre de Nos Seigneurs les Archevêques des provinces ecclésiastiques de Québec de Montréal et d'Ottawa," pp. 685-86.

aussi *le plus puissant levier* pour relever le niveau de l'école. Qu'on écarte donc tout projet qui tendrait à en entraver et à en diminuer l'action.[22]

But perhaps the Church's largest single commitment to primary education was her teaching corps of brothers and sisters. In his official report, in 1913, the Inspector General wrote in commendation of the zeal and ability of the 3,886 sisters and 1,463 brothers, who constituted 53 per cent of the teachers in Catholic primary schools, and 85 per cent of the teachers in intermediate and higher classes,

> This choice body, quite an army of high-class teachers both as regards morals and pedagogics, constitutes the strongest support of our school system.   The divisional inspectors are unanimous in recognizing the zeal and ability of the members of the religious communities whose permanence in the teacher's career makes them true educators.[23]

It seems that there can be little doubt of the sincerity and seriousness of the Church's intention to improve the general level of primary education in the province, but what, in fact, was accomplished during the pre-war period? Was there any truth in the boast of Premier Gouin, so often repeated in Catholic newspapers, that Quebec without recourse to compulsory education was succeeding in attaining a higher school attendance than the other provinces which had such legislation?   Indeed, claims based on the official statistics found in the report of the Superintendent asserted that, in 1910, 96 per cent of the children in the 7–14 age bracket were registered at school and that their average school attendance was between 75 and 80 per cent.[24]

---

[22] Letter of Abbé Émile Roy to Sir Lomer Gouin, Premier, November 28, 1912, Gouin Papers, Document Nos. 006414-15. These same papers contain several letters from bishops and priests thanking the premier for particular grants made to schools and normal schools or congratulating him on various initiatives which he has taken to improve education.   All are of a very favourable nature—which would lead one to believe the observation made to him by Curé G.-A. Picotte of Lanoraie that many of the high and low clergy were grateful to him for the great work he had done for temperance and education and that he should not believe the press which delighted in saying that the clergy is unfavourable to him (Letter of Curé G.-A. Picotte to Sir Lomer Gouin, February 19, 1912, Document No. 006373).

However, the choir was not all singing the same tune; for we find Mgr Cloutier of Trois-Rivières warmly congratulating the intransigent, ultra-montane editor of *l'Action sociale*, Abbé d'Amours, for meriting a public rebuke from Gouin for his criticism of his political tactics.   The bishop believes that the premier and his Liberal party will put truth and error on the same footing if necessary to stay in power.   He feels that had the bill for compulsory education succeeded in passing, it would have been an entry "dans le système scolaire de la Révolution" (copy of letter of Mgr Cloutier to Abbé d'Amours, editor of *l'Action sociale*, December 15, 1912, EATR).

[23] "Reports of Inspectors-General," *Sessional Papers*, XLVII (1913), Part I, No. 8, p. 444.   The Protestant schools, grouping all non-Catholic children, constituted only about 8.9 per cent of the total population in the elementary schools.   In general, we do not discuss their development in this study.

[24] For example, see *le Canada*, October 18, 1912, where Arthur Saint-Pierre argues this against Senator Dandurand, who had claimed that it was more likely that about 60 per cent were at school regularly.

These statistics are highly dubious since no accurate school census had been established in the big cities, and the percentage of children given as enrolled in school was often little more than an optimistic guess on the part of the school officials.[25] They were obviously too optimistic, for the estimate of children in the 5–16 age bracket made by the federal census of June 1911 indicated 70,421 more children than did the school census taken the previous September, and 58,017 more than the school census in the following September.[26]

Relying on the data of the federal census, which perhaps have a small negative bias, we find that school attendance in 1911 was high in 7–13 age bracket, ranging between 73.59 and 90.24 per cent, but fell off rapidly in the 5-6 and 14–17 age brackets. It is also clear that prolonged absences of younger children from school were common, ranging as high as 32 per cent for the 5-year olds and 19 per cent for the 6-year olds, probably because of the long cold winters and the bad roads (see Table VII). If we consider the 7–14 age bracket—the one to which a law of compulsory attendance at school usually applies—we find that 80.92 per cent of these children were enrolled in school and that 76.41 per cent of those enrolled attended school for a period of 7 to 9 months of the year.[27] Ontario, which had compulsory education, had 84.2 per cent of its children enrolled in school, or about 3 per cent more than Quebec, but had an average attendance of only 74.35, or 2 per cent lower than in Quebec. The comparable figures for Canada taken as a whole were 79.78 and 69.51 per cent, both lower than in the province of Quebec.[28]

However, perhaps a more reliable indication of progress achieved in education in the province is the fact that the percentage of people over 5 years of age who were unable to read or write fell in the decade 1901–1911 from 17.71 to 12.66. "Of all the Eastern Provinces, in the decade 1901–1911, it is Quebec that has

---

[25] "Report of the Superintendent on Public Instruction," *Sessional Papers* XXXIII (1900), Part II, No. 5, p. VIII.

[26] See C.-J. Magnan, *A propos d'instruction obligatoire*, p. 21; and Gérard Filteau and Lionel Allard, "Un siècle au service de l'éducation, 1851–1951," II, 63-64.

[27] Dominion of Canada, *6th Census 1921*, Population, II, 693. If we compare the census data of June 1911 with the school enrolment of September 1911 instead of that of September 1910, the percentage of the total number of children enrolled would be increased to 84.5 per cent. Over the period, average attendance at the Protestant schools was consistently a few points lower than in the Catholic schools, and was generally lower among British and foreign-born than among Canadian-born children. Attendance at private schools was consistently much higher on the average than in public schools (see *Statistical Year Book*, II [1915], 298).

[28] *Ibid.*

TABLE VII

School Attendance of the Population from 5 to 24, in 1911*

Ages	Total	ALL CLASSES, 5 TO 24 YEARS				
		Percentage for any period		Number at school per month		
		At school	Not at school	1–3	4–6	7–9
5–20	717,192	51.05	48.95	8,043	19,010	339,281
5	54,073	18.79	81.20	1,643	1,653	6,866
6	52,699	49.55	50.45	2,055	3,227	20,829
7	52,121	76.37	23.63	1,138	2,817	35,848
8	50,512	86.66	13.34	636	1,935	41,204
9	47,430	90.10	9.90	382	1,497	40,854
10	47,490	90.24	9.76	330	1,337	41,186
11	43,140	89.66	10.34	307	1,275	37,097
12	44,931	84.60	15.40	348	1,498	36,166
13	43,335	73.59	26.41	404	1,145	30,074
14	43,276	54.55	45.45	372	1,043	22,190
15–17	123,310	19.96	80.04	374	1,144	23,096
18–20	115,275	3.55	96.45	54	169	3,879
21–24	143,906	1.04	98.96	36	54	1,410

*Source: *Statistical Year Book* II (1915), 298.

increased the most considerably the number of those who know how to read and write";[29] she remained below the national average of 10.5 per cent of illiteracy and was surpassed by 4 of

---

[29] *Bulletin XV of the Federal Census*, p. 1, cited by C.-J. MAGNAN, *A propos d'instruction obligatoire*, p. 31.

the 8 other provinces.[30] Considering that the period was one
of vast population movements and that Quebec had a much
higher percentage of young children than the other provinces,
the French Canadian cannot be said to have been at this time
significantly less literate than the average English Canadian.[31]

This improvement had been achieved by cooperative efforts
of the government, the Church, and the municipalities. In the
period 1895–1914, the annual number of graduates of normal
schools increased almost five-fold, from 239 to 1,087, owing to
the opening of nine new normal schools under the direction of
the sisters;[32] the number of teachers receiving diplomas from the
Catholic Central Board of Examiners rose from 615 to 1,520
annually (1898–1914);[33] regional pedagogical conventions for
teachers and for school commissioners began to be organized
regularly. But there remained an essential weakness in the
system, apparently based almost wholly on the simple fact that
neither the people nor the government was willing to pay the
price of education; and while the devotedness of the brothers and
sisters helped to bridge this gap in the short run, their presence
in the teaching profession also helped to consecrate the current
abuse of vastly underpaying the teachers. This was the major
cause that drove men other than the brothers—out of the
profession, and caused the annual turnover of teachers to be as
high as 50 per cent. Because of the frequent changes of teachers
and the prolonged absences of children, in 1912 failure to pass
grades annually was still as high as 38 per cent in the Catholic
schools under the Council of Public Instruction.[34]

[30] *5th Census 1911*, II, XIV.
[31] However, a healthy dose of skepticism is in order as to the exact meaning of these statistics—especially when we find the Assistant Commissioner of the Census, Thomas Côté, writing to Bishop Labrecque of Chicoutimi, in 1901, to ask for his co-operation and that of the clergy in getting an "exact" census. He claims that former censuses have been hurt because some French Canadians thought they were held in order to raise taxes or for other reasons prejudicial to their race. So now he asks the curés to tell the people "à déclarer sans hésitations qu'ils savent lire et écrire du moment qu'ils sont en position de signer leur nom, afin qu'au point de vue de l'éducation la province de Québec puisse au moins marcher à l'égal des autres parties du pays." (Letter of Thomas Côté, Assistant Commissioner of the Census, to Mgr Labrecque, Bishop of Chicoutimi, February 17, 1901, EAC.) The net effect of such interventions—which probably took place elsewhere in Canada as well—is ambiguous; but they may well have served to exaggerate somewhat the progress achieved in reducing illiteracy in any one decade.
[32] *Statistical Year Book*, II (1915), 284.
[33] *Ibid.*, p. 285.
[34] "Reports of Inspectors-General," *Sessional Papers*, XLVII (1913), Part I, No. 8, pp. 437-38. However, low wages—they were generally about one-half those paid in the Protestant school system—were not the only cause for the high turnover among teachers. French Canadian girls are primarily homemakers, and long after the wages were raised, the turnover among teachers remained unusually high, as they seemed to prefer marriage to money earned in the teaching profession. Wages of female teachers in the elementary classes rose from about $98 to $157 (1896–1912), but still remained about one-third the average of an unskilled day-labourer. Men teachers in these grades received about $527. about the wage of an unskilled labourer (*Statistical Year Book*, XX [1915] 286).

Largely through the increase of brothers and sisters teaching in the intermediate and superior grades, the percentage of children frequenting the former rose from 34 to 42.6, and of those frequenting the latter from 14.7 to 29, over the period 1897–1913.[35] But still, in 1913, in the city of Montreal, only .97 per cent of the children registered at school were in 8th or final grade.[36] And in the rural areas, the situation was much worse; in the Ottawa region, *no* student out of a total of 5,560 was registered in the 8th grade; in the Quebec-Portneuf-Montmorency region, 14 out of a total of 8,736; in the Saint-Hyacinthe-Rouville-Bagot region, 5 out of 7,300, etc.[37] As Inspector General Magnan stated so clearly,

> Voilà le point faible: *les élèves de nos écoles primaires, règle générale, quittent trop tôt la classe.* N'ayant pas l'instruction suffisante, ils ne songent pas à franchir le seuil de l'école spéciale: *agricole, commerciale, technique.*[38]

If the brothers and sisters helped to correct the instability in the teaching profession, ironically they were unwittingly somehow partially responsible for it. If local school commissions could acquire brothers or sisters, who were esteemed the best teachers, at very low salaries, why should they pay young school mistresses more? And it was considered by the Catholic people as out of harmony with the vocation of religious brothers and sisters for them to become at all demanding in salaries. The government also was only too happy to shirk an unpopular responsibility. As Premier Flynn explained to the legislature in 1897, the government spent less on education in the province of Quebec than in the province of Ontario, because of the assistance of the brothers and sisters:

> Nous avons les couvents et les collèges qui donnent l'éducation à un prix très modique, et dans certains cas presque gratuitement... Sans leur généreux concours et leur dévouement inaltérable, nous serions obligés de donner le triple de ce que nous donnons aujourd'hui pour l'éducation.[39]

---

[35] "Report of the Superintendent of Public Instruction," *Sessional Papers* XLVIII (1915), Part III, No. 8, p. XXXIII.

[36] "Report of School Inspectors," *Sessional Papers* XLVIII (1915), Part III, No. 8, p. 109. This percentage probably has a downward bias owing to the fact that it did not allow for the children in two of the private schools and in the equivalent grades in the three classical colleges in the city.

[37] J.-C. MAGNAN, "Premier rapport de l'Inspecteur général des écoles catholiques de la province de Québec," *L'Enseignement primaire* (1911-1912), pp. 472-73. These figures exclude students in the equivalent grade registered in private schools and in the classical colleges.

[38] *Ibid.*, p. 473.

[39] L'Honorable E.-J. FLYNN, premier ministre, *L'éducation dans la province de Québec*, A speech addressed to the Legislative Assembly, January 7, 1897 (Québec: 1897), pp. 34-35.

The succeeding Liberal government seems at times to have been enamoured of major educational reforms, and did give bigger grants for school construction, normal schools, and school inspection, yet it long hesitated to implement the demand of the Catholic School Committee, and in particular of Mgr Bruchési, that an obligatory minimum wage for teachers be established which would have greatly contributed to the teaching profession.[40] It was only in 1912 that the annual government grant to the primary schools finally exceeded $1 per child, and then only by 3 cents.[41]

In brief, primary education seems to have been starved for lack of sufficient funds. One is tempted to agree with the veteran teacher, Edmond Saucier, who wrote in 1908 that Quebec had no reason to boast about a system of education that was built on the devotedness of religious men and women and, therefore, cost 5 times less than elsewhere.[42] Without belittling the difficulty of overcoming in the short run the innate antipathy of the French Canadian to pay higher taxes for any project whatsoever, we must say that the evidence seems to indicate that this attempt to run the school system on devotedness rather than money was perhaps its chief weakness. Had these two powerful forces been intelligently combined in Quebec, probably no other Canadian school system could have competed with it.

SECONDARY EDUCATION AND CLASSICAL COLLEGES

The 21 classical colleges founded by the Church between 1665 and 1911 represented Catholic secondary education in Quebec. In the school year 1913–1914 they had a total of 8,444 students; however, 16 of them also taught elementary commercial courses, which were taken by 3,030 of these students. These colleges had 686 religious and 40 lay professors, the vast majority of the former being priests who worked for token salaries, and they were thus able to provide tuition and board to their students for the meagre sum of $125–150 per annum. The total expenses of all these schools for the year 1913-1914 was $800,019.[43] After 1908, 18 of them received an annual grant of $1,000 each from the government.

[40] Pierre BOUCHER DE LA BRUÈRE, *Le Conseil de l'Instruction publique*, pp. 226-27. He was the Superintendent at this time. He claims the government, on three different occasions, refused the recommendation to impose a minimum wage for school teachers.

[41] The total contribution of the local government to all education, including the technical schools and the universities, increased from about $1.42 per head to $3.05 in the period 1897-1913 (*Statistical Year Book* II [1915], 295).

[42] Edmond SAUCIER, *Éducation moderne et entraînement professionnel*, p. 34.

[43] *Statistical Year Book*, II (1915), 308-309.

The educational value of these colleges has always been a highly controversial subject.[44] They tend to evoke warm admiration or bitter negative criticism according to what role people expect them to play in French Canadian society. Historically, they have had "pour objet immédiat et principal de former des prêtres ... Cependant, on ne refuse pas d'y admettre même ceux qui ... veulent faire un cours classique pour embrasser plus tard une carrière libérale."[45] They professed to keep their students abreast of modern developments in science, but, this same author warned, "... ne confondons pas le séminaire [the colleges are often called "seminary" or "minor seminary" because of their historical origin] avec l'école commerciale, l'école polytechnique, l'école industrielle. Confondons-le moins encore avec l'école de réforme."[46] Nevertheless, as time passed these colleges came to have a monopoly on Catholic secondary education and caused the priesthood and the liberal professions to become the most prized vocations in French Canadian society.[47]

With the arrival of industrialization, many people looked to these esteemed schools to prepare French Canadian industrial leaders just as in the past they had ensured "la survivance" of the race by successfully preparing religious and political leaders. The Church did not see her way clear to doing this, for such a preparation seemed to involve substantially changing the entire system of classical education. How could the system within which she prepared her priests also prepare businessmen, who obviously needed a much more technical basic preparation than did doctors or lawyers? Her position, as indicated in the bish-

---

[44] The program in the classical section of these colleges consisted of an eight-year course leading to a BA in classics and philosophy. To the essential courses of Latin, Greek, and French composition and literature, and scholastic philosophy, were added courses in English, mathematics, astronomy, botany, chemistry, geology, zoology, mineralogy, mechanics, and physics; however, these latter courses were usually concentrated in the last two years and were only followed by those who completed the whole course (cf., for example "Cours d'étude," *Année académique, 1913-1914* [Trois-Rivières: le Séminaire Saint-Joseph], pp. 4-6). This course at Trois-Rivières remained unchanged during the period 1896-1914.

[45] "Nos collèges séminaires," *Revue ecclésiastique*, VI (Valleyfield: 1899), 110.

[46] *Ibid.*, p. 112.

[47] This is how Professor Esdras Minville, former director of l'École des Hautes Études, put it in a personal interview, March 1962. If a son told his father that he wanted to become a priest, the father would be deeply moved and proud, and his money would support all his son's preparation and later missionary works; if the son said he wanted to be a doctor or a lawyer, the father would be happy and willing to pay for his education; if he told his father he wanted to go into business, the father would be satisfied—he would make his own way. A typical example of how deeply this judgment entered into the thinking of the time is found in the listing of all the 3,211 graduates of Collège de Joliette, 1846-1897. After listing the number of priests, brothers, professors, judges, deputies, lawyers, pharmacists, civil engineers, accountants, farmers, and merchants, the list ends with the simple remark, "Les autres sont ou des industriels ou exercent un métier." (*Répertoire et compte rendu des noces d'or du Collège de Joliette*, 1846-1897, [Joliette: 1897], p. 254.)

ops' pastoral letter of 1894 and constantly repeated thereafter, is clearly stated by Abbé Camille Roy of the Séminaire de Québec:

> Outillons-nous donc, outillons-nous donc puisqu'il le faut; fondons des écoles de hautes études pratiques; que nos gouvernements suppléent à l'initiative privée qui manque de ressources; développons même en ce sens utilitaire l'enseignement de nos universités. Mais ne demandons pas... à nos collèges classiques... de se transformer en usines où l'on prépare les apprentis de tous les métiers.[48]

In the sequel, the programme of the colleges was not substantially altered. The excuse offered by a historian for not entering into a detailed account of the evolution of the programme of the college of Saint-Hyacinthe over the period 1809–1899, namely, that "le Séminaire n'a point et n'a jamais eu d'autre programme" continued, by and large, to be valid for the colleges during the next twenty years.[49] The letter addressed by Archbishop Bruchési of Montreal to the Superiors of the classical colleges of his diocese in 1899, recommending that they adapt their science programme to facilitate the entrance of their students into the polytechnical school and that they direct a few students to this institute each year, did not seem to have any marked effect on the programme offered, though it did coincide with an increase of students attending the polytechnical school.[50] At the congress of secondary education held at Quebec in June 1914, Abbé Alex Maltais could still impatiently report that the teaching of such subjects as mathematics was far from adequate:

> Nos collèges et nos petits séminaires doivent donner un enseignement qui permette à nos élèves de passer de plain-pied dans les Facultés de l'Université ou dans les écoles spéciales techniques ou de génie.
> Notre enseignement littéraire et philosophique répond à ce besoin. L'enseignement des mathématiques manque d'orientation, a vieilli, ne correspond plus aux besoins actuels. La nécessité d'une réforme fut admise en principe au Congrès de 1911. Mais nous n'avons rien fait depuis.
> Notre enseignement des mathématiques est inférieur à celui que l'on donne en France pour l'examen du baccalauréat ès-lettres; inférieur à celui que donnent les institutions anglaises d'enseignement secondaire, tant en Angleterre qu'au Canada. Il ne prépare pas suffisamment à l'admission dans les écoles spéciales régies par l'université Laval elle-même.

---

[48] Cited in *l'Annuaire de l'Université Laval de Montréal de 1910-1911*, p. 265.
[49] *Séminaire de Saint-Hyacinthe: Aperçu historique* (Saint-Hyacinthe: 1899), p. 9.
[50] Mgr BRUCHÉSI, *MLPC* (Montreal, Circular No. 11, February 10, 1899). It should be noted that the classical colleges are often largely autonomous and not directly under the authority of the local bishop.

> Ce n'est pas une augmentation de programme qu'il faut, mais une nouvelle orientation. Mettre de côté une foule de problèmes, de rébus et de casse-tête à peu près inutiles à la formation des élèves; leur substituer des démonstrations, des discussions de problèmes généraux. Notre enseignement est indigeste, en algèbre surtout; manque d'enchaînement logique.[51]

The basic question being asked was well phrased by Abbé Groulx, a professor of philosophy at the college of Valleyfield:

> Qu'on nous permette une réflexion: habitués à regarder nos collèges comme les pourvoyeurs naturels des grands séminaires, ne sommes-nous pas trop tentés de les organiser selon cette fin unique, comme si nous n'avions pas assumé la tâche de préparer aussi la jeunesse catholique aux carrières du siècle ?[52]

The plea of Abbé F.-A. Baillairgé of Collège de Joliette, made in 1892, that the Canadian clergy "si influent dans la régie des destinées du pays" devote themselves to the study of social questions, and that his new economics text-book be introduced into the final years of both the commercial and the classical courses seems not to have had any great response; at least, such a course does not appear in the programmes.[53] Looking back on his own years in a classical college, Édouard Montpetit, the first trained French Canadian economist, as we have already noted, would reflect on this lack of a practical bent in the classical course:

> Notre enseignement a vécu longtemps au delà de la réalité, dans le domaine de l'esprit. Il a été surtout littéraire et philosophique, d'une philosophie livresque, sans contact avec la vie.[54]

This attitude was reflected in the French Canadian literature of the time, and in 1901 merited the following severe, and not wholly unbiased judgment of the sociologist Léon Gérin, who made a survey of it for the Royal Society of Canada. He writes in his conclusion,

---

[51] *Congrès de l'enseignement secondaire à Québec, les 20 et 21 juin, 1914: résumé des travaux* (Québec: 1914), p. 15.

[52] Abbé L.-A. GROULX, "La préparation au rôle social," *Revue ecclésiastique,* XVII (1910), 248.

[53] Abbé F.-A. BAILLAIRGÉ, *Traité classique d'économie politique,* p. IX. We also find *l'Action sociale* (October 28, 1908) highly recommending Abbé J. Schrijvers' *Manuel d'économie* to the professors of moral philosophy in the classical colleges. It is unlikely that many of the priests had much acquaintance with economics. At least before 1911, as seminarians they had made no formal study of social questions except for an incidental treatment in moral theology. In 1911, some of the religious orders had begun to organize study circles on these questions among their seminarians: this was at the time when the École sociale populaire was founded in Montreal (Joseph P. ARCHAMBAULT, S.J., "Clergé et études sociales," *Institut social populaire,* No. 24 [1913], p. 12).

[54] Édouard MONTPETIT, *Les Forces essentielles,* pp. 22-23.

... le mouvement intellectuel de notre classe supérieure (suffisamment actif) n'est pas parfaitement équilibré, ne se fait pas dans le sens le plus utile. Abstraction faite des ouvrages professionnels ou officiels, notre production écrite est presque toute de sentiment, d'imagination et de légèreté.[55]

The notable exceptions to this pattern are the writings of Gérin himself, who was an ardent promoter of the social sciences in the province, and Errol Bouchette, who wrote extensively on the theme of French Canadian economic independence. As was to be expected, the newspapers were more in tune with the times than were the intellectual reviews. In the brief period 1896–1904, six small towns founded papers entitled *le Progrès* and the vast majority of the local newspapers, both secular and Catholic, followed the economic developments closely. But what was still clearly lacking was a sense of patient observation and exact statement of fact.[56]

L'Association catholique de la Jeunesse canadienne-française, the nationalistic movement of Catholic youth founded in the colleges in 1903 under the influence of some catholic journalists and some professors of the colleges, whose purpose was to prepare an elite to defend the interests of the Catholic faith and the French Canadian race, seemed to be aware of this deficiency in the training of the youth; each of their congresses devoted to special problems was prepared for by very detailed questionnaires and investigations.[57] This was the beginning of a corrective, but the youth were primarily crusaders and observed facts could still make little headway against such universal "dogmas"

[55] Léon GÉRIN, "Notre mouvement intellectuel," *Proceedings and Transactions of the Royal Society of Canada* VII, Series II (1901), Section I, 171-72. The titles published over the next decade do not indicate any marked change in the type of literature being published by French Canadian intellectuals prior to World War I (see N.-E. DIONNE, "Inventaire chronologique des livres, brochures, journaux et revues publiés dans la province de Québec de 1764 à 1904," *Proceedings and Transactions of the Royal Society of Canada* X, Series II (1904), Section IV, Supplementary volume, pp. 1–175; and *Inventaire chronologique de livres, brochures, journaux et revues publiés en diverses langues dans et dehors de la province de Québec: premier supplément 1904–1912* (Québec: 1912), p. 72).
[56] This did not mean that the intellectual reviews, for example, *la Revue canadienne*, were in any way hostile to such economic preoccupations. This review, with which the clergy were closely associated, first published all Bouchette's articles on economic independence, and it warmly welcomed the work of the new École des Hautes Études, *la Revue économique canadienne* (see, for example, *la Revue économique canadienne* III (May-June, 1914), 419). But somehow the writers and editors of this influential review manage to remain serenely detached from the surge of economic activity that is rapidly creating the "new" Montreal right under their noses.
[57] See, for example, *Étude critique de notre système scolaire: congrès des Trois-Rivières, les 28, 29, 30 juin et 1er juillet 1913.*

as that the introduction of free and compulsory schools into Quebec would have for its inevitable corollary, "God-less" schools.[58]

If there seemed to be little in the classical programme of studies that prepared a student for other than the liberal professions and the priesthood, yet there are certain anomalies that are not easily explained. This was the training that a Laurier, a Tarte, a Curé Labelle, a Curé Corbeil, a Mgr Lapointe had received, and yet they turned out to be builders of great economic vision. This was the ordinary education of the clergy; in fact, many of them had spent some part of their career teaching in the colleges; nevertheless, when they took over the responsibilities of bishop or curé they usually became very practical men and even entrepreneurs to the extent that their vocation permitted it. Likewise, it was the colleges that furnished the polytechnical institute and the École des Hautes Études with the majority of their students and with their best students.[59] But perhaps the most interesting anomaly is that all but five of the classical colleges combined on the same premises with their "impractical" classical studies a very pragmatic commercial course, in which almost half of their students were enrolled. It was much the same course as the intermediate and higher courses conducted by the brothers in their model and academy schools, which were later severely condemned by many educators as being excessively "practical" and "utilitarian."

This "commercial" course, undertaken after three years of elementary school, usually consisted of a five-year course, which emphasized English, arithmetic, bookkeeping, penmanship, commercial law, bank operations, etc. These courses were conducted wholly or in part in English, and in many of the colleges there was a students' bank managed by the students to

---

[58] *Premier congrès de l'A.C.J.C.*, p. 10. It is interesting to hear Joseph Versailles, the first general president of this Catholic Action group, two decades later, when he had become a successful banker and one of the most ardent promoters of French Canadian industry and finance, admonish his fellow country men on the obstacles that prevent them from succeeding in business; he says, "... la première de ces difficultés est notre manque de goût pour les chiffres et pour l'exactitude. Par atavisme, nous avons pris l'habitude de nous contenter d'à peu près... On a trop cru jusqu'à présent que le succès était le résultat du hasard, de la chance. Le succès dans les affaires, comme la réussite dans les professions libérales, est dû à la compétence." (*Le problème industriel au Canada français*, p. 105.)

[59] See, for example, A.-J. DE BRAY, "L'enseignement commercial au Canada," *Revue économique canadienne I* (1911), p. 18. However, as de Bray notes, this achievement of the colleges may be due simply to the inadequacy of the commercial schools of the time to prepare students for the specialized schools. Besides, the classical colleges undoubtedly attracted the best students. Nevertheless, it is interesting to find a thesis written at the École des Hautes Études in 1921, demonstrating that the classical college prepares students adequately for higher commercial education (J. ARBOUR, "Le cours classique et les études commerciales supérieures" [unpublished thesis, École des Hautes Études, 1921], p. 3).

familiarize them with all the operations involved and to give them a sense of the value of money. The optimistic description of this course in the prospectus of Collège de Valleyfield is typical, and reveals at once the attitude and ambition which these priest-professors had for their students and also their lack of a realistic knowledge and acquaintance with the world of business and industry. It reads in part,

> The Commercial Course whose object is to initiate young men into the secret difficulties of a business life, comprises the following program:
>> It covers a period of five years and fulfils all the requirements necessary to insure to any young man, who has completed it, sure access to all the commercial, industrial, and administrative careers of life.
>> This course may be completed in less than five years, according to the knowledge a pupil has on entering the college.[60]

In most of the colleges the last year was called the "business class" and was supposed to launch successful students directly into the world of business.

There is no doubt that the results of this commercial course fell far short of its stated purpose, but no one could deny that the priests and brothers were exceedingly anxious to give this group of students a "practical" education and to make them conscious of the world of money. It had originally been organized to relieve the overcrowded liberal professions, but when the École des Hautes Études commerciales appeared on the scene after 1907, the graduates of these commercial schools were not adequately prepared to enter it. They both fostered and were the offspring of the widespread idea that all a boy needed to become a business man was a commercial academy education and to be able to speak English.[61] And, unfortunately, the fact that they were closely associated with the reputed classical colleges led parents to believe all too easily that the commercial course was of the same calibre as the celebrated classical course. These commercial schools were, in fact, too immediately utilitarian. In 1920, the new programme for the primary schools drawn up by Mgr Ross recommended that these commercial courses become more generally cultural and that an anxiety to teach the boys in English not be allowed to interfere with their obtaining a firm grasp on their own mother tongue, as it had often done in the past. The new programme was aimed at removing the bias

---

[60] *Annuaire du Collège de Valleyfield* (1904-1905), p. 11. The programme of the commercial course is given in English.
[61] Mgr F.-X. Ross, *Questions scolaires: le nouveau programme primaire*, p. 27.

which had long oriented the primary schools excessively towards commerce.[62]   This was simply the fruit of a reaction, which had begun much earlier in Catholic circles, towards endeavouring to persuade parents not to congest further the liberal and commercial professions but rather to direct their children to the truly productive fields of agriculture and industry.[63]

It became more and more evident that what was lacking in the system were continuation schools outside the classical colleges, which would permit non-classical students to enter more easily into the applied sciences and the specialized schools. The problem of drop-outs in the classical course was serious. Since the science courses tended to be concentrated in the last two years of the programme, this meant that many students left the classical college after several years still almost totally unprepared to enter on any practical career whatsoever.   That is why throughout the period there was great reserve on the part of many local curés and the Catholic press towards both the classical colleges and the commercial schools, for, with the new wave of prosperity, parents tended to send a son off to college with little regard to his disposition, interests, or capacity.

UNIVERSITIES

Quebec had, at this time, three private universities; two were English Protestant, McGill founded in 1821, and Bishop's College founded in 1845, and the third was Université Laval, the only French Catholic University, which had been founded in 1852, with an affiliate, Laval de Montréal, founded later in 1876. We consider here only Université Laval and its affiliates and only their faculties more immediately related to economic development.

If we compare the over-all student body in the universities, we find the English minority far better represented in the universities than the French Canadian majority; however, the latter were improving their position at a much faster rate than the former.   In the period 1896–1913, attendance at the English universities increased by 83 per cent, from 952 to 1,762, while attendance at Laval increased by 875 per cent, from 281 to 2,260.   The rate of increase of attendance in the science course, the polytechnical school, and the forestry school of Laval is

---

[62] *Ibid.*, p. 29.
[63] See, for example, *l'Action sociale*, December 22, 1913.

particularly impressive; here enrolment increased from 39 to 351, almost a tenfold increase, while at McGill enrolment in the more practical fields did not quite double from 340 to 608. And in medicine, pharmacy, and the veterinary school, attendance at Laval increased from 344 to 477, while in the English schools it fell from 493 to 373.[64]

All the universities were private and government aid to them was a minimum. In 1896, the total government grant to higher education was $16,200; by 1913 it had increased only to $77,500, with some small additional grants to the specialized schools.[65] Because of its apprehension of government control, Laval, though poor, was very jealous of its independence. In 1872, it had returned a grant to the government after having accepted it the previous year to establish courses in science and economics, just as it had in 1864 on the same grounds refused a grant to present courses in mathematics and science in the interests of improving agriculture. Again, in 1876, it refused the offer of a navigation school. But in 1885 it accepted government help to open a veterinary school, and two years later it affiliated the polytechnical school in Montreal, both of which continued to receive government subsidy.[66] Only at the turn of the century did utilitarian and practical education become a more serious preoccupation of the faculty. The Rector, Mgr Olivier-E. Mathieu, at the convocation of June 1906, emphasized this preoccupation by quoting the celebrated statement of Richelieu: "En un État bien réglé, il faut plus de maîtres ès Arts mécaniques que de maîtres ès Arts libéraux," and he pointed out that this truth had special relevance for Quebec.[67]

In 1907 the university opened a surveying school for which it obtained a grant of $4,000 from the hesitant Premier Gouin, who wanted more direct control over the school. Assisted by the persevering initiatives of Mgr Laflamme, Laval opened a school of forestry in 1910. Later the agricultural colleges of Oka and Sainte-Anne-de-la-Pocatière were affiliated to give them

---

[64] *Statistical Year Book* II (1915), 289. Even if we were to include all 3,137 of the students over 16 years of age attending the classical colleges, which, in fact, lead to the baccalaureat, it is clear that the great discrepancy between English and French representation in the universities is not much reduced. However, these statistics remain only approximations, for if the number of French Canadians attending university is overstated by including all the students over 16 years of age attending the classical colleges, the English Protestant attendance at university is also clearly overstated, for the statistics here include also the English Catholics and French Canadians attending these schools.

[65] *Ibid.*, p. 288.

[66] Abbé Honorius PROVOST, *Historique de la faculté des arts de l'Université Laval, 1852-1952*, pp. 26, 35, 36.

[67] *Ibid.*, p. 58, citing *l'Annuaire de l'Université Laval*, (1906-1907), p. 166.

greater prestige.   And, finally, in 1913 the new École des Hautes
Études was also affiliated.   But it was only in 1932 that steps
were taken to introduce systematic courses in the social sciences,
and it was 1943 before a special faculty of social sciences was
organized.

It may seem that there was a certain sluggishness in adapt-
ing to pressing needs, but there was also a serious lack of finances
and a constant fear of excessive government control, just as was
true for the primary school system.   The university operated on
a shoestring, the priest professors receiving a nominal salary of
$400 and the lay professors only $1,200, while the students' fees
remained ridiculously low.[68]   The Catholic press was forever
admiring the English Canadian industrialists and millionaires
who made generous gifts to McGill University and especially to
MacDonald Agricultural College.   The latter, in a few short
years, had received more than $7 million from the tobacco
magnate whose name it bore.   The editors of *l'Action sociale*
continually ask why French Canadians were not more generous
to Laval.   They pointed out that the English understand that
the competition is becoming more and more scientific and that,
unless the French Canadians want to stay at the bottom in all
industry, they must be generous to Laval, which at that time
was still depending largely on special collections made in the
churches and on the low salaries paid its staff.[69]   And finally,
when the university officials of Laval de Montréal had sufficiently
overcome their fear of government control and came with cap
in hand to beg for government subsidies, it is not at all clear
that the government was ready to cooperate with them.   In a
letter of January 25, 1912, the Vice-Rector, G. Doucette, wrote
to Premier Gouin describing in detail all the university had done
with insufficient funds and told him that as things then stood,
the teachers' salaries were poor, their number had to be increased,
laboratories had to be better equipped for practical research; in
brief, they could only get on with the task of promoting progress
in education and of assuring the province of leaders in all the
professions including agriculture and industry if the government gave them more generous help.[70]   We do not know the
tenor of Gouin's reply, but there is no indication that his government raised the school's annual grant above the $25,000 which
it had been receiving in previous years.

[68] Provost, *Historique de la faculté des arts de l'Université Laval*, pp. 22, 59, 60, 80.
[69] For example, see *l'Action sociale*, February 17, 1909.
[70] Letter of the Vice-Rector of Laval de Montréal, G. Doucette, to Premier Lomer
Gouin, January 25, 1912, Gouin Papers, document Nos. 011391-98.

A word now on the specialized schools affiliated to Laval University.

POLYTECHNICAL INSTITUTE

This school was founded in 1870, and was affiliated to Laval in 1887. It graduated 79 engineers in the period 1870–1898, but after the turn of the century the number of graduates rose steadily from one, in 1898, to 30, in 1911, and fell off slowly thereafter, not reaching the number of 30 again before 1933. Thus over the period 1899–1915 the school graduated an average of 14 engineers annually as compared with an average of 4 in the previous 25 years. It also graduated 24 architects in the brief period, 1911–1915.[71]

This increase in the number of graduates coincided roughly with Mgr Bruchési's recommendation to the superiors of classical colleges that they direct some students to the polytechnical school each year in order to open up certain careers to French Canadians which had hitherto been almost closed to them; however, the new wave of industrialization was probably a more important determining cause of an increased interest in engineering. Later *l'Action sociale* did some propaganda work in favour of the school, but more often it grouped the school's work under its general promotion of technical education.[72] Most of the increase of students did actually come from the colleges, for the simple reason given by the principal in his letter addressed to the superiors of the colleges, which accompanied that of Mgr Bruchési: the colleges were the only schools that ordinarily taught "quelques matières d'ordre scientifique."[73]

However, it did not seem at all easy for the French minority to break into the engineering field. Rightly or wrongly, the conviction was already widespread, as Honourable G.-A. Nantel, Commissioner of Public Works, stated in 1893, that even the best graduates had trouble finding good jobs.

> La position faite aux élèves de l'École Polytechnique est due à notre état social et économique, à nulle autre cause. Les grandes industries, les grandes entreprises de chemin de fer, d'aqueducs et d'éclai-

---

[71] *Diplômés polytechniques* (Montréal: L'Association des Diplômés de Polytechnique, 1911), pp. 135-36, 151.

[72] For example, see *l'Action sociale*, December 21, 1908, where a full page of pictures and history is devoted to the polytechnic institute.

[73] M. BALÈTE, *MLPC* (Montreal, February 10, 1899), pp. 137–41. "Notice sur l'École Polytechnique de Montréal." Later, the brothers' school of Mont-Saint-Louis began to furnish competent students after they had given more depth their commercial course.

rage sont en général entre les mains de compatriotes qui tiennent, et je ne puis pas les en blâmer, à employer leurs nationaux de préférence aux autres, tout compétents, tout honorables qu'ils peuvent être.[74]

Moreover many young French engineers who did start out with industry did not stay there long but soon turned to government employment, seemingly because they became distressed at being alone in the closed English communities of higher industrial personnel, often disowned by their own people as traitors, if not Masons. They were, therefore, easily attracted by the security of government employment among their own ethnic group.[75]

SURVEYING AND FORESTRY SCHOOLS

These were achievements of which Université Laval can be justly proud, for they were desperately needed if the work of settlement and the timber industry were not to continue to cause great destruction to both timber and land because of ignorance and partisan politics. The most effective pioneer in this field was Mgr J.-C.-K. Laflamme, a priest-scientist, who was responsible for interesting both the bishops and the government in what the science of forestry could do to conserve the wealth of the province's forest, land, and water-power. He was elected a director of the Canadian Forestry Association in 1906, and read widely publicized papers at their conventions of 1906 and 1908. He received the complete backing of the Catholic press in his energetic campaign to fight the three enemies of national wealth, which for him were: "*Ignorantia vulgaris, Indifferentia communis,* et *Influentia politica.*"[76] It was through his influence that Archbishop Bruchési of Montreal attended the convention of the Forestry Association in 1908, and publicly committed the clergy to furnish forestry missionaries, just as they had in the past furnished colonization, agricultural, and temperance missionaries. Their task would be to teach the people how to conserve the province's forest wealth. The archbishop pointed out that this action was in keeping with the clergy's past policy

---

[74] Honorable G.-A. NANTEL, *Discours sur l'instruction publique* (Quebec: June 5, 1893), p. 19.

[75] Personal interview with Hector Cimon in March 1962. Mr. Cimon was a graduate of the polytechnical school, in 1916. He spent his life working for the Price Brothers Company and later was named vice-president of the company. He was one of the few French Canadian engineers to persevere and succeed in a large English company.

[76] "La colonisation et la forêt," *Convention forestière canadienne* (Montreal: March, 1908), p. 17. *L'Action sociale,* March 12, 13, and 14, 1908, reproduces his paper in full.

of not separating the national cause from the religious cause, of always defending the material interests of their people, and of remaining "indifférents à rien de ce qui fait le bonheur des familles et la prospérité du pays." [77] Later, Mgr Bruchési was himself elected a vice-president of the Canadian Forestry Association.

At his death in July 1910, Mgr Laflamme was warmly eulogized by the editors of the *Pulp and Paper Magazine* for his work of education in resource conservation, which they pointed out had led him even to translate and circulate at his own expense a pamphlet produced by their magazine on the relation between the forests and the pulp and paper industry. They write in part,

> His work in this field will be gratefully remembered by the pulp and paper manufacturers of Canada, and particularly those of Quebec, and there is no doubt that the plea he put forth for the preservation of the forests of Quebec had a most important bearing on the policy that has since been adopted by the Government and on the grasp which the people now have of this question. [78]

To Mgr Laflamme and the clergy is due much of the credit for having finally convinced the French Canadian settler that the forest is not an enemy to agriculture, but rather its friend and ally, and in itself a permanent source of revenue for the woodsman and farmer alike.

AGRICULTURAL SCHOOLS

The clergy were intimately associated with all the beginnings and the improvements of formal agricultural education in Quebec. [79] The first agricultural school was founded by Abbé Pilote, in 1857, at the classical college of Sainte-Anne-de-la-Pocatière. [80] The classical college of L'Assomption founded a second agricultural school, in 1866. In 1869, Abbé Nazaire Leclerc had published a *Catéchisme d'agriculture* for the school children. [81] In 1893, the Trappists of Oka, at the request of the government, opened an agricultural school which was soon

---

[77] "Discours par Mgr Bruchési," *Convention forestière canadienne*, p. 6.

[78] *Pulp and Paper Magazine*, August, 1910, p. 184.

[79] Cf., for example, Firmin LÉTOURNEAU, *Histoire de l'agriculture (Canada français)*, pp. 238–63; also Marc-A. PERRON, *Un grand éducateur agricole: Édouard-A. Barnard 1835–1898*. Perron shows how the pioneer efforts of Barnard in agricultural education were everywhere supported by the clergy.

[80] LÉTOURNEAU, *Histoire de l'agriculture*, pp. 238–40.

[81] Abbé Nazaire LECLERC, *Catéchisme d'agriculture ou la science agricole mise à la portée des enfants*.

to have an impact on the province through its publications, lecturers, and experimental farm.[82] It was another classical college, the Séminaire de Saint-Hyacinthe, that offered land and lent $5,000 to promote the founding of the first school of dairying, in 1892.[83] The Dairymen's Association had already established its laboratory at the seminary, in 1888, under the direction of Abbé C. Choquette, a post which he continued to occupy for the next twelve years.[84] We have already seen how the domestic science schools for girls spread rapidly after the successful example provided by the Ursuline school and experimental farm founded at Roberval, in 1882. In 1914, there were 43 such schools with 4,777 pupils, and a new normal school had been founded in the preceding year to prepare teachers for these specialized schools.[85] Their general purpose was to teach girls to be efficient and thrifty housewives, especially in the rural areas.[86] The teaching of the elements of agriculture was also introduced into the programmes of the rural elementary schools and, in 1914, there were 284 school gardens cared for by 9,308 elementary school children under the supervision of their teachers.[87] And, of course, the agricultural missionaries continued to move about the province promoting agricultural projects of every kind.

However, the limited amounts of capital invested in the agricultural schools by both parents and the government were not at all proportionate to the zeal of their promoters. Prejudice about such education was still too deep and irregular attendance at school too common among the students. Far too often the graduates felt that they, like other "educated" people, should not have to return to manual work, and this caused some reaction against the training. Undoubtedly, here too the problem of Church versus state control stopped not a few dollars from coming to the aid of these schools, and decisive action was further thwarted by prolonged hesitation on the part of the government in deciding exactly what kind of agricultural school it wanted.[88] Thus as usual negative and destructive criticism was much more in evidence than supporting dollars.

But there *was* genuine progress, and when the government began steadily to raise its total subsidies to these schools, from

---

[82] LÉTOURNEAU, *Histoire de l'agriculture*, pp. 243–48.
[83] *Ibid.*, p. 254.
[84] *Ibid.*, p. 255.
[85] *Statistical Year Book*, II (1915), 291.
[86] It is not by accident that even today one often discovers that it is the wife and not the husband who keeps the household accounts in the French Canadian family.
[87] *Statistical Year Book*, II (1915), 291.
[88] See LÉTOURNEAU, *op. cit.*, p. 250 ff.

$12,000 in 1908 to $88,925 in 1913, and subsidized some new construction, they were able to become more selective, all the vacancies were quickly filled, and at last Quebec had a team of efficient, well-trained agronomes.   But the monks of Oka and the priests of Sainte-Anne must often have envied the lot of their English Canadian counterpart, MacDonald College, which had been founded by the Montreal tobacco manufacturer, William C. MacDonald, in 1907.   Through his generous gifts, amounting to over $7 million, this school in a few short years had facilities second to none in the province and a student body almost as large as the two Catholic schools put together.   Dollars seemed to have worked much faster and more efficiently than dollarless devotedness—but then it is one thing to educate those who want to be educated, it is quite another to convince a people that they need an education in order to farm more efficiently.

HIGHER COMMERCIAL EDUCATION AND THE TECHNICAL SCHOOLS

With the new wave of industrialization at the turn of the century, French Canadians became very much aware that their educational system did not provide for technical instruction. Many blamed their traditional educators, the clergy, for not having furnished them with technical schools.   The latter, though keenly aware of this gap in the system, did not see how they could provide for it.   They were great promoters of the evening classes in arts and manufacturing and the adult education courses organized in the big cities, and they continually urged workers to attend them in order to better themselves.[89] In Montreal, Mgr Bruchési was himself among the donors of prizes for these schools.[90]   But as late as 1913, only 2,634 were enrolled in these courses in arts and manufacturing and 6,836 in adult education courses, and attendance averaged only about 50 per cent.[91]   Technical schools were essential, and the bishops in their pastoral letter on education in 1894 had clearly stated that they would look with a favourable eye on the foundation of such specialized schools provided only that they did not

---

[89] For example, see *l'Action sociale*, October 5, 1908; October 4, 1909; October 9, 1911.   The editors, like the curés, renewed their promotion campaign at the opening of each school year.

[90] *Conseil des arts et manufactures de la province de Québec: règlements des classes de dessin industriel du soir, 1901-1902* (Montréal: La Patrie, 1901), p. 36.

[91] *Statistical Year Book*, II (1915), 316.

jeopardize the necessary work accomplished by the traditional classical colleges. But they held that the Church was not in a position to furnish these new schools, and the typical reply made to those who blamed them for not doing so was that the Church did not have the necessary resources and that it was only by stretching the devotedness of her teachers to the limit that she was able to do what she was now doing in education. The editor of *la Semaine religieuse de Québec* made this point in 1902:

> Oui, le clergé voudrait, à ce superbe édifice de notre système éduca-tionnel, ajouter le couronnement scientifique et industriel dont il voit la nécessité. Par exemple, ses ressources ne lui permettent pas de s'engager dans cette entreprise.
>
> Quant à se donner lui-même et à mettre tout son dévouement au service de l'œuvre, il est tout disposé à le faire. Que le gouverne-ment ou les particuliers fassent pour cet objet appel à son concours personnel, et l'on verra combien il est disposé à servir, sur ce terrain aussi, les intérêts du peuple canadien-français.[92]

Other members of the clergy were more forward in urging the government to take the lead. For example, at the annual convention of the Dairymen's Association in 1902, Abbé Cho-quette confronted the Honourable E. Bernier publicly on the floor of the convention hall: "The Minister of Interior Revenue spoke of the utility of technical schools: but he would not promise to provide us with any! Still it seems that our two governments might found and support one!" And he went on to explain how important a school of practical chemistry was if inspectors of butter and cheese were to have the knowledge necessary to carry out their work efficiently.[93] In 1905 the Superintendent of Public Instruction urged the legislature to begin finally to do something for technical education, and cited the initiative of Séminaire Saint-Charles of Sherbrooke,

> ... at Sherbrooke, a manufacturing town, which has a smiling future before it, the authorities of the St. Charles Seminary have laid the foundation of a technical school and only await the favour of the Legislature to impart to this new branch of education all the desirable guarantees of stability.[94]

In 1906, when it was clear that industry left to itself would not take any direct responsibility for such education, the Gouin government undertook to build a school of higher commercial studies in Montreal as well as large technical schools in both

---

[92] *La Semaine religieuse de Québec*, September 27, 1902, p. 83.
[93] "The Twentieth Annual Report of the Dairymen's Association," *Sessional Papers*, XXXVI (1903), Part I, No. 3, p. 70.
[94] "Report of the Superintendent of Public Instruction," *Sessional Papers*, XXXVIII (1905), Part II, No. 5, p. XII.

Montreal and Quebec. The whole project was to cost almost $2 million, about three times the government's annual budget for education of all types. Soon after arose the ever latent problem of whether these schools were to be "neutral" or "Godless," that is, free of all Church control and supervision. Were these schools to be the first clear victory for the anti-clericals and the Masons on French-Canadian soil? The adjective "neutre" was anything but "neutral" in French Canada—it was the dread adjective chosen to describe the "écoles athées" of France.

Archbishop Bruchési and Canon Dauth of Laval de Montréal immediately gave their approval to the new "université commerciale." But the archbishop clearly betrayed the secret wishes of the hierarchy to have this new school affiliated to Université Laval in the unanimously adopted resolution he proposed to the Catholic School Committee (in which all the bishops were *ex officio* members):

> Que ce comité a appris avec plaisir les démarches faites à Montréal, par la chambre de commerce, par le clergé, et un grand nombre de citoyens, pour la fondation d'une école des hautes études commerciales et serait heureux de voir cette école incorporée à l'Université Laval.[95]

The foundations were laid, the cornerstones were publicly blessed by high Church dignitaries, the Catholic press and the clergy urged parents to send their children to these schools, and the students began to graduate all under the warm applause of the clergy for Premier Gouin's energetic accomplishments in this field.[96] And yet through it all, on another level, particularly that of the editorials of *l'Action sociale*, the government was attacked for making these schools "neutral." Each time a high Church official praised the new schools or was present at one of their functions, the Liberal newspapers, especially *le Canada* and *le Soleil*, would rouse the ire of the intransigent editor of *l'Action sociale* Abbé d'Amour, by citing this as evidence of the Church's full acceptance of these "neutral" schools. And each time this able logician and theologian would comment on their naïveté in thinking these schools were therefore on the same footing as other Catholic schools; he reminded them that crucifixes

---

[95] "Rapport de l'instruction publique, 1906-1907," p. 428, cited in *Le gouvernement Gouin et son œuvre*, p. 101. Likewise, when l'École des Hautes Études was affiliated to Laval, in 1915, the speaker, Mr. Isaïe Préfontaine, claimed that the school had always enjoyed the support of Archbishop Bruchési and Mgr Dauth, among other religious authorities (cited in *Le gouvernement Gouin et son œuvre*, p. 100).

[96] See, for example, *l'Action sociale*, October 23, 1908; October 5, 1909; May 10, August 10, and September 9, 1911; May 31, 1912; June 21, 1913; etc.

on the walls, priests on the staff, good competent Catholic lay professors, the Premier's personal assurance of the uprightness of his intentions could not make these schools "Catholic"; to be "Catholic" the Church must have juridical rights over them. He approved of the material layout of these schools and of their personnel, and he encouraged parents to send their children to them.   But it hurt his logical and theological sensitivities to hear anyone call them "Catholic."[97]   *L'Action sociale* and its backers won a partial victory.   In 1914, l'École des Hautes Études sought affiliation with Laval, but the technical schools remained "neutral" so that they could benefit by federal subsidies.   The Catholic editors enthusiastically endorsed the new industrial school opened by the Marist Brothers in 1913, and gave their unqualified praise to the government for subsidizing the industrial training programme initiated by the Séminaire de Sherbrooke.[98]   Thus, contrary to a widespread opinion held by English Canadians,[99] the Church never directly opposed commercial and technical education as such.   As *l'Action sociale* correctly stated, in June 1909, not a single voice was raised in the Catholic press to oppose it.   What was being discussed was, rather, methods and the atmosphere in which such instruction should take place.[100]

In spite of this appearance of slowness in the development of technical and higher commercial education in the province of Quebec, in reality this province was not behind the other Canadian provinces in equipping herself with facilities for this kind of education.   According to the engineer J.-P. Buteau, a professor of the Quebec technical school, who made a survey of faculties in both Quebec and Ontario in 1916, Halifax became in 1906 the first city in America to have a technical school built by government funds, preceeding the state of Massachusetts by two months.[101]   In 1901, the University of Toronto had launched a not-too-successful higher commercial course, and technical courses of a kind were available in Toronto after 1899, and especially after 1904; Hamilton had built a big technical

---

[97] For example, see *l'Action sociale*, May 3 and 31 1912; July 16, 1913; Jan. 20, 1914; etc.

[98] *Ibid.*, October 3, 1913.

[99] For example, see *Collier's Magazine*, June 12, 1909.

[100] See *l'Action sociale*, June 15, 1909, where the article which appeared in *Collier's Magazine* is refuted.   The author has found no general evidence to support the statement of Mason Wade that the commercial academies hesitated to introduce industrial courses, which business had offered to subsidize, because the big new technical schools were under criticism for being "neutral."   (Mason WADE, *The French Canadians*, p. 611).

[101] J.-P. BUTEAU, *Notre enseignement technique: ses avantages, coup d'œil à l'étranger*, p. 25.

school in 1909. But it was only in 1911 that Ontario adopted comprehensive legislation on technical education, and thereafter it progressed rapidly. It was the judgment of Buteau that Quebec with her two large technical schools, her school of higher commercial studies, and her several smaller regional technical schools was only slightly behind Ontario for first place in the Dominion.[102] Earlier, in 1911, the Belgian principal of l'École des Hautes Études, A.-J. de Bray, had considered Quebec as the Canadian leader and believed that Ontario's Industrial Education Act of that year had been influenced by the example of Quebec's new technical schools.[103]

But buildings, however well equipped, do not of themselves educate. The neutral-school issue may have caused confusion in the minds of some parents and kept them from sending their children to these schools, yet it is not clear that their presence there at this time would have been very profitable.[104] Indeed it was soon evident that the simple fact that these schools were born under non-Church auspices did not automatically guarantee their success. In the case of l'École des Hautes Études, the chairman wrote confidentially to Premier Gouin in March 1916 to deplore the entire situation as very unsatisfactory. He complained of the general lack of orderly discipline in the school as well as of the unbecoming conduct of the principal, the professors, and the students, and concluded, "Je considère que si ce résultat était connu du public, l'enseignement de l'École serait sévèrement critiqué."[105] But the chief culprit both here and in the technical schools seems to have been no particular person or persons, but rather "le manque de préparation des élèves."[106] The Royal Commission on Industrial Training and Technical Education of 1911 had these observations to make on Ontario's education system:

> General complaint was made that the public school education of the present is not practical enough; that it tends to draw boys away

---

[102] *Ibid.*, p. 27.

[103] A.-J. DE BRAY, *L'essor industriel et commercial du peuple canadien*, p. 206. He likewise believed that Toronto was copying the example of Montreal in her new school of higher commercial studies (*ibid.*, p. 213).

[104] Préfontaine noted that the attendance at l'École des Hautes Études increased temporarily to 86 after the school was affiliated to Laval, but it is not clear whether this affiliation enhanced the prestige of the school or simply guaranteed its "orthodoxy" in the eyes of Catholic parents; and this increase disappeared as quickly as it came (Letter of I. PRÉFONTAINE to Premier Lomer Gouin, March 9, 1916, Gouin Papers, Documents Nos. 001552-65).

[105] *Ibid.*

[106] See, for example, *ibid.*, Documents Nos. 001534-38; and also J.-P. BUTEAU, *Notre enseignement technique*, p. 34. The three bigger technical schools in Montreal, Quebec, and Shawinigan had by 1917 still granted only 130 full-course diplomas (BUTEAU, p. 12).

from the industrial pursuits and towards professions, while at the
same time it does not turn them out adequately trained in matters
of spelling, writing, punctuation, arithmetic and other elementary
subjects...

Among the general conclusions it reached was the following,
" ... the present school curriculum is not suited for children who
will earn their living in industries."[107]   But though these remarks are concerned with Ontario, they are typical of their
observations on public education in Canada as a whole at this
time.

Ontario, it is true, did have some continuation or high
schools with a more practical bent than the classical colleges,
which could open the way to other higher specialized studies;
Quebec, in general, had only her much criticized "commercial"
colleges and academies which ordinarily led to nothing beyond
themselves.   And offers such as that of Brother Landry of
Collège Mont-Saint-Bernard in Sorel, to open a preparatory
school to help bridge this gap and provide competent students
for the technical, commercial, and specialized schools did not
seem to find any immediate echo in government circles.[108]

The basic fact of the matter was that neither the people nor
even the majority of industrialists were as yet sufficiently convinced of the need for technical training and for "scientific"
businessmen.[109]   Moreover, it was a mistake to start at the
top rather than at the bottom and try to build a sophisticated
technical and commercial education on a faulty general education.   For this adequate funds and adequate teaching were
essential.   Dr. William Peterson, Principal and Vice-Chancellor
of McGill University, who had served for fifteen years on the
Protestant School Committee in Quebec, aptly observed before
the Royal Commission that the whole problem boiled down
largely to a matter of money, and this author's own research
fully confirms his statement:

> Until more money is forthcoming for schools, you will not have
> in the Province of Quebec an education really worth the name.

---

[107] *Royal Commission on Industrial Training and Technical Education, Report of the
Commissioners*, IV, 2054, 2059.

[108] Letter of Brother Landry, director of Collège Mont-Saint-Bernard, Sorel, to
Premier Lomer Gouin, March 6, 1912, Gouin Papers, Documents Nos. 002152-3.

[109] For example, it was only after 1910 that the *Pulp and Paper Magazine* began to try
to convince its readers that a knowledge of mathematics, chemistry, and physics was "a
necessary groundwork for practical paper-making" (*Pulp and Paper Magazine*, December
1910, pp. 300-301).   In 1913 we find the editors deploring the fact that chemists are so
little appreciated in the industry (*ibid.*, October 15, 1913, p. 679).   One of the old-time
chemists in the industry recalls that at the turn of the century there were only two
chemists in the whole of the industry and even they were very little appreciated (*ibid.*,
"50th Anniversary of the *Pulp and Paper Magazine*," May 1953, pp. 166-67).

Teachers must have adequate remuneration, and must be competent, and until public opinion justifies spending more on education, the search for technical education may lead us far afield, for we shall have a people asking for technical education who are unable to profit by it.[110]

EDUCATION IN SAVING AND THRIFT[111]

The clergy lent their wholehearted support to any initiative aimed at teaching the French Canadians how to be savers, for they early recognized that lack of personal savings was one of the chief reasons why so many of their fellow countrymen had been forced to take the road to the factories of New England. Many of them had lost their patrimony through indebtedness to money-lenders. It was, therefore, a relatively easy task for Alphonse Desjardins to win the complete support of the clergy for the *caisses populaires.* These he founded at the turn of the century to be a school of saving to teach his people to overcome their prevalent faults of excessive individualism, extravagant spending, and lack of foresight; ultimately also they were to provide a means of gaining economic independence for the French Canadians and of enabling them to put their own money into productive investment. From the beginning, his cardinal rule for these banks was that loans should be made only for productive purposes and not for extravagant consumption.

The clergy were not only Desjardins' defenders and intercessors before the provincial and federal governments, they also soon became the chief propagandists of the movement, and, after some little hesitation, they even became his most reliable "bankers."[112] It was the bishops who promoted the change in the educational law in 1909 to permit the establishment of students' banks in all the primary schools, and it was Cardinal Bégin who allayed personally the scruples of the sisters and brothers, who felt that their "banking" activities might be in conflict with their vow of poverty. It was likewise Cardinal Bégin who took the responsibility after 1910 of permitting his clergy to manage

---

[110] *Report of the Commissioners*, IV, 1891.

[111] For much of the following discussion I am indebted to the excellent study of Yves ROBY, *Alphonse Desjardins et les caisses populaires 1854–1920* (Montreal: Fides, 1964), pp. 149.

[112] Among the bishops who at first hesitated to give their full support to the new banks was Mgr Bruchési of Montreal, who left his clergy free to promote the banks or not as they thought best. But later he too began to promote them actively in his diocese (see, for example, "Le congrès sacerdotal de Montréal," *La Semaine religieuse de Montréal*, January, 1913, p. 119).

the local *caisses* despite a general Church ruling issued against it by Rome in that year—an unorthodox situation for which he won the approval of the Pope in 1913.[113]

What did these *caisses* represent and how deeply were the clergy involved in them? The first years were difficult. Between 1900 and 1907 only 3 banks were founded, mostly because of lack of sympathy for the movement on the part of the government, the violent opposition of the commercial banks, and the general need of an educational campaign in favour of the new banks. But once the *caisses* won legal recognition by the provincial government, in March 1906, progress became much faster. In the period 1907–1916, 159 *caisses* were founded. Desjardins, after a brief experience, adopted the principle that he would not open a *caisse* in a parish unless the local curé asked him to do so and himself participated in its founding. There are no general statistics available for this early period of operations; however, Roby describes the activities of the mother-bank at Lévis as typical. In 1913-1914, it had a total capital of $177,100. In the period 1901–1912 it had made 5,111 loans nearly all for less than $100; however, the average loan increased to $182 in the following period, 1915–1920.

The weakness of this system of banks was that prior to Desjardins' death in 1916 individual banks tended to restrict their activity too narrowly to the parish within which they operated and were too dependent on the people's confidence in the person who founded and operated them; as often as not this was the local curé himself. Indeed a few *caisses* actually collapsed when the curé wanted major loans to build a church or a school and the depositors withdrew their savings to meet his needs. The curé's hand was everywhere in evidence. As Roby sums it up,

> D'après des statistiques incomplètes que nous possédons, 126 curés occupent un poste dans le conseil d'administration ou la gérance des 171 caisses fondées de 1900 à 1920. Il faut ajouter à ce chiffre déjà impressionnant les noms de 12 vicaires qui se substituent à leur curé. Environ 80% des curés participent donc activement à la bonne marche de la société. De plus, à compter de 1914, nous pouvons affirmer que, si les curés ne sont pas dans le conseil d'administration, ils siègent soit à la commission de crédit, soit au conseil de surveillance. Peut-être en était-il ainsi auparavant, mais le

---

[113] PIE X, *Decretum de Vetita Clericis Temporali Administratione,* November 18, 1910, cited by Roby. Roby cites a letter of Cardinal Bégin to A. Desjardins of November 4, 1916, in which he explains how he arranged the matter with the Pope.

manque de données nous empêche de l'affirmer. On peut toutefois conclure que dans presque 100% des cas, le curé collabore directement au fonctionnement des caisses.[114]

The more glaring weaknesses of the system were removed after 1916, when the banks were organized into a federation; now loans could be more easily centralized and efficient lay administrators trained. The *caisses populaires* were still concerned primarily with the provision of productive loans for seed, tools, machinery, etc., and these loans were ordinarily confined to the workers and farmers of the local parish; it was not their policy to provide funds for either big industry or commerce. The thousands of small loans they supplied both in the cities and in the countryside saved many families from ruin and provided many others with the funds necessary to set themselves up in farming or in a trade. The editor of *l'Action sociale*, probably somewhat presumptuously, claimed that the new credit facilities provided by the *caisses* had helped Quebec weather the financial crisis of 1914 better than the rest of Canada.[115]

How completely the bishops and their clergy were won to this form of economic education is well demonstrated by the example of Bishop Émard of Valleyfield, who, in his New Year's greeting to his people in 1913, recounted how delighted he had recently been to have met a little girl of the diocese who had proudly showed him her bank book which indicated that she had a deposit of $151—the fruit of hard work and thrift, for her family was large and not rich. He concluded, underlining each word, *"Parents chrétiens, enseignez à vos enfants la petite épargne."*[116] That the lesson was well learnt is evidenced by the fact that, in 1963, as we have seen, Quebec had 1,248 *caisses* with total assets of $1,010,023,000 serving 1,539,000 members.[117]

SOCIAL WELFARE

We may note here, without entering into detail, that throughout this period the Church carried out a successful campaign against the increased use of alcohol, which she con-

---

[114] ROBY, *op. cit.*, pp. 113-14. Of the curés directly involved, 74 were presidents; 1 secretary; 16 secretary-managers; 5 managers; and 30 president-managers. And of the assistant priests, 6 were presidents; 2 vice-presidents; 3 secretary-managers; and 1 manager.

[115] *L'Action sociale*, February 18, 1914.

[116] Mgr ÉMARD, "Les Souhaits d'un Pasteur," *MLPC* (Valleyfield, December 30, 1912), p. 403.

[117] *Statistical Year Book*, XLVI (1963), 569-70.

sidered harmful both to virtue and to material progress. Through the efforts of the Church, supported by those of the other Christian churches as well as of the government, in the decade 1901–1911, while the population increased by 21.5 per cent, the number of hotels, restaurants, and stores licensed was reduced by 16.75 per cent, and in 853 out of a total of 1,230 municipalities there was no liquor trade.[118]   She even introduced anti-alcohol teaching into the programme of the schools. Mgr Bruchési himself introduced the resolution to the Catholic School Committee that the Superintendent should provide local teachers with general guidelines for anti-alcohol teaching.[119]

She was also ever active in the struggle against tuberculosis which was ravaging the cities and especially Montreal. In 1911, the rate of infant mortality in Montreal was 242 per 1,000, a rate exceeded only by Calcutta's 252, while the average for other major cities was only 112.   The Church promoted clinics to provide free milk in an attempt to cut down this abnormally high death rate among newborn children.[120]

Other themes that keep recurring in sermons and the Catholic press are an encouragement to hard work and an appreciation of manual labour; the avoidance of lawsuits, extravagant spending, and gambling; the practice of honesty and justice in all business and commercial dealings as a duty to the common good.   Mgr Émard points out the importance of fair dealing in a pastoral letter,

> L'industrie et le commerce sont devenus de puissants facteurs de prospérité nationale et sont à la base des grandes questions patriotiques.   Or, il en est d'un peuple comme d'un particulier: de sa réputation de justice et d'honnêteté dans ses opérations industrielles ou dans ses tractations commerciales dépendra son succès définitif, et cette réputation commune constitue un patrimoine public; c'est chacun en particulier qui doit y concourir par une probité personnelle à l'abri de tout reproche.[121]

Finally, it should be mentioned that social welfare services such as hospitals, etc., in French Canadian society, were still organized under Catholic auspices and received some subsidy from the government for carrying out this work so essential in rapidly developing urban and industrial areas.

---

[118] *Le gouvernement Gouin et son œuvre*, p. 59; *Statistical Year Book*, II (1915), 408.

[119] *L'Enseignement primaire* (1906-1907), p. 623.

[120] Joseph GAUVREAU, "La goutte de lait," *Institut social populaire*, No. 29 (1914), p. 13. Dr. Gauvreau attributed the reduction in the death rate of children in Montreal in the following few years in part to this new programme.

[121] Mgr ÉMARD, "Lettre pastorale sur la justice," *MLPC* (Valleyfield, December 25, 1901), p. 69.

AGRICULTURALISM

Under the title of education we must also ask what was the Church's attitude and what attitude did she communicate to the people towards industrialization and urbanization, over which she and they alike had so little control, especially in Montreal, where both capital and industry were almost exclusively in Anglo-Saxon Protestant hands? This question is important, for it has been repeatedly stated in recent times, as we noted earlier, that the Church in the past has been hostile to industry and industrialization, that for a century now the clergy along with the vast majority of the intellectuals have been "agriculturalists." For example, the French-Canadian historian, Michel Brunet, writes,

> Tous les principaux dirigeants de la société québécoise, dans les milieux laïcs et ecclésiastiques, ont adhéré avec enthousiasme, unanimité et crédulité à tous les enseignements et à toutes les illusions de l'agriculturalisme. Seule une très petite minorité tenta à réagir.[122]

Brunet defines agriculturalism as a philosophy of life and a reaction against the materialism and technology of the present day.

> L'agriculturalisme est avant tout une façon générale de penser, une philosophie de la vie qui idéalise le passé, condamne le présent et se méfie de l'ordre social moderne. C'est un refus de l'âge industriel contemporain qui s'inspire d'une conception statique de la société. Les agriculturalistes soutiennent que le monde occidental s'égare en s'engageant dans la voie de la technique et de la machine. Ils dénoncent le matérialisme de notre époque et prétendent que les générations précédentes vivaient dans un climat spiritualisé. Selon eux, l'âge d'or de l'humanité aurait été celui où l'immense majorité de la population s'occupait à la culture du sol. Avec nostalgie et émoi, ils rappellent "le geste auguste du semeur."[123]

Brunet, who believes that Quebec is still an "underdeveloped" region from the point of view of economic equipment, explains the fact that some industrialization did come about by claiming that the propaganda of the agriculturalists "n'a pas, heureusement, empêché les lois économiques de fonctionner," and that the heed paid these prophets by the politicians was not so servile as to prevent them from opening the province wide to foreign capitalists.[124]

---

[122] Michel BRUNET, "Trois dominantes de la pensée canadienne-française...," p. 45.
[123] *Ibid.*, p. 43.
[124] *Ibid.*, p. 58.

A full investigation of this thesis would take us far afield. Here we can only investigate whether this "agriculturalist" attitude was as universal among the clergy during the pre-war economic spurt as is sometimes claimed.

The most compact and forceful embodiment of the so-called "agriculturalist" attitude in this period seems to be in the oft-quoted sermon of Abbé (later Monsignor) Louis Paquet, preached on June 23, 1902, during the celebrations of the 50th anniversary of Université Laval. His theme was "La vocation de la race française en Amérique," and he identifies that vocation as the fostering of religion and thought:

> Notre mission est moins de manier des capitaux que de remuer des idées; elle consiste moins à allumer le feu des usines qu'à entretenir et à faire rayonner au loin le foyer lumineux de la religion et de la pensée...

And again,

> Pendant que nos rivaux revendiquent, sans doute dans des luttes courtoises, l'hégémonie de l'industrie et de la finance, nous ambitionnerons avant tout l'honneur de la doctrine et les palmes de l'apostolat.[125]

The sermon has been often interpreted as an attempt by Abbé Paquet to steer his fellow French Canadians away from playing their rightful role in industry. This is a possible interpretation. It is also plausible to interpret it as a rationalization of the poor showing which his fellow countrymen were making in the new wave of industrialization. And again, it is possible to see in it merely an eloquent plea on the part of a priest who earnestly wishes to remind his people of that age-old teaching of Christ that riches can never be an ultimate goal, but only a means to higher values. Later in his sermon, Abbé Paquet says that he does not want his audience to think that he is preaching "un renoncement fatal" of the new age of progress, which he then proceeds to describe in equally glowing language. He concludes, "La richesse n'est interdite à aucun peuple ni à aucune race; elle est même la récompense d'initiatives fécondes, d'efforts intelligents et de travaux persévérants." But his deep concern is that a thirst for gold and pleasure may deaden their noble aspirations and that gross materialism may rivet them to

---

[125] Mgr L.-A. PAQUET, *Le bréviaire du patriote canadien-français*, pp. 52, 59. One reason why this sermon is well known by contemporary French Canadians is that 23 years after it was preached it was re-published by Canon Chartier and was later often studied in the classical colleges as embodying the French Canadian nationalistic preoccupations that dominated their thinking in the twenties and the thirties. In my extensive reading in the pre-1914 literature I have found it quoted verbatim only once (see *l'Enseignement primaire* (1906-1907), p. 218).

material things.   And he goes on to counsel them how to use this new wealth and progress, in which he obviously assumes they intend to share fully:

> Usons des biens matériels, non pour eux-mêmes, mais pour les biens plus précieux qu'ils peuvent nous assurer; usons de la richesse, non pour multiplier les vils plaisirs des sens, mais pour favoriser les plaisirs plus nobles, plus élevés de l'âme; usons du progrès, non pour nous étioler dans le béotisme qu'engendre trop souvent l'opulence, mais pour donner à nos cœurs un plus vigoureux élan.[126]

Rhetoric apart, Abbé Paquet seems here to be merely spelling out that qualification of "véritable" or "vrai," which the bishops always add when they claim that the Church and they themselves favour and are actively working to promote progress.[127]   For the rest, it is not particularly surprising that French Canadians, like their French ancestors, should despise what they regard as the grubbing materialistic ways of the Anglo-Saxon and of his American cousin!

It is, of course, one thing stoutly to refuse to make a god of riches but quite another deliberately to refuse industrialization and the consequent urbanization in favour of agriculture.   Yet this is the accusation often made against the Quebec clergy.   Is it sound ?

As we have already seen, Quebec had long suffered from the problem of surplus population, which forced hundreds of thousands of French Canadians to emigrate to the United States. The clergy as well as many politicians soon came to realize that the opening of new areas for settlement and the improvement of agriculture were urgently required not only as the necessary economic base of the province, but also as an essential condition of the survival of the French Canadians as a separate ethnic group—and hence also of their Catholic religion, which they had come to consider as almost inherently dependent on the maintenance of their French language and culture as a bulwark against

---

[126] *Ibid.* p. 57.   In the case of Abbé Paquet personally, there seems little doubt that in his later writings he indulged fully in the agriculturalist theme.   In 1917, he clearly stated that he was very concerned that there were people who were trying to uproot the French Canadian soul and bend it towards a new destiny (Mgr L.-A. PAQUET, *Études et appréciations: mélanges canadiens*, pp. VI-VII).

[127] See, for example, Mgr CLOUTIER, "Le véritable progrès," *Le Bien public*, January 3, 1911: or "Lettre pastorale de Nos Seigneurs les Archevêques des provinces ecclésiastiques de Québec, de Montréal et d'Ottawa," March 19, 1894), p. 690, where the bishops maintain that the Church not only does not oppose but emphatically favours "tous les progrès bien entendus."   As Father LALANDE, S.J., expressed it in his lecture at Trois-Rivières (*Le Bien public*, November 30, 1909) and repeated it often elsewhere in the province, the French Canadians should not set an upper limit to their pursuit of riches, "car là, comme ailleurs, il n'est jamais bon de rester volontairement au second rang quand on peut être au premier," provided only that they are ever mindful of "la noblesse de nos origines sur cette terre d'Amérique."

Anglo-Saxon Protestantism.   Only by rapidly increasing their voting power in the Confederation could they defend their minority rights in view of the endless flood of non-French immigrants now pouring into Canada.   Inevitably, watchwords and clichés entered the French Canadian vocabulary and came to be mouthed at the slightest provocation.   Among them were such phrases as, "Emparons-nous du sol" (this saying was first attributed to George-Étienne Cartier, who as well as being one of the chief architects of Confederation was also involved in railway expansion); "Nous sommes essentiellement une race de terriens"; "La mission du Canadien-français est d'être agriculteur"; "Ne l'oublions jamais: avant tout, ce qui nous enrichira, c'est la charrue."[128]   If emigration was to be stopped and if the people were to be kept on the land, farming had to be made into a successful vocation and the people had to be taught to attach a certain prestige value to an occupation vital for the causes of both race and religion.   In fact, the bishops had assigned a group of priests the special role of colonization and agricultural missionaries to carry out this work, often at the request of the government, which at times paid some of them a regular salary.   In 1894, as we saw, Bishop Bégin spelt out clearly to his agricultural missionaries what they were to teach the farmers:

> Il s'efforcera de faire aimer l'agriculture, d'en faire ressortir la noblesse, les avantages, la supériorité sur les diverses professions libérales et sur les différents métiers et industries; et cela à divers points de vue: au point de vue matériel, au point de vue de la famille, et au point de vue national.[129]

And so, over the next two decades, even though the bishops themselves scarcely ever referred directly to agriculture and were more immediately preoccupied with a new set of problems arising out of rapid industrialization, this group of zealous missionaries continued in times of prosperity as in times of recession to preach the gospel of agriculture and colonization.   The Catholic press took up the cause every now and then, especially each year about the time of the annual convention of these missionaries, or when the question of agriculture or of colonization came up for discussion in the legislature.   On these occasions, the editors usually fell back briefly on the various clichés mentioned above.   But for the rest, they were content to devote a section of their paper to agriculture in which though preaching occasionally occurs, it

---

[128] *L'Action sociale*, March 18, 1909; June 3 and July 14, 1911.
[129] Mgr Bégin, "Notes à l'usage des missionnaires agricoles," p. 177.

is obviously meant only to encourage the farmers or settlers. When economic reasoning is invoked, as it is on rare occasions, it invariably has a physiocratic flavour.

For example, Abbé Michaud reasons as follows: agriculture is the basis of the nation's riches; unlike commerce, agriculture and industry are productive, yet agriculture has this advantage over both the others, for "Quant au commerce et à l'industrie, *ils travaillent sur des matières existantes, tandis que l'agriculture travaille pour produire ce qui n'existe pas.*"[130] And he manages so to reconstruct history as to be able to draw the pertinent universal lesson that the prosperity and happiness of a nation are in direct relation to the number and prosperity of its farmers. Michaud, like his fellow agriculturalist, Abbé Georges Dugas, who is fond of citing Sully to the effect that agriculture and grazing are the breasts of France,[131] fears lest the necessary equilibrium between production and consumption be endangered, since productivity in agriculture is not keeping pace with productivity in industry. Father Adélard Dugré tried to state this balance mathematically and explained that the industrial crisis of 1913 was caused by the fact that there were only 119 persons in rural areas for every 100 persons in the city, whereas, in 1901, there were still 165 in the countryside for every 100 in the city.[132]

Such economic reasonings as these are generously interspersed with biblical quotations and references to the Fathers of the Church, but they cannot in any meaningful way be said to represent the economic thinking of the Church at this time. Her economic thinking was quite unsophisticated—she simply wanted to keep the French Canadians in the province and to help to

---

[130] Abbé MICHAUD, *L'agriculture et l'état agricole*, pp. 27, 28. *L'Action sociale,* as we noted earlier, reduces the same argument to: "We can live without electricity; we cannot live without bread." And the editor spells out the argument more moderately as follows: we should rejoice at the progress and perfection achieved in our industrial equipment, but "Sachons ... garder en cela une juste mesure, et n'allons pas, au milieu du bruit assourdissant des machines, oublier que la base de toute prospérité industrielle et commerciale, c'est l'agriculture. Pas de récoltes, pas d'argent; pas d'argent, pas de commerce." The "bad" years are the years when the farmers have no money to buy the products of industry which soon finds itself in crisis (*L'Action sociale*, June 3, 1911).

[131] Abbé George DUGAS, "De la vocation des Canadiens à l'agriculture," *Rapport du congrès de la colonisation tenu à Montréal, les 22-24 novembre 1898*, p. 78. Abbé Dugas had formerly been a missionary in the Canadian Northwest and there seems, like Mgr Laflèche, to have acquired his passionate love for agriculture.

[132] Adélard DUGRÉ, S.J., *La désertion des campagnes: ses causes et ses remèdes*, p. 5. It is interesting to find the federal Board of Enquiry into the Cost of Living, in their report of 1915, talking almost the same language. They explain that the prices of food products have increased because of the decrease in the proportion of persons engaged in producing the food supply. Concentration in the cities "has increased the proportion of non-producing food consumers." And they recommend a policy of land settlement and better education in agriculture (*Report of the Board*, I, 12, 79).

provide the material base to make this a real possibility.   At no time do the bishops themselves indulge in theoretical economic reasoning.

It is interesting to note that with the industrial crisis of 1913 and the outbreak of war the following year, the editors of *l'Action sociale* stepped up their campaign in favour of colonization and improved agriculture.   Here the preoccupation is neither economic nor religious, it is racial.   Economic and religious arguments are merely rallied to strengthen conclusions reached on "nationalist" reasoning.

Among these agriculturalist priests there is much rhetoric; they are used to rising to the occasion as special pleaders whenever required.   But they themselves are seldom men of narrow vision.   A one-time colonization missionary, Curé Corbeil, can on occasion give a lecture in Quebec City calling the desertion of the land a "lèse-nationalité," while at the same time he himself is busy building a pulp-and-paper-mill town at La Tuque, where the word "agriculture" scarcely enters his vocabulary.[133]   Curé Cimon of Saint-Alphonse (Bagotville) can, in 1900, plead the cause of agriculture and decry the evils of the manufacturing towns at a "fête agricole," held in the new pulp mill at Jonquière,[134] and a few years later can equally revel in the success of the new all-French-Canadian mill at Chicoutimi, and be among the most ardent promoters of turning Ha Ha Bay into a major seaport to the benefit of his parish.[135]   The agricultural and colonization missionary who overshadowed and gave the example to all others, Curé Labelle, while he took as the slogan on his coat of arms *"Pater Meus Agricola"* seemed to be as much at home in inviting French capitalists and industrialists to come to Canada, and promoting local railroads, manufacturing, mining, and tourism as in extolling the noble vocation of agriculture.

To what extent did the promotion of agriculture and colonization involve depreciating the newly developing manufacturing cities?   The chief goal in all this campaign of the clergy was effectively to stop emigration to the manufacturing towns of the United States, and especially to those of New England.   Hence these towns were often excoriated.   In their joint pastoral letter of 1893, the bishops had them in mind when they talk of the crowds foolishly rushing headlong towards "les Babylones

---

[133] *L'Action sociale*, March 18, 1909.
[134] *Le Colon du Lac Saint-Jean*, September 27, 1900.
[135] *Le Soleil*, November 29, 1903, which reproduces a letter of Curé Cimon to the directors of the Chicoutimi mill congratulating them on their great achievement.

modernes" and their chief recommendation is to make agriculture sufficiently profitable to weaken the temptation to emigrate to the United States.[136]   Nowhere during this period can one find either the bishops or the clergy directly attacking French Canadian cities by name, although one suspects that Montreal was often at least implicitly included with those of New England.   The clergy of the rural areas may rhetorically praise agriculture and the quiet peacefulness of the countryside at the expense of the noise and restless bustle of the city, but by the clergy of the cities there is certainly no general decrying of industrialization.[137]   Rather, as we noted earlier, the bishops set themselves the task of helping to promote the better economic and social organization of their respective cities, and we find the local Catholic press in such cities as Chicoutimi, Trois-Rivières, and Quebec City rejoicing at every local gain in industry, modernization of public utilities, and population.   Unfortunately, no official Catholic newspaper was published in Montreal and we are thus handicapped in not being able to follow the day-to-day reactions of the local clergy to the city's rapid developments.   *L'Action sociale* and other outside Catholic papers from time to time expressed some reservations concerning the rapid growth of the metropolis, but these seem to stem primarily from a concern with racial survival.   Montreal was considered too costly in health, energy, human life, and particularly in infant mortality—all of which were questions of life-and-death for the French Canadian race.[138]

The major goals sought by the clergy, in descending order of their importance, seem to have been the following: (1) to keep

----

[136] "Lettre pastorale des Évêques établissant l'Œuvre des missionnaires agricoles," p. 97.

[137] In the first plenary council of the Canadian bishops, which was held in Quebec in 1909, the preoccupation of the bishops was chiefly to promote and safeguard Catholic education; and the three major evils they selected to fight were abuse in the use of alcohol, the growing practice of mixed marriages, and Catholics' participation in "neutral" societies. Rapid industrialization and urbanization were neither excoriated nor praised ("L'esprit chrétien dans l'individu, dans la famille, et dans la société," *Lettre pastorale des pères du premier concile plénier de Québec* [Québec: 1909], p. 33).

[138] For example, see *l'Action sociale*, October 1, 1909; December, 1911.   In this concern they were not exaggerating.   We have already seen that Montreal's rate of infant mortality was 242 per thousand second only to that of Calcutta, which was 252, the highest in the world.   And, in 1909, Dr. Valin reported to the Royal Commission inquiring into the causes of tuberculosis, "Montréal est la plus insalubre de toutes nos villes à cause de son atmosphère pleine de poussière soulevée par les automobiles et les tramways; de la fumée vomie par les cheminées de ses nombreuses usines; à cause de ses *nombreuses habitations insalubres*; de sa population considérable d'immigrants qui se tassent dans des logements malpropres, infectés et humides et dans des quartiers insalubres par leur vétusté; enfin à cause du tassement des maisons et de l'étroitesse des rues."   (Cited by Gustave Tremblay, "Le logement ouvrier," unpublished thesis at l'École des Hautes Études, 1924, p. 13.) Valin also points out that, as late as 1922, 10 per cent of the deaths occurring in Montreal were due to tuberculosis (*ibid.*).

the French Canadians from emigrating to the United States;
(2) to keep them in the province of Quebec; and (3) only where
possible, to keep them on the land. *L'Action sociale* clearly
recognizes that the way to get French Canadians to return from
the United States was to invite them to return not to farm, but
to work in the more prosperous industries in Quebec.[139]

It usually seems to be among the more intellectual members
of the clergy, among the journalists and the professors of classical
colleges and seminaries, and not among the bishops and the curés,
that we find men sufficiently removed from immediate involvement in economic life to endorse ardently the more unrealistic
tenets of pure agriculturalism; though these people often live
in the cities they seem to be the most removed of all from industrial reality. That some of these priests were fervent agriculturalists is evident from the fact that the economist Édouard
Montpetit recounts that he personally was advised at this time
by one of his professors at a classical college in Montreal that
the best thing he could do in life was to become a farmer and
settle on the good soil of French Canada.[140] Errol Bouchette,
too, claims that at the turn of the century there was in several
of the colleges a current of thought that held that French Canadians were unfitted for business.[141] He also recalls an old
professor whose common theme ran as follows,

> Le commerce, l'industrie, ... sont des occupations matérielles; nous,
> Canadiens-français, sommes faits pour quelques chose de plus noble;
> soyons cultivateurs comme Cincinnatus, orateurs comme Cicéron
> et Bossuet; la charrue, la tribune, la chaire nous appellent; laissons
> le gain matériel aux natures plus grossières.[142]

Brunet suggests that hundreds of other young men were
probably counselled similarly to take up the plough, the tribune,
or the pulpit.

At least prior to 1914, this seems highly unlikely, though we
have not sufficient evidence to deny its truth categorically.[143]
What is true is that the Catholic Action movement, founded in
the classical colleges in 1903, did seem to adopt a certain agriculturist bias, already found among some of the priest-professors

---

[139] For example, see *l'Action sociale*, April 21, 1908.
[140] Édouard MONTPETIT, *Souvenirs* (Montréal: 1944–1949), I, 21.
[141] Errol BOUCHETTE, "L'évolution économique dans la province de Québec," *Proceedings and Transactions of the Royal Society of Canada* VII, 2nd Series (May, 1901), Section 1, 120.
[142] *Ibid.*, p. 122.
[143] The author questioned a few graduates of classical colleges in Montreal and elsewhere on this matter; all denied categorically that any of their professors had tried to direct them towards agriculture.

and journalists who promoted it—among others, especially J.-P. Tardivel, the editor of *la Vérité*. Because Catholic Action was a French Canadian nationalist movement to promote French Canadian interests, above all those of religion, language, and culture, the vital question of the promotion of agriculture and colonization found a place in its programme even before the serious problems arising out of rapid industrialization and urbanization, despite the fact that the majority of the students involved were attending classical colleges in the larger cities.[144] However, neither in the movement's congresses nor in its official publication, *le Semeur*, do we find any recommendations that the students should turn their back on industry and city life and return to the farm. And its congress on education in 1913 strongly recommended that primary education be adapted to the milieu in which it was given, the rural schools being adapted to the needs of country folk and the city schools adapted to the needs of city folk.[145]

Nor does this particular aspect of the agriculturalist theme appear anywhere in the Catholic press, although parents are asked not to push their children into the overloaded fields of the liberal professions and commerce, but rather to direct them into the more productive occupations of agriculture and industry.[146] Indeed the prevalent complaint seems to run in the opposite direction. The classical and commercial colleges are blamed for taking the children away from the farms and teaching them the ways of the city, thus causing them to lose their taste not only for agriculture but for manual work of any type. Besides, it was a common opinion, recurring again and again, that the proximity of an agricultural school to a classical college not only hurt the effectiveness of the former but did positive damage to the dignity of agriculture, a conviction about which these schools were endeavouring to instil in their pupils.[147] Finally, it should be noted that if such counsel was, in fact, occasionally given, it seems to have been quite ineffective. Montpetit became Quebec's first professional economist; Bouchette had long been his unofficial predecessor and one of the few at the turn of the century who clearly realized that "la survivance" to be complete had to include French Canadian control over big industry; Joseph Versailles, the first president of the Catholic Action movement, who can rightly be supposed to incarnate the spirit

---

[144] See *Premier congrès de la Jeunesse catholique et canadienne-française*, p. 6.
[145] *Étude critique de notre système scolaire*, p. 160.
[146] For example, see *l'Action sociale*, December 22, 1913.
[147] For example, see Marc PERRON, *Un grand éducateur agricole*, p. 276; also pp. 259-60.

of the classical college élite of this period, became not a farmer, but a successful Montreal banker and the genuine successor to Bouchette, forever urging the French Canadians to fight systematically for their economic independence.[148]   There is no record of college graduates dutifully turning back to the plough, although, as we shall see later, with the liberal professions overloaded and the channels into the business world practically blocked to him, it is not at all clear that the average college graduate contributed more as an insignificant lawyer or notary to the Gross National Product than did his fellow countryman, the successful farmer!

One suspects that the agriculturalist spirit was everywhere at this time, in the sense of a nostalgia for a French Canadian Catholic state where French Canadians would control their own religious, political, and economic history—the type of Laurentian state about which Mgr Laflèche dreamed, or the rosy French Canadian Kingdom of the Saguenay conjured up by the priest editors of *l'Oiseau Mouche*.   Interestingly enough, both dreams included industry—in the former figured the textile cities of New England, in the latter the mighty future industrial and commercial cities of the Canadian north.   Doubtless too, the appeal of claiming the Canadian North and peopling it with French Canadians free from the control of foreigners ever clung to the colonization and agricultural movement.   But, by and large, the clergy, and particularly the bishops and the local curés, were down-to-earth realists, and, during the two decades of rapid economic development that preceded World War I, they not only adapted themselves to a quickly changing situation, but even eagerly taught their people how to benefit from it to the extent of their possibilities.   Only a small group, composed chiefly of professors, orators, and journalists, who were usually less immediately involved in the day-to-day struggle with economic realities, could harbour actively and at times express publicly the full-blown philosophy of agriculturalism.   It was to these that the people turned on special occasions, such as their national feast of St. Jean Baptiste, to have them conjure up in flowing rhetoric their long suppressed ambition of becoming one day a beacon to the people of the new world just as their "Mother" France had long been to the old—not merely a struggling minority held fast in the chains of economic slavery.

---

[148] At the congress of 1921, Versailles was acclaimed as perfectly embodying the spirit of the movement (*Le problème industriel au Canada français*, p. 115).

CHAPTER VIII

CONCLUSION

This concluding chapter will summarize the key attitudes and initiatives adopted by the Church during the spurt in economic development in the period 1896–1914, note how they changed or were modified during this period, and attempt to evaluate very roughly their significance for the economic development that actually occurred. It will then relate this study to the more general discussion on the relevance of religion for economic development, and, finally, conclude by making some suggestions about possible lines of future research which will fill out the exploratory work reported here.

ATTITUDES AND INITIATIVES OF THE CHURCH

General Perspective

It is important to remember that we have been dealing only with those attitudes and initiatives which are relevant from the economic point of view. To keep a perspective, it must be recalled that these always remain a relatively small part of the preoccupations of bishops and priests as a group, since the majority of them quite naturally deal more often with the theological, pastoral, and administrative problems of leading the Church. However, in this limited area, the basic principle that has guided the Catholic hierarchy as well as the lower clergy in Quebec over the past century, and earlier, has been to promote and support every attitude and project that seemed to them to aid "la survivance," that is, the survival of the French Canadian people in its Catholic religion, its French language and culture, and its material prosperity, and to oppose energetically all that seemed to hurt this cherished cause.

This was a time when many French Canadian spokesmen seriously believed that "la survivance" was being threatened on all sides—by massive non-French immigration into Canada, which was interpreted as, and at times may actually have been, a plot to reduce the French in Canada to a small powerless minority; by a continual flouting of what were considered the

French Canadians' constitutional school and language rights
in the English Canadian provinces and territories; by Great
Britain's adoption of a form of economic imperialism which
not only menaced Canada's economic autonomy but even required that her soldiers and ships be enlisted to bolster the Empire's
armed might; by a constant barrage of bitter, ill-informed
attacks in the Protestant Anglo-Saxon press on what was branded
as the "backwardness" and "illiteracy" of the French Catholics;
by scurrilous sallies against the clergy by a small group of French
Canadian anti-clericals, who championed the final dissolution
of the Church's monopoly of education and the initiation of
"neutral" schools; by the insults and mockery directed by the
frustrated organizers of the American International unions
against the local clergy when they found themselves powerless
to organize the "priest-ridden" workers of Quebec; by the occasional flagrant abuse of French religious and cultural traditions
on the part of both "foreign" entrepreneurs and labour union
leaders; by the criticism levelled by Irish and English Catholics,
and even by their priests and prelates, against the French clergy's
habit of identifying the Catholic religion too closely with the
preservation of the French language in Canada; by the blind
absolute loyalties instilled by the federal political parties that
seemed to turn even staunch French Canadian deputies against
the vital interests of their race and religion; by the increasing
control of what little industry they possessed or had initiated
by English or Americans; and, finally, by some subtly organized
plot on the part of international Freemasonry ultimately to
destroy the French Canadian Catholic race in America (a suspicion fostered by rhetorical orators and journalists who, quite
unhampered by the hard facts of the case, managed to interpret
Quebec's peaceful day-to-day life in the context of France's
recent unattractive history of religious persecution). This
complex of threats—real or imaginary—to "la survivance"
naturally bred, over the years, an increasingly strong but narrow
French Canadian nationalism, which would reach its peak with
the conscription issue during World War I. The growing
nationalist consciousness found its best expression in the speeches
of the flamboyant French Canadian orator and politician, Henri
Bourassa, but it was equally apparent in the Catholic Action
movement organized among the students of the classical colleges
in 1903, and in the clerically sponsored *Société du Bon Parler
français*, founded about the same time.

   In practice, they generally do not separate the national or
racial from the Catholic or religious cause. They are ardent

promoters of what they call "genuine" or "true" progress, a qualification which can imply a whole spectrum of nuances of meaning ranging all the way from the basic teaching of Christianity that progress and the pursuit of material riches involved must always be in harmony with and never be allowed to vitiate the Christian's more essential pursuit of final union with the Creator of such riches, to the implicit suggestion that "true" progress is best embodied in a prosperous French Canadian Catholic enterprise, such as Dubuc's large pulp mill at Chicoutimi, which has been solemnly blessed by the Church and over which proudly flies the "drapeau Carillon Sacré-Cœur," the distinctive French Canadian Catholic flag.[1] Besides, the basic Christian teaching often seems to be coloured in French Canada by an ill-concealed anxiety lest a growing hankering after material wealth might eventually turn French Canadians into the sordid ways of the Anglo-Saxon Canadians and Americans and cause them to forget their first and more noble vocation which is to civilize and Christianize nations, a providential vocation inherited by them from "Catholic" France which has now, itself, betrayed it. The distinctions between religion, language, culture, and race are thus constantly blurred by the clergy, and the attitudes and initiatives adopted by them in this period can only be fully understood if seen in this context.

Religious values were quite freely put on nationalist goals, for the latter were believed always to include explicitly or implicitly what was best for Catholicism. A non-Catholic French Canadian was at least an incongruity, if not an open contradiction; and a Catholic Anglo-Saxon always remained somewhat of a mystery to Quebec, for his language was "Protestant." Needless to say, much precious energy and talent was committed during this period to the defence of the French Canadian Catholic citadel against many and incessant "attacks," energy that might well have been employed to build a bigger, richer citadel—but it would probably have been less French and less Catholic.

Any attempt to reduce the attitudes and initiatives of the bishops and the clergy to a simple common denominator is vain. A procrustean unanimity thus achieved would not at all reveal the wealth of variety and nuance indicated by the available evidence. The reality would be better portrayed by a type of

---

[1] Mason Wade describes this flag as follows: it is "a mythical standard supposedly flown at Ticonderoga in 1758, but actually divised by a romantic abbé at the Seminary of Quebec under the inspiration of Fréchette's poem (*Légende d'un Peuple* [1887]) and messianic nationalism." (Mason WADE, *The French Canadians*, p. 516.)

scatter diagram representing all the shades of opinions, through which a trend or regression line might be drawn approximating the opinions and initiatives voiced and recommended by the hierarchy in their more sober and less rhetorical pastoral letters. Even with such a scatter-diagram approach one would have to be wary of the ever present temptation to give undue weight to the more vocal, often less immediately involved element of the clergy, that is, the professors, the writers, the journalists, and the orators of special occasion whose influence among the non-literary Catholic masses of society, at least in the short run, was not at all comparable to that of the more authoritative voice of the bishop and the ubiquitous guiding voice and bustling initiative of the local curé.   For this reason this study tries to give equal and even greater weight to this less vocal and more active element of the clergy, since we are here interested less in fascinated ideas, abstract plans, imaginative dreams, and formulated ideologies than in the motives of action and initiative.

The Bishops

There is no evidence of any sudden, dramatic, or substantial changes in the bishops' attitudes towards economic development during the economic spurt 1896–1914; though many minor changes did come about.   They were not out of harmony with past attitudes and initiatives already expressed and adopted. Since 1850, as has been said in previous chapters, the French Canadian bishops' direct involvement in economic development seems to have stemmed primarily from their preoccupation with the massive French Canadian emigration to the United States which began to be a serious problem about that time.   When they understood that the future of their people as well as of their Catholic religion was thereby imperilled, they began to concern themselves and their clergy with ways to halt this wasting tide. The chief methods used were moral suasion, measures to improve local agriculture, and especially the opening up of new settlement areas in Canada.   The bishops personally used all their prestige and influence with governments and businessmen alike to win support for their particular projects of agricultural schools, the building of roads and railways, the settling of new areas, etc., to which they unstintingly devoted their priests, their religious congregations, and their finances.   And, in return, they lent their full support to governments and businessmen who, directly or indirectly, helped them to achieve these goals.   Their more detailed programme involved teaching the farmers the virtues of hard work, thrift, foresightedness, solidarity, temperance, and progressive agriculture; commissioning priests to organize the settlement of particular new areas; and even bringing back families from the United States to resettle them under more suitable and more prosperous conditions. They readily put a religious value on both agriculture and colonization. They accepted the logging industry as the natural counterpart of their settlement work and considered the English and American entrepreneurs not as enemies but as benefactors, who merited their encouragement, help, and at times even their warm friendship. They did not attack or minimize the importance of industry. In fact, where the "foreign" Protestant entrepreneur so desired he could always establish with the bishops a relationship of mutual respect and harmony not unlike that cultivated between the French Canadian bishops and their English rulers after the conquest of 1759.

During the "depression" of the 1870's and 1880's, the bishops renewed their efforts to foster better agriculture and more rapid settlement and were quick to urge their people to switch from the cultivation of cereal crops to more remunerative dairy farming. At this time, they renewed their attacks on American cities—those modern "Babylons" that were ruinous to their race and religion alike. But with the return of industrial prosperity and the dropping off of emigration in the late 1890's their personal involvement in the promotion of colonization and agriculture declines. Those who have industrial centres in their dioceses, such as the bishops of Montreal, Trois-Rivières, Chicoutimi, and Quebec, begin to turn their attention to the new problems arising out of rapid industrialization and urbanization. Once more there is no expression of hostility to either industry or industrialization, only an honest attempt to face the problems they bring that bear on both race and religion.[2] They give their encouragement, their blessing when it is sought,

---

[2] One suspects that both bishops and priests were, at that time, at once more voluntaristic in their ethics and more liberal in their economic thinking than they tend to be today. Economic changes were regarded merely as the occasion and not the cause of evil and misery in the burgeoning, overcrowded cities, for evil itself could dwell only in the human will. As an anonymous Jesuit priest wrote in 1903, there was obviously no question of trying to change the new economic situation, "... puisqu'elle est amenée par la force des choses. Il faut donc chercher le remède dans un changement moral et religieux, ..." (*La Croix* [Montréal], June 28, 1903). The same idea was expressed by Archbishop Bruchési in his Labour Day sermon to the English-speaking Catholics of Montreal, in 1906. He spoke in part as follows: "While this economic and industrial progress of which we are so proud has brought us new forms of physical, intellectual, and moral trouble, let us be grateful to God for having given us His Church, which can revive all the energies of the Christian faith in accordance with the needs of the time." (*La Vérité*, September 10, 1906).

and even their active co-operation and help to modern industry'
which they would clearly like to spiritualize and ennoble as they
had agriculture.³ Somehow the new industry seems to foster
misery, jealousy, egoism, cupidity, all of which run counter to
their creed; nevertheless, they are generally willing to gamble
their hopes on any Christian industrialist who shows the least
willingness to try to improve the situation, especially, of course,
if he be a French Canadian!

All are enthusiastic promoters of the prosperity of both
their cities and their industries. In 1899, they sought and
obtained an indult from Rome to suppress three Catholic holydays—the feasts of the Assumption, Corpus Christi, and Saints
Peter and Paul—which meant that thereafter these days became
regular work days and the obligation to assist at Mass was
dropped.⁴ In Chicoutimi, a diocese formerly committed to
agriculture and where now a new pulp industry was initiated
under French Canadian auspices, the bishop has little more to
say about agriculture and gives his full encouragement and
blessing to the new industry. In fact, in his 1910 report to
Father Hudon, S.J., who conducted a province-wide survey on
the new situation caused by rapid industrialization, the bishop
was openly enthusiastic on the changes brought about by industry in his diocese during the past decade.⁵ In the other
dioceses, where industry continues to be the hegemony of "foreigners" and "Protestants," it still receives all the encouragement
it could ask for from the bishop and could have the Church's
public blessing if it so desired. Most big businessmen were on
personal and even friendly terms with the local bishops, but, in
the bigger cities, especially in Montreal, the bishops were inevitably more removed from big industry, which had for a time been
ruled almost exclusively by Anglo-Saxon businessmen and
financiers.

However, if the bishops accept "foreign" capital and capitalists readily, they, like the industrialists, do not accept "foreign"

---

³ It is perhaps only since World War II that the full theological significance of industrialization in Christian life is becoming sufficiently clear. Today a bishop in an underdeveloped area might well tell Catholic parents that to give their child to engineering or
industry is "to give him to God," as the bishops of old used to say so easily of agriculture.
But this is a universal phenomenon and not in any way limited to the French Canadian
Catholic Church.

On this wishful, hopeful attitude of the Church towards modern industry at the turn of
the century, see, for example, Abbé A. BAILLAIRGÉ, *Traité classique d'économie politique*,
p. 76.

⁴ For example, see Mgr Paul LaRocque, *MLPC* (Sherbrooke, Circular No. 29, May 15,
1899).

⁵ "Rapport du diocèse de Chicoutimi sur la situation, etc., des ouvriers," December 19,
1910, EAC.

labour unions, for these organizers are set on influencing the ideas of the local workers and not merely on organizing their labour power. Particularly when these organizers fall to decrying clerical control in education and to promoting free, compulsory education, they incur the enmity of the bishops, who determine to supplant their unions eventually with French Catholic unions, which will be more in harmony with the particular situation existing in French Canada. Nevertheless, the bishops do reverse one of their earlier positions, and now energetically defend the rights of the workers to organize, although they continue to do all in their power to prevent strikes and even offer their personal services and those of the clergy to arbitrate any strikes that do occur.

In the meantime, the impetus which they have already given to both settlement and agriculture continues to produce fruit. If the bishops personally no longer try to persuade the farmers to stay on the soil, the local curés do, not only because they do not want to lose their parishioners, but because they are fully aware that there is no shortage of labour in the cities and that good jobs are not easy to obtain.

In education the situation is more ambiguous. At the turn of the century the clergy is under attack for not providing the people with more practical and technical education. The more virulent attacks come from a small but vocal group of anticlericals who would like to see the clergy's monopoly on education overthrown and the new French pattern of "neutral" schools adopted. The bishops' reaction is to refuse to change, in any substantial way, the secondary education provided by the classical colleges on which they depend for candidates for the priesthood and the liberal professions. However, Archbishop Bruchési of Montreal recommended to the superiors of the classical colleges that they try to equip their students with the mathematics and science necessary to permit a few of them, at least, to pursue studies at the polytechnical school. The bishops refuse adamantly to accept the "French" formula of "free, compulsory, uniform" primary education, which they firmly believe will inevitably lead to "neutral" or "God-less" education. But they give their full support and devote their manpower and finances to the improvement of attendance at school and the quality of the education provided, and especially to the introduction of greater stability into the teaching profession by increasing the number of brothers and sisters engaged therein and by promoting the construction of normal schools in each diocese. Attacks on the clergy and the religious who teach

in the schools were confined to a few small, anti-clerical papers;
when they became obnoxious, their editors were given formal
warning, and if they failed to desist the more intransigent among
them saw their papers formally condemned by the Church.

The bishops are obviously embarrassed by the lack of
technical and "practical" education in the school system.   Their
concern for technical education is not new but rather quite in
harmony with their earlier views.   They repeatedly declare
that they favour such education, but they have neither the
means nor the personnel to provide it.   Nevertheless, they
promise to lend their full support to any public or private initiative to promote it and they continue to commend the evening
trade schools to their people.   They likewise continue to foster
the agricultural schools as well as the "commercial" courses
provided by the priests and brothers in their colleges, for which
they seem to entertain unrealistic hopes.   They commend the
brothers for trying to adapt their schools to the needs of the time,
and they foster the new courses of domestic economy provided by
the sisters in their schools.

When in 1906 the government finally took the initiative in
building a school of higher commercial studies and two big
technical schools, the bishops quickly endorsed these schools
in principle, and they never withdrew this endorsement, even
though they were conceived by the government as "neutral"
institutions, in which the Church would have no legal jurisdiction.   They were the first of their kind in Quebec and, quite
naturally, among their most ardent promoters were to be found
well-known anti-clericals and "Masons," who saw in these
schools a first breach in the ecclesiastical control of education.
While the bishops' representatives blessed the schools and
commended them to Catholic parents, dialectical war continued
to rage openly between the anti-clerical and liberal press, on the
one hand, and the Catholic press, on the other, concerning the
exact status of these new schools—a situation that could not
help sowing at least some confusion in the minds of the faithful.

The bishops quickly became enthusiastic promoters of the
caisses populaires and urged their establishment in each parish to
foster French Canadian economic independence as well as the
practice of Christian virtue.   They concerned themselves with
the campaign to conserve the natural resources of the province,
especially the forests, and waged endless campaigns against the
abuse of alcohol and the widespread disease of tuberculosis,

which was ravaging the overcrowded cities. They sponsored programmes to help reduce the high rates of infant mortality, especially in Montreal.

They urged the government to promote economic development. The catechism statement of their position, made in 1909, is unambiguous:

> Les dépositaires du pouvoir civil doivent aider au développement des ressources naturelles du pays: 1) En stimulant le zèle de ceux qui les exploitent; 2) En encourageant tous les travaux qui peuvent contribuer au progrès de l'agriculture, du commerce, de l'industrie... etc.; 3) Enfin, en assurant à tous les citoyens, par une sage administration, la protection dont ils ont besoin pour vaquer en paix à leurs travaux et à leurs affaires.[6]

They favour government initiative in most areas of economic development and tend to bewail its miserliness and half-heartedness in promoting agriculture, communication facilities, and colonization. But, in two areas, that of education and of welfare services, they continue to be wary of government interference and to look to the government for subsidies but not control. It is ever their aim to remove these two areas from what they believe to be the instability and vagaries of partisan politics. They firmly believe that their people had "survived" because of their vigilance against overzealous governors and legislators in the past. And the bogy that France's recent history could easily be repeated in French Canada is never wholly absent from their thinking.

The Curés [7]

The ordinary Catholic and non-Catholic alike knew the Church through the person of the local parish priests, who together with their assistant priests, in 1914 ruled the 942 parishes and 195 mission posts throughout the province.[8] The quality that is perhaps at once most striking and most typical of the French Canadian curé is how completely he tends to identify himself with the needs, hopes, and aims of his parish, no

---

[6] *Manuel du citoyen catholique: ouvrage spécialement recommandé par NN. SS. les Évêques de la Province de Québec* (4th ed., Saint-Boniface: 1909), p. 13.

[7] A discussion of the role and attitudes of the teaching brothers and sisters is not possible for lack of space and lack of evidence. In general, it can be assumed that they second all the initiatives of the local curé, but the influence exercised by this silent group of workers merits much more careful study: it was ubiquitous.

[8] The number of parishes increased from about 764 to 942 in the period 1896–1913. And the total number of priests increased from about 1,807 to 2,730. About 1,000 of these priests were occupied with teaching and administrative tasks of various kinds and the remainder were engaged in parish work (see *Canada ecclésiastique*, 1914, pp. 40–265; and Hormisdas MAGNAN, *Monographies paroissiales*, p. 3).

matter what his past upbringing and experience has been.   This
phenomenon did not escape the careful observer Léon Gérin, who
knew his people and his province as no other scholar of his
generation.   He has a fine description of a variety of situations
met by a variety of curés:

> Même l'observateur pressé et superficiel ne pouvait qu'être frappé de
> l'étroite corrélation qui se manifestait dans toute la région entre le
> milieu économique et social de la paroisse et son chef ecclésiastique.
> Le type social des divers curés était en rapport direct d'une part
> avec les conditions du milieu soit rural soit urbain où s'était écoulée
> leur enfance, et d'autre part avec celles du milieu,—ou semblable ou
> différent,—dans lequel s'exerçait leur ministère.
>   Ainsi, dans les campagnes à culture relativement riche de la rive
> fluviale, se rencontrait fréquemment le curé de belles manières, à
> l'esprit fin et cultivé; le curé de grande allure faisant à de nombreux
> visiteurs les honneurs d'un vaste presbytère; ou encore le curé lettré
> et chercheur, fouilleur d'archives; enfin, le curé aux goûts artis-
> tiques, collectionneur de beaux tableaux.   Dans les campagnes
> aisées, mais isolées de la terrasse, c'était le curé hospitalier, à la vie
> modeste mais encore large, souvent préoccupé de progrès industriel
> ou commercial, ou même de construction de voies ferrées.   Dans les
> vallons du haut pays, on pouvait même relancer le curé défricheur,
> solidement bâti, aux "poignets de frêne," pour parler la langue d'Al-
> phonse Daudet, cultivant ses champs, rentrant ses récoltes ou char-
> riant ses produits dans les chantiers à bois.[9]

On the parish level, the curé, like his bishop, does not in
practice separate religious interests from those of race and
language; for him they tend to form a single complex whole.
All the teachings and attitudes of the bishops reappear but now
in action and coloured by the local circumstances of each parish.
The curé's direct role in parish life increases in proportion as we
leave the bigger cities, where the municipalities are already well
organized, and travel towards the remoter industrial towns and
farm villages that have just been hewn out of the woods; it
changes from the role of a spiritual leader and perhaps a builder
of churches and schools to the more comprehensive role of a
leader and organizer of a village's entire spiritual, material,
and social life.   The degree of his involvement will, of course,
also vary according to his own disposition and ability, but
personal inclination is quite secondary to the role he is permitted
and even expected to play in each given situation.   Should he
show excessive zeal, he will be checked by his bishop; should he
fail to concern himself with the temporal prosperity of his parish,
he is likely to be invited by his bishop to be more diligent.   The

---

⁹ Léon Gérin, *Le type économique et social des Canadiens*, pp. 104-105.

local curé's chief economic preoccupation during this period of prosperity, 1896–1914, is to see that his parish continues to grow and to prosper, and to keep his people in it. He realizes full well that the prosperity of the Church's institutions, the church building, the parish hall, the schools, the hospital, and even the size of his own income, are usually in direct proportion to his people's material welfare.

If his is an agricultural parish, he promotes better agriculture, and is probably wont to thunder against the evils of American cities and even, at times, of cities in general, for they always pose the temptation of emigration to some of his parishioners. But if his parish is in a little town or village that can benefit by industry, he may well become a promoter of industry to provide his people with employment and even bring in new parishioners from other "rival" parishes. *Ex officio*, he is usually the intermediary between the industrialist—be he French Canadian, English, or American—and the local workers. Any industrialist can have all the favours of the Church for the asking, provided he does not openly flout local French Canadian Catholic customs. A curé in open opposition to an industrialist, even when the latter has shown outright intransigence, is seemingly unknown; like his bishop, he is sufficiently realistic to see that the prosperity of his parish is at stake, and that if he is not to compromise it he must seek other means than an open clash with a local industrialist to remedy an ugly situation.

The curé supports all the efforts of his bishop to promote local education, often accepting elected office on the school commission; and it is a proud feather in his cap if he can succeed in getting a sisters' convent school for the girls and a *collège* directed by the brothers for the boys, for both are believed to be excellent educators and the latter to give a more "practical" education. His is a continual battle with the town council to reduce the number of liquor licences issued in the parish and with the local school commission to have them exact and collect adequate school taxes. He is likely to be not only interested in the local *caisse populaire* and agricultural club, but to be actually managing both. The *caisses*, the agricultural clubs, the budding co-operatives, etc., are all considered as effective means of fostering economic solidarity and of fighting the common weakness, found everywhere among French Canadians, of an exaggerated individualism which drives them into frequent and expensive lawsuits, seemingly as easily as other people's weaknesses drive them to drink. Perhaps most important of all, at least in the more remote regions, is the curé's invaluable role of channelling into this closed society new ideas, new methods, even new industries and industrialists with the sanction and even the blessing of the Church, in which these people have complete trust.   In his sociological study on the French Canadian village of Saint-Denis-de-Kamouraska, Horace Miner of the University of Chicago remarked how the curé could acclimatize his people to new ideas quickly and without shock. We may not accept without reservation his methodology of studying French Canadian society as a primitive peasant society but his point is well taken about the priest as innovator:

> Attention should be called to the fact that acculturation—the adoption of rational beliefs from the urban centers particularly—differs in St. Denis from the situation in Haiti or Mexico.   The difference lies in the fact that in St. Denis innovations enter sanctioned by a church, which is the most powerful force in the native community. In the acculturation between people of entirely different backgrounds, the entrance of a new church is a factor.   As it is new itself, it has not the same power as the native church in assisting the entrance of other new ideas.   St. Denis is being acculturated from a similar society, but a society two centuries more advanced along the lines of Western civilization.   The fact that the parish finds support for the new ideas from within itself, in the person of the priest, explains the ready acceptance of rational procedures in matters of birth and sickness. This is the opposite situation from that found in the urbanization of most folk societies, where contacts are with an entirely different type of culture.   It suggests that the sophistication of rural French Canada will take place more rapidly and more completely than in these other regions.[10]

Professors, Writers, Journalists, Orators, Missionaries

This catch-all group of the clergy overlaps that of both the bishops and the curés, but is, nevertheless, a group sufficiently different to merit separate consideration.   The professors and writers, as we saw, are among the less directly involved members of the clergy and so are freer to indulge in speculation, criticism, and even daydreaming; and, because of their loftier positions, their opinions and views tend to range over a wider gamut of interests than those of the bishop and ordinary curé.   Besides, being classical scholars, they can bring to bear all the resources of rhetoric and literature to the expression of their ideas.   From their ranks emerge men such as Mgr Laflamme, who probably did more at this time than any other single person in the province of Quebec to promote reliable surveying, scientific forestry, and the popularization of the elementary ideas of forest, land, and water-power conservation; Mgr Lapointe, who not only dreamed

---

[10] Horace MINER, *St. Denis: A French Canadian Parish*, p. 140.

about but actually worked for a French Canadian industrial and agricultural kingdom in the Saguenay; Abbé Baillairgé, who produced the first economics textbook in Canada; the Trappist monks of Oka, who year by year improved the standards of their agricultural college and published many learned tracts on agriculture. But in this group we also find diffident men, prophets of doom, who seemed more familiar with the daily happenings in ancient Rome and Greece and modern France than those which were taking place in the province and cities where they lived; men who, with the best of goodwill could naively lead parents to believe that a four- or five-year elementary commercial course could equip their sons to enter on any commercial or industrial career whatsoever; agriculturalists, who without ever having put their hand to the plough and quite innocent of any realistic knowledge of the farming resources of the province could from their ivory towers direct their race further northward onto the rocks of the forbidding Canadian Shield, steadfastly refusing to accept the hard facts of industrialization and urbanization that were swirling around them; rabid nationalists who, in spite of episcopal cautions to the contrary, set about teaching a whole generation of college students to tighten still closer the race-religion binomial and to reject every semblance of compromise; journalists who, like some of their lay contemporaries, often seemed to delight more in endless dialectical battles with their adversaries, especially on the question of educational reform, than in proposing positive alternatives and mutually acceptable *ad hoc* solutions such as the bishops and the curés, closer to reality, were forced to find; orators who could, on special occasions, make the French Canadians forget their inferior position in both society and industry in Canada with the tempting myth—which found an echo in every French Canadian heart—that somehow they were still successfully carrying out that providential mission, inherited from "Catholic" France, of civilizing and Christianizing the peoples of the world, and that after all they, and not the "money-grubbing" Anglo-Saxons, had in spite of all appearances to the contrary the far greater destiny. Finally, in the group were the colonization and agricultural missionaries, many of whom were also curés. These men were by designation "special pleaders," and were thus allowed full freedom to put spiritual and nationalist values on their particular goals of teaching the people to appreciate better the dignity of intelligent agriculture and the glory of conquering new uninhabited forest lands for their race and religion.

Summary

If we try to summarize the major groups of attitudes and initiatives of the clergy—those which lie closest to our imaginary regression line—they can perhaps be reduced to four:

1. There was a growing tendency to identify racial and religious goals, a confusion easily extended into the area of material prosperity and economic development.

2. There was a concerted effort to promote the growth and material prosperity of a healthy French Canadian population inside the borders of the province of Quebec—a project more easily identified with improved agriculture and the opening of new areas of settlement to both farming and industry, for here future French Canadian control was better ensured. It is significant that the more extreme elements of agriculturalism are in vogue among the clergy at either end of the industrial boom—prior to 1896 and after 1913—a phenomenon that suggests that this philosophy may be strongly correlated with longer industrial cycles.

3. By and large, there was a realistic acceptance of both industrialization and urbanization and even their positive promotion by the clergy immediately involved in these areas. Foreign capital was welcomed but foreign labour organization was not. With nationalist sentiment on the rise during this period one could well expect that in the near future foreign entrepreneurs and capitalists might increasingly come to be considered as rivals, and even enemies, to French Canadian economic independence; but, for the time being, they still occupied the envied position of being considered benefactors and enjoyed almost unlimited freedom of action provided only they did not grossly violate local customs and traditions.

The most important changes adopted by the Church at this time were the acceptance of the principle of trade unionism and the promotion of various kinds of cooperative economic associations among the French Canadians to teach them to overcome through group-action the glaring economic disadvantages to which their rugged individualism had always exposed them in the past, as well as to protect them from the undesirable influences of "neutral" and American associations. The ebb in agricultural interest represented a recognition and a gamble that industrialization would provide an alternative solution to mass emigration to the United States, but enthusiasm for it was tempered in proportion as the French Canadians had less say in its organization. As long as they continued to comprise the mass of unskilled labour, ever subject to sudden unemployment, the agricultural interest would have a potential preference, not primarily for religious reasons but simply because here the French Canadians were in control, masters of their own destiny, and more economically secure.

4. In education, the Church was throwing her full weight, manpower, finances, and devotedness into improving both the school attendance and the quality of primary education, but she was adamantly refusing to see the State wrestle from her any of her predominant influence by introducing compulsory, free, uniform education or by putting education under a Minister of Education, selected from the ranks of the party in power. Likewise, she was holding fast to the program of the classical colleges and insisting that the new technical education should be organized parallel to these colleges and without changing them into specialized schools.

EVALUATION OF THE ECONOMIC SIGNIFICANCE OF THE CHURCH'S ATTITUDES AND INITIATIVES

We now have a rather clear idea of the role of the clergy in economic development during the pre-war period. But the economist can still ask, what was its economic significance? Did the clergy actually contribute to the rate of growth of the Gross National Product or did they all unwittingly slow that rate of growth? It is far from my intention to attempt to make a quantitative estimation in this matter. I shall merely bring together the more relevant considerations involved which will perhaps permit us to form a very general tentative judgment on whether in particular areas their influence was, on balance, positive, negative, neutral, or insignificant. Only very detailed research in well-defined areas might possibly permit a more refined evaluation and the scope of the present study does not permit me to undertake such research. It must be admitted that the feasibility of such research is very much open to question where so many variables are involved and so few quantitative data are available. And the task of measuring influence, especially moral influence, remains a frustrating and hazardous one at best.

There is a second important question intimately related to this first question, and still more complicated; did the Church positively or negatively influence the role which the French Canadians themselves played in the production of the actual

Gross National Product? It is not my intention to answer this second question, except in so far as it impinges on the first; again, not enough information is available and I can merely suggest some general lines of future research which should prove fruitful. Hence, much of the following discussion is inevitably tentative and suggestive rather than conclusive.

Population

We saw how the Church for both racial and religious reasons began early in the last century to try to build a Chinese wall between Canada and the United States. Later this wall came more and more to coincide with the borders of Quebec, as it became clear that the English Canadian majority did not intend to guarantee to scattered French Canadian minorities school and language rights outside this province. The Church also promoted large families; this was apparently a deep tradition, probably stemming more directly from racial than religious motivation. In any case, there is little evidence that the practice of birth control was a serious pastoral concern.

These influences, combined with the recurring waves of foreign immigration, helped to create a situation of constant surplus population in the province even during the industrial spurt at the turn of the century. Labour shortages were practically unknown, and the greatest joy a French Canadian could hope for was to have job security with one of the better known English companies. Strikers, even when they were specialized workers such as at the Angus railway shops in Montreal, could seemingly be easily replaced in short order by workers recruited in England, Scotland, and the United States.[11]

The massive emigration that had taken place in past decades to the United States was not, of course, a total loss to the province; it turned out to be perhaps the chief way in which French Canadians learned the textile and shoe-making trades; and their successful mastery of the latter trade gradually gained them control of much of the shoe industry in the province. Besides, they certainly brought or sent back much of their earnings to their families and relatives in Quebec.

---

[11] See, for example, in *l'Action sociale*, the reports on the strike that took place in these shops from August to October 1909. These reports were confirmed in my interviews with three men who took part in this strike, Clarence Wales, George Musgrove and William Walsh. Because of this invasion of imported skilled workers recruited by the company, the strike was a total loss; all the strikers lost their seniority with the company and about one-third their jobs as well (personal interviews, February 1963).

The decision to try to keep the French Canadians in Quebec was not primarily an economic one, but it did make economic sense. As Curé Labelle repeatedly said, it was a sad waste to raise and educate a child to manhood and then lose his talent to a foreign country. Here lay certainly one of the reasons why, in 1911, 51.32 per cent of the total population in the province was either under 20 or over 70 years of age, compared with a corresponding figure for Ontario of 42.87 per cent, and for Canada as a whole of 45.39 per cent.[12] This meant that Quebec had approximately 8.5 per cent less of her people available for her labour force than did the neighbouring province of Ontario, and this quite independently of any differences that may have existed in the attitudes of their respective populations towards gainful labour. A higher birth rate and the after effects of massive emigration were definitely harmful to the immediate growth of per capita income in Quebec, even if the increase in population served to stimulate agriculture, construction, transportation, and consumer goods industries such as processed foods, textiles, shoes, clothing—all of which still loomed large among Quebec's manufacturing industries.[13] It is clear, too, that population pressure had the advantage of forcing both government and Church officials to foster the opening of new areas of settlement, with all the investments of social capital involved, and to improve the province's stagnant agriculture. There was poverty and hardship, but no starvation; in fact, the years 1896-1914 were everywhere considered as the "good years," after the crisis in the logging industries during the preceding decades. And the proof that people were sharing in the new wave of prosperity is that emigration to the United States during this period dropped drastically. In short, the losses in

[12] *Census of Canada, 1921*, Population, Vol. II, Table 5, p. 20. The comparable percentages for those under 15 and over 70 years of age for Quebec and Ontario, in 1911, were 41.30 and 33.10 respectively. Moreover, these percentage figures for Quebec have a downward bias through the inclusion of the non-French population which had fewer children and had not been exposed to same pattern of emigration, as is clearly indicated by the corresponding percentage figure for the city of Montreal, which was only about 26 per cent (*Statistical Year Book* II [1915], 146).

[13] See Kenneth BUCKLEY, "The Role of Staple Industries in Canada's Economic Development," "*Journal of Economic History* XVIII (December 1958), pp. 448-49. This well-known Canadian economist claims here that he has found "an apparent relationship between the swings in Roman Catholic births in Quebec and transportation development in Canada from 1824 to 1918, and also a relationship between the birth swings and building activity in Montreal—the data suggest that there is an economic link and the present approach suggests that it is provided through the movement of labour and population." This hypothesis would certainly square with my own findings on population pressures as a stimulant to economic action in the province. However, one is inclined to suggest that the birth rate itself is not a very reliable indicator in the province of Quebec, especially when one recalls that the rate of infant mortality in Montreal, in 1910, was still about 242 per 1,000. But this could easily be allowed for in the hypothesis.

immediate per capita income and consumption did not seem to be too high a price to pay for a big investment in their province's future. If population in Canada was still considered to be so scarce that the federal government continually subsidized new waves of immigration of strangers, surely high birth rates among native citizens were only to be encouraged. Besides, increased population provided perhaps the biggest single incentive to rouse the French Canadians out of their lethargy and cause them to set about improving their economic circumstances as well as their degree of literacy.

Agriculture

That the clergy played a positive and effective role in the improvement of both the quality and the quantity of Quebec's agricultural products is now too evident to require further comment here. It is to be regretted that their endeavours to promote better agricultural education were so hampered by lack of adequate funds. If their devotedness had been amply assisted by substantial government grants and stricter qualifications required of both professors and students, much more would have been accomplished and much sooner. In this case the government, torn between a small vocal force favouring strictly state-controlled schools and the vast majority supporting the proven devotedness of the Church schools, talked much, but really did little. The result was that MacDonald Agricultural School with more adequate financial resources could rapidly overtake and even surpass the hard-won accomplishment of decades of devotedness and self-sacrifice on the part of dozens of priests, monks, and lay professors.

New Settlement

Was the clergy's ardent involvement in the movement of new settlement a sound economic investment as well as a good racial and religious policy?   It is not clear that it was wholly a matter of free choice; there were simply not sufficient openings in industry or in the already settled farming areas, and the ultra-laissez-faire policy of the local government provided no other means of accommodating population. Albert Faucher and Maurice Lamontagne seem to be correct in claiming that Quebec promoted agriculture not primarily because of some traditional philosophy, but *"because there was nothing else to do."*[14]

This settlement movement in the northern forests required heroic courage and perseverance to eke out a bare subsistence

---

[14] A. FAUCHER and M. LAMONTAGNE, "History of Industrial Development," p. 28 (their italics).

for several years before the new crops arrived in sufficient quantity to provide surplus income. Here religion, patriotism, rhetoric, politics, and ignorance all played a role. There seems little doubt that it was not always a successful economic venture, for, at times, it was excessively wasteful of resources both human and natural. The French Canadian *habitant* had over the years quite naturally come to think of the tree as an enemy to agriculture, and the forest as a wall to be continuously pushed back as the settler advanced to the attack with his axe and his plough. His habits were often wasteful, even if not to be compared with those of the English and American wood merchants who for almost a century had ravaged Quebec's pine forests with little thought of the needs of future generations. For some reason, there was abroad a common *a priori* belief that under the forests of the rugged Laurentian Shield lay millions of acres of potentially fertile farm land, such as was found in the Canadian West and in Western Europe, both of which were at higher latitudes than much of the province of Quebec. It was to prove a costly illusion which was still not fully laid to rest even at the outbreak of World War I.

In 1912, when Henri Laureys, the new Belgian professor of economics at l'École des Hautes Études, made a serious assessment of the province's agricultural resources based on the data available at the time, he could still only conclude that agriculture offered a fine example of development:

> De tout ce qui précède il est logique de conclure que la province de Québec offre un bel exemple de développement agricole, développement qui, si l'on tient compte de l'immense étendue de territoire restant encore à exploiter, est loin d'être arrivé à son apogée.[15]

His professional opinion differed little from the still cherished view of the exuberant Premier Honoré Mercier, who three decades earlier in a time of industrial recession had stated that agriculture was the foundation of prosperity:

> L'agriculture est, surtout pour la province de Québec, la fondation première de la prospérité publique. On peut chercher à détourner le cours des fleuves et des rivières; on peut, par des travaux artificiels, réussir, pendant un certain temps, à produire des résultats temporairement satisfaisants; mais on ne peut empêcher une province d'être ce qu'elle est, tant sous le rapport du climat que sous celui des ressources agricoles. Or, la province de Québec a une population qui est nécessairement portée vers l'agriculture.[16]

---

[15] H. LAUREYS, "Les ressources agricoles de la province de Québec," *Revue économique canadienne*, II (1912), 25.
[16] Cited by Alfred PELLAND, "La colonisation dans la province de Québec," *Revue économique canadienne*, II (1912), 87.

Nor did his study discredit the opinion of Honourable G.-A. Nantel, who as Minister of Lands, Forests, and Fisheries, had had the responsibility of assigning forest lands to settlement, and who in 1903 before the Colonization Commission had maintained that it really did not matter what lands were opened up to the settlers.

> On n'a pas besoin d'être si difficile pour les terrains.   Je dis que dans les plus mauvais cantons, dans les plus mauvais terrains, cinquante arpents sur une terre de cent arpents sont amplement suffisants pour faire vivre une famille.[17]

The Commission did not seem to be overly impressed by such testimony; even the accuracy of the reports of the official surveyors was questioned:

> There are exceptions, of course, but, as a rule, the reports made by the surveyors respecting the nature and the qualities of the soil and its fitness for cultivation are lamentably inaccurate. How many settlers have been deceived, discouraged, ruined, so to say, through errors and false representations arising from this fruitful source of trouble, of deception and of hardship of every kind.[18]

Obviously, to the extent that they acted on this kind of generalized ignorance and substituted rhetoric for knowledge owing to the need to conjure up anticipations of a "promised land" for prospective settlers, the colonization missionaries bear some of the responsibility with the government for opening areas that were totally unfit for agriculture and that should have been conserved as forest limits for the timber merchants.[19]

But the poor soil, the severe climate, and the distant markets would finally assert themselves.   In 1943, Professor E. Minville suggested that Quebec's agriculture was the least advantageous in North America, and that only 35–40 million acres were capable of being farmed, or about 7 per cent of total land area of the province.[20]   In fact, in 1959, the area of improved farm land was

---

[17] *The Colonization Commission, Report*, Annex, *Enquête à Montréal*, pp. 376-77. He based his statement on the experience of settlement north of Montreal as well as in the Vosges and Switzerland, where the climate, he claims, is not more severe than in Quebec. His principle is that successful agriculture does not depend on the quality of the land, but rather on the way in which it is cultivated.

[18] *The Colonization Commission, Report*, p. 40.

[19] See, for example, Mgr LAFLAMME, "La colonisation et la forêt," p. 13, where he scores this practice as a recognized fact and gives as an example the region between Trois-Rivières and La Malbaie on the southern lip of the Canadian Shield and suggests that certain areas near Nominingue and north of Trois-Rivières and along the Lake St. John railway are in the same category.   Likewise, the Abbés Ivanhoe Caron and Jean Bergeron both take their predecessors—even such great men as Curé Labelle and Père Lacombe—to task for their disastrous policy: "pour avoir un peu exagéré les avantages de certaines régions et avoir passé sous silence les misères qui attendent les colons un peu partout, ces deux apôtres de la colonisation se sont créé de graves difficultés." ("Le problème de colonisation au Canada français," pp. 160, 171.)

[20] See E. MINVILLE, "La Colonisation," p. 330.

only 8,629,835 acres—not substantially different, even allowing for changes in definition, from what it was in 1911, namely 8,147,633 acres, or about 2.5 per cent of the total area of the province.[21]

As we saw, Mgr Laflamme considered the enemies of the forests to be especially three: *"Ignorantia vulgaris, Indifferentia Communis,* and *Influentia Politica."* He believed that of these three scourges the third was the greatest—governments which played politics with the province's forest wealth; which never really adopted a comprehensive settlement plan until the 1930's; which for political reasons consistently failed to come to grips with the problem of the "false" settler, who occupied land not to farm but to make quick profits by cutting the wood thereon; and which despite numberless recommendations had never clearly divided the fertile areas destined for settlement from the crown timberlands for logging, a policy of drift that had the inevitable consequence of providing a fruitful source of misunderstandings between the settlers and the wood merchants at the expense of both parties and of the province as a whole.

But if through ignorance and enthusiasm costly mistakes were made in conserving Quebec's timberlands, we must remember that the science of forestry was still in its infancy, and that largely because of the energetic campaign of Mgr Laflamme Quebec was one of Canada's first provinces to be endowed with both a surveying and a forestry school, and the energies of the Church were engaged to educate the local people on how to conserve the province's forests and water power. In the sequel, few areas opened to genuine farm settlement have been in fact abandoned; subsistence and sub-subsistence agriculture usually joined forces with the timber and the tourist industry to make many of these areas which had once been considered failures, quite prosperous a few decades later.

Needless to say, much of the road work, etc., directly undertaken by the clergy was of necessity patchwork, but it often effectively served to open the way to markets in areas where the government was still unwilling to do the job once and for all. And these new settlements were usually advantageous to the timber and the pulp and paper industry, providing them with efficient woodsmen in the winter and with readily available agricultural products. One need only recall the name of Brother

[21] See N.R. RICHARDS, "Production Possibilities and Technology, Fertility and Soil Management in Eastern Canada," *Resources for Tomorrow* (Ottawa: Queen's Printer, 1961), I, 60; and *Statistical Year Book*, II (1915), 423.

Moffet who, in the new settlement areas of Temiscaming, occasionally organized caravans involving as many as 100 men and 200 teams of horses to supply the needs of the surrounding logging camps and, at the same time, conveniently to dispose of the new settlers' farm products in this region where there was still no organized market for them.[22] How happy the timbermen were to have these French Canadians at hand to work in their camps is well indicated in the years immediately preceding the war, when such lumberjacks were becoming scarcer and labour costs were soaring as employers tried to replace them with European immigrants. The *Pulp and Paper Magazine* drew attention in 1913 to the withdrawal of men from the woods:

> A further circumstance, which should be viewed with keen apprehension by the trade, is the fact that throughout Eastern Canada, the Frenchman who is by training the best lumber-jack probably in the world, is rapidly giving up his traditional vocation for employment in the smaller towns or construction and other activities. This is developing to such an alarming extent that several companies in these districts are feeling its effects. The withdrawal of men from such work who by natural disposition and training are the best suited, and substituting in their places men of about 60 per cent their producing capacity and at a higher wage, must tend to increase the price of pulp wood to home and foreign consumers.[23]

If we allow for the fact that the science of forestry was still in its infancy, it would seem that on balance land settlement was a sound investment both in the short and in the long run, though it would be hazardous to try to substantiate Mgr Lapointe's guarantee to the government that any investment it might make in colonization would bring a return of 50 per cent over and above the interest rate.[24] Since the government's annual investment in this field was usually trifling, it certainly did earn a high return! And if at times the province's resources seemed to be squandered for a small immediate return, it should be remembered that this was the common experience of the whole of America in this period. New land settlement helped not only to keep the province's population from emigrating and thus to increase the percentage of its people available for productive economic activity, it also rendered a vital service in opening up the remote areas of the province to both agriculture and the timber industry, as well as to mining and the develop-

---

[22] Eugène NADEAU, O.M.I., *"Un homme sortit pour semer..."— Le Frère Joseph Moffet, O.M.I., 1852–1932*, p. 142.
[23] *Pulp and Paper Magazine*, March 1913, p. 180. See also *ibid.*, February 1914, pp. 94-95.
[24] See" Le problème de colonisation au Canada français," p. 54.

ment of water power by initiating a system of communications which could meet the industrial needs for cheap abundant labour. Even under the worst conditions, which prevailed in a few exceptional cases, if settlement did not greatly add to the annual Gross National Product, it at least provided a subsistence living for hundreds of people who otherwise would have been unemployed or would have become emigrants. One can only regret here again that the government did not better support private initiative in this venture and provide it with the professional "know-how," which it often lacked and which could have made it a much more productive effort—but it was far from obvious that the government at that time was either interested in or capable of doing so! Only a philosophy of national economic planning could have made this support possible, and the prevalent laissez-faire philosophy of those days tended to make colonization subsidies a matter of votes rather than of economic growth.

Industry and Education

The evidence already discussed would seem to indicate that even in industry the Church had a positive, though much more marginal role. Nevertheless, it was probably not negligible, particularly in the more remote areas of the province and in such enterprises as cheese and butter factories, sawmills, local pulp mills, etc. The clergy were active also in bigger towns and cities such as Chicoutimi, Trois-Rivières, and Quebec City in encouraging tax-exemption for new industry, investments in overhead capital such as local utilities, electricity, transportation facilities, construction, schools; by reducing the number of religious holydays they increased the number of work days. They indirectly contributed to the economic boom in industrial centres such as Montreal, Hull, Chicoutimi, Trois-Rivières, and Saint-Hyacinthe by sustaining the population and keeping it from dispersing when disastrous fires wiped out whole quarters of these key cities between 1900 and 1912.[25] But, in Montreal, where, as we saw, almost 50 per cent of the total manufacturing production was concentrated, there is little evidence to show that

---

[25] See Eugène LECLERQ, *Statistiques rouges* (Québec: E. Tremblay, 1932), pp. 17–26. He lists for the period 1896–1914, 85 major fires in the province involving schools, colleges, churches, many whole villages—in addition to the big fires listed above, where losses run into the millions, the worst being that of Hull which left 18,000 homeless and represented a loss of capital of about $10 million. These frequent fires explain why curés were always fostering plans of mutual insurance.

the Church had any direct significant influence on industry.[26] Although even here the bishop promotes general improvements that indirectly reflect on the economic progress of the city, there is no official Catholic press to follow and favour each new industrial or commercial gain as there was in many other centres. In all areas, the clergy promoted with varying degrees of success the habits of hard work, thrift, saving, temperance, and led campaigns against disease and the premature death of infants, and both promoted and provided welfare and health facilities, all of which contributed to improving the quality of the labour force.   Probably little if any of the funds of the *caisses populaires* found their way into larger industrial investment, but they did help to finance the local dairy industry, individual worker's tools, etc., and to maintain consumption at higher levels than would have otherwise existed in times of unemployment.   Much more important was whatever truth lay behind the firm belief that the fiduciary funds of dioceses, parishes, and religious orders and congregations formed a substantial part in the estimated 60 per cent of French Canadian total savings that regularly found their way for greater safety into the English Canadian banks, much to the chagrin of French Canadian bankers, for these funds undoubtedly were more easily channelled into large-scale industrial investment than they otherwise would have been.[27]

A key area in which the Church exercised influence was in fostering an atmosphere of industrial peace.   In many cases, the clergy were directly responsible either for the avoidance or the settlement of costly strikes, and their increased hostility to the "neutral" unions certainly helped to weaken the latter's power.   It was the proud boast of cities and of whole regions in the province that strikes were almost unknown, and this fact was openly exploited by both the power companies and city officials to encourage new industry to settle there.   In all these activities, the influence of the Church, however marginal, was conducive to industrialization.

With a surplus labour market in every city, no strong case can be made that the pleas of the rural curés to keep their people

---

[26] We lack a reliable estimate of Gross National Product in Quebec at this time against which to compare the value of Montreal's total manufacturing output.   However, the fact that in 1911 about 10 per cent of the total labour force, 67,840 out of a total of 653,241, were employed therein, gives us an approximate if downward biased estimate of the relative importance of this sector in the total Gross National Product (personal estimates from *Statistical Year Book*, II [1915], 171–79, 509).

[27] See, for example, *Le problème industriel au Canada français*, p. 114, where this estimate is made by the Montreal banker, Joseph Versailles, and the practice deplored.

on the land or to have them settle in "new" Quebec rather than in the cities had any significant negative effect on industrialization. In fact, on balance, they probably helped to reduce the number of the unemployed and underemployed in the province. Besides, there were equally powerful forces working in the opposite direction. Because of the commercial schools of the brothers and the commercial courses offered by the classical colleges, a sizable group of better educated youths continually made their way to the cities, where they could more profitably employ their training in the elements of bookkeeping, banking, mathematics, and perhaps most of all, their "working knowledge" of English.

We have already shown that the Church's campaign against Sunday work in the pulp and paper mills was substantially unsuccessful. Ironically, the Church did not succeed in gaining for the French Canadians what the international unions had already fought for and won in the United States. For the time being, employers could continue to exploit a situation where French Canadian opinion instinctively revolted at any legal measure that appeared to promote a puritan, Anglo-Saxon Sunday. However, it would be hard to show that it was in the interest of a nation's long-run economic development to allow companies to work labourers seven days a week.

There remain two key areas to explore where the situation is not at all clear, those of the Church's influence on French Canadian entrepreneurship and on labour productivity. It is particularly in these areas that critics have suggested that the Church through her educational system has had a decidedly negative influence. Here, as already noted, we separate the already complicated question of whether the Church's educational system had a negative influence on entrepreneurship and labour productivity, thus actually reducing the Gross National Product at this time, from the still more complicated question of whether this influence merely handicapped French Canadians economically.[28]

French Canadian Entrepreneurship

One thing is certain, the number of French Canadian entrepreneurs of any notable importance is small. In fact, only three big names continue to appear in the literature of this period:

---

[28] It is interesting to note that Kindleberger thinks that the loss of Church control over education is a necessary condition for economic development, though he implies that this becomes less true as such education becomes less antithetical to development (Ch. P. KINDLEBERGER, *Economic Development*, p. 66).

Senator Louis-Joseph Forget and especially his nephew, Sir Rodolphe Forget; Alfred Dubuc; and the Honourable Georges-E. Amyot.   Rodolphe Forget, like his uncle, who taught him his profession, was a financial genius and industrial promoter.   He was called "the young Napoleon of Saint-François-Xavier Street," then the financial heart of Montreal and of the whole Dominion.   He seems to have been the only French Canadian of his time to mix freely with the English Canadian industrialists and financiers.   He was elected chairman of the Montreal Stock Exchange in 1908.   His English biographer does not exaggerate when he writes,

> His connections with the largest financial and industrial enterprises of the Dominion were so many and of such a varied character that it seemed as if there were hardly an important venture of any kind which did not owe an appreciable portion of its prosperity to his able direction of affairs or sympathetic interests.[29]

Dubuc, as we saw, was primarily a banker turned industrialist, who later concentrated his energies in the pulp and paper industry of the Saguenay.   Georges Amyot operated on a still smaller scale, and though serving on the executive of several other companies, his major achievement was the modern prosperous Dominion Corset Industry in Quebec City.   All three were self-made men, apparently owing little to the formal education which they had received in the colleges.   Like most other big businessmen of their time they had had relatively little education and no formal technical or specialized education. Dubuc had left college to enter a bank at the age of 16 and Forget at the age of 13 to enter his uncle's office; the two major English Canadian (born American) industrial and financial giants of the day, Lord T.G. Shaughnessy, President and Chairman of the Canadian Pacific Railway, and Sir William C. Van Horne, former President of the same railway and President of a dozen or more other companies, had left public school at the ages of 14 and 15 respectively to work on the railway.   These three French Canadian industrialists and financiers remained closely attached to the Church, were on terms of warm friendship with the bishops and other members of the clergy, and openly received their encouragement and blessing and even distinctive Church honours.[30]

---

[29] *The Storied Province of Quebec*, ed. W.C.H. Wood, I, 189.   The author notes 28 major companies across Canada of which Forget was or had been President, Vice-President or Director, besides other companies with which he was merely associated.

[30] In passing it might be noted that Lord Shaughnessy, the genius behind the promotion of the Canadian Pacific Railway at this time, was a devout Roman Catholic and a close friend of Mgr Bruchési—but considerations of this kind remain outside the scope of the present study.

Can it realistically be said that the dearth of successful French Canadian entrepreneurs served actually to reduce the Gross National Product during this period? It is not at all evident. Rather we find a pattern of substitution; budding and weak French Canadian entrepreneurs are continually being bought out or gobbled up by American, English, and English Canadian entrepreneurs with their superior financial resources and easier access to "know-how." Had the French Canadians been more successful, the "foreigners" would probably have gone elsewhere or entered into ruinous competition. Especially when we consider that Ontario, which is usually regarded as the model of economic leadership, with its telling advantages of proximity to iron and coal, was not experiencing a rate of growth in manufacturing production noticeably greater than that of Quebec with all its purely economic handicaps, the assumption that lack of French Canadian entrepreneurship was a major deterrent to economic growth simply dissolves. The pattern of successful Anglo-Saxon entrepreneurship had already been long established, and was accepted and encouraged even by French Canadians and their institutions. Probably the only significant impediment to growth caused by this situation consisted in the sporadic make-shift attempts of the French Canadians to break into industry—attempts that all too often ended in bankruptcy. Nevertheless, it could be argued that these failures, besides providing a necessary school of experience, were often turned to the benefit of economic development, for usually a stronger Anglo-Saxon later picked up the pieces if the project seemed to have a future—a sequence of events which we saw repeated again and again in the Saguenay. The extreme laissez-faire attitude on the part of the government, local municipalities, and even the Church with regard to Anglo-Saxon industrialists allowed the latter, who had the added advantage of a surplus labour market, to exploit any clearly profitable situation for which they could raise the necessary capital. If opportunities were missed, they were probably marginal, and, in any case, these were usually left to the French Canadians to develop in peace, if not with the greatest efficiency.

French Canadian Labour Productivity

What was the influence of the Church's education system, if any, on the labour productivity of the French Canadian workers? If there was a weakness, it could only have been at the level of competence and know-how, for certainly the Church

constantly instilled in the French Catholic workers a spirit
of hard work, justice, obedience, peacefulness, and temperance
that was openly appreciated by employers and greatly encouraged them to locate their factories in Quebec.   Indeed, they
often congratulated themselves on their good fortune in contrast
with their fellow employers in the Anglo-Saxon world around
them who were being plagued with labour troubles and unrest.
Since with the present state of research we do not know in any
exact way the nature of the relationship which existed between
the various kinds of education and labour productivity at that
time, the following discussion can only be general and tentative.

That specialized labourers, engineers, chemists, etc. were
lacking among the French Canadians is evident.   It is equally
clear that the school system did not change this situation substantially during the period under study, though many important
initiatives were taken that would have an impact in the future.
The problem was realized and many of the necessary facilities
provided, but it turned out that it had been scarcely touched,
and much of the criticism of the opposition party as well as
of the Catholic press proved to be well-founded.   The elementary
school system had still not been geared to prepare students for
the big city technical schools nor had the work of popular education been sufficiently advanced to make people appreciate the
benefits of these usually distant schools.   And if the existence
of these fine facilities proved an added incentive towards providing them with competent students, it, unfortunately, also
served to create the illusion in political circles that the problem
was already solved.

The essential weakness of the elementary education system
was, as we saw, the instability and poor qualification especially
of its lay staff, owing to the miserly salaries paid them and the
desire of French Canadian girls to marry young.   The result
was that even if a boy did happen to stay in school until the
age of 14, it was most unlikely that he would have completed the
8-year elementary course.   Even if he did, the course was still
not sufficiently oriented towards specialized training to open
the door easily to him to pursue higher studies in the applied
sciences.   The popular commercial colleges and academies,
which initially were thought able to provide adequately for the
preparation of businessmen and bankers, furnished the boys with
some practical if not very sophisticated tools: "English"—the
language of business and commerce,—a sense of the value of
money, bookkeeping, etc.   They thus supplied a better equipped
work force particularly in the service and commerce industries,

where some degree of bilingualism was essential, for the Anglo-Saxon felt no inclination or necessity to speak French in "an English-speaking country." Very slowly, under the prodding of the Superintendent and the Catholic School Committee, the religious as well as the lay teachers were convinced that in the primary schools they should teach drawing as the rational base for the child's later training in manual work, and not merely to permit him to be able to appreciate the fine arts.[31]

How serious for economic development was the lack of more technical training on the part of the French Canadian workers? While it is true that appropriate technical training could undoubtedly have improved the efficiency of thousands of the workers, yet, in the context of French Canada at this time, it is not at all certain that economic development was hampered more seriously here than in other areas of Canada by this lack of skilled native workmen. Quebec had its major technical institutions and the higher commercial school as early as Ontario and earlier than most of the other provinces. The French Canadians had their well-recognized skills as lumberjacks, carpenters, masons, and through their migratory sojourns in New England had acquired other skills, especially in the leather and textile industries. In the newer industries, the Anglo-Saxon employers had the best of two worlds. They could easily bring in English-speaking skilled labourers, engineers, etc., from the United States or Britain, or select such workers at leisure from the steady flow of immigrants through the cities of Montreal and Quebec; and for their unskilled and semi-skilled labour they could use the cheaper sturdy French Canadians. But should the Anglo-Saxon workers become unwieldy or too demanding, they could in the last resort always quickly train the cheaper French Canadian labourers to replace them. If industrialists gave only token encouragement to the project of building technical schools, it was because by and large they still did not keenly feel the need of such training. That is why, with few exceptions, the system of apprenticeship had fallen into disuse. Employers themselves were just beginning to appreciate the benefits of more scientific as opposed to rule-of-thumb methods of production. This situation is well illustrated in the booming pulp and paper industry, which was rapidly

---

[31] For example, see BOUCHER DE LA BRUÈRE, *Le Conseil de l'Instruction Publique*, pp. 100, 151. The author, who was the superintendent of public instruction at this time, indicates how slowly this change came about. As early as 1876, the Catholic Committee had taken the first initiative to give this orientation to drawing in the primary schools, but it was only in 1911 that it began to be successfully implemented.

beginning to dominate the whole industrial scene in the province. For example, at the eminently prosperous Laurentide Paper Company in Grand'Mère, as we saw, owing to a strike among the American skilled paper makers, and at the Chicoutimi Pulp Company in the Saguenay owing to nationalist aspirations, the French Canadians early came to occupy efficiently the key positions in the production of pulp and paper. But this was far from the general picture, as is well revealed by the investigation made by the American Tariff Board in 1911 into the efficiency of labour in Canada in the American-owned mills.

The question had arisen why the Canadian mills, benefiting from the latest American plants, still had average labour-costs only about 8 cents lower per cwt. than in the United States. They concluded that the colder winter in Canada was partially responsible, but that the major cause was the failure of mill managers to train their unskilled French Canadian labour. The American managers, when questioned, claimed that the French Canadians fresh from the farms and forest were still too inefficient and irresponsible. But the report continues,

> The answer to the statements of the inefficiency of the French Canadian labourers was the pointing out of numerous instances of efficiency of a high order in the higher grades of employment. It is charged that American-trained superintendents give preference to Americans in the skilled positions and that no opportunity has been afforded to French Canadians to advance and it was pointed out that where strikes occurred and the French Canadian was given a chance he had succeeded.[32]

From the campaign undertaken by the *Pulp and Paper Magazine* after 1910, it is quite clear that not scientific training but rather rule-of-thumb production procedures pervaded the industry and that it would still be several years before the chemist and university graduated engineer would find his full role.

Would a law compelling parents to leave their children at school until the age of 14—a measure long opposed by the Church —have much improved the productivity of French Canadian workers? What at first sight seems obvious becomes less clear when the situation is examined in more detail. On the basis of the census of 1911, the claim of the Church that the Catholic system of education in Quebec was doing as well as any other

---

[32] U.S., Tariff Board, *Report on the Pulp and Newsprint Paper Industry* (Washington: Government Printing Office, 1911), p. 55. As we saw at Laurentide, the Wayagamack, and at Chicoutimi, the Church leaders eagerly favoured such French Canadian advancement in the industry, but ordinarily they were helpless to bring it about.

system in the Dominion in the matter of actual attendance of the children in the 7–14 age bracket at school appears well founded. That the government of Quebec could have succeeded in accomplishing more by law than the Church by moral suasion and censure at this time is at least doubtful. And as long as the government was not disposed to increase substantially its grants to primary education and at least to double the minimum salaries of teachers, it is not clear that much was to be gained by forcing all the children to stay in school. There is abundant evidence to show that what was required of a French Canadian to be "educated" in industrial and financial circles was not merely an ability to read and write, but primarily an ability to speak, read, and write English, the language of business and commerce. This fact emerged from the author's interviews with several older workers in the Saguenay and St. Maurice regions as well as in Montreal. Promotion for a French Canadian depended ordinarily not on the number of years he had spent in school but on his ability to use English. The man who could speak English was often created a gang foreman on the spot. This is confirmed by the evidence of the Principal of the Shawinigan Technical Institute, John V.L. Morris, before the Royal Commission on Technical Education in 1913. He pointed out that the most skilled technicians in Shawinigan had been trained not in Canadian schools but in evening technical schools in England or through English correspondence courses. He claimed that he saw no discrimination at Shawinigan, but that very few French Canadians rise into better positions "due to their ignorance of English, and meagre education in general."[33] He rightly puts the "meagre education" in second position, for it usually could only be put to use if it included a knowledge of English. As we noted earlier, despite its ambitious pro- gramme, the major immediate goal sought by the new technical institute inaugurated by the local companies in Shawinigan was, in its early years, to teach the French Canadians English.

Among the older workers interviewed, those who had succeeded in being promoted to skilled jobs or posts of authority had usually learned their English at the local brothers' com- mercial schools, but more often they had either passed some time at an English Protestant school or had associated much with English people. It is not impossible that the most rentable feature of the primary school system was the smattering of

[33] Royal Commission on Industrial Training and Technical Education, *Report of the Commissioners*, IV, 1875-1876.

English that the French Canadians learned in these very commercial courses which were so much decried for their failure to provide a general education and an adequate knowledge of the mother tongue. As we pointed out earlier, the French Canadian engineer who entered industry, had to be not only a competent engineer, he had also to be at least bilingual, and his success often was in proportion to his ability to become an "Englishman."[34]

Likewise, the system of hiring generally employed at the time, which gave the foreman, ordinarily an Anglo-Saxon, almost complete power over hiring and firing, was weighted in favour of workers of his own ethnic background and culture whom he could more easily know, understand, and trust. The system of giving preference in the distribution of new jobs and in the acceptance of boys into apprenticeship to the sons and nephews of their skilled workers was also weighted against the French Canadians; for initially the majority of skilled workers had usually been recruited from Britain or the United States, and they could by this system easily perpetuate their majority hold on the better jobs as well as the opportunities to get technical training within the companies. There was at this time always a group of American "boomers," young skilled workmen, who used work as a means to see the country, but the English employer was only too anxious to benefit from their skills as long as their owners did not become too unruly or try to bring in their unions with them; it saved him the expense and removed his motivation to train his local French Canadian labour—except always as a last resort.

[34] What E. Hughes discovered in his study of the French Canadian industrial town of Cantonville (in reality, Drummondville), undertaken much later, was already true before World War I. He writes, "In general, there is probably a strong bias in favour of appointing for higher positions a man of the kind liked and trusted by the appointing group. Ethnic background, religion, and even 'the old-school tie' might enter into the case—not in the spirit of looking after one's friends but with the conviction, which might be true, that efficiency is best served so.

"In our community it is evident that French Canadians as a group do not enjoy that full confidence of industrial directors and executives which would admit them easily to the inner and higher circles of the fraternity—and fraternity it is—of men who run industry. This situation prevails throughout the province." (E.C. HUGHES, *French Canada in Transition*, p. 53).

Or as Monique Lortie describes the situation, "The English owner establishing himself in Quebec saw the advantage of labour which was cheap, docile, demanding little because it did not know what to demand. He did not entrust responsibilities to these peoples. In brief, a majority of French language and culture is invaded by an English-speaking minority which gives it work, but at the same time keeps it in subordinate positions. Only a small number of French Canadians can rival the English, and it seems that these are French Canadians who are anglicized, that is to say who have adopted this impersonal attitude in business." (Monique LORTIE, "Les relations biculturelles au Canada," *Contribution à l'étude des sciences de l'homme*, pp. 323-24, cited by N. KEYFITZ in Mason Wade, ed., *Canadian Dualism*, p. 138.)

The basic fact that emerges from even a cursory study of these matters of entrepreneurship and labour productivity among the French Canadians is that the industrial and financial world was essentially English. This was not a new situation, as we noted already in the timber industry of the Saguenay and the St. Maurice valleys. Lord Durham, in his *Report* to the English Parliament after the uprisings of 1837-1838 in Upper and Lower Canada, had recommended that His Majesty's government adopt a policy of assimilation as the only effective method of saving the French Canadian minority from "hopeless inferiority." He wrote prophetically in an Anglo-Saxon racist strain— though somewhat underestimating the French Canadians' dogged will to survive:

> I know of no national distinction marking and continuing a more hopeless inferiority. The language, the laws, the character of the North American Continent are English; and every race but the English (I apply this to all who speak the English language) appears there in a condition of inferiority. It is to elevate them from that inferiority that I desire to give the Canadians our English character. I desire it for the sake of the educated classes, whom the distinction of language and manner keeps apart from the great Empire to which they belong At the best, the fate of the educated and aspiring colonist is, at present, one of little hope, and little activity; but the French Canadian is cast still further into the shade, by a language and habits foreign to those of the Imperial Government. A spirit of exclusion has closed the highest profession on the educated classes of the French Canadians, more, perhaps, than was absolutely necessary; but it is impossible for the utmost liberality on the part of the British Government to give an equal position in the general competition of its vast population to those who speak a foreign language. I desire the amalgamation still more for the sake of the humbler classes. Their present state of rude and equal plenty is fast deteriorating under the pressure of population in the narrow limits to which they are confined. If they attempt to better their condition, by extending themselves over the neighbouring country, they will necessarily get more and more mingled with an English population: if they prefer remaining stationary, the greater part of them must be labourers in the employ of English capitalists. In either case it would appear that the great mass of the French Canadians are doomed, in some measure, to occupy an inferior position, and be dependent upon the English for employment. The evils of poverty and dependence would merely be aggravated in a tenfold degree, by a spirit of jealous and resentful nationality, which would separate the working classes of the community from the possessors of wealth and employers of labour.[35]

The classical training provided by the colleges and minor seminaries made a virtue out of necessity, and not only did

---

[35] C.P. Lucas, *Lord Durham's Report*, II, pp. 292-93.

not equip the élite for industry and finance, but gave them a
training that largely removed them from the world of economic
forces.   Already, in 1846, in his *Charles Guérin*, Pierre Chauveau
reveals how aware college graduates were of the limited horizons
open to them:

> ... Il faut être médecin, prêtre, notaire, ou avocat.   En dehors de
> ces quatre professions, pour le jeune Canadien instruit, il semble
> *qu'il n'y a pas de salut.*   Si par hasard quelqu'un de nous éprouvait
> une répugnance invincible pour toutes les quatre; s'il lui en coûtait
> trop de sauver des âmes, de mutiler des corps ou de perdre des for-
> tunes, il ne lui resterait qu'un parti à prendre, s'il était riche, et deux
> s'il était pauvre: ne rien faire du tout, dans le premier cas, s'expatrier
> ou mourir de faim, dans le second.[36]

In general, the boy emerging with his BA at the delayed
age of 20 or older was ordinarily not equipped with sufficient
mathematics and science, nor provided with sufficient finances
to pass easily into engineering school, even if he wanted to.
Errol Bouchette, a keen critic of the traditional education of
the bourgeoisie claimed it was designed to reduce their economic
and social influence to a minimum and certainly bar them from
effective entrepreneurship.   He asks himself the question, why
did so many families possessing a high degree of virtue, moral
qualities, intellectual culture, and public spirit have so little
economic and social influence and, consequently, so little lasting
influence on national life?   His answer is brutally frank and
appears to be substantially true; he claims this intellectual
training renders the French Canadian elite void of economic
and social power and influence:

> Par malheur cette formation offrait l'inconvénient, qui n'est pas
> inhérent au système, mais seulement à la manière de l'appliquer—de
> ne porter presque aucun des sujets formés par elle vers les carrières
> commerciales ou industrielles, et cela au point de créer un préjugé
> contre le commerce, même dans les familles qui lui devaient leur
> élévation.   Nous sommes donc en présence des sujets détachés du
> sol par la perte de leurs terres et inaptes à l'industrie par leur for-
> mation première: les deux carrières qui créent la richesse leur sont
> dès lors fermées, de même que le commerce par lequel la richesse
> s'accumule.   Il s'en suit qu'ils n'exercent aucune influence sur les
> transports qui distribuent et font circuler la richesse acquise.   Il
> leur est par conséquent pratiquement impossible de faire l'immense
> effort de travail, d'épargne, de progrès industriel et commercial qui
> seul permet de mener à bien les grandes entreprises et même de
> transformer une région, comme le font constamment les grands
> agriculteurs, les grands industriels, et ceux qui possèdent les moyens
> de transporter les produits de ces industries dans le pays même, ou

------

[36] Pierre CHAUVEAU, *Charles Guérin* (Montréal: 1853), p. 2.

jusqu'à l'étranger. Chez eux la fortune matérielle demeure toujours médiocre; ils ne savent ni la créer ni la répandre. Les jeunes de cette classe se découragent de leur impuissance et ne se livrent pas aux occupations sérieuses. C'est ainsi que l'on tarit les sources de la pensée comme celles de la richesse. Il leur reste encore, il est vrai, l'action politique et surtout l'influence si haute que leur donnent le sacerdoce, la magistrature, les professions et les cultures intellectuelles, mais cette influence est de sa nature même indirecte et exclusivement morale.[37]

But Bouchette seems implicitly to assume that the industrial and financial giants of the day were the products of their formal education, which was simply not true. They were much more the products of the hard school of experience and apprenticeship with men already highly successful in their field. And it would be to miss completely the heart of the problem of why the French Canadians were in an inferior economic position if one failed to realize fully that, from the time of the conquest until the middle of the last century, they, the earliest Canadians, were usually considered in practice, if not in official policy, as "outsiders," whom the British hoped eventually to assimilate. Their modern economic inferiority stems primarily from their decision to "survive" as a distinct people at any price and England's grudging assent to their determination. The laissez-faire policy of the government and the keen individualism of the French Canadians themselves theoretically put them on an equal basis of competition with the Anglo-Saxons, but, in reality, the latter had already a long start and had besides relatively easy access to English and American capital.[38] When the French Canadian leaders built their "language" wall around their people they left the English world of business outside. While English and American entrepreneurs, capitalists, skilled workmen, as well as their technical publications and trade journals, all rallied to build the new English Canadian economic world, the minimum entrance fee to this world for the French Canadians was to become bilingual—no small task in a young country where education was still very rudimentary! The competition would have been more equal had France come, even belatedly, to the assistance of the French Canadians with capital, engineers, entrepreneurs, skilled labour and technical know-how. But in spite of the efforts of successive govern-

---

[37] Errol BOUCHETTE, "Les débuts d'une industrie et notre bourgeoisie," *Proceedings and Transactions of the Royal Society of Canada*, IV, 3rd Series, (1912), Section I, p. 156.
[38] The proportion of Canadian domestic investment financed by foreign capital rose steadily over this period until, in 1913, it was roughly two-thirds and amounted to $541,-700,000 (see Richard E. CAVES and Richard H. HOLTON, *The Canadian Economy*, p. 96).

ments—and even the personal invitations extended by Curé Labelle—France's contribution in this area was never significant. For most Frenchmen, Canada was still, if not the land of ice and snow from which they had been driven almost two centuries earlier, at least the rugged Lake St. John country of Maria Chapdelaine, which chilled any enthusiasm for serious immigration. The description of a genuine entrepreneur such as Alfred Dubuc being forced literally to range over whole continents to try to find sufficient capital to sustain his successful pulp industry in the Saguenay only confirms how difficult it was for a budding French Canadian entrepreneur to acquire capital. The only help seriously offered by France at this time was in education. But neither the Church nor French Canadians generally were inclined to believe in the professed disinterested nature of the offer of this anti-clerical government, which was busy at home destroying the last remnants of Catholic education.

Given this situation, it would appear that French Canadians could still have succeeded had they grouped together to foster and to back their own latent entrepreneurial ability and especially their successful businessmen. But this was too great a challenge for their native individualism. In fact they were much more prone to wasteful lawsuits than to concerted economic action. As we saw, a Forget and a Dubuc were more inclined to want to supplant one another than to work together for a common goal. The first real education in economic co-operation that appeared was provided by the agricultural clubs, the *caisses populaires*, and the co-operatives, so strongly promoted by the clergy. But it was already far too late to pool rapidly sums of capital comparable to those easily available to their English and American rivals.

Had the French Canadians been fully logical—and if the English had permitted them to be—they might have adopted a French Canadian national economic policy to promote and even subsidize the efforts of budding French Canadian industrialists.[39] Thus they would have helped to dissipate an atmosphere of economic inferiority among French Canadian entrepreneurs and have stimulated would-be French Canadian engineers and technicians by offering them a bright future inside their own race and tradition, as the Quebec government has

---

[39] Errol Bouchette seems to have been almost alone in realizing and proposing this. See *L'indépendance économique du Canada français*, p. 277. See also on this whole discussion François-A. ANGERS, "Naissance de la pensée économique au Canada français," Revue d'Histoire de l'Amérique française, XV (September 1961), 204–29.

finally begun to do today. This would have removed perhaps the biggest single obstacle to ambition and initiative on the part of French Canadians—the lack of incentive. They could not realistically believe in the possibility of dramatically improving themselves. Instead, the local government was anything but a "socialist" or "planning" government. In fact, "Quebec was the only province to adopt a strict laissez-faire position."[40] Politicians seemed to believe that their duties to economic development were acquitted provided they satisfied the whims of English and American big business and generously entrusted to their benevolent care the rich resources of the province.

What French Canadian leaders did not understand was that they could not hope to build a linguistic and cultural wall around their people without also protecting them economically as well as politically. The Trojan-horse which was their undoing was their own native individualism and their inherited philosophy of laissez-faire, which permitted the English entrepreneur to take advantage of the natural riches of their province and to occupy every important position of economic influence and advantage without appearing to violate the accepted rules of fair play. Unfortunately, the Church with her easily roused suspicions of the state, bred of her recent tangled experience in Europe, could hardly be a good teacher of civics, though it is not clear that the clergy would not have accepted a much bigger economic role on the part of the state had it been conceived as a "nationalist program of progress" for the French Canadians. Certainly the clergy were the severest critics of the government's policy of niggardliness towards land settlement, agriculture, and communication and transportation projects of all types.

---

[40] Kenneth BUCKLEY, *Capital Formation in Canada, 1896–1913*, p. 55. He adds later (*ibid.*, p. 57) "Quebec occupied a unique position. In comparison with every other provincial government, the government of Quebec was relatively inactive in the investment field over the whole period under review. Developmental policies had little place in the provincial budget. The public works undertaken were for the most part those that could not be avoided. At the time when the Dominion was engaged in the construction of the National Transcontinental, and the other provinces were rapidly expanding their public programmes and supporting developments in the railway and other utility fields, Quebec was expanding its public works programme slowly and leaving utilities to others. Quebec had been active in the railway field during the seventies and eighties. The modest growth in debt resulting from the railway subsidies and the construction of the Quebec, Montreal and Ottawa (later sold) was followed by reaction. Despite buoyant revenues after 1900 a conservative policy prevailed and budget surpluses were applied to the cost of necessary capital works. The provincial debt was small relative to the debts of other provinces.
"Quebec contributed less than 10 per cent of total provincial investment during the first decade covered by the estimates. If utilities were included in the total, the percentage would be considerably reduced. Highway policy was virtually confined to grants to municipalities. Construction outlays increased after the passing of the Good Roads Act in 1912 which authorized provincial road construction for the first time. By 1915, the province incorporated 1,600 miles of road into a provincial system and spent $7 million (excluding grants)."

Seen in this wider perspective, it can be truthfully said that the French labourer was less specialized, and perhaps less productive in certain of the newer industries, and this was due in part to the non-technical and unstable nature of the education system. However, this lower productivity of the French Canadian worker should not be exaggerated. In the timber industry, which still remained the largest industry in Quebec and which had regained vigour with the construction boom in housing and manufacturing, he knew no equal. Professors Caves and Holton confirm A.R.M. Lower's contention that a major reason why Canada's timber industry began to lose out in international competition at this time was that French Canadian woodsmen emigrated to better paying urban industry and employers were obliged to replace them with unseasoned and unskilled immigrant labour.[41]

The editors of the *Pulp and Paper Magazine* estimated in 1913, as already noted, these immigrant labourers had only about 60 per cent the productive capacity of the French Canadians, even though they had to be paid a higher wage.[42] Likewise, in the construction, textile, clothing, tobacco, food, and service industries the French Canadians were easily able to hold their own. But it was particularly in the new industries such as electrical supplies, metal-work, chemicals, etc. that they had no experience and no training. Yet, in the big railway shops of Montreal, to cite only one example, it is interesting to find that the French Canadians dominated in the construction and repairing of freight and passenger cars, where they could use their wood skills, while the English Canadians, mostly new arrivals from the railway shops of England, Scotland, or the United States, were generally employed in the construction and repairing of locomotives, boilers, etc. But in most industries engineers were, by and large, English-speaking and British or American trained; here there was no French Canadian tradition and though the number of French Canadian engineers steadily increased during the period they were nearly all civil engineers and easily attracted to government or city employment.

If one can easily see how the education system could have been improved to provide a better general and more practical education, it is also clear that it could not have been realistically expected to produce in the short run such major transformations as would have permitted the French Canadian elementary

---

[41] Richard E. CAVES and Richard H. HOLTON, *The Canadian Economy*, p. 40.
[42] *Pulp and Paper Magazine*, March 1913, p. 180.

education to equip a boy to compete on an equal basis with an English Canadian boy, who had just emerged from a similar school—for the simple reason that to have as good an education as his English rival the French boy would have had to be at least partly bilingual. As to the comparable quality of the education, neither my interviews, nor my research into the history of various companies, nor the *Report of the Royal Commission on Technical Education* indicates that the English Canadian primary school at this time was clearly doing a better job of preparing boys for industry than was the French Canadian.[43] But the English Canadian had the great advantage that his mother tongue was the language of technical know-how. Besides, his father or his uncle was probably a boiler maker or a practical engineer who had had his apprenticeship in the shipyards, railway shops, or cotton mills of Scotland or England. His interest and potential skill probably stemmed more from his father or his uncle than from the boy's own schooling. And because of his father's or his uncle's position, he himself had easy access to a job opening or an apprenticeship in the newer industries and skills. All that was asked of his schooling was that he be able to read and have some elementary notions of arithmetic.

The French Canadians obviously did not yet have an educational system, either at the elementary or the secondary level, that could successfully equip their youth for the newer industries. The result was that they often did not appear to appreciate the skills necessary to organize, equip, and run a successful business and still tended to consider it largely a matter of luck. They were improvisers and "make-shifters." Perhaps the greatest irony of the whole situation was that because the majority of college graduates tended to be poorly equipped and uninterested, it often fell to their fellow collegian, the local curé, to improvise and fill the lacuna of economic leadership that often existed outside the bigger towns and cities. Had the French Canadians been as fortunate as the English Canadian neighbours, a constant immigration of French and Belgian capitalists, entrepreneurs, engineers, and skilled workmen would have bridged this gap in technological knowledge for them.

---

[43] In a widely publicized address to the St. James Literary Society of Montreal, in March 1900, Mr. Henry Miles developed this theme at length. He maintained that the educational system of Canada was giving the least possible help to youths entering commercial or industrial life. And he dwelt on the picture of practical helplessness presented by the university graduate armed with his BA degree and now entering business as an apprentice (Henry MILES, *Commercial Education*, [Montreal: March 22, 1900], reprint, pp. 3-15).

Summary

We can now assert fairly confidently that the Church's role in economic development in the pre-war spurt was, on balance, positive, without being either decisive or determining. If her formal educational system did not prepare entrepreneurs— it is not clear that the English Canadian system was doing this either, for they seemed at this time to be mostly self-made men of meagre education—this scarcity of successful entre- preneurial skill among the French Canadians does not seem to have had any marked significance for the economic develop- ment of the province at this time, for the more apt English Canadians and foreigners simply substituted for them, and manufacturing production grew at rates not significantly dif- ferent from those found in the leading province of Ontario, in spite of the latter's great locational advantages and more seasonal climate.   If, in certain newer industries, the French Canadian youth was partly handicapped owing to the untechnical nature of his education, this seems to have been more than compensated for by his skills in other large industries and by his spirit of hard patient work at lower wages; and, in fact, here again the pattern of substitution appeared, for these new jobs were not ordinarily filled by inefficient and untrained French Canadian workers but by English and American trained technicians— often even in cases where the former were equally capable of filling them if given the chance by their English and American masters to prove it.   If the Church had some responsibility in this matter, it is certainly mitigated by the fact that she shared it jointly with the more directly culpable English and American entrepreneurs who often did not train their French Canadian workers or offer them any strong motivation to acquire training; with the government which did not suffi- ciently second the efforts of the Church to improve elementary education with substantial subsidies to bring more stability to the teaching profession; with the people who still did not sufficiently comprehend the value of either education or of technical training to be willing to be taxed at rates high enough to pay for it; and with a general situation that put the French Canadian at the disadvantage of having to be bilingual even to profit by his general education however meagre it might be. The central fact remains that during this period the energetic, "less spoilt" local labour combined with the more skilled tran- sient and immigrant labour to permit Quebec to achieve as big an industrial spurt as any of the other more prosperous regions of Canada at this time, although these other regions were far less hindered by the problems arising out of a bilingual, bi-cultural labour market. No doubt the problem would have been more serious had Canada's industries not been still largely of the more staple and less intricate kind. But, as it was, employers thought themselves not hindered but rather blessed with an industrious, peaceful labour force, and were only beginning to become more conscious of the possibilities of increasing labour productivity by specialized education and training, after the successful example of many European countries.

But when the question is asked in the purely French Canadian context, whether the Church's educational system hindered French Canadians from becoming entrepreneurs and advanced skilled workers, the answer would seem to have to be in the affirmative. (I merely suggest lines along which further research into this interesting question might be pursued.) It would seem that an educational system not more directly adapted to actual industrial needs was one element of a much deeper and more complex problem that came in the wake of the much earlier decision of the French Canadians to "survive" as a separate people on the North American continent with a distinct language and culture. It is generally admitted that it was the steadfast leadership and determination of the Catholic Church that turned this dream into a concrete reality, but the fact that their economic independence was already compromised was not clearly recognized. This weakness could have been surmounted best by a compact economic grouping among themselves, which their native individualism prevented; by national economic planning on the part of the provincial government—a concept wholly out of line with its prevalent laissez-faire policy; or perhaps most effectively by direct economic aid from France in the form of capital, entrepreneurs, engineers, skilled labour, etc.—a policy that did not interest France and which, in any case, might well have been wholly unacceptable to Great Britain and the English Canadian majority in the Dominion. A more practical system of education would have powerfully aided any of these policies, but left to itself, almost financially destitute, and largely under the influence of the clergy who tended by their training and profession to have more faith in devotedness and hard work than in technical know-how, the actual system could not overcome this glaring economic weakness in the dream of French Canadian independence. The bishops themselves calmly admitted that they could not provide technical and specialized training, but would support any attempts on the part of the government and private groups to provide it.   Unfortunately, from France, the only modern nation that was fully open to French Canada at this time, came only trouble, for any educational reform was seen by the extreme ultramontane as of masonic origin, and extreme reformers instead of advancing the situation only hurt it by exaggerating the faults in the educational system and talking of totally overthrowing the Church's jurisdiction in education.

The editors of one of the radical papers, *le Pays*, raised a fundamental question in one of their editorials of July 1911 under the title "Faire de l'argent."   They write in part,

> ... nous ne croyons pas que les religieux puissent développer sérieusement chez nos paysans l'ambition, l'esprit pratique, le désir de faire de l'argent,—toutes choses auxquelles ils ont renoncé par serment.   Nous ne croyons pas davantage aux Frères pour donner à l'enseignement commercial dans notre province la tendance, l'orientation et l'efficacité qui lui ont manqué jusqu'ici.   Ces braves religieux dont nous reconnaissons, sans la moindre arrière-pensée, l'esprit de dévouement et de désintéressement ne savent pas ou connaissent mal les besoins de la société moderne.   Un jeune homme qui sort d'un collège commercial catholique devrait pouvoir se mesurer à armes égales avec un élève qui sort des 'high schools'.   Or, il ne le peut pas.   On ne l'a pas dressé à la vie positive, au sens des affaires, à l'initiative; on ne lui a pas prêché que dans le commerce il faut travailler dans le but de s'enrichir; on n'a pas cultivé toutes ses aptitudes; on n'a pas préparé la mise en valeur de ses énergies...
> Ceux qui lui ont formé l'esprit sont détachés, par vocation et par état, des biens de ce monde.   Ont-ils, alors, l'entraînement et la mentalité nécessaire pour pousser sûrement nos jeunes dans la voie des conquêtes matérielles ?
> C'est une question qui souffre discussion.[44]

The matter does bear discussion and careful research. Ironically, however, much of the criticism levelled at the commercial colleges at this time was of a very different nature. They were considered too grossly utilitarian and practical. Indeed, some of the clergy were even scandalized at the existing situation, believing that the lesson on how to make money was being more indelibly imprinted on the boys' minds because imparted by the members of religious congregations, who often served as the "bankers" for their students' *caisses*, which the bishops insisted be organized in the elementary and secondary schools to teach the children thrift and the sense of money.   If this study has shown anything it has indicated the wisdom of

---

[44] Cited by *l'Action sociale*, July 25, 1911.

caution against any *a priori* judgment that the Church and her clergy, religious as well as secular, are by vocation detached from material progress and uninterested in economic development. Still, it is often apparent that the clergy, owing to their classical, philosophical, and theological formation, tend to put much more emphasis on devotedness, hard work, patience, and perseverance, than on efficiency, know-how, and money, which traditionally have not been part of their French Canadian world. They made heroic attempts by moral suasion, improvisation, and deep personal involvement, but these alone could not bridge the gap. The astonishing thing is that they did so well and that a new generation of French Canadians seem to blame them for not having done more! One can only imagine what a major difference it would have made had there been more Mgr La-Flammes in their ranks—priests and brothers fully trained and competent in the positive and applied sciences as well as a few economists and sociologists, who might have provided the constant factual corrective to their perpetual temptation to have excessive recourse to rhetoric and *a priori* reasoning, which however compelling risked easily leaving too much of reality outside the syllogism. Thus the vicious circle of lack of acquaintance with and appreciation of technical know-how in the educational system could have been decisively broken once and for all, and more attempts might have been made to study concrete local situations rather than to import from France or elsewhere ready-made problems together with solutions.

When all is said and done, one is inclined to suspect that if, from the economic point of view, the Church was at fault, it was precisely for having built and maintained the Chinese wall around her people to preserve their culture, language, and religion integrally. But this decision was not made on its economic merits. It is open to debate whether the wall needed to be built so high and so thick and to have so few gates and lookouts in order to achieve its goal, but from this first decision more than from any other minor later decisions or particular faults in the educational system stems French Canadian inferiority, for the real enemy was always lack of communication. This people continued to speak and move outside the Anglo-Saxon world of business. And only today has the government finally determined to support the efforts of budding French Canadian entrepreneurs, engineers, and scientists, and to help put them on a footing of competition with their long-ensconced, long-privileged Anglo-Saxon rivals.

RELEVANCE OF THE STUDY

Among the more interesting findings of this study are the following. The Catholic Church in Quebec, which has commonly been portrayed in Anglo-Saxon circles as being perhaps the major negative force impeding economic development in that province, has in reality been more concerned about and more deeply involved in the promotion of such development than most Churches in Anglo-Saxon countries. In Quebec the Church's attitudes and initiatives that bear on economic development seem to have been more immediately related to French Canadian nationalist, cultural, and language interests than to theological or strictly religious teachings. There is a wide variety among the concrete interpretations which different bishops and priests put on the one absolute Christian qualification to economic progress, namely, that it must not be permitted to turn men away from their primary goal in life, which is union with God. Perhaps most interesting of all is the amazing adaptability of the local curé, who quite independently of his past upbringing and experience usually manages to blend his life with the needs and aspirations of his parish and to become its intermediary with the outside world and with the world of Anglo-Saxon businessmen. Finally, one is struck by the obvious lack of proportion between the Church's ceaseless endeavours to foster a multitude of initiatives having a direct or indirect bearing on economic development and the relatively meagre results which these seem to have achieved. Clearly the major levers of rapid economic development and especially of rapid industrialization are not to be sought in the attitudes and initiatives of the Catholic Church, however great her influence, but rather in more prosaic economic factors such as entrepreneurship, abundant capital, and technical know-how.

Our study provides little basis for the categoric affirmations of such authors as V.A. Demant, for whom religion is a purely negative force in economic development,[45] and S.D.Clark, for whom "The promotion of the religious interest in itself has involved a weakening of the economic interest because of the fundamental antagonism of one for the other."[46] It rather tends to confirm clearly the thesis of Father Mario Zanartu that there is no necessary inconsistency between "the present day Roman Catholic ethic" and "the economic development ethos."[47]

[45] V.A. DEMANT, *Religion and the Decline of Capitalism*, p. 177ff.
[46] S.D. CLARK, "Religious Factor in Canadian Economic Development," p. 95.
[47] Mario ZANARTU, S.J., "Roman Catholic Ethic and Economic Development," p. 260.

It would also seem to indicate serious reservations about the approach used by such authors as Gerard Lenski, who resort to the method of counting heads among "Catholics" and assuming far too easily that common traits found in their economic attitudes are traceable to their Catholic faith—especially if they be known to be "pious," "loyal," or "orthodox."[48] Nakedly stated, their assumption seems to be that "Catholicism" is a concept univocal in its economic elements over time, and that "to be a Catholic" is to be more or less the same type of economic man anywhere in the world; for authors, however hesitatingly they may initially construct their hypotheses, usually end up attempting to generalize their conclusions on a global scale over time. For example, Lenski feels he can conclude from his study carried out recently in the city of Detroit, that

> In view of the social heritage of contemporary Catholicism, it seems unlikely that in the foreseeable future any devoutly Catholic state will become a leading industrial nation—one in the forefront of economic development and progress. Catholicism seems to contain too many elements which are incompatible with such a role. As an extension of this proposition, it would appear that as the Catholic segment of a pluralistic nation increases, this will tend to reduce the rate of economic growth.[49]

The present study suggests that it is exceedingly difficult to isolate economic influence exercised by the religious as distinct from the racial, the cultural, and the minority factors in a given situation. Further, that if in an area as small and homogeneous as that of French Canada within the brief span of two decades we find no clear unanimity among the attitudes of the clergy, and if we can discern their attitudes being modified considerably according to the economic status of the French Canadian Catholic minority in particular regions, it is feasible to suppose that a similar and even greater variety of economic attitudes exists among lay Catholics.

SUGGESTED LINES FOR FUTURE RESEARCH

The lines of research indicated in order to make this study more general and complete would seem to be the following: (1) to study the attitudes and initiatives of the English-speaking Catholic minority over this period in French Canada; (2) to attempt to pursue much more carefully the study of the signifi-

---

[48] Gerard LENSKI, *The Religious Factor*, p. 52ff.
[49] G. LENSKI, *op. cit.*, p. 315.

cance of the Catholic "monopoly" of education and the question
whether priests, brothers, and sisters are in fact by their un-
wordly vocation not the best persons to prepare students integrally for their role in society as future citizens, and to what
extent the classical system of education is responsible for a
certain neglect and lack of appreciation of technical and scientific know-how; (3) to pursue research in more detail in the
Montreal area, especially in such suburbs as St. Henri and
Lachine, where there is some evidence that the same pattern
of Church action found in the smaller centres throughout the
province is repeated; and (4) to complement the fragmentary
discussion here of Church properties, revenues, and investments
with more detailed research into these areas.

Finally, on the international level, the results of this study
seem to suggest that another Catholic country should be studied
in a comparable period of economic development; but it should
preferably be a country where the elements of nationalism,
racial survival, and minority consciousness are not so intimately
linked with the interests of the Catholic religion, and where
industrialization depends primarily on local Catholics and not
on an outside group. Such a study would enable us to understand better to what degree the religious factor is separable
from the racial or national factor in the process of economic
development. We could also thus discover whether the Church
has the ability to adapt its educational system to immediate
practical needs more rapidly when her control is not in jeopardy
and the language of business and commerce is her own; to what
extent, in these different circumstances, the local priest continues
to fill the role of being an intermediary between outsiders and
new ideas and ways and his own people who trust his leadership
and judgment; and finally, to what extent the philosophy of
agriculturalism is present and swings in intensity with the
swings of the industrial cycle, as it seems to do in French Canada.

An accumulation of such studies would permit better understanding of how to enlist the manifest energies of the Church
to promote economic development in the Catholic underdeveloped countries today and to reduce to a minimum the latent
obstacles which she might put in its way—obstacles, as this
study clearly suggests, that usually do not stem from her essential
theology and teaching but rather from concrete circumstances.

APPENDIX I

MANUFACTURING AND AGRICULTURAL STATISTICS

MANUFACTURING STATISTICS

Until recently, relatively little work had been done on Canadian manufacturing statistics for the period 1870–1917. Only since 1917 have annual statistics been available on industrial production. For the earlier years we must rely on the data provided by the decennial censuses, which have serious weaknesses for inter-decade comparisons, since both the definitions of industries and the coverage change from decade to decade. The censuses for 1901 and 1911, which are of special interest for this study, offer three particular difficulties. From 1871 to 1891 coverage is complete, but in 1901 and 1911 only firms employing five or more employees are included in the census data. The first postal census of 1906 claimed total coverage, but the second postal census of 1915 excludes all firms with a total production of less than $2,500. Only in 1917 is there again total coverage. The result is that the total number of firms reporting in the various censuses in the province of Quebec presents an inconsistent pattern. For 1881, 15,754 firms reported; for 1891, 23,034; for 1901, 4,845; for 1905, 4,965; for 1910, 6,584; for 1915, 7,158; and for 1917, 10,042; only the data for the years 1881, 1891, 1906, and 1917 claimed total coverage of all firms regardless of the number of employees involved.

Likewise, after 1891, on the pretext of protecting manufacturers, industrial data were not reported separately in industries in which there were less than three firms either at the provincial level or at the comprehensive national level, but rather all such industries were lumped into the catch-all category "all other industries." Again, the coverage is inconsistent. In 1901, all butter and cheese factories and all brick and tile works were included independently of the number of employees engaged in them, and one suspects that the decision whether to include other plants withlessthan five employees when they appeared sufficiently important was often left to the individual census collector. And, in 1911, this total coverage was by way of exception extended to include all sawmills, shingle mills, and other firms producing lumber products; fish curing plants; flour and grist mills; and lime kilns. Finally, the census data include several industries which would be considered today as belonging to services and trades, as well as the construction and electric light and power industries which today are also excluded from the category of manufacturing industries.

For these reasons, I have thought it necessary to re-tabulate the data on manufacturing for the census years 1901 and 1911, which provide the most complete and meaningful data available to describe the development spurt of 1896–1913; we have no annual data for the year 1896, and the spurt had ended in 1913 and the war had had time to haves its initial impact on the recovery before the postal census of 1915 was taken. I have therefore (1) redistributed the more than two hundred industries classified in these censuses into the more meaningful and comparable seventeen industrial classifications adopted in the Standard Industrial Classification, in 1948, by the Dominion Bureau of Statistics; (2) distributed as many as possible of the "all other industries" classification into these seventeen industrial groups; (3) adjusted the data for both 1900 and 1910 to full coverage of all firms; (4) omitted, where possible, all industries which are not considered manufacturing industries in the more recent Standard Industrial Classification; and (5) adjusted the data to constant dollar values (1900 = 100) for gross value of production and value added at both the provincial level and at the level of the individual industry groups so that it will be possible to make a better estimate of the rates of real growth in manufacturing for the decade.

After carefully studying the data on capital formation, I decided to forego a discussion and re-tabulation of them in this appendix, as being disproportionate to my purpose which is here merely to find a few reliable indicators of the quantitative proportions of the industrial spurt that took place in Quebec at the turn of the century. Gross production and value added in manufacturing serve this purpose adequately. As for the census data on capital formation in industry, one cannot be sure exactly what they mean or how they were collected. Thomas K. Rymes, of the Dominion Bureau of Statistics, who has long occupied himself with the statistics on capital formation in Canada, writes concerning the early data on capital invested in manufacturing,

> The conceptual basis for the valuation of capital invested is never, to my knowledge, clearly stated in the various censuses. Thus one is at a loss to know whether fixed reproducible capital is valued gross or net, at original cost or current market prices.[1]

The method of evaluating capital goods seems to have been left entirely to the ingenuity of the individual census collector or manufacturer, for there is no record of particular instructions having been issued to them on this matter. Rymes adds elsewhere, "... in my opinion, the data with respect to 'capital invested' are of questionable reliability."[2]

Nor do I concern myself in detail with the exact number of firms in manufacturing or the exact number of workers employed in each industry, for it is clear from the postal census of 1906 that the reporting unit varied from census to census according as firms were reported as one or several firms when they produced products falling into different industrial classifications.[3] Moreover, employment seems often to have been exaggerated by employers who reported the number of men who had worked any time during the year rather than the number of jobs in their firm, as is suggested by the fact that employment figures usually exceed occupational figures where these are available for comparisons; and, besides, salaried workers were not consistently included among the number of employees in the different censuses.[4]

---

[1] Thomas K. RYMES, "Some Comments on the Pre-Annual Census of Industry data with respect to Manufacturing in Canada 1870–1915" (typewritten manuscript, Dominion Bureau of Statistics, Ottawa, 1960), p. 4. This manuscript represents the author's own views and not necessarily those of the Dominion Bureau of Statistics.
[2] *Ibid.*, p. 14. I am indebted to Mr. Rymes for the opportunity to consult his manuscript and for his suggestions. I am also indebted to the paper of G.W. BERTRAM, "Historical Statistics on Growth and Structure of Manufacturing in Canada, 1870–1957." Both have recently tackled some of these problems in the early manufacturing statistics at the national level. Bertram also attempted to redistribute the category "all other industries" at the provincial level for the years 1901 and 1911.
[3] *Manufactures of Canada, 1907*, Census and Statistics Bulletin II, p. vii.
[4] *Ibid.*

The method used to redistribute the category "all other industries" was, wherever possible, to find Quebec's production as a residual after subtracting out the production of other provinces which happened to have at least three firms, and, therefore, had a definite statistic in a given industry. Happily, this was frequently possible, since Ontario and Quebec often shared an industry between them containing as they did over 80 per cent of Canadian manufacturing production. Where there were less than three firms in the industry in other provinces as well as Quebec, I subtracted out the production of all provinces having at least three firms, and then divided the residual production equally among the remaining number of firms for which the total value of production as a residual was available. The national production was also divided equally among the three firms where there was a statistic available only at the national level. For cases in which Quebec contained one or two of the less than three firms in a particular industry in the whole of Canada, no separate production figure could be distributed. Only in the important new industry of aluminum was another source of data used. Omitted from the re-tabulation were such census industries as dyeing and cleaning; electric light and power; gas, heating, and lighting; house building; interior decorating; printing and glazing; photography; and plumbing and tinsmithing. Following this method I succeeded in reducing the category "all other industries," for 1900, from 13 to 3.3 per cent of gross value of production, and for 1910, from 10.6 to 4.3 per cent.[5]

The problem of adjusting to full coverage proved more difficult and the results less satisfactory. Some authors, such as Raynauld and Caves and Holton, though conscious of the problem raised by incomplete coverage, have neglected it in their calculations for Quebec manufacturing, probably on the assumption that it did not substantially modify their picture of the general evolution of economic development in Quebec.[6] Firestone, Rymes, and Bertram have used various techniques to adjust the national census data on manufacturing to full coverage. Firestone estimated that in 1900 the census data accounted for only 82.37 per cent of total Canadian manufactures. His method was to attribute the average output per man in 1900 to all those listed as gainfully employed in manufacturing in the separate occupational statistics provided by the census for that year. Thereafter, he assumed that the percentage of output provided by firms with less than five employees fell steadily at a constant rate from 17.63, in that year, to 2.85 in 1915.[7] Bertram's technique is more radical and simple. He suggests that this percentage fell steadily from 81.5 in 1890—a statistic derivable from the census data—to Firestone's estimate of 2.85 per cent in 1915.[8] Rymes used information derivable from the census of 1901 and the postal census of 1906 to obtain by industry the proportion of total production accounted for by firms employing five hands or over for 1890 and 1905 respectively, and applied these proportions as blow-up factors to the census data of 1901 and 1911 in order to adjust them to full coverage.[9]

[5] The results are in substantial agreement with those of Professor Bertram ("Historical Statistics on Growth and Structure of manufacturing in Canada," Table 7, p. 34).

[6] A. RAYNAULD, *Croissance et structure économiques*, p. 596; R. CAVES and R.H. HOLTON, *The Canadian Economy*, p. 190.

[7] O.J. FIRESTONE, *Canada's Economic Development*, pp. 291-92. It is not clear from his brief description how he arrived at this last estimate.

[8] G. BERTRAM, "Historical Statistics," p. 5.

[9] T.K. RYMES, p. 8. Bertram also used a similar technique in his first retabulation on an industry group basis, but for his final estimate of total manufacturing production he fell back on his assumption that the percentage of output provided by firms with less than five employees decreased at a constant rate from 81.5 to 2.85 per cent in the period 1890–1915. He felt that his former estimates were too small.

TABLE VIII

Quebec's Manufacturing Industries Reclassified According to the Standard Industrial Classification Including Redistribution of the Census Category. "All Other Industries," 1900–1910*

	Gross-value of manufactures (in thousands current dollars)		Value added	
	1900	1910	1900	1910
I. Foods and beverages	33,099	55,751	7,931	14,719
II. Tobacco and tobacco products	8,231	18,292	5,749	8,265
III. Rubber products	39	165	12	85
IV. Leather products	20,325	29,699	8,024	13,339
V. Textile products	12,352	24,072	5,545	10,510
VI. Clothing (textile and fur)	16,542	38,061	8,188	18,132
VII. Wood products	16,340	42,783	8,669	21,304
VIII. Paper products	6,461	16,318	3,706	9,019
IX. Printing, publishing, etc.	3,510	5,733	2,560	4,043
X. Iron and steel products	12,842	28,351	6,808	15,496
XI. Transportation equipment	8,058	28,228	3,264	12,957

* The data represent the census data covering only firms with five or more employees. The reclassification was carried out following the manual, Dominion Bureau of Statistics, *Standard Industrial Classification*, 1951.

XII.	Non-Ferrous metals	1,497	10,678	767	6,863
XIII.	Electrical apparatus, etc.	1,815	7,923	1,355	4,496
XIV.	Non-metallic mineral products	1,630	5,975	1,127	4,866
XV.	Products of petroleum and coal	245	899	42	146
XVI.	Chemical products	4,138	8,748	1,805	4,008
XVII.	Miscellaneous manufacturing industries	1,342	3,675	841	2,041
	Total Reclassified and Redistributed Manufacturing Production	148,457	325,349	66,393	150,289
	Total Manufacturing Production in Census Data	153,574	340,117	68,593	159,111
	Manufacturing Data still remaining in "All other Industries"**	5,108	14,767	2,190	8,822

** In 1900, this residual of $5,107,783 in gross value of production includes errors involved in the redistribution technique being used here, together with the following firms for which no separate estimate was available: 1 bicycle repairs, 1 railway car wheels, 2 church ornaments, 1 costumier and hairdresser, 1 cottolene, 1 cotton and wool waste, 1 dyes and colors, 1 graphite, 1 miscellaneous, 1 patterns, 1 pottery and painted ware, 1 prepared flour, 1 rice cleaning and polishing, 1 sausage casings, 1 spinning wheels, 1 washing blue.

In 1910, the residual of $14,767,445 in gross value of production that remained undistributed besides errors includes the following firms: 1 beekeeper's supplies, 1 bells, 1 belting and hose leather, 1 carbonic acid gas, 1 clothes pins, 1 costumier and hairdresser, 2 dyes and colors, 1 fountain pens, 1 hay baled, 1 oxygen gas, 1 paper blue print, 1 flour paste, 1 phosphorous, 1 pins, 2 pottery and painted ware, 1 sausage casings, 2 school supplies, 2 stationery, 1 polished stone, 1 time recorders, 1 typewriters, 1 washing blue, 1 window fixtures. Obviously, some of these industries would have been excluded from the standard industrial classification if there were any way to approximate their particular share of the residual total.

This problem of undercoverage has not, to my knowledge, been tackled on the provincial level. Yet it obviously cannot be overlooked if we wish to estimate the growth in manufacturing in the decade 1900–1910. If, as Firestone estimates, the census data on the national level accounts for only 82.37 per cent of total manufacturing in 1900, whereas it accounts for 100 per cent in 1890, quite clearly the glowing prosperity of the decade 1900–1910 has been artificially enhanced at the expense of exaggerating the "depression" of the decade 1890–1900. And the situation can be expected to be analogous at the provincial level.

In estimating full coverage at the provincial level, or more precisely at the Quebec level, one is more handicapped than at the national level. Occupational data are not available separately at the provincial level in the census of 1901, and neither in 1901 nor in 1906 are there comparable data at the provincial level from which to derive the proportion of total output accounted for by firms employing less than five employees in 1890 and 1905.[10] It is unwise to assume a decline at a constant rate in the percentage of output provided by firms with less than five employees, partly because such an assumption neglects the available information that in 1900 and 1910 several important industries were by exception given full coverage in the census data, and especially because there are no data at the provincial level from which to estimate how these proportions changed in each particular industry and not merely for manufacturing as a whole. I decided, therefore, to adopt with certain important modifications Ryme's technique of applying the proportions of total production produced by firms with under five employees in 1891 and 1906 as blow-up factors to the census data of 1901 and 1911 respectively to arrive at full coverage. This method offers the advantage of adjusting each particular industry by a blow-up factor derived from its own peculiar history. And besides the justification of simple availability, the use of these proportions as blow-up factors can also be justified on other grounds. Since the decade 1890–1900 was one of recession and the spurt did not get seriously underway until after 1896, these proportions of 1890 can be quite realistically applied to the industrial data of 1900. And since, claims of the compilers to the contrary, all who have worked with data provided by the postal census of 1906 suspect undercoverage, the proportions of that year can on these grounds be more confidently applied to the data of 1910.[11]

The assumption that Quebec's manufacturing industries reflected the national proportions of total output produced by firms with less than five employees in any particular industry reasonably well, is justified by the fact that Quebec accounted for about 30 per cent of Canadian manufacturing at this time, and together with her neighbouring province of Ontario accounted for over 80 per cent of the national total, both operating under geographical conditions so similar that they are often studied together as a single economic region. The blow-up adjustments were applied to total output in individual industries, but the value added for the increment was

---

[10] See *Census of Canada, 1901*, III, Table XXIII; and *Manufactures of Canada, 1907*, Bulletin II, Table II.

[11] *Manufactures of Canada, 1907*, p. V; T. RYMES, p. 10; G. BERTRAM, p. 5. Firestone makes no use or reference to the postal census of 1906 in this context (p. 292)—perhaps on the assumption of incomplete coverage. The number of firms reporting in Quebec varied as follows: 4,845 in 1900; 4,965 in 1905; and 6,584 in 1910. This variation already rouses suspicions of undercoverage in 1905, the only year for which total coverage is claimed. However, the compilers themselves explain that the reporting units chosen in 1905 often grouped several units reporting separately in 1900 (*Manufactures of Canada, 1907*, p. VII). Nevertheless, here the coverage in 1905 in Quebec appears to have been better than for Canada as a whole for which the number of firms reporting varied more inconsistently from 14,285 in 1900 to 12,059 in 1905, and 18,447 in 1910.

estimated by the proportion existing between total output and value added in firms with five or more employees in each particular industry for the census years 1900 and 1910 themselves in order to allow for changes in productivity. In general, where the 1890 proportions were lacking in the data, the average proportion of the industry group was used. But in the case of new industries appearing for the first time in 1900, the 1905 proportion was used instead of the 1890 proportion on the grounds that the latter was irrelevant to the new industry; and where less than three firms were reported in an industry no adjustment was made on the grounds that it was unlikely that there existed firms with less than five employees, since these were usually highly specialized industries. An exception was made in the case of the iron and steel products industry group. Here the average proportion of that industrial group for 1890 was applied for though this classification appeared as a "new" industry in 1900, yet in reality it merely regrouped many small industries which had formerly appeared under separate names. Where no proportion was available for an industry with one or two firms in the whole of Canada no adjustment was made. And finally, in industries where full coverage was clearly indicated by the instructions issued to the census collectors no adjustment was made.

The new estimates suggested that the census data in 1900 accounted for only 83.0 per cent of the gross value of manufacturing in Quebec and for only 84.2 per cent of the total value added, and that, in 1910, the census data accounted for 98.7 and 98.3 per cent of these respective totals. But closer examination of these initial results suggested that certain further modifications should be made in the blow-up factors for at least four industries—flour and grist mills; bread, biscuits, and confectionery; fish curing plants; and boots and shoes.

1. *Flour and grist mills.* Here it is not clear what coverage was given the mills in 1900. The account given in the census itself is ambiguous. The census of 1911 suggests that the exception of full coverage "might have been applied in the case of flour and grist mills," but it is not clear whether this expression implies the likelihood that they were so covered or merely that they could or should have been so covered.[12] The census of 1901 itself states clearly in one place that they were not given full coverage, but elsewhere seems to call into question the degree of fidelity with which the rule of excluding firms with less than five employees was followed out in practice. The compiler writes, "... the limitation being conventional it is no doubt the case that some industries (flour and grist mills and electric plants, for example) have been enumerated with sufficient fullness."[13] In fact, on the national level, where there are separate occupational statistics, we find that the census data of 1901 for flour and grist mills already accounted for 3,445 out of a total of 3,816 workers claiming to be gainfully employed in this industry. Even allowing for a turnover of 10 per cent in the work force, the manufacturing statistics on workers would still account for 81.3 per cent of those gainfully employed in the industry, who would surely account for more than 59.9 per cent of the total production in the industry, as suggested by the blow-up factor. Thus I adopted as a more realistic blow-up factor the proportion of 81.3 per cent suggested by the employment picture.

[12] *Census of Canada 1911*, III, VII. This ambiguity led Rymes to include flour and grist mills and fish curing plants as fully covered in the census of 1901 (Part I, Appendix I, Table D2).
[13] *Census of Canada 1901*, III, XXIII.

2. *Fish curing plants.* The census data in this industry were not adjusted because of our lack of sufficiently clear information. We have no separate complete occupational statistics for this industry at the national level, and all the other data available are inconsistent. In 1900, there were 121 firms with 1,071 employees (supposedly all with five employees or more) producing a total product valued at $565,527, while in 1910, when there is full coverage, 554 firms with 2,191 employees reported a total product worth only $785,677, despite the fact that they represented in current value a capital investment 6 times as great and the price of fish had increased by about one third during the decade. The data for 1905 offer no help—they evidently reveal undercoverage, reporting only 50 firms with a total product valued at $320,541. Given these inconsistencies, I decided to include the census data without adjustment.

3. *Bread, biscuits and confectionery.* Here it seems that the census collectors could not decide in practice what firms to include in this industry. In this decade of very rapid urbanization, we find that the number of workers, including salaried workers, in firms reported in the industry fell from 2,180 to 2,170. On a national basis, allowing for a 10 per cent turnover in the number of workers reported in the manufacturing statistics, we still find that the census manufacturing data in 1900 account for only 67.4 per cent and in 1910 for only 59.9 per cent of those reported in the occupational statistics as gainfully employed in this industry as bakers and candymakers. Again the data of 1905 offer no help, for though claiming total coverage they account for only 1,728 wage earners. Confronted with these inconsistencies in the census data, I decided simply to report the data without adjusting them to full coverage.

4. *Boots and shoes.* This industry seems to have been transformed from an industry of small artisan shops to one of sizable factories much more rapidly than the blow-up factor derived from the statistics in the industry in 1890 would suggest. The latter indicate that, in 1900, 66.9 per cent of the boots and shoes were still being made in establishments employing less than five persons. But the national occupational statistics suggest a quite different picture. Even allowing for a turnover of labour of 10 per cent the manufacturing labour statistics for factories with five or more employees accounted for 13,743 out of 14,038 or 88.3 per cent of those reported as gainfully occupied in this industry in 1900. Since the national picture in this industry adequately represents its situation in Quebec, as this province was producing 76 per cent of Canadian boots and shoes at the time, the proportion suggested by the employment picture of 1900 rather than the production picture of 1890 was accepted. The chances are that this latter proportion of 88.3 per cent is still biased downward, for workers employed in small poorly equipped shops are usually less productive than workers equipped with modern machinery in new factories.

When these new adjustments were made, the final estimates suggested that the census manufacturing data for 1900 accounted for 89.7 instead of 83.9 per cent of the gross value of manufacturing production, and for 88.2 instead of 84.2 per cent of the total value added as the first estimate indicated; and the corresponding estimates for 1910 were 98.8 instead of 98.7 per cent for gross value of production, and 98.4 instead of 98.3 per cent for value added.

The census data for this early period did not include in the costs of materials an allowance for fuel and electricity, and therefore overestimated the value added in industry. The census of 1901 provides information on miscellaneous expenses by industry on a provincial level.[14] By combining the categories of "rent of power and heat" and "fuel and light" and adjusting them to total coverage we can estimate that in 1900 these costs amounted to $2,416,328, or 1.39 per cent of gross value of production, and 2.48 per cent of total costs of materials. The equivalent data for 1910 provided only the cost of oil and other fuel, but omitted any cost allowance for electricity, although the latter was becoming an increasingly important cost in all industry.[15] The cost of electricity used in industry can be estimated as follows. The amount of electric horsepower used in Quebec in 1910 can be calculated at 172,306 hp.[16] If this statistic is divided into the gross value of production in the electric light and power industry (which is fully covered in the census data), each electric horsepower will be valued at $45.69. From the statistics on mechanical power used in manufacturing it appears that 76,462 electric horsepower were used in industry, or 44.4 per cent of the total electric power delivered that year by the electric power industry.[17] Allowing for an additional 5.6 per cent for lighting and electricity used in electrical reduction in the new aluminum and carbide industries, we arrive at the estimate that 50 per cent of all electricity developed was used in industry in 1910.[18] Thus the total fuel and electricity bill in industry for 1910 when adjusted for total coverage amounted to $8,131,364 in current dollars, or 2.4 per cent of gross value of production, and 4.2 per cent of total material costs. Allowance is made for these additional costs of fuel and electricity in estimating the rates of growth in total manufacturing over the decade, but since they exaggerate the growth in value added over the whole decade by only about 3.5 per cent on a total increase of 75.6 per cent, I did not feel the gain of this small difference warranted the extra work and assumptions required to distribute it on an individual industry basis.

Finally, the data were deflated to measure the rates of growth over the decade at both the industry-group and the total provincial level. For a deflator I first used H. Mitchell's "Index numbers constructed for 70 commodities with base 1900."[19] His general index number for 1910 was 118.5. But because I suspected that his general index of wholesale prices gave too much weight to the group "animals and meats" for our purposes, and because I wanted to estimate the rate of growth for each particular industry group more exactly, I decided to deflate each industry group separately.[20] Where Mitchell's commodity groups were found to coincide fairly well with the Standard Industrial Classification groups, his indexes were used and elsewhere the wholesale prices of individual commodities were used to deflate particular industries. Unless otherwise indicated I used the indexes of wholesale prices or indexes constructed from the wholesale prices available for many individual commodities in the *Report* of the Board of Inquiry into the Cost of Living, which was published in 1915.[21]

---

[14] *Census of Canada 1901*, III, Table IV.

[15] *Census of Canada 1911*, III, Table III.

[16] *Statistical Year Book of Quebec*, II (1915), 519. It is assumed that the electric power developed by the Ottawa River was equally divided between Quebec and Ontario.

[17] *Census of Canada 1911*, III, Table VI.

[18] Cf. O.J. FIRESTONE, p. 292. He uses this same ratio when calculating electricity costs for the whole of Canadian industry, but he does not indicate how he arrived at it.

[19] K.W. TAYLOR and H. MITCHELL, *Statistical Contributions to Canadian Economic History*, II, "Statistics of Prices," 54–56.

[20] *Ibid.*, p. 56. His index for 1910 for this group is 145, indicating a very rapid price increase in meats over the decade.

[21] Canada, Board of Inquiry into Cost of Living in Canada, *Report of The Board*.

Our deflators for the seventeen industry groups are as follows:

I. *Foods and Beverages:* bread, biscuits and confectionery (119.9), cocoa and chocolate (109.1), dairy products (120.8), coffee and spices (117.4), preserved fish (132.6), flour and grist mills (136.6), distilled liquor (121.1), malt liquors (102.2), vinegar and pickles (75.5), refined sugar (108.7), and malt (123.3). These indexes were constructed from Canadian wholesale prices—where available, from Montreal quotations—of either individual commodities or of the major commodity in a group. For slaughtering and meat-packing Mitchell's index was used (145). The other component industries of this industry group were deflated by the average of the other price indexes (116.8).

II. *Tobacco and Tobacco Products:* the price of tobacco (100.4).

III. *Rubber Products:* the price of rubber (196.2).

IV. *Leather Products:* Mitchell's index (116.7).

V. *Textile Products:* R.H. Coats' index for textiles (114.6) (*Wholesale Prices in Canada*, p. 3).

VI. *Clothing* (textiles and furs): price of furs (175); clothing (129.5), derived from the average increase in prices of standard overcoats and suits; hats and caps and furs (152.8), the average of the above two indexes.

VII. *Wood Products:* the average price of lumber (139).

VIII. *Paper Products:* the price of newsprint (82.2); wood pulp (68.1), derived from the price of mechanical wood pulp. The latter was deflated separately because of the wild cyclical swings in its price during this decade.

IX. *Printing, Publishing and Allied Industries:* The price of paper (82.2).

X. *Iron and Steel Products:* (92.7), the average of Mitchell's index for iron and steel products (80.9) and Coats' index for implements (104.4).

XI. *Transportation Equipment:* Since the building and repairing of railway rolling stock accounted for about 85 per cent of the total of this industry group, I used indexes derived from the price variations in standard Canadian Pacific equipment constructed at the Angus Shops in Montreal at this time. On the assumption that prices changed regularly over time, it was found that the cost of building the Type D-4 locomotive rose by 136.7 per cent in the decade; and the cost of the standard 30-ton freight car rose by 120.5 per cent (Source: The Office of Canadian Pacific Rolling Stock Department, Windsor Station, Montreal.) The Type D-4 steam locomotive rose in cost from $8,280 in 1897 to $13,321 in 1912; and the cost of the 30-ton freight car rose from $732 in 1900 to $912 in 1912. Although the census data do not indicate it specifically, the construction of steam locomotives during the decade was very important. In the Angus Shops alone, some 391 steam locomotives were built in the decade, and 764 in the period 1896-1914 (Omer S.-A. Lavallée, *Delormier and Angus* [Montreal: Canadian Railroad Historical Association, 1962], pp. 21–32).

The index was weighted by the occupational statistics for locomotive builders and other workers in car building and repairs. For the other 15 per cent of the industry group, the index of freight car prices was used, since at this time these cars were still largely made of wood and used other materials roughly in the same proportion as they were used in ship building and repairs. The same index was applied to the carriage and wagon industry on the same grounds; it accounted for only 6.3 per cent of the industry group at this time.

XII. *Non-Ferrous Metals:* Mitchell's index (86.6). The value of the output of new aluminum industry was not deflated. An estimate of its production had to come not from the census data but from company records, for, being a single firm, it fell into the "all other industries" category. Its production was 9,679,980 pounds in 1910 (M.E. Gooding, "The History of Reduction Plants at Shawinigan Falls," [unpublished manuscript, Aluminum Company of Canada, Shawinigan Falls], Appendix A, p. 95). It was valued at the price quoted on the New York market—which Coats gives as the Canadian price—of 22.7 cents. Deflation would exaggerate the importance of the industry, since the price of aluminum had been falling sharply since 1886 when it was still valued at $12 a pound.

XIII. *Electrical Apparatus and Supplies:* (98.8). Since no prices were available, an average was taken of the indexes of iron and steel products, implements, non-metallic and metallic products. At this time, all major electrical equipment was still being imported from the United States, England, and Switzerland.

XIV. *Non-Metallic Products:* brick and tile (167.3), cement and cement blocks and tiles (56.5), lime (117.1), cut mica (177), glass (71), plaster (111)—all derived from their respective wholesale prices. For the rest of the components of the industry group, these indexes were averaged to get an index of (117.1).

XV. *Products of Petroleum and Coal:* (110.4) Mitchell's index for non-metallic minerals and their products. This category is happily small, for the census data lumps such dissimilar products as vegetable oils and petroleum into the same industry group.

XVI. *Chemical Products:* Mitchell's index (110.3).

XVII. *Miscellaneous Manufacturing Industries:* (116.6), derived as an average from all
the above indexes less that of food and beverages.
Fuel and Electricity: fuel (110.4), electricity (84.2), derived from their respective price
changes over the decade.

The difference discovered in the growth rates of gross manufacturing
production and value added over the decade when deflated by separate
deflators rather than by Mitchell's general index seemed to confirm the
suspicion that his index was too heavily weighted by the "animal and meat"
group for our purposes. The deflators being used indicated that the total
gross value of manufactures increased by 74.9 instead of 69.7 per cent, as
suggested by his index; and the increase in value added in manufactures
was 81.6 rather than 75.6 per cent, as his index indicated.

This technique for attaining total coverage had the result of reducing
the annual real growth rate in gross manufacturing product from 8.69 to
7.49 per cent and that of value added in manufacturing from 9.79 to 8.16
per cent for the spurt-decade 1900–1910. At the same time the previous
decade 1890–1900 had restored to it some of its industrial vigour which
had been artificially removed from it by the undercoverage of the census
data in the latter terminal year. It now shows an annual average increase
in gross value of manufactures (in constant dollars) of 2.6 rather than .86
per cent as indicated by the census data, and an annual increase in value
added of 2.45 rather than the original percentage of only .96—thus some
of the basis for interpreting it as a decade of "deep depression" has been
removed.[22]

In fact, the whole period 1870–1900 was remarkably buoyant in Quebec
manufactures for a period usually considered by historians as one of "deep
depression." The gross value of manufactures (in constant dollars, 1900 =
100) for the three decades showed increases of 47; 51.7; and 26 per cent
respectively. And in value added there were correspondingly significant
increases of 40.6; 69.6; and 24.5 per cent—levels of real growth hardly
characteristic of deep depression, even though the decade 1900–1910 retains
its peculiar character of presenting both the most dynamic spurt of the
whole period and the most far-reaching structural changes in Quebec
manufactures.

---

[22] Growth estimates for the period 1870–1890 are based on Bertram's redistribution of the census data into
industry groups which make them comparable with my own work, since at that time the problems of undercoverage and the "all other industries" category did not exist ("Historical Statistics," pp. 33-34).

TABLE IX

Total and Rates of Growth for Incomplete Coverage (Current Dollar Value) and Complete Coverage (Deflated Dollar Value) in Gross Value of Manufacturing Production, 1900–1910*

(in thousands of dollars)

	Incomplete Coverage 1900	Incomplete Coverage 1910	Percentage Increase	Complete Coverage 1900	Complete Coverage 1910	Percentage Increase
I. Food and beverages..........	33,099	55,751	68.4	35,429	40,821	15.2
II. Tobacco and tobacco products	8,231	18,292	122.2	8,367	18,327	119.0
III. Rubber products..........	39	165	322.8	42	84	99.7
IV. Leather products..........	20,325	29,699	46.1	25,255	26,129	3.3
V. Textile products..........	12,352	24,072	94.9	12,445	21,029	69.0
VI. Clothing (textile and fur)	16,542	38,061	130.1	18,310	28,986	58.3
VII. Wood products..........	16,340	42,783	161.8	18,939	30,870	63.0
VIII. Paper products..........	6,461	16,318	154.1	6,504	20,659	217.6
IX. Printing, publishing, etc.	3,510	5,733	63.3	3,794	7,277	91.8

* Only results are included, as the detailed work sheets would add too much bulk to the study.

X.	Iron and steel products..........	12,842	28,351	120.8	14,993	31,245	108.4
XI.	Transportation equipment......	8,058	28,228	250.3	8,936	22,750	154.6
XII.	Non-ferrous metals............	1,497	10,678	613.4	1,838	12,109	558.7
XIII.	Electrical apparatus, etc.	1,815	7,923	336.6	1,958	8,019	309.7
XIV.	Non-metallic products..........	1,630	5,975	266.5	1,817	6,509	258.2
XV.	Products of petroleum and coal..	245	899	266.6	293	849	189.3
XVI.	Chemical products.............	4,138	8,748	111.4	5,611	8,242	46.9
XVII.	Miscellaneous manufacturing....	1,342	3,675	173.9	1,569	3,269	108.3
	Total for 17 industry groups....	153,574	340,117	121.5	171,208**	299,459***	74.9

** This statistic includes $5,107,783 in addition to the total for the 17 industry groups and represents the gross value of production which could not be distributed.

*** This statistic includes the corresponding undistributed total gross value of $14,767,445 deflated by Mitchell's general index, 118.5.

TABLE X

Total and Percentage Increase for Incomplete (Current Dollar Value) and Complete Coverage (Deflated Dollar Value) in Total Value Added in Manufacturing Production, 1900–1910 (in thousands of dollars)

	Incomplete coverage 1900	Incomplete coverage 1910	Percentage increase	Complete coverage 1900	Complete coverage 1910	Percentage increase
I. Food and beverages	7,931	14,719	85.6	9,546	12,362	29.5
II. Tobacco and tobacco products	5,749	8,265	43.8	5,845	8,287	41.8
III. Rubber products	12	85	605.1	13	43	228.1
IV. Leather products	8,024	13,339	66.2	9,728	11,732	8.5
V. Textile products	5,545	10,510	89.6	5,590	9,358	67.4
VI. Clothing (textile and fur)	8,188	18,132	121.4	9,200	14,049	52.7
VII. Wood products	8,669	21,304	145.8	10,242	15,375	50.1
VIII. Paper products	3,706	9,019	143.4	3,730	11,430	206.4
IX. Printing, publishing, etc.	2,560	4,043	57.9	2,767	5,133	85.5

X.	Iron and steel products..............	6,808	15,496	127.6	8,010	17,086	113.3
XI.	Transportation equipment..........	3,264	12,957	297.0	3,813	9,482	148.7
XII.	Non-ferrous metals....	767	6,863	794.9	983	7,785	691.6
XIII.	Electrical apparatus, etc..	1,355	4,496	231.9	1,453	4,550	213.2
XIV.	Non-metallic products.............	1,127	4,866	331.6	1,174	5,322	353.3
XV.	Products of petroleum and coal.......	42	146	248.3	50	138	174.5
XVI.	Chemical products..	1,805	4,008	122.1	2,502	3,739	49.5
XVII.	Miscellaneous manufacturing........	841	2,041	142.6	918	1,994	117.3
	Total for the 17 industry groups.....	66,462	151,110	127.4	75,337*	136,816**	81.6

* Includes $2,190,101, undistributed value added, less $2,416,328, allowance for fuel and electricity adjusted to total coverage.

** Includes $8,821,644, undistributed value added deflated by Mitchell's general index, 118.5, less the total adjusted fuel and electricity bill deflated by their individual deflators—which left a total of $8,492,983. When the complete coverage was deflated by Mitchell's general index (118.5) and fuel and electricity were allowed for, value added showed an increase of 75.6 per cent Without allowance for fuel and electricity it showed an increase of 72.1 per cent. Hence, the gain achieved by using individual deflators is clear.

TABLE XI

Rank and Percentage of Total Gross Value of Manufacturing Production by Industry Groups for Selected Years: 1870–1959 Current Dollar Value*

	1870	1880	1890	1900	1910	1959
I. Food and beverages	1 (26.1)	1 (23.6)	1 (23.0)	1 (20.7)	1 (17.0)	1 (17.7)
II. Tobacco and tobacco products	9 (1.9)	10 (1.71)	11 (2.6)	8 (4.9)	8 (5.9)	14 (2.7)
III. Rubber products	15 (.8)	15 (.8)	13 (1.22)	17 (.002)	17 (.05)	16 (.9)
IV. Leather products	2 (19.0)	2 (20.7)	2 (13.5)	2 (14.8)	4 (9.3)	17 (.18)
V. Textile products	7 (3.4)	6 (4.9)	7 (5.6)	6 (7.3)	7 (7.3)	5 (7.7)
VI. Clothing (textile and fur)	5 (7.8)	4 (10.2)	5 (10.1)	4 (10.7)	3 (11.9)	6 (7.1)

* Percentages are in brackets.

VII. Wood products.............	3 (17.1)	3 (13.9)	3 (13.3)	3 (11.1)	2 (13.0)	10 (4.6)
VIII. Paper products.............	13 (1.3)	12 (1.6)	10 (2.8)	9 (3.8)	9 (5.0)	2 (10.8)
IX. Printing, publishing, etc.	11 (1.7)	9 (1.9)	12 (1.6)	11 (2.2)	14 (1.8)	12 (3.3)
X. Iron and steel products.	4 (9.3)	5 (9.2)	4 (11.1)	5 (8.8)	5 (8.8)	4 (8.5)
XI. Transportation equipment........	6 (3.9)	7 (3.49)	6 (7.2)	7 (5.2)	6 (8.6)	9 (4.9)
XII. Non-ferrous metals...........	14 (1.2)	13 (1.3)	14 (1.17)	13 (1.07)	10 (3.3)	3 (9.6)
XIII. Electrical apparatus...........	(0)	(0)	16 (.30)	12 (1.14)	12 (2.4)	11 (4.2)
XIV. Non-metallic products.........	10 (1.8)	11 (1.18)	9 (2.9)	14 (1.06)	13 (1.9)	13 (2.8)
XV. Products of petroleum and coal...	16 (.30)	16 (.30)	(0)	16 (.17)	16 (.30)	8 (5.5)
XVI. Chemical products............	8 (3.0)	8 (3.46)	8 (3.0)	10 (3.3)	11 (2.8)	7 (6.0)
XVII. Miscellaneous...............	12 (1.4)	14 (1.1)	15 (.50)	15 (.92)	15 (1.2)	15 (1.9)

TABLE XII

Percentage Increase in Quebec Manufactures by Decade, 1870–1910 (In Constant Dollars, 1900 = 100)*

	1870–1880	1880–1890	1890–1900	1900–1910
Total gross value of man-ufacturing production:	47.0	51.7	8.6 (incomplete coverage) 26.0 (complete coverage)	74.9
Total value added in man-ufactures:	40.6	69.6	9.6 (incomplete coverage) 24.5 (complete coverage)	87.8

* For the decades 1870-1890, these percentages are based on Bertram's redistribution of the census data deflated by Mitchell's general index with base 1900. The decades 1890-1910 show the author's adjustment of the census data to total coverage deflated by separate deflators for each industry group. The costs of fuel and electricity are not allowed for in the total material costs from which value added is calculated.

AGRICULTURAL STATISTICS

TABLE XIII

**Total Value of Quebec's Production of Butter and Cheese
(Domestic and Creamery in Constant Dollars) 1870–1910
(in thousands of dollars)**

		Percentage increase
1870...............	4,435.0	
		35.8
1880...............	6,022.9	
		38.0
1890...............	8,309.8	
		94.9
1900...............	16,193.0	
		4.7
1910...............	16,954.0*	

* This table is based on the series reconstructed by A. RAYNAULD, *Croissance et structure économiques*, Table 21, p. 587. For all years except 1910 Mitchell's index for dairy products ("Statistics of Prices," p. 56) was used for deflation. For 1910, it was by the index of wholesale prices for Montreal dairy products, 120.8. Had Mitchell's general index for Canadian dairy products been used there would have been a decrease in dairy production for the decade 1900–1910 amounting to 3 per cent. The increase of 4.7 per cent is in harmony with the 3.9 per cent increase indicated in gross value of manufactured butter and cheese.

TABLE XIV

**Revenue From Quebec's Field Crops in Constant Dollars
1870–1910* (in thousands of dollars)**

		Percentage increase
1870..............	28,940	
		20.3
1880..............	34,804	
		14.5
1890..............	39,853	
		36.9
1900..............	54,574	
		15.5
1910..............	64,049**	

* Source: A. RAYNAULD, *Croissance et structure économiques*, Table 22, p. 588.

** The year 1910 does not seem to have been a good year for agriculture in Quebec. If we choose 1911 as the terminal year for the decade rather than 1910, we get a quite different picture. Following Raynauld's reconstructed series for the combined products of both dairy farming and field crops, we find for the period 1900–1911 a healthy annual rate of growth in agricultural produce of about 3.5 per cent in constant dollars (Table 25, p. 590).

SELECTED BIBLIOGRAPHY

*In the interests of brevity only a selected bibliography is included here.
With few exceptions, the more than two hundred parish histories and monographs
consulted have been omitted. A complete separate listing of this collection is
available at the provincial archives in Quebec City. A detailed listing of the
published and unpublished directives, letters, etc. of the Catholic bishops is not
given and they receive only a general reference. Detailed references are available
in the footnotes for the more important documents in these collections.*

MANUSCRIPT COLLECTIONS

Canada

Canada, Public Archives. The Gouin Papers. These extensive papers
were examined only on a few specific subjects through the use of the
index: education, correspondence with the Catholic hierarchy and
clergy, agriculture, railways, anti-alcoholism, immigration and re-
patriation, relations between the Liberal Party (and its press) and the
Catholic press, especially *l'Action sociale.*

Canada, Public Archives. *Standard Rates and Wages and Hours of Labour
in Canada, 1900–1913.* This is an unpublished collection of the original
reports sent in by companies to the Department of Labour of Canada.

United States

United States, National Archives. Despatches from U.S. Consuls in
Montreal, Quebec, and Trois-Rivières, 1890–1915, in the *Register of
Consular Correspondence.* Much of this documentation is now available
on microfilm. Occasional reports on the economic situation in the
province of Quebec as well as on local demographic and health problems.

Ontario

Pembroke, Episcopal Archives of the Diocese of Pembroke. Correspondence of Curé E. CORBEIL with Mgr N.-Z. LORRAIN, 1909–1912.

Quebec

Chicoutimi, Archives of la Société historique du Saguenay. Excellent
collection of published and unpublished documents concerning the
regional history of the Saguenay. Includes several private collections.

Chicoutimi, Archives of the Séminaire de Chicoutimi. Especially the
private correspondence, papers, and manuscripts of Mgr Eugène
Lapointe. Among others, "Litige de Val-Jalbert," collection of the
relevant documents by Mgr LAPOINTE; LA FÉDÉRATION OUVRIÈRE
DE CHICOUTIMI, "Procès verbaux des assemblées générales et des
assemblées du conseil de direction de la Fédération ouvrière de Chicoutimi et histoire de sa fondation," unpublished manuscript, 1907–
1914; LAPOINTE, Mgr E., "Recueil de Souvenirs," unpublished handwritten diary.

Chicoutimi, Episcopal Archives of the Diocese of Chicoutimi. Personal correspondence of the successive bishops with their clergy, government officials, and businessmen on all questions having a bearing on economic development for the period 1878–1915.

Chicoutimi, Private collection of the Dubuc family. A rich collection of the letters, books, and papers of J.-E.-A. DUBUC, general manager of the Chicoutimi Pulp Company.

Grand'Mère, Private collection of Mrs. M.E. Browne, daughter of G. Chahoon, former manager of the Laurentide Paper Company. Includes correspondence between Curé LAFLÈCHE and Mr. CHAHOON, as well as some of the latter's speeches, statements, etc.

Trois-Rivières, Archives of the Séminaire de Trois-Rivières. Excellent collection of published and unpublished documentation on the regional history of the St. Maurice Valley. Includes personal correspondence and papers of early bishops and many private collections of manuscripts, clippings, etc. Among others, BOUCHER, T., "La Grand'Mère," unpublished manuscript, 1952.

Trois-Rivières, Episcopal Archives of the Diocese of Trois-Rivières. Personal correspondence of successive bishops with their clergy, government officials, and businessmen on all questions having a bearing on economic development for the period 1896–1915.

La Tuque, Archives of the Presbytery. A small collection of manuscripts and papers of Curé Eugène CORBEIL.

PUBLISHED EPISCOPAL DOCUMENTS

Les Mandements, Lettres pastorales, Circulaires, etc. This rich, voluminous collection contains all the official directives, letters, and circulars issued either separately or jointly by the bishops of the province of Quebec. They also usually include official directives and letters received by the bishops from the Pope and the various sacred congregations of the Roman Curia.

These documents are bound in chronological order and indexed separately by diocese, and are available at least in the respective chanceries, but usually also in the libraries of larger seminaries, etc. They were consulted for the various dioceses for the following years: Chicoutimi, 1878–1914; Joliette, 1908–1914; Montreal, 1850–1915; Nicolet, 1885–1914; Quebec, 1850–1915; Rimouski, 1890–1914; Saint-Hyacinthe, 1893–1917; Sherbrooke, 1890–1915; Trois-Rivières, 1890–1915; Valleyfield, 1892–1917.

GOVERNMENT PUBLICATIONS

Canada

Canada, Census Office. *Census of Canada 1901.* Vol. III. Ottawa: Queen's Printer, 1905.

Canada, Department of Agriculture. *Census of Canada 1890–1891.* Vol. III. Ottawa: Queen's Printer, 1894.

Canada, Department of Agriculture. Census and Statistics Office. *Postal Census of Manufactures 1906.* Ottawa: King's Printer, 1907.

Canada, Department of Trade and Commerce. Census and Statistics Office. *Postal Census of Manufactures 1916.* Ottawa: King's Printer, 1917.

Canada, Department of Trade and Commerce. Census Office. *Census of Canada 1911*. Vol. III. Ottawa: King's Printer, 1913.

Canada, Department of Labour. *The Labour Gazette*. The official journal of the Department of Labour of Canada. Published monthly in English and French. Ottawa, 1900–1914.

Canada, House of Commons. *Debates*. Ottawa: Session of 1883, May 17.

Quebec

Province of Quebec, Provincial Secretary's Department. *Statistical Year Book*. Quebec: 1914–1960 inclusive.

Province of Quebec, *The Sessional Papers*. Vols. XXX-XLVIII (1896–1914). Quebec: King's Printer. This valuable collection of documents contains the annual reports of the various governmental departments to the Legislature, and, therefore, includes either in text or in appendix such documents as the following: the annual reports of the activities of the Department of Agriculture and Colonization; the annual reports of the activities and expenditures of the agricultural clubs and societies; the annual reports of Quebec's Dairymen's Association as well as of their annual convention; the annual reports of the Superintendent of Public Instruction as well as of the individual school inspectors; the minutes of the meetings of the Catholic and Protestant Committees that make up the Council of Public Instruction; an account of all the monies spent by the executive branch during the past year; etc.

NEWSPAPERS, REVIEWS, AND BULLETINS

L'Action sociale. 1907–1914 (years relevant to this study). This is the official Catholic daily newspaper of the province, founded by Cardinal Bégin, Archbishop of Quebec, in 1907.

Le Bien public. 1909–1914 (years relevant to this study). This is the official Catholic newspaper of the diocese of Trois-Rivières, founded by Mgr Cloutier, in 1909.

Canada ecclésiastique. Montréal: Librairie Beauchemin, 1896–1915 inclusive. This annual Church catalogue gives the names of each parish and mission of the Catholic Church in Canada, as well as the date of its foundation and the number of parishioners belonging to it.

The Canadian Annual Review of Public Affairs. Edited by John C. Hopkins and Others. Toronto, 1902–1916 inclusive.

Le Colon du Lac Saint-Jean (Roberval). 1900-1901. On file in the Archives of la Société historique du Saguenay.

La Défense (Chicoutimi). 1898–1904. On file in the Archives of la Société historique du Saguenay.

Le Digester [*sic*]. 1918-1919. A newspaper issued by the Laurentide Paper Company for the benefit of the population of Grand'-Mère. On file in the Laurentide Division of the Consolidated Paper Corporation.

L'Écho paroissial du Sacré-Cœur. 1911–1916. Monthly bulletin edited by the Eudist Fathers for the workers' parish in Chicoutimi. On file in the Archives of la Société historique du Saguenay.

L'Enseignement primaire. 1899–1916 inclusive. This educational magazine was sent gratuitously to all the teachers of primary schools in the province. It was supervised by the Conseil de l'Instruction publique, and subsidized by the government.

Le Lac Saint-Jean. 1898-1899. Roberval's first newspaper. On file in the Archives of la Société historique du Saguenay.

Le Nouvelliste (Trois-Rivières). Collection of clippings on the regional history of the St. Maurice Valley, Archives of the Séminaire de Trois-Rivières.

L'Oiseau Mouche. 1893–1902. Newssheet of the Séminaire de Chicoutimi. On file in the Archives of la Société historique du Saguenay.

Le Progrès du Saguenay (Chicoutimi). 1896–1915. On file in the Archives of la Société historique du Saguenay.

Pulp and Paper Magazine. 1903–1916 inclusive. A monthly review first published in Toronto and then at Gardenvale, Quebec.

La Semaine religieuse de Montréal. 1896–1914. A weekly news bulletin edited by the chancery, devoted chiefly to religious news, but occasionally touching on economic questions.

La Semaine religieuse de Québec. 1896–1914. A weekly news bulletin edited by the chancery, devoted chiefly to religious news, but occasionally touching on economic questions.

Le Semeur. 1904–1914. The monthly bulletin of l'Association catholique de la Jeunesse canadienne-française.

BOOKS

L'Agriculture. Group Study by the professors of l'École des Hautes Études commerciales and l'Institut agricole d'Oka. ("Études sur notre milieu." Collection directed by Esdras Minville.) Montréal: Éditions Fides, 1943.

ALLAIRE, J.-B.-A. *Dictionnaire biographique du clergé canadien-français.* 4 vols. Saint-Hyacinthe: Courrier de Saint-Hyacinthe, 1934.

AUCLAIR, Abbé Élie-J. *Le Curé Labelle.* Montréal: Librairie Beauchemin, 1930.

BAILLAIRGÉ, Abbé F.-A. *Traité classique d'économie politique selon la doctrine de Léon XIII, avec applications au Canada.* Joliette: Privately printed, 1892.

BLANCHARD, Raoul. *Le Canada français,* Montréal: Librairie A. Fayard, 1960.

——*Les Études canadiennes.* Vol. I: *L'est du Canada français* (2 tomes). Vol. II: *Géographie générale.* Vol. III: *Le centre du Canada français.* Vol. IV: *L'ouest du Canada français, Montréal et sa région.* Vol. V: *L'ouest du Canada français, les pays de l'Ottawa, l'Abitibi, Témiscamingue.* Montréal: Librairie Beauchemin, 1935–1954.

——*La Mauricie.* Trois-Rivières: Éditions du Bien public, 1950.

BOISSONNAULT, Charles-M. *Histoire politique de la province de Québec (1867–1920).* Québec: Éditions Frontenac, 1936.

BOUCHER, Thomas. *Mauricie d'autrefois.* ("Collection régionale," No. 11.) Trois-Rivières: Éditions du Bien public, 1952.

BOUCHETTE, Errol. *L'indépendance économique du Canada français.* Montréal: Wilson et Lafleur, 1913.

BRACQ, Jean C. *The Evolution of French Canada.* New York: Macmillan Co., 1924.

BRAY, A.-J. DE. *L'essor industriel et commercial du peuple canadien.* Montréal: Librairie Beauchemin, 1912.

BROUILLETTE, Benoît. *Le développement industriel de la vallée du Saint-Maurice.* ("Pages trifluviennes," Série A, No 2.) Trois-Rivières: Éditions du Bien public, 1932.

BRUÈRE, Pierre BOUCHER DE LA. *Le Conseil de l'Instruction publique.* Montréal: Le Devoir, 1918.

BRUNET, L.-A. *La famille et ses traditions.* Montréal: Sénécal, 1881.

BUCKLEY, Kenneth. *Capital Formation in Canada, 1896–1930.* ("Canadian Studies in Economics," No. 2.) Toronto: University of Toronto Press, 1955.

BUIES, Arthur. *Le Saguenay et le bassin du Lac Saint-Jean.* 3rd ed. Québec: Côté, 1896.

BUTEAU, J.-A. *Notre enseignement technique industriel.* Québec: Le Soleil, 1919.

CADEN, José. *L'an 1 de Shawinigan (mai 1901–mai 1902).* Trois-Rivières: Éditions du Bien public, 1961.

CAIRNCROSS, A.K. *Home and Foreign Investment, 1870–1913: Studies in Capital Accumulation.* Cambridge: Cambridge University Press, 1953.

CARON, Abbé N. *Deux voyages sur le Saint-Maurice.* Trois-Rivières: Ayotte, 1900.

CARRIER, Hervé, S.J. *Le sociologue canadien Léon Gérin, 1863–1951.* ("Cahiers de l'Institut social populaire," No. 5.) Montréal: Éditions Bellarmin, 1960.

CARRUTHERS, G. *Paper in the Making.* Toronto: Garden City Press Co-operative, 1947.

CARUFEL, Abbé D.-O.-S. *Notes sur la paroisse de Notre-Dame-du-Mont-Carmel.* Trois-Rivières, 1907.

CAVES, R.E. and HOLTON, R.H. *The Canadian Economy.* ("Harvard Economic Studies," Vol. CXII.) Cambridge: Harvard University Press, 1961.

CHOQUETTE, Robert. *Le Curé de village.* Montréal: Granger Frères, 1936.

Codex Juris Canonici. Rome, 1918.

DALES, John H. *Hydroelectricity and Industrial Development in Quebec, 1898–1940.* Cambridge: Harvard University Press, 1957.

DEMANT, V.A. *Religion and The Decline of Capitalism.* London: Faber and Faber, 1952.

DESBIENS, Lucien. *Au cœur de la Mauricie (La Tuque).* ("Pages trifluviennes," Série A, No 8.) Trois-Rivières: Éditions du Bien public, 1933.

DESILETS, Auguste. *La Grand'Mère.* ("Pages trifluviennes," Série A, No 10.) Trois-Rivières: Éditions du Bien public, 1933.

DOUVILLE, Raymond. *Visage du vieux Trois-Rivières.* (Collection "L'histoire régionale," No 18.) Trois-Rivières: Éditions du Bien public, 1955.

DUPIN, Pierre. *Anciens chantiers du Saint-Maurice.* ("Pages trifluviennes," Série B, No 7.) Trois-Rivières: Éditions du Bien public, 1935.

EASTERBROOK, W.T. and AITKEN, H.G.J. *Canadian Economic History.* Toronto: Macmillan Co. of Canada, 1956.

ELLIS, L.E. *Print Paper Pendulum, Group Pressures and Price of Newsprint.* New Brunswick: Rutgers University Press, 1948.

FALARDEAU, Jean-Charles, ed. *Essays on Contemporary Quebec.* Québec: Presses universitaires Laval, 1953.

FANFANI, A. *Catholicism, Protestantism, and Capitalism.* New York: Sheed and Ward, 1955.

FILTEAU, Gérard. *L'épopée de Shawinigan.* Shawinigan: Guertin and Gignac, 1944.

———*Organisation scolaire de la province de Québec.* Montréal: Centre de psychologie et de pédagogie, 1954.

FIRESTONE, O.J. *Canada's Economic Development, 1867–1953, with Special References to Changes in the Country's National Product and National Wealth.* (International Association for Research in Income and Wealth, Income and Wealth Series, VII.) London: Bowes and Bowes, 1958.

La Forêt. Group Study by l'École de Génie forestier de Québec and l'École des Hautes Études commerciales. ("Études sur notre milieu." Collection directed by Esdras Minville.) Montréal: Éditions Fides, 1944.

GARIGUE, Philippe. *Études sur le Canada français.* Montréal: Université de Montréal, 1958.

GÉRIN, Léon. *Le type économique et social des Canadiens.* 2nd ed. Montréal: Éditions Fides, 1937.

GÉRIN-LAJOIE, A. *Jean Rivard, le défricheur.* 2nd ed. Montréal: Librairie Beauchemin, 1913.

———*Jean Rivard, l'économiste.* 2nd ed. Montréal: Librairie Beauchemin, 1913.

GIRARD, Alex. *La province de Québec.* Québec: Dussault & Proulx, 1905.

GOODWIN, Craufurd D.W. *Canadian Economic Thought: The Political Economy of a Developing Nation, 1814–1914.* Durham, N.C.: Duke University Press, 1961.

GUTHRIE, J.A. *Newsprint Paper Industry.* Cambridge: Harvard University Press, 1941.

HAMON, E., S.J. *Les Canadiens français de la Nouvelle-Angleterre.* Québec: N.-S. Hardy, 1891.

HARVEY, Vincent, O.P., ET AL. *L'Église et le Québec.* Montréal: Les Éditions du Jour, 1961.

HÉMON, Louis. *Maria Chapdelaine: A Tale of the Lake St. John Country.* Transl. W.H. Blake. New York: Macmillan Co., 1921.

HOPKINS, J.C. *French Canada and the St. Lawrence.* Philadelphia: J.C. Winston Co., 1913.

HUGHES, E.C. *French Canada in Transition.* Chicago: University of Chicago Press, 1943.

HULLIGER, Abbé Jean. *L'enseignement social des évêques canadiens de 1891 à 1950.* ("Bibliothèque économique et sociale.") Montréal: Éditions Fides, 1958.

KINDLEBERGER, Ch. P. *Economic Development.* New York: McGraw, 1958.

LACASSE, Le Père, O.M.I. *Une mine produisant l'or et l'argent.* Québec: C. Darveau, 1880.

LANGLOIS, Georges. *Histoire de la population canadienne-française.* ("Documentations historiques.") Montréal: Éditions Albert Lévesque, 1934.

LEBON, Mgr W. *Histoire du collège de Sainte-Anne-de-la-Pocatière*. Vol. II. Québec: Charrier & Dugal, 1949.

LEMAN, Beaudry. *Hier et demain: recueil de causeries*. Montréal: Banque canadienne nationale, 1952.

LENSKI, G. *The Religious Factor: A Sociologist's Inquiry*. New York: Doubleday, 1961.

LÉTOURNEAU, Firmin. *Histoire de l'agriculture (Canada français)*. Oka: Printed privately, 1959.

LEWIS, W.A. *The Theory of Economic Growth*. Homewood, Ill.: Irwin, 1955.

LOWER, A.R.M. *Settlement and the Forest Frontier in Eastern Canada*. Vol. IX of *Canadian Frontiers of Settlement*, edited by W.A. Mackintosh and W.L.G. Joerg. Toronto: Macmillan Co. of Canada, 1936.

LUCAS, C.P. *Lord Durham's Report*. 3 vols. Oxford: Clarendon Press, 1912.

MAGNAN, C.-J. *Au service de mon pays: Discours et conférences*. Québec: Dussault & Proulx, 1917.

——*Éclairons la route*. Québec: Librairie Garneau, 1922.

——and AHERN, G. *Mon premier livre*. 2 parts. Québec, 1900.

MAGNAN, Hormisdas. *Monographies paroissiales*. 2nd ed. Québec: Ministère de la Colonisation, Mines et Pêcheries, 1913.

MAILLOUX, Alexis. *Le manuel des parents chrétiens*. Québec: L'Action sociale, 1910.

MARSHALL, Herbert ET AL. *Canadian-American Industry*. New Haven: Yale University Press, 1936.

McCLELLAND, David. *The Achieving Society*. New York: D. Van Nostrand Co., 1961.

MENDELS, M.M. *The Asbestos Industry of Canada*. ("McGill University Economic Studies," No. 14.) Toronto: Macmillan Co. of Canada, 1930.

MINER, Horace. *St. Denis: A French Canadian Parish*. Chicago: University of Chicago Press, 1939.

MONTPETIT, Édouard. *La Conquête économique*. Vol. I: *Les Forces essentielles*. Vol. II: *Perspectives*. Vol. III: *Étapes*. Montréal: Bernard Valiquette, 1939–1942.

——*Souvenirs*. 3 vols. Montréal: Éditions de l'Arbre, 1944–1949.

NADEAU, Eugène, O.M.I. *"Un homme sortit pour semer... "—Le Frère Joseph Moffet, O.M.I., 1852–1932*, Montréal: Éditions Beauchemin, 1939.

O'BREADY, Mgr Maurice. *Histoire de Wotton, comté de Wolfe, 1848–1948*. Sherbrooke: Printed privately, 1949.

OTIS, Abbé L.-E. *Saint-Alexis-de-Grande-Baie, 1838–1938*. Chicoutimi: La Société historique du Saguenay, 1938.

PANNETON, Chanoine G., and MAGNAN, Abbé A. *Le diocèse de Trois-Rivières, 1852–1952*. Trois-Rivières: Éditions du Bien public, 1953.

PAQUET, Mgr L.-A. *Droit public de l'Église: l'organisation religieuse et le pouvoir civil*. Québec: L'Événement, 1912.

——*Études et appréciations; mélanges canadiens*. Québec: Imprimerie Franciscaine Missionnaire, 1918.

PERRON, Marc-A. *Un grand éducateur agricole. Édouard-A. Barnard, 1835–1898*. Québec: Printed privately, 1955.

POULIOT, Léon, S.J. *Mgr Bourget et son temps*. Montréal: Librairie Beauchemin, 1955.

RAYNAULD, André. *Croissance et structure économiques de la province de Québec.* Québec: Ministère de l'Industrie et du Commerce de Québec, 1961.

REICH, Nathan. *The Pulp and Paper Industry.* ("McGill University Economic Studies," No 7.) Toronto: Macmillan Co. of Canada, 1926.

ROBERTSON, H.M. *Aspects of the Rise of Economic Individualism.* Cambridge: Cambridge University Press, 1933.

ROBY, Yves. *Alphonse Desjardins et les caisses populaires, 1854–1920.* ("Bibliothèque économique et sociale.") Montréal: Éditions Fides, 1964.

ROSS, Mgr F.-X. *Questions scolaires, le nouveau programme primaire.* Montréal: Le Devoir, 1920.

ROSTOW, W.W. *The Stages of Economic Growth.* Cambridge: Cambridge University Press, 1960.

RUMILLY, Robert. *Histoire de la province de Québec.* Montréal: Centre de psychologie et de pédagogie, 1953.

——*Histoire de la province de Québec.* Various editors. Especially vols. VII–XVIII (1892–1914). Montréal: 1943–1961.

SAIT, Edouard McChesnay. *Clerical Control in Quebec.* Toronto: The Sentinel, 1908.

SAMUELSSON, K. *Religion and Economic Action.* New York: Basic Books, 1961.

SAUCIER, Edmond. *Éducation moderne et entraînement professionnel.* Louisville: Librairie Beauchemin, 1909.

SELLAR, Robert. *The Tragedy of Quebec: The Expulsion of its Protestant Farmers.* Toronto: Ontario Press, 1910.

SÉNÉCAL, G. *La Tuque et le haut Saint-Maurice.* ("Études économiques." Vol. III.) Montréal: École des Hautes Études, 1932.

SIEGFRIED, André. *Canada: An International Power.* Transl. Doris Hemming. 2nd. ed. New York: Duell, Sloan & Pearce, 1947.

——*The Race Question in Canada.* Transl. London: Eveleigh Nash, 1907.

Situation de la recherche sur le Canada français. Edited by Fernand Dumont and Yves Martin. Québec: Les Presses universitaires Laval, 1962.

SKELTON, O.D. *Life and Letters of Sir Wilfrid Laurier.* 2 vols. London: Oxford University Press, 1922.

LA SOCIÉTÉ HISTORIQUE DU SAGUENAY. *L'histoire du Saguenay depuis l'origine jusqu'à 1870.* ("Publications de la Société historique du Saguenay," No 3.) Chicoutimi: La Société historique du Saguenay, 1938.

The Storied Province of Quebec. Edited by William C.H. Wood *et al.* 3 vols. Toronto: Dominion Publishing Co., 1931, 1932.

SYLVAIN pseud. *Horizons mauriciens.* Trois-Rivières: Éditions du Bien public, 1962.

TAWNEY, R.H. *Religion and the Rise of Capitalism.* New York: The New American Library, 1960.

TAYLOR, K.W., and MITCHELL, H. *Statistical Contributions to Canadian Economic History.* Vol. II. Toronto: Macmillan Co. of Canada, 1931.

TESSIER, Mgr Albert. *Jean Crête et la Mauricie.* (Collection "L'histoire régionale," No. 20.) Trois-Rivières: Éditions du Bien public, 1956.

——*Trois-Rivières, 1535–1935.* Trois-Rivières: Le Nouvelliste, 1935.

THÉRIAULT, Yvon. *Trois-Rivières: ville de reflet.* (Collection "L'histoire régionale," No 15.). Trois-Rivières: Éditions du Bien public, 1954.

THOMPSON, Norman. *Canadian Railway Development from the Earliest Times.* Toronto: Macmillan Co. of Canada, 1933.

TRUDELLE, Pierre. *L'Abitibi d'autrefois, d'hier, d'aujourd'hui.* Amos: 1937.

VATTIER, G. *Essai sur la mentalité canadienne-française.* Paris: Honoré Champion, 1928.

——*Esquisse de la colonisation de la province de Québec, 1608–1925.* Paris: Honoré Champion, 1928.

VIEN, Rossel. *Histoire de Roberval, cœur du Lac-Saint-Jean, 1855–1955.* ("Publications de la Société historique du Saguenay," No 15.) Chicoutimi: La Société historique du Saguenay, 1955.

VINEBERG, Solomon. *Provincial and Local Taxation in Canada.* New York: Columbia University Press, 1912.

VINER, Jacob. *Canada's Balance of International Indebtedness, 1900–1913.* Cambridge: Harvard University Press, 1924.

WADE, Mason, ed. *Canadian Dualism: La Dualité canadienne.* Toronto: University of Toronto Press, 1960.

WILLSON, Beckles. *Quebec: The Laurentide Province.* London: Constable & Co., 1913.

PAMPHLETS

L'Action sociale catholique et l'œuvre de la presse catholique: motifs—programme —organisation—ressources. Québec: E. Marcotte, 1907.

ANON. *Canadiens, méfiez-vous. Une expérience de vingt ans.* Montréal: La Revue canadienne, 1900.

ANON. [OBLATE FATHERS.] *Manuel du citoyen catholique.* 4th ed. Saint-Boniface, Manitoba: 1909.

ANON. *Saintes comédies par?* Vol. II, *Le cléricalisme au Canada.* Montréal: Privately printed, 1896.

BAILLAIRGÉ, Abbé F.-A. *La nature, la race, la santé, dans leurs rapports avec la production du travail: applications à la province de Québec.* ("Petites lectures sur l'économie politique," No 1.) Joliette: Printed privately, 1890.

BERNARD, Henri. *La Ligue de l'Enseignement (Histoire d'une conspiration maçonnique à Montréal.)* Montréal: Privately printed, 1904.

BOIVIN, Abbé Léonce. *Le catéchisme social.* Québec: L'Action sociale, 1913.

BUIES, Arthur. *Le chemin de fer du Lac Saint-Jean.* Québec: Léger Brousseau, 1895.

Le Canadien Émigrant. Edited by Abbé A. Racine. Québec: Côté et Cie., 1851.

CARON, Abbé Ivanhoe. *L'Abitibi, esquisse générale, cantons ouverts à la colonisation, moyens de transport.* Québec: Ministère de la Colonisation, Mines, et Pêcheries, 1915.

——*Centres de colonisation du nord-ouest de la province de Québec, le Témiscamingue, l'Abitibi.* Québec: Ministère de la Colonisation, Mines, et Pêcheries, 1912.

CARUFEL, L.-E. DE. *Quelques-unes des industries indispensables à l'avancement de la colonisation et utiles à l'immigration dans la province de Québec.* Québec: La Société de colonisation de Montréal, 1914.

CAZES, Paul DE. *L'instruction publique dans la province de Québec.* Québec: Dussault & Proulx, 1905.

CHAPAIS, Thomas. *Les congrégations enseignantes et le brevet de capacité.* Québec: Léger Brousseau, 1893.

CHAREST, Abbé J.-B. *La colonisation dans les Cantons de l'Est.* Saint-Hyacinthe: Presses à Vapeur du Courrier de Saint-Hyacinthe, 1871.

THE CITIZEN'S ASSOCIATION OF THREE RIVERS. *The City of Three Rivers.* Three Rivers: Printed privately, 1910.

Collège Ste-Marie, Archives. A very rich collection including hundreds of pamphlets published in Canada, and particularly in the province of Quebec, in the last 150 years.

"La Constitution de l'École sociale populaire." *Institut social populaire,* No. 1 (1911).

DAVID, L.-O. *Le clergé canadien: sa mission, son œuvre.* Montréal: E. Sénécal et Fils, 1896.

Diplômés Polytechniques. Montréal: L'Association des Diplômés de Polytechnique, 1961.

DUGRÉ, Adélard, S.J. *La désertion des campagnes: ses causes et ses remèdes.* Québec: Ministère de l'Agriculture de la province de Québec, 1916.

FLYNN, The Hon. E.-J., premier ministre. *L'éducation dans la province de Québec.* (Speech given before the Legislative Assembly, January 7, 1897.) Québec: Imprimerie Générale, 1897.

GARON, J.-E. *Histoire de la colonisation dans la province de Québec de 1825–1940.* Québec: Privately printed, 1940.

GOUIN, Sir Lomer, Premier. *Résumé d'un discours sur un projet de loi concernant la fréquentation obligatoire des écoles chez les protestants.* (A speech given before the Legislative Assembly, November 26, 1912.) Québec: Le Soleil, 1913.

Le gouvernement Gouin et son œuvre: onze années de progrès et de saine administration. Québec: 1916.

GREENING, W.E. *Paper Makers in Canada: A Record of Fifty Years of Achievement.* Cornwall, Ontario: International Brotherhood of Paper Makers, 1952.

INSTITUT DES FRÈRES DE L'INSTRUCTION CHRÉTIENNE. *Notice historique.* Laprairie: Privately printed, 1911.

LALANDE, Hermas, S.J. *L'instruction obligatoire, principes et conséquences.* Montréal: Imprimerie du Messager, 1919.

LECLERC, Abbé Nazaire. *Catéchisme d'agriculture ou la science agricole mise à la portée des enfants.* Québec: Darveau, 1869.

LECLERQ, Eugène. *Statistiques rouges.* Québec: E. Tremblay, 1932.

LEFRANC, J.-P. [Canon P. Grondin.] *Catéchisme des caisses populaires.* Québec: La Vérité, 1910.

LEMIEUX, Le Juge. *Sobre et Riche.* Québec: L'Action sociale, 1910.

LEMIEUX, A.-J. *La Loge d'Émancipation.* Montréal: La Croix, 1910.

LEMIEUX, Hon. R. *Une industrie: une région: un homme.* Montréal: Librairie Beauchemin, 1916.

MAGNAN, C.-J. *A propos d'instruction obligatoire.* Québec: L'Action sociale, 1919.

MARCHAND, Hon. F.-G., premier ministre. *Discours sur la loi de l'instruction publique.* (A speech before The Legislative Assembly, December 28, 1897.) Québec, 1897.

MICHAUD, Abbé. *L'agriculture et l'état agricole.* Québec: Ministère de l'Agriculture de la province de Québec, 1915.

MONTIGNY, Le Recorder Testard DE. *La colonisation: le nord de Montréal ou la région Labelle.* Montréal: Librairie Beauchemin, 1895.

MONTPETIT, Édouard. *Les survivances françaises au Canada.* (A lecture given at l'École libre des sciences politiques in Paris.) Paris: Plon-Nourrit & Cie., 1914.

PAQUET, Mgr L.-A. *Le bréviaire du patriote canadien-français.* Edited by Canon Émile Chartier. Montréal: Bibliothèque de l'Action française, 1925.

PARENT, E. *Importance de l'étude de l'économie politique.* (Paper read before l'Institut canadien, November 19, 1846.) Montréal: Privately printed, 1846.

PROULX, Abbé J.-B. *Le Canada, le Curé Labelle, et la colonisation.* Paris: Imprimerie de l'Œuvre de Saint-Paul, 1885.

PROVOST, Abbé Honorius. *Historique de la faculté des arts de l'université Laval, 1852–1952.* Québec: Presses universitaires Laval, 1952.

Règlement du Comité catholique du Conseil de l'Instruction publique de la province de Québec. Revised in 1915. Québec: 1915.

ROULEAU, Abbé C.-E. *L'émigration, ses principales causes.* Québec: Privately printed, 1896.

SAINT-PIERRE, Arthur. *L'avenir du Canada-français.* Montréal: Le Messager, 1909.

Shawinigan Technical Institute, 1912–1913. Shawinigan, 1912.

ARTICLES

ALEXIS [Dr J.-A. COUTURE.] "Le roman d'un Canadien français," *L'Événement* (Québec), December 30, 1916, and January 3, 1917.

ANGERS, François-A. "Naissance de la pensée économique au Canada français," *Revue d'histoire de l'Amérique française*, XV (September 1961), 204–21.

ANON. "Nos collèges séminaires," *Revue ecclésiastique*, VI (1899), 108–12.

AUDET, L.-P. "Le centenaire du système scolaire de la province de Québec." *Cahiers du service extérieur d'éducation sociale*, IV, No. 8 (1947). Faculté des Sciences sociales de l'université Laval.

——"La querelle de l'instruction obligatoire," *Les Cahiers des Dix*, No. 24 (1959), 132–50.

BERTRAM, Gordon W. "Economic Growth in Canadian Industry, 1870–1915: The Staple Model and The Take-off Hypothesis," *Canadian Journal of Economics and Political Science*, XXIX (May 1963), pp. 159–84.

BOUCHETTE, Errol. "Les débuts d'une industrie et notre classe bourgeoise," *Transactions and Proceedings of the Royal Society of Canada.* VI, 3rd Series (1912), Section I, 143–57.

——"L'évolution économique dans la province de Québec," *Proceedings and Transactions of the Royal Society of Canada*, VII, 2nd Series (1901), Section I, 97–116.

BOULDING, Kenneth. "Religious Foundations of Economic Progress," *Harvard Business Review*, XXX, No. 3. (1952), 33–40.

BRAY, A.-J. DE. "L'enseignement commercial au Canada," *Revue économique canadienne*, I (1911), 4–19.

BRUNET, Michel. "Trois dominantes de la pensée canadienne-française: l'agriculturalisme, l'anti-étatisme, et le messianisme. Essai d'histoire intellectuelle," *Écrits du Canada français*, III (1957), 33–117.

BUCKLEY, Kenneth. "The Role of Staple Industries in Canada's Economic Development," *Journal of Economic History*, XVIII (December 1958), 439–50.

CARON, Maximilien. "La province de Québec est-elle un État?" *Actualité économique*, XIV (May 1938), 121–32.

CHAPAIS, J.-C. "Three Centuries of Agriculture," *Canada and its Provinces*. Vol. XVII: *Province of Quebec*. Edited by Adam Short. Toronto: Glasgow Brook, 1914–1917.

CLARK, S.D. "Religion and Economic Backward Areas," *American Economic Review*, XL (Papers and Proceedings, 1951), 258–65.

——"The Religious Factor in Canadian Economic Development," *Journal of Economic History*, VII (Supplement, 1947), 89–103. Also reprinted under the title "The Religious Influence in Canadian Society," in his book *The Developing Canadian Community*. Toronto: University of Toronto Press, 1962.

——"The Religious Sect in Canadian Economic Development," *Canadian Journal of Economics and Political Science*, XII (November 1946), 439–53. Also reprinted in his book *The Developing Canadian Community*. Toronto: University of Toronto Press, 1962.

DESMARCHAIS, Philémon, "La paroisse, facteur d'économie," *Revue trimestrielle canadienne*, XXIV (1938), 300–327.

DESROSIERS, Léo-P. "En relisant les mandements," *Les Cahiers des Dix*, No. 8 (1949), 65–86.

FALARDEAU, J.-C. "Rôle et importance de l'Église au Canada français," *Esprit*, (August, 1952), 214–29.

FILTEAU, Gérard. "L'éducation en Mauricie, 1634–1852," *Rapports de la Société canadienne d'histoire de l'Église catholique* (1951-1952), 75–84.

FINLAYSON, H.M. "Hydrology of the St. Maurice River," in *Engineering Features of the Shawinigan System*. Montreal: The Shawinigan Water and Power Company, 1957, 9–11.

GENDRON, Gérard. "La contribution financière du clergé à l'enseignement dans la province de Québec," *Actualité économique*, XXIII (July, 1947), 266–84.

GÉRIN, Léon. "Notre mouvement intellectuel," *Proceedings and Transactions of the Royal Society of Canada*, VII, Series II (1901), Section II, 145–72.

——"La vulgarisation de la science sociale chez les Canadiens français," *Proceedings and Transactions of the Royal Society of Canada*, XI, Series II (1905), Section I, 66–88.

GOSSELIN, Abbé A. "L'Abbé Holmes et l'instruction publique," *Proceedings and Transactions of the Royal Society of Canada*, I, Series III (1908), Section I, 127–72.

GROULX, Abbé L.-A. "La préparation au rôle social," *Revue ecclésiastique*, XVII (1910), 236–50; 267–77.

GUINDON, Hubert. "The Social Evolution of Quebec Reconsidered," *Canadian Journal of Economics and Political Science*, XXVI (November 1960), 533–51.

HARE, John. "Nationalism in French Canada and Tardivel's Novel 'Pour la Patrie'," *Culture*, XXII (December 1961), 403–12.

HARTLAND, Penelope E. "Factors in Economic Growth in Canada," *Journal of Economic History*, XV, No. 1 (1955), 13–22.

HEILBRONER, "The Literature of Development," *Harper's*, May 1961, pp. 96-97.

HELLEINER, K.F. "Moral Conditions of Economic Growth," *Journal of Economic History*, XI, No. 2 (1951), 97–116.

HUGHES, E.C. "Industry and the Rural System in Quebec," *Canadian Journal of Economics and Political Science*, IV (August 1938), 341–49.

KEYFITZ, Nathan. "The Growth of the Canadian Population," *Population Studies*, IV (June 1950), 47–63.

LAFLAMME, Mgr J.-C.-K. "La colonisation et la forêt." (Speech given before the Canadian Forestry Associations' Convention March 11-12, 1908.) *L'Action sociale*, March 12, 13, and 14, 1908.

LAFORCE, J.-E. "Mgr Calixte Marquis, colonisateur," *Rapports de la Société canadienne d'histoire de l'Église catholique*, (1943-1944), 113–36.

LANGLOIS, Conrad. "Cultural Reasons Given for the French Canadian Lag in Economic Progress," *Culture*, XXI (June 1960), 152–70.

LAPIERRE, Laurier-L. "Joseph Tarte: Relations between the French Canadian Episcopacy and a French Canadian Politician, 1874–1896," *Reports of the Canadian Catholic Historical Association*, (1957-1958) 23–38.

LAPOINTE, Mgr Eugène. "Le travail du dimanche dans notre industrie," *La Semaine sociale*, II (1922), 132–49.

LAUREYS, H. "Les ressources agricoles de la province de Québec," *Revue économique canadienne*, II (1912), 12–32.

LEMELIN, Charles. "Social Impact of Industrialization on Agriculture in the Province of Quebec," *Culture*, XIV (1953), 34–46; 156–69.

MARION, Séraphin. "Jules-Paul Tardivel, pionnier de la presse indépendante et catholique au Canada français," *Rapports de la Société canadienne d'histoire de l'Église catholique*, (1954-1955), 13–24.

MINVILLE, Esdras. "L'aspect économique du problème canadien-français," *Actualité économique*, XXVI (April 1950), 48–77.

MONTPETIT, Édouard. "L'indépendance économique du Canada français," *Revue économique canadienne*, III (1913), 370–84.

PELLAND, Alfred. "La colonisation dans la province de Québec," *Revue économique canadienne*, II (1912), 85–95.

PELLETIER, Gérard. "La Société canadienne-française et l'Église," *Le Magazine Maclean*, (September 1961).

ROY, Antoine. "Bibliographie des monographies et histoires de paroisse," *Rapport de l'Archiviste de la province de Québec pour 1937-1938*, XVIII (1938), 252–383.

SAINT-PIERRE, Arthur. "Le socialisme à Montréal," *Messager canadien du Sacré-Cœur*, (March 1910), 109–11.

TREMBLAY, Mgr Victor. "La Paroisse et la race canadienne-française," *Rapports de la Société canadienne d'histoire de l'Église catholique*, (1947-1948), 73–86.

——"La pulperie de Jonquière," *Centenaire de Jonquière, 1847–1947*. Jonquière, 1947.

THÉRIAULT, Yvon. "Mandements des évêques de Trois-Rivières," *Rapports de la Société canadienne d'histoire de l'Église catholique*, (1951-1952), 53–64.

WADE, Mason. "Social Change in French Canada," *Tradition, Value and Socio-Economic Development*. Edited by Ralph Braibanti and Others. ("Duke University Commonwealth Studies"), Durham, N.C.: Duke University Press, 1961, 276–96.

REPORTS

L'ASSOCIATION CATHOLIQUE DE LA JEUNESSE CANADIENNE-FRANÇAISE. *Le congrès de la jeunesse à Québec.* A Report on the Congress held in Quebec in 1908. Montréal: Le Semeur, 1910.

——*Étude critique de notre système scolaire.* A Report on the Congress held in Trois-Rivières, June 28-July 1, 1913. Montréal: Bureau de l'A.C.J.C., 1913.

——*Premier congrès de la Jeunesse catholique et canadienne-française.* Report on the Congress held in Montreal, June 25, 1903. Montréal: Printed privately, 1903.

——*Le problème de la colonisation au Canada français.* Report on the Congress held in Chicoutimi, June 29-July 2, 1919. Montréal: Bureau de l'A.C.J.C., 1920.

——*Le problème industriel au Canada français.* Report on the Congress held in Quebec, July 1–3, 1921. Montréal: Secrétariat général de l'A.C.J.C., 1922.

UN AMI DE L'ÉDUCATION [Abbé T.-B. PELLETIER.] *Considérations sur l'agriculture canadienne au point de vue religieux, national, et du bien-être matériel.* A Report presented to the deputies composing the Committee on Agriculture. Québec: 1860.

BOARD OF INQUIRY INTO THE COST OF LIVING IN CANADA. *Report of the Board.* 2 vols. Ottawa: King's Printer, 1915.

THE COLONIZATION COMMISSION. *Report.* Quebec: King's Printer, 1904.

LE COMITÉ SPÉCIAL. *Premier et second rapport du comité spécial, nommé pour s'enquérir des raisons qui retardent la colonisation des townships de l'est du Bas-Canada.* Québec: Queen's Printer, 1851.

LE CONGRÈS DE L'ACTION SOCIALE. *Compte rendu du premier congrès d'action sociale du diocèse des Trois-Rivières, 1912.* Trois-Rivières: Le Bien public, 1912.

LE CONGRÈS DE LA COLONISATION. *Rapport du congrès de la colonisation, tenu à Montréal, les 22–24 novembre 1898.* Montréal: Société de la colonisation et de repatriement de la province de Québec, 1900.

LE CONGRÈS DE L'ENSEIGNEMENT SECONDAIRE. *Résumés des travaux.* Report on the Congress held in Quebec, June 20, 21, 1914. Québec: 1914.

Fragmentary reports are available for the following Quebec companies, for the period 1896–1916, in the "Corporation Records Collection," Baker Library, Harvard Business School: Laurentide Paper Company Ltd., Montreal Light, Heat and Power Company, Price Brothers and Company, Ltd., Shawinigan Water and Power Company and the Wabasso Cotton Company, Ltd.

KING, W.L. Mackenzie, Deputy Minister of Labour, Commissioner. *Report on the Royal Commission to Inquire into Industrial Disputes in the Cotton Factories of the Province of Quebec.* Ottawa: King's Printer, 1909.

LA LIGUE ANTI-ALCOOLIQUE. *Contre l'alcoolisme.* First annual report. Montréal: Imprimerie du Messager, 1913.

MAROIS, Félix, greffier, conseiller de conciliation et d'arbitrage. *Rapport adressé à l'Honorable L.-A. Taschereau, ministre des travaux publics.* A Report on the official investigation made into the common complaint that unnecessary Sunday work was being carried on in the pulp and paper mills of the province. Quebec: King's Printer, August 3, 1914.

ROYAL COMMISSION ON INDUSTRIAL TRAINING AND TECHNICAL EDUCATION.
Report of the Commissioners. Ottawa: King's Printer, 1913.
LA SOCIÉTÉ DE REPATRIEMENT ET DE COLONISATION DU LAC SAINT-JEAN.
Rapports Annuels. 1899, 1901, 1902, 1905. Archives of la Société
historique du Saguenay.
LA SOCIÉTÉ DE COLONISATION DU DIOCÈSE DE MONTRÉAL. *Rapport du
Rév. M.-A. Labelle, curé de Saint-Jérôme, à Sa Grandeur Mgr E.-C.
Fabre, Archevêque de Montréal.* Saint-Jérôme: J. Chapeau et Fils, 1887.
UNITED STATES, TARIFF BOARD. *Report on the Pulp and Newsprint Paper
Industry.* Washington: 1911.

UNPUBLISHED MATERIAL

ARBOUR, J. "Le cours classique et les études commerciales supérieures."
Unpublished thesis, École des Hautes Études, Montréal, 1921.
BERTRAM, Gordon W. "Historical Statistics on Growth and Structure of
Manufacturing in Canada, 1870–1957." Paper read before the Cana-
dian Political Science Association, McMaster University, Hamilton,
Canada, June 11, 1962. (Mimeo.).
CADENHEAD, A.F.G. "History of Shawinigan Chemicals Ltd., 1916–
1946." Unpublished manuscript, 1947. Private copy of J.S. Whyte,
Shawinigan. (Mimeo.).
"Cahiers d'annonce de la paroisse Saint-Dominique de Jonquière." Un-
published, handwritten notebooks. Archives of the Presbytery of
Jonquière.
"Cahiers de prône et d'annonces de la paroisse de Sainte-Famille de Kéno-
gami." Unpublished, handwritten notebooks. Archives of the Pres-
bytery of Kénogami.
La Commission scolaire de Grand'Mère. "Livre des minutes de la Commission scolaire de la municipalité du village de Grand'Mère, du 9
août 1900 au 14 février 1916." Unpublished, handwritten volume.
Archives of the School Commission of Grand'Mère.
La Commission scolaire de La Tuque. "Livre des délibérations." Vol. I
(1908–1920). Unpublished, handwritten volume. Archives of the
School Commission of La Tuque.
FILTEAU, Gérard, and ALLARD, Lionel. "Un siècle au service de l'éducation,
1851–1951." 2 vols. Unpublished manuscript, 1951. Archives of
the Séminaire de Trois-Rivières. (Mimeo.).
GAVIN, Mortimer, S.J. "Labor Union Policies in the United States Primary
Pulp and Paper Industry." Unpublished Ph.D. thesis, St. Louis
University, St. Louis, 1950.
GOODING, M.E. "The History of Reduction Plants at Shawinigan Falls."
Private history circulated in the company, 1947. Files of the Alumi-
num Company of Canada, Shawinigan.
JOHNSTON, G.M. "The Historical Geography of the Saguenay Valley."
Unpublished Master's dissertation, McGill University, Montreal,
1950.
JONES, R.L. "History of Agriculture in Canada." Unpublished Ph.D.
thesis, Harvard University, Cambridge, 1938.
LEMELIN, Charles. "Agricultural Development and Industrialization of
Quebec." Unpublished Ph.D. dissertation, Department of Economics,
Harvard University, 1951.

LIEFF, Mrs. Pearl J. "The Urbanization of the French Canadian Parish."
    Unpublished Master's dissertation, McGill University, Montreal, 1940.
MAHEUX, Mgr Arthur. "William Price et la Compagnie Price, 1810–
    1954." Unpublished typewritten manuscript, 1954. Archives of
    Price Brothers and Company, Quebec.
MIVILLE-DECHÈNE, Mme Louise, "William Price, 1810–1850." Un-
    published Licentiate thesis, Institut d'Histoire, université Laval,
    Québec, 1964.
MOLESWORTH, H.N. "Canada Iron Foundries Limited." Unpublished
    manuscript. Files of the Canada Iron Foundry, Trois-Rivières.
O'BREADY, Mgr Maurice. "Jean ou John Holmes." Unpublished man-
    uscript. Université de Sherbrooke Library. Date not specified.
Québec. Le ministère de l'Industrie et du Commerce. "L'expansion
    industrielle de la province de Québec de 1900 à 1953." A study present-
    ed to the Royal Commission on constitutional problems. Québec:
    Service Bureautech, 1953. (Mimeo.).
——"L'évolution de l'industrie manufacturière de la province de Québec
    depuis 1880." Memoir presented to the Royal Commission on con-
    stitutional problems. Québec, 1954. (Mimeo.).
RYMES, Thomas K. "Some Comments on the pre-Annual Census of In-
    dustry Data with respect to Manufacturing in Canada." Typewritten
    manuscript. Dominion Bureau of Statistics, Ottawa, 1960.
SMART, J.C. "Notes on the Early Days of the Shawinigan." Unpublished,
    typewritten mémoires. Date unspecified. Files of the Shawinigan
    Light and Power Co., Montreal.
The Technical Institute of Shawinigan. "Minutes Book." Unpublished,
    handwritten volume (1911–1919). Files of the Technical Institute
    of Shawinigan.
TÊTU, Michel. "Les premiers syndicats catholiques canadiens (1900–1921)."
    Unpublished Ph.D. dissertation, université Laval, Québec, 1961.
UREN, P.E. "An Historical Geography of the Saint Maurice Valley with
    a special reference to Urban Occupance." Unpublished Master's
    dissertation, McGill University, Montreal, 1949.
ZANARTU, Mario, S.J. "Roman Catholic Ethic and Economic Devel-
    opment." Unpublished Ph.D. thesis, Faculty of Political Science,
    Columbia University, 1962.

BIBLIOGRAPHIES

DIONNE, N.-E. "Inventaire chronologique des livres, brochures, journaux,
    et revues publiés dans la province de Québec de 1764 à 1904," *Proceed-
    ings and Transactions of the Royal Society of Canada*, X, Series II (1904),
    Section IV, Supplementary volume, 1-175.
——*Inventaires chronologiques de livres, brochures, journaux, et revues publiés
    en diverses langues dans et en dehors de la province de Québec: premier
    supplément, 1904–1912.* Québec, 1912.
GARIGUE, Philippe. *A Bibliographical Introduction to the Study of French
    Canada.* Montréal: Department of Sociology and Anthropology,
    McGill University, 1956.

INDEX

PRINTED BY

L'IMPRIMERIE LAFLAMME LIMITEE
QUEBEC CITY

AUGUST 30, 1966